C

B Y   E X A M P L E

800 East 96th Street
Indianapolis, Indiana 46240

Greg Perry

C by Example

Trademarks

Warning and Disclaimer

Publisher
John Pierce

Acquisitions Editor
Todd Green

Development Editor
Laura Bulcher

Technical Editor
Louis C. Lowe

Managing Editor
Thomas F. Hayes

Project Editor
Karen S. Shields

Copy Editor
Victoria Elzey

Indexer
Becky Hornyak

Proofreader
Jeanne Clark

Interior Design
Karen Ruggles

Cover Design
Radar Design

Layout Technicians
Steve Geiselman

Eric S. Miller

Team Coordinator
Julie Otto

Media Developer
Jay Payne

Contents at a Glance

Table of Contents

About the Author

Greg Perry is a speaker and writer on both the programming and the application sides of computing. He is known for his skills at bringing advanced computer topics down to the novice's level. Perry has been a programmer and trainer since the early 1980s. He received his first degree in computer science and a master's degree in corporate finance. Perry is one of the most prolific computer-title authors today, having written more than 60 books and sold more than two million books worldwide. Perry co-designed the current *by Example* series and was the author of the first several books in the original *by Example* series developed by Que nine years ago. His book titles include *QBasic by Example, Access by Example,* and *Using Visual J++.* In addition, he's written other books for Macmillan USA, including *Sams Teach Yourself Visual Basic in 21 Days* and *Teach Yourself Programming in 24 Hours.* He also writes about rental-property management and loves to travel.

Dedication

Ironic as it may be, this programming text is dedicated to Dr. Gary North, a man who's taught me more about the nature of programming in a single year than all the years I spent in school, industry, and life. Thanks, Dr. North; you have probably done more to help my family than any other man alive today.

Acknowledgments

My sincere thanks go to the editors and staff at Que who strive to produce computer books that teach all levels of computer users from beginners to experts. The people at Que take their jobs seriously because they want readers to have only the best books possible.

The one who had to turn my writing mess into this helpful book is Laura Bulcher. Laura, I want to thank you for the diligence you show. I hope we work together for many more books.

Todd Green had the most impact on the early stages of this book when he had to take over the acquisition job at the last moment. This book is much better due to Todd's early suggestions. In addition, Todd's patience with this frustrating author makes him shine even more.

Other editors and staff at Que who produced this book. Louis Lowe had the unfortunate job of locating the bugs in my code and writing, and I thank him for that. Karen Shields, Victoria Elzey, and Jeanne Clark did their best in the middle and end development cycles of this book and are also responsible for this book's excellence. I alone am responsible for any problems in the text, if any exist.

My lovely and gracious bride, Jayne, keeps me flying high with her 10 years of love that seem like fleeting moments. Thanks also to my Dad and Mom, Glen and Bettye Perry, who are my biggest fans. I love you all.

Greg Perry

We Want to Hear from You!

As the reader of this book, you are our most important critic and commentator. We value your opinion and want to know what we're doing right, what we could do better, what areas you'd like to see us publish in, and any other words of wisdom you're willing to pass our way.

As an associate publisher for Que, I welcome your comments. You can email or write me directly to let me know what you did or didn't like about this book—as well as what we can do to make our books better.

Please note that I cannot help you with technical problems related to the topic of this book. We do have a User Services group, however, where I will forward specific technical questions related to the book.

When you write, please be sure to include this book's title and author as well as your name, email address, and phone number. I will carefully review your comments and share them with the author and editors who worked on the book.

Email: feedback@quepublishing.com

Mail: Greg Wiegand
Que Publishing
800 East 96th Street
Indianapolis, IN 46240 USA

For more information about this book or another Que title, visit our Web site at www.quepublishing.com. Type the ISBN (excluding hyphens) or the title of a book in the Search field to find the page you're looking for.

Introduction

The *by Example* Series

How does the *by Example* series make you a better programmer? The *by Example* series teaches programming using the best method possible—examples. The text acts as a mentor, looking over your shoulder, providing sample programs, and showing you new ways to use the concepts covered in each chapter. While the material is still fresh, you will see example after example demonstrating ways to use what you just learned.

The philosophy of the *by Example* series is simple: The best way to teach computer programming is with multiple examples. Command descriptions, format syntax, and language references are not enough to teach a newcomer a programming language. Only by taking the components, immediately putting them into use, and running sample programs can programming students get more than just a feel for the language. Newcomers who learn only a few basics using examples at every step of the way will automatically know how to write programs using those skills.

Who Should Use This Book

This book teaches C programming to brand new C programmers, people who may have never seen a C programming statement. Programming concepts are described, such as looping, data storage, and naming conventions, but the reader should have some knowledge of another programming language. Perhaps you have programmed some in QBasic, a batch language, a macro language such as Visual Basic for Applications, or even keyboard macros that appear in the Microsoft Office suite of applications. You do not have to be an expert, but the very introductory and fundamental programming concepts are not described in great detail. Nevertheless, the C language is described thoroughly and if you are new to C—if you can't even *spell* C—this book is for you.

This Book's Organization

This text focuses on programming correctly in C by teaching structured programming techniques and proper program design. Emphasis is always placed on a program's readability rather than "tricks of the trade" code examples. In this changing world, programs should be clear, properly structured, and well documented—and this book does not waver from the importance of this approach.

C by Example teaches you C by using a holistic approach. In addition to learning the mechanics of the language, you'll learn some tips and warnings, how to use C for different types of applications, and a little of the history and interesting asides about the computing industry.

Many other books build only one application, adding to it a little at a time with each chapter. The chapters of this book are standalone chapters, showing you complete programs that fully demonstrate the commands discussed in the chapter. There is a program for every level of reader. The final chapter contains a large, complete application tieing together all of the previous applications discussed in the book.

Not only does this book contain almost 200 sample program listings, but these programs are useful—not just meaningless examples. These programs show ways that you can use C for personal finance, school and business record keeping, math and science, and general-purpose applications beneficial to almost everybody with a computer. This wide variety of programs shows you that C is a very powerful language but is still easy to learn and use.

Please visit the by Example Web site for code examples or additional material associated with this book: `http://www.quecorp.com/series/by_example`.

Conventions Used in This Book

This book uses several common conventions to help teach the C programming language. Here is a summary of those typographical conventions:

- Commands and computer output appear in a special `monospaced` font.

- Words you type appear in **boldfaced** computer font.

In addition to typographical conventions, the following special elements are included to set off different types of information to make them easily recognizable:

NOTE
Special notes augment the material you read in each hour. These notes clarify concepts and procedures.

TIP
You'll find numerous tips offering shortcuts and solutions to common problems.

CAUTION
The cautions warn you about pitfalls that sometimes appear when programming in C. Reading the caution sections will save you time and trouble.

What's Next

C is the basis for many languages in use today, including C++ and the Internet-based language called Java. As the first chapter explains, knowledge of C is necessary for mastering these other languages. It is now time for you to turn the page and begin learning C programming—by example, of course.

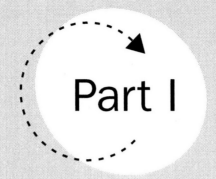

Part I

Welcome to C

What C Is All About

Your future programming career is sure to get a boost when you learn the C programming language. C is the cornerstone of languages, the building block language on which so many of today's more modern languages are based. After you learn C, you will be ready to tackle just about any programming language and environment.

This chapter teaches you the following:

- The reasons for learning C
- C's influence on other languages
- The history of the C language
- The compilation process
- The look of a C program

C Is Fundamental

Just a few years ago, C was the most popular programming language being used. Programmers wrote C code for PCs, mainframes, and supercomputers. C was standardized so that the same program would run on every kind of computer using every kind of operating system available.

Today, the use of C has dramatically decreased. Rarely will a project be written in C. Programmers are using languages such as C++ and Java to create applications that run on standalone, networked, and Internet-based machines. Yet, when learning to program, C is considered to be the one language it is imperative a programmer master before moving on to the other languages in use today.

TIP

Due to the Internet's phenomenal growth, new languages are appearing to handle the different challenges that Internet-based processing requires. Companies looking for programmers in these newer, and sometimes obscure, languages often advertise for C programming skills. The companies know that someone well-versed in C can pick up these offshoot languages rapidly. Therefore, learning C will boost your career potential even if you are never hired to write C-based code.

The reason for C's recommended mastery, despite its low levels of actual use, is that C is the common denominator of many of today's languages; learn C and these languages will be simple to learn. Languages such as C++ and Java are based on C. In fact, many of the statements and commands in these newer languages are identical to the ones found in C. Overall, C is much simpler to learn than these languages because it carries with it a much slimmer toolkit of add-on procedures.

CAUTION

When some people attempt to learn C, even if they are programmers in other languages, they find that C can be cryptic and difficult to understand. This does not have to be the case. When you are taught to write clear and concise C code, in an order that builds on fundamental programming concepts, C is no more difficult to learn or use than any other programming language.

The History of C

Before you jump into C, you might find it helpful to know a little about the evolution of the C programming language. Bell Labs first developed this language in the early 1970s, primarily so that Bell programmers could write their *UNIX* operating system for a new DEC (Digital Equipment Corporation) computer. Bell Labs designed UNIX to run efficiently on small equipment, and it was the first operating system to be written entirely in a high-level programming language. Until that time, operating systems were written in *assembly language*, the computer's low-level, hardware-based language that is tedious, time-consuming, and difficult to change. The Bell Labs designers knew they needed a higher-level programming language to implement their project quicker and make its code easier to maintain.

Because other high-level languages at the time (COBOL, FORTRAN, PL/I, and Algol) were too slow to use for an operating system's code, the Bell Labs programmers decided to write their own language. They based their new language on Algol and BCPL, two high-level but efficient languages used throughout the European markets, but rarely in America. BCPL strongly influenced C, although BCPL did not offer the various data types that the makers of C required. After a few versions, these Bell programmers developed a language that met their goals very well. C is efficient (it is sometimes called a *high low-level language* due to its speed of execution) and flexible, and contains the proper constructs enabling it to be maintained over time.

How C Differs

If you have programmed before, you should understand a little about how C differs from other programming languages on the market. (Today's new C-based languages, such as Java, also contain many of C's nuances.) Besides being a very efficient language, C is known also as a *weakly typed* language; that is, the data types you assign to variables do not necessarily require that same type of data. (Proper coding techniques learned in this book, however, will help to eliminate this problem.) If you declare a numeric variable, and then decide to put a letter into it, C enables you to do this. The data may not be in the format you expect, but C does its best. This is much different than stronger-typed languages such as COBOL and Pascal. These languages require rigid conformity to consistent data types; you cannot store, for example, a character in a numeric storage location. Although you can get into trouble a little more easily, C enables you to view the same data in different ways.

C's weakly typed nature places much more responsibility on the programmer. C is an extremely flexible language—particularly if it is to be used to write operating systems. At any one time, an operating system does not know what is coming down the line. If, for example, an operating system expects a number but instead receives a letter, the language used must be flexible enough to handle this different data without aborting.

NOTE

C's philosophy is this: Trust the programmers—they must know what they're doing!

The added responsibility of the weakly typed, flexible C language adds to the programmer's burden of being careful while programming. Although the programmer has more freedom with data storage, the languages do not check data type accuracy for the programmer. The trade-off is worth it, however. The designers of C did not want to hamper C programmers by adding lots of strict rules to the language.

C is a small, block-structured programming language. C has fewer than 40 keywords. To make up for its small vocabulary, C has one of the largest assortments of *operators*, such as those used for calculations and data comparisons. (The C-based languages have more operators than virtually every other language in existence, second only to APL.) The large number of operators in C could tempt programmers to write cryptic programs that do a lot with a small amount of code. As you learn throughout this book, however, making the program more readable is more important than squeezing out bytes. This book teaches you how to use the C operators to their fullest extent, while maintaining readable programs.

C's large number of operators (more than the number of keywords) requires a more judicious use of an *operator precedence* table that states the order in which C processes multiple operators inside a single statement.

✔ Appendix B, "C's Precedence Table," page 476, contains C's operator precedence table that you can refer to as you learn C.

Unlike most other languages that have only four or five levels of precedence, C has 15. As you learn C, you need to master each of these 15 levels. The precedence table is not as difficult as it sounds, but its importance cannot be overstated.

C also has no input or output statements. (You might want to read that sentence again!) C has no commands that perform input or output. This is one of the most important reasons why C and C-based languages are available on so many different computers. The *I/O* (input and output) statements of most languages tie those languages to specific hardware. QBasic, for instance, has almost 20 I/O commands—some of which write to the screen, to the printer, to a modem, and so on. If you write a QBasic program for a microcomputer, chances are sky-high that the program cannot run on a mainframe.

C's input and output is performed through the abundant use of *function calls*. With every C compiler comes a library of standard I/O functions that your program calls to perform input and output. These standard routines are *hardware independent*, because they work on any device and on any computer that conforms to the ANSI C standard (as most do).

To master C completely, you need to be more aware of your computer's hardware than most other languages require you to be. You certainly do not have to be a hardware expert, but understanding the internal data representation makes C much more usable and meaningful. You also should eventually become familiar with binary and hexadecimal numbers. If you do not want to learn these topics, you can still become a very good C programmer, but knowing what goes on "under the hood" will make C more meaningful to you.

✔ Appendix A, "Memory Addressing, Binary, and Hexadecimal," page 460, contains a tutorial on these topics before you start to learn the C language.

The C Programming Process

To give C programming instructions to your computer, you need an *editor* and a *C compiler*. An editor is similar to a word processor; it is a program that enables you to type a C program into memory, make changes (such as moving, copying, inserting, and deleting text), and save the program more permanently in a disk file. After you use the editor to type the program, you must compile it before you can run it. The compiler takes the C instructions you write and converts those instructions to code the computer can understand.

Many of today's compilers come with their own built-in editor, as well as a *debugger* to help locate and correct errors (called *bugs*) that creep into most people's programs at one time or another during the writing stage. Unless the only language in your background is an interactive language such as QBasic, or a macro language such as those found in major software applications such as Microsoft Office, it is most likely that you've used a debugger. Only after compiling the C program that you write can your computer run the program and show the results from that program.

NOTE
Actually, you might have a difficult time even locating a C compiler today. Generally, C is included with C++ compilers since C++ is based on C and uses a technique called *object-oriented programming, OOP,* in which data values perform actions that the programmer gives them. Therefore, a compiler such as Visual C++ or Borland C++ will recognize your C code once you've set the proper options to inform the compiler that you are writing C programs.

CAUTION
Today's compilers are often Windows-based. UNIX computers also run windowing environments. To write and execute a C program, you'll have to run the program in a text window. Otherwise, you have to not only learn C, but also programming for the graphical user interface, such as Windows, as well—which is quite a feat. This book teaches C in a text-based environment so that you can concentrate on learning the language and all its nuances. However, where you apply that knowledge is often in a windows environment—after you learn the proper techniques for programming in a windowed environment.

While you are programming, remember the difference between a program and its output. Your program contains only the C instructions that you write. But the computer follows your instructions only after you run the program. Throughout this book's examples, you will often see a *program listing* (that is, the C instructions in the program) followed by the results that occur when you run the program. The results are the output of the program, and they go to an output device such as the screen, the printer, or a disk file.

All C programs use the .C filename extension. One way that C++ compilers know that you are compiling a C program is the .C filename extension as opposed to the .CPP extension C++ programs require.

Proper Program Design

You must plan your programs before typing them into your C editor. When builders construct houses, for example, they don't immediately grab their lumber and tools and start building. They first find out what the owner of the house wants, draw up the plans, order the materials, gather the workers, and then they start building the house.

EXAMPLE

The hardest part of writing a program is breaking the problem into logical steps that the computer can follow. Learning C is a requirement, but C is not the only thing you should consider. There is a method of writing programs—a formal procedure you should learn—that makes your programming job easier. To write a program you should

1. Define the problem to be solved with the computer.

2. Design the program's output (what the user should see).

3. Break the problem into logical steps to achieve this output, including determining the input required by the program. Often, the input comes from a user at the keyboard or from a data file.

4. Write the program (using the editor).

5. Compile the program.

6. Test the program to make sure it performs as you expect.

As you can see from this procedure, the typing of your program occurs toward the end of your programming. This is important, because you first need to plan how to tell the computer how to perform each task. Designing the program in advance makes the entire program structure more accurate, and helps to keep you from having to make many changes later. A builder, for example, knows that a room is much harder to add after the house is built. So, if you do not properly plan every step, it is going to take you longer to create the final, working program. It is always more difficult to make major changes after your program is written.

Planning and developing according to these six steps becomes much more important as you write longer and more complicated programs. Throughout this book, you learn helpful tips for program design. But now it's time to launch into C, so you can experience typing in your own program and then seeing it run.

NOTE

This book teaches the *ANSI C* standard programming language, programs that adhere to the standard C programming language adopted by the American National Standards Institute (ANSI), and makes no attempt to tie in specific editor or compiler commands—there are too many on the market to cover them all in one book. As long as you write ANSI C–specific programs, the tools you use to edit, compile, and run those programs are secondary. Your goal of good programming is the result of whatever applications you produce, not the tools you use to do it.

The Compile Process

After you type and edit your C program's source code, you must compile the program. The process you use to compile your program depends on the version of C and the computer you are using.

NOTE

Each program in this book contains a comment that specifies a recommended filename for the source program. You do not have to follow the file-naming conventions used in this book; the filenames are only suggestions. If you use a mainframe, you need to follow the dataset-naming conventions set up by your system administrator.

Unlike many other programming languages, your C program must be routed through a *preprocessor* before it is compiled. C source code can contain *preprocessor directives* that control the way your programs compile.

You may have to refer to your compiler's reference manuals or to your company's system personnel to learn how to compile programs for your programming environment. Again, learning the programming environment is not as critical as learning the C language. The compiler is just a way to transform your program from a source code file to an executable file.

Your program must go through one additional stage after compiling and before running. It is called the *linking*, or the *link editing*, stage. When your program is linked, the compiler sends runtime information to your program such as the memory addresses where variables and code will be stored when your program executes. You can also combine several compiled programs into one executable program by linking them. Most of the time, however, your compiler initiates the link editing stage and you do not have to worry about controlling the linking process.

Figure 1.1 shows the steps that your C compiler and link editor perform to produce an executable program. Again, many of today's C compiling systems perform most of these steps behind your back so you can be left concentrating on the source code.

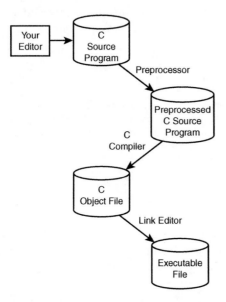

Figure 1.1: Compiling C source code into an executable program.

Running a Program

One of the most important tasks you can perform now is to start your C compiler, enter a program, and see the results. This may or may not be a trivial task depending on your compiler. Some Windows-based compilers are loaded with so many features that doing something *simple*, such as compiling a small, text-based C program, might require a study of the documentation until you locate the options necessary to compile and view the executable results of a source program that ends with the .c extension.

NOTE
Be sure to install your compiler and familiarize yourself with your compiler's editor. Entering a program should be relatively simple because an editor works like a simple word processor for programs that you enter.

EXAMPLE

Starting with Chapter 2, "Analyzing C Programs," you should put all your concentration into the C programming language and not worry about using a specific editor or compiling environment. Therefore, start your editor of choice and type the program in Listing 1.1 into your computer. Be as accurate as possible—a single typing mistake could cause the C compiler to generate a series of errors. You do not have to understand the program's content at this point; the goal is simply to give you practice in using your editor and compiler.

Listing 1.1: This C program is simple to give you practice with your C compiler.

```
/* Filename: C1FIRST.C

    Requests a name, prints the name 5 times, and rings a bell */


#include <stdio.h>
#define BELL '\a'


main()
{
    int ctr=0;                   /* Integer variable to count through loop */
    char fname[20];              /* Define character array to hold name    */

    printf("What is your first name? ");           /* Prompt the user */
    scanf(" %s", fname);                  /* Get the name from the keyboard */
    while (ctr < 5)                           /* Loop to print the name */
    {                                         /* exactly 5 times        */
      printf("%s\n", fname);
      ctr++;
    }
    printf("%c", BELL);                      /* Ring the terminal's bell */
    return 0;
}
```

Again, be as accurate as possible. In most programming languages—and especially in C—the characters you type in a program must be accurate. In this sample C program, for instance, you see parentheses, ( ), brackets, [ ], and braces, {}, but you cannot use them interchangeably.

The *comments* (words between the two symbols, /* and */) to the right of some lines do not need to end in the same alignments that you see in the listing. However, you should familiarize yourself with your editor and learn to space characters accurately so you can type this program exactly as shown.

Compile the program and execute it. Granted, the first time you do this you might have to check your reference manuals or contact someone who already knows your C compiler. But do not worry about damaging your computer: Nothing you do from the keyboard can harm the physical computer. The worst thing that may happen is your computer will freeze and you'll have to reboot and restart your C compiler.

The program from Listing 1.1 asks the user for his or her first name, prints the entered name five times, and beeps the computer's speaker. Here is a sample execution of the program:

OUTPUT   What is your first name? **Terry**

```
Terry
Terry
Terry
Terry
Terry
<Beep>
```

Handling Errors

Because you are typing instructions for a machine, you must be very accurate. If you misspell a word, leave out a quotation mark, or make another mistake, your C compiler informs you with an error message. The most common error is a *syntax error*, and this usually implies a misspelled word.

When you get an error message (or more than one), you must return to the program editor and correct the error. If you don't understand the error, you may have to check your reference manual or scour your program's source code until you find the offending problem. Often, a built-in debugger helps you locate and correct errors.

After you have typed your program correctly using the editor (and you get no compile errors), the program should run properly by asking for your first name, and then printing it five times on the screen. After it prints your name for the fifth time, you hear the computer's bell ring.

GETTING THE BUGS OUT

One of the first computers, owned by the military, refused to print some important data one day. After its programmers tried for many hours to find the problem in the program, a programmer by the name of Grace Hopper decided to check out the printer.

She found a small moth lodged between two important wires. When she removed the moth, the printer started working perfectly (although the moth did not have the same luck).

Grace Hopper is now a retired admiral from the Navy and, although she is responsible for developing many important computer concepts (she was the author of the original COBOL language), she may be best known for discovering the first computer bug.

Ever since Admiral Hopper discovered that moth, errors in computer programs have been known as computer bugs. When you test your programs, you might have to *debug* them—get the bugs (errors) out by correcting your typing errors or changing the logic so your program does exactly what you want it to do.

What's Next

Now that you've entered, compiled, and executed your first C program, you are ready to dive into the language itself to learn how the details of C programming. After you complete the next chapter, you'll understand more about the format of C programs, and you'll have a better grasp as to why the cryptic nature of C is not so difficult to understand after all.

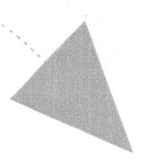

Analyzing C Programs

Once you complete this chapter, you'll better understand just why a C program looks the way it does. A C program is rather cryptic until you familiarize yourself with its structure, even if you understand other programming languages. C's heavy reliance on special characters, as opposed to a heavy use of commands, makes C programs rather mysterious to newcomers.

This chapter teaches you the following:

- The fundamentals of C program structures
- The two kinds of C comments
- Variable and constant locations
- Simple math operators
- Textual screen output format

Studying a Program

Figure 2.1 shows a high-level look at a C program. The figure contains no commands or variables; instead, the figure illustrates the simple, general structure to which all C programs adhere. Although there is much more to a C program than Figure 2.1 implies, the figure is a great place to begin studying the examples that appear in the rest of this book.

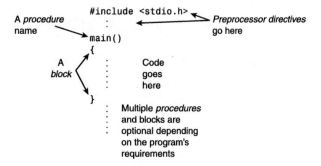

Figure 2.1: Begin analyzing C programs with this general outline.

TIP

As you progress through this book, remember that many other languages, such as Java and Visual J++, are based on C. The structure of these other programs often mimics that of C programs, so you're gaining valuable insight into more than just C.

EXAMPLE

To get acquainted with C programs as quickly as possible, you should look at a C program in its entirety. Listing 2.1 contains a program for your study. The program is simple so you can start easy. Although the program does not do a lot, it enables you to see the general nature of C programming. The next few sections discuss elements from this and other programs. You may not understand everything in this program, even after finishing this chapter, but the program is a good place to start.

Listing 2.1: A simple C program gives you general insight into the nature of the C language.

```
/* Filename: C2FIRST.C

    Initial C program that demonstrates the C comments

    and shows a few variables and their declarations */

#include <stdio.h>


main()
{
    int i, j;    /* These 3 lines declare 4 variables */
    char c;
    float x;
```

```
  i = 4;        /* i and j are assigned integer values */
  j = i + 7;
  c = 'A';      /* All character constants are
                       enclosed in single quotes */
  x = 9.087;    /* x requires a floating-point value since it
                       was declared as a floating-point variable */
  x = x * 4.5; /* Change what was in x with a formula */

/* Sends the values of the variables to the screen */
  printf("%d %d %c %f", i, j, c, x);

  return 0;     /* End programs and functions with return */
}
```

OUTPUT

The output of this program is minimal—it simply displays four values on the screen after performing some assignments and calculations of values, as shown here:

```
4 11 A 40.891499
```

Just concentrate on the general format at this point. Begin to familiarize yourself with the structure of C program code. See whether or not you can understand part of all of the program in Listing 2.1. Since you are not completely new to programming, you already know that the computer looks at each line of the program, starting with the first line, and work its way down until the computer has carried out all the instructions in the program. (Of course, the computer does nothing with this code until you issue the command to compile, link, and execute the program as the previous chapter described.)

✔ Chapter 1, "What C Is All About," page 4, describes the complete compile process.

The Format of a C Program

You can include as much *white space* (separating lines and spaces) in your C programs as you wish. The more readable your program is, the easier your program is to maintain when you have to change the program. Insert as many blank lines in your programs as you wish. Blank lines help separate the sections of the program from each other.

NOTE

C is called a *free-form* language—unlike some other languages, such as COBOL—because programming elements can begin in any column of any line.

The sample program shown in Listing 2.1 is called C2FIRST.C (you'll find the name of each program in this book in the first line of each program listing). C2FIRST.C contains several blank lines to help separate parts of the program from each other. In a simple program such as C2FIRST.C, this separation is not as critical as it might be in a longer and more complex program.

EXAMPLE

Your goal should not be to make your programs as compact as possible. Your goal should be to make your programs as readable as possible. For example, the C2FIRST.C program shown in Listing 2.1 could be rewritten as in Listing 2.2 with the same executable results but with dramatically more difficult maintenance headaches.

Listing 2.2: By eliminating extra space, you greatly reduce a program's readability.

```
/* Filename: C2FIRST.C Initial C program that
demonstrates the C comments and shows a few variables
 and their declarations */
#include <stdio.h>
main() {int i,j;/* These 3 lines declare 4 variables */
char c;float x;i=4;/* i and j are assigned integer values */
j=i+7;c='A';/* All character constants are enclosed in
single quotes */x=9.087;/* x requires a floating-point
value since it was declared as a floating-point variable */x=
x*4.5;/*Change what was in x with a formula */ /* Sends the values of the
variables to the screen */printf("%d %d %c %f",i,j,c,x);return 0;/* End programs
and functions this way*/}
```

To your C compiler, the two programs are exactly the same, and they produce exactly the same result. However, to people who have to read the program, the first style is much more readable. Granted, Listing 2.2's compressed version is an extreme example of a program lacking in white space and readability.

Readability Is the Key

As long as programs do their job and produce correct output, who cares how well they are written? Even in today's world of fast computers and abundant memory and disk space, you, the programmer, should still care. Even if nobody else ever looks at your C program, you might need to make a change at a later date. The more readable you make your program, the faster you can find what needs changing, and then make your changes.

If you work as a programmer for a company, you can almost certainly expect to modify someone else's source code—and others can certainly modify yours. In programming departments, it is said that long-term employees write readable programs. Given this new global economy and all the changes that will face business in the years ahead, companies are seeking programmers who write for the future, that is, people whose programs are straightforward, readable, full of white space, and devoid of hard-to-read "tricks" that make for messy programs.

TIP

You can break a line just about anywhere except between a quoted phrase. To continue a quoted phrase on the next line (to keep a single statement from becoming too lengthy), end the first line with a backslash, like this:

```
printf("This is a very, very, \
very, very, very long line.");
```

Use lots of white space so you can have separate lines and spaces throughout your programs. Notice that the first few lines of C2FIRST.C start in the first column, but the body of the program is indented from the left. This indention helps programmers "zero in" on the important code. When you write programs that contain several sections (called *blocks*), your use of white space helps the reader's eye drop down to, and recognize, the next indented block.

Uppercase Versus Lowercase

Your uppercase and lowercase letters are much more significant in C than in most other programming languages. You can see that most of C2FIRST.C is lowercase. The entire C language is in lowercase. For example, you must type the keywords int, char, and return into programs using lowercase characters. If you use uppercase letters, your C compiler produces many errors and refuses to compile the program until you correct the errors. Not one C command uses uppercase letters.

CAUTION

Turn off that Caps Lock key while programming in C!

Many C programmers reserve uppercase characters for some words and messages sent to the screen, printer, or disk file; they use lowercase letters for almost everything else. There is, however, one exception to this rule that you will read about in Chapter 5, "Preprocessor Directives." This exception is the #define *preprocessor directive*, a statement that modifies your actual source code before the C compiler turns your program into an executable format.

NOTE

The line that appears before `main()` in most C programs, that is, `#include <stdio.h>`, is also a preprocessor directive and not a C statement.

Braces and `mainx()`

All C programs require the following lines:

```
main()

{
```

The statements that follow `main()` are the first statements executed. The section of a C program that begins with `main()`, followed by an opening brace (`{`) is called the *main function*. A C program is actually a collection of *functions* (small sections of code). The function called `main()` is always required and always the first function executed.

In the sample program, almost the entire program is `main()` because the matching closing brace that follows `main()`'s opening brace is at the end of the program. Everything between two matching braces is called a *block*. You read more about blocks later. For now, you only need to realize that this sample program contains just one function, `main()`, and the entire function is a single block because there is only one pair of braces.

All *executable* C statements must have a semicolon (`;`) after them so C knows where the statements end. Because the computer ignores all comments, do not put semicolons after your comments. Notice that the lines containing `main()` and braces do not end with semicolons either, because these lines simply define the beginning and ending of the function and do not execute.

As you become better acquainted with C, you learn when to include the semicolon and when to leave it off. Many beginning C programmers learn quickly when semicolons are required; your compiler certainly informs you if you forget to include a semicolon where one is needed.

TIP

Many programmers use *program templates* that are nothing more than skeleton programs with the typical `main()` and other C program elements already in the code. Instead of typing the same required portions of the program every time the programmer begins, the programmer loads the template program into the editor and then modifies whatever needs changing for the particular job at hand.

Figure 2.2 repeats the sample program shown in Figure 2.1. It contains additional markings to help acquaint you with these new terms as well as other items described in the remainder of this chapter.

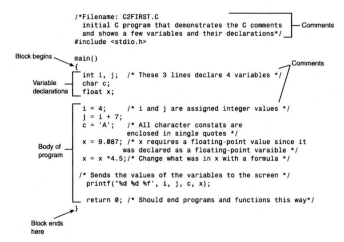

Figure 2.2: A skeleton outline of a simple C program that illustrates the key elements.

C Comments

As a programmer in another language before you began learning C, you know the difference between a program and its output. Most users of a program do not see the program's instructions, the *source code*, itself; they see the output from the execution of the program's instructions. Programmers, on the other hand, look at the program listings and add new routines, change old ones, and update for advancements in computer equipment.

As explained previously, the readability of a program is important so that you and other programmers can look through it easily. Nevertheless, no matter how clearly you write C programs, you can always enhance their readability by adding comments throughout.

Comments are messages that you insert into your C programs, explaining what is going on at that point in the program. For example, if you write a payroll program, you might put a comment before the check-printing routine that describes what is about to happen. You never put C language statements inside a comment, because a comment is a message for people—not computers. Your C compiler ignores all comments in every program.

NOTE

C comments begin with a /* symbol and end with a */ symbol. An optional method, preferred by many of today's programmers, enables programmers to begin comments with two forward slashes, //.

Comments can span more than one line. Notice in the sample program, C2FIRST.C, that the first three lines are actually a single comment. This comment explains the filename and a little about the program.

Comments can also share lines with other C commands. There are several comments to the right of much of the C2FIRST.C program, explaining what the individual lines do. Use abundant comments, but remember who they are for: people and not computers. Use comments to help explain your code, but do not over-comment.

EXAMPLE

Even though you may not be familiar with C yet, the following statement is easy: It prints "C By Example" on the screen.

```
printf("C By Example");   /* Print C By Example on the screen */
```

This comment is redundant and adds nothing to your understanding of the line of code. It would be much better, in this case, to leave out the comment. If you find yourself almost repeating the C code, leave out that particular comment. Not every line of a C program should be commented. Only comment whenever code lines need explaining—in English—to the people looking at your program.

Comments Are for You

It does not matter if you use uppercase, lowercase, or a mixture of both in your comments because C ignores them. Most C programmers capitalize the first letter of sentences in comments, just as you would in everyday writing. Because only people read comments, use whatever case seems appropriate for the letters in your message.

CAUTION

Do not nest C comments by embedding one comment within another comment. If you do, the C compiler gets confused when it sees the first comment end in the middle of a second one.

EXAMPLE

The section of a C program that follows is illegal because one comment resides within another:

```
sales = 3456.54 * bonus;
/* This is an example of a C program
   /* It does NOT
      comment correctly! */
The first comment did not end before the second began. */
```

This sometimes confuses programmers who are just learning C, but who know another programming language. In C, you cannot *comment out* large sections of code just by inserting /* at the beginning of the section and */ at the end if any lines within that section already have comments. In some languages, programmers can comment out several lines in a program so that those lines do not execute. This enables the programmer to test remaining lines independently from those commented out. If you were to try this in C—and nested comments result—your compiler might confuse a comment with code and produce compile errors.

EXAMPLE

1. Suppose you want to write a C program that produces a fancy boxed title containing your name with flashing dots around it (like a marquee). The C code to do this might be difficult to understand and might not be understandable—by itself—to others who look at your program later. So, before such code, you might want to insert the following comment:

```
/* The following few lines draw a fancy box around
     a name, then display flashing dots around the
     name like a Hollywood movie marquee. */
```

This would not tell C to do anything because a comment is not a command, but it would make the next few lines of code more understandable to you and others. The comment explains in English, for people reading the program, exactly what the program is getting ready to do.

2. You should also put the disk filename of the program in one of the first comments. For example, in the C2FIRST.C program shown earlier, the first line is really the beginning of a comment:

```
/* Filename: C2FIRST.C
```

The comment would continue to the subsequent lines, but this part tells you in which disk file the program is stored. Throughout this book, programs have comments that include a possible filename under which the program can be stored. They begin with Cx, where x is the chapter number in which they appear (for example, C6VARPR.C and C10LNIN.C). This naming convention helps you to find these programs when they are referred to in another section of the book.

The New Comment: //

C++ is sometimes called a "better C." Some programmers don't necessarily agree with the "better" label, but almost every programmer does agree that C++ introduced a new style of commenting into the language that is often preferable to C's /*...*/ style. As a matter of fact, after the C++ style was introduced, most C compiler manufacturers changed their compilers to recognize the new comment style, and all C major compilers today recognize both the old and new comment style.

The new style requires only that a comment begin with two forward slashes (//) and continue until the end of the line. You can mix the two commenting styles if you wish. A number of reasons occur for the new style's popularity:

1. C programmers can forget to terminate the older style of comments, resulting in several lines of comments that were meant to be code. This commented-out code can sometimes be difficult to debug.

2. C programs require less typing because the new style of comments requires no characters to end them.

3. Mainframe programmers used to *JCL* (*Job Control Language*, a batch-like language used to control processing on mainframes) like the new style of C comments because JCL comments also begin with //.

4. Commenting several lines out of a program, leaving the code but turning the section of code into one long comment for testing purposes, is simpler and less error-prone with the new style of C comments.

Listing 2.3 contains a program that uses the new style of C comments exclusively.

Listing 2.3: The new style of C comment is often simpler to use.

EXAMPLE

```
// Filename: C2COMM.C
// This program contains the new comments
//
#include <stdio.h>
main()
{
   int age = 30;    // Declare variable and assign value
   printf("Your age is %d years old\n", age);

// Now, print a closing message
   printf("%d is still young!\n", age);
   return 0;
}
```

Notice that the new comments can appear by themselves on a line or anywhere to the right of a statement.

CAUTION

Unlike the old style of C comments, the new style does not enable you to put executable code to the right of a comment. A comment in the new style must be the final item on the line.

Studying the Sample Program

Now that you have an overview of a C program, its structure, and its comments, the rest of this chapter walks you through the entire sample program. Do not expect to become a C expert just by completing this section—that is what the rest of the book is for. For now, just sit back and follow this walk-through of the program code.

As described earlier, this sample program contains several comments. The first three lines of the program are comments:

```
/* Filename: C2FIRST.C

   Initial C program that demonstrates the C comments

   and shows a few variables and their declarations */
```

This comment tells you the filename and explains the purpose of the program. This is not the only comment in the program; others appear throughout the rest of the code.

The next two lines (following the blank separating line) are shown here:

```
main()

{
```

This begins the main() function. Basically, the main() function's opening and closing braces enclose the body of this program and the instructions that execute. C programs often contain more than one function, but they must always contain a function called main(). The main() function does not need to be the first one, but it usually is. The opening brace begins the first and only block of this program.

When this program is compiled and run, the computer looks for main() and starts executing whatever instruction follows main()'s opening brace. Here are the three lines that follow:

```
int i, j;     /* These 3 lines declare 4 variables */

char c;

float x;
```

These three lines *declare variables*. A variable declaration describes all variables used in that block of code.

A C program processes data into meaningful results. All C programs include the following:

- Commands
- Data

Data is made up of variables and constants. As the name implies, a *variable* is data that can change (become variable) while the program runs. A *constant* remains the same. In life, a variable might be your salary. It increases over time (if you are lucky). A constant would be your first name or social security number, because each remains with you throughout life and does not (naturally) change.

Chapter 3, "Variables and Constants," fully explains these concepts. However, to give you an overview of the sample program's elements, the following discussion explains variables and constants in this program.

C enables you to use several kinds of *literal constants*, often just called *constants* or *literals* throughout the rest of the book. A C constant is any number, character, word, or phrase. The following are all valid C constants:

```
5.6
-45
'Q'
"Mary"
18.67643
0.0
```

As you can see, some constants are numeric and some are character-based. The single and double quotation marks around two of the constants, however, are not part of the constants themselves. A single character constant requires single quotation marks around it; a string of characters, such as "Mary", requires double quotation marks.

Look for the constants in the sample program. You can find these:

```
4
7
'A'
9.087
4.5
```

A variable is like a box inside your computer that holds something. That "something" might be a number or a character. You can have as many variables as your program needs to hold data that changes in the program. After you put a value into a variable, it stays in that variable until you change it or put something else into it.

Variables have names so you can tell them apart. You use the assignment operator, the equal sign (=), to assign values to variables. The following statement

```
sales=25000;
```

puts the constant value 25000 into the variable named sales. In the sample program, you can find the following variables:

```
i
```

```
j
```

```
c
```

```
x
```

The three lines of code that follow the opening brace of the sample program declare these variables. This variable declaration lets the rest of the program know that two integer variables named i and j as well as a character variable called c and a floating-point variable called x appear throughout the program. The terms *integer* and *floating-point* basically refer to two different types of numbers: Integers are whole numbers, and floating-point numbers contain decimal points.

You can see the variables being assigned values in the next few statements of the sample program:

```
i = 4;      /* i and j are assigned integer values */
j = i + 7;
c = 'A';    /* All character constants are
              enclosed in single quotes */
x = 9.087;  /* x requires a floating-point value since it
              was declared as a floating-point variable */
x = x * 4.5; /* Change what was in x with a formula */
```

The first line puts 4 in the integer variable i. The second line adds 7 to the variable i's value to get 11, which then gets assigned to (or put into) the variable called j. The plus sign (+) in C works just like it does on calculators. The other primary math operators are shown in Table 2.1.

Table 2.1: The primary math operators.

Operator	Meaning	Example
+	Addition	4 + 5
–	Subtraction	7 – 2
*	Multiplication	12 * 6
/	Division	48 / 12

The statements that appear before Table 2.1 require only slight explanation. The character constant A is assigned to the c variable. The number 9.087 is assigned to the variable called x, and then x is immediately overwritten with a new value: itself (9.087) multiplied by 4.5. This helps illustrate why computer designers use an asterisk (*) for multiplication and not a lowercase x as people generally do to show multiplication; the computer would confuse the variable x with the multiplication symbol, x, if both were allowed.

NOTE

If mathematical operators are on the right side of the equal sign, the math is completely carried out before the assignment is performed.

The next line (after the comment) includes the following special—and, at first, confusing—statement:

```
printf("%d %d %c %f", i, j, c, x);
```

When the program runs and gets to this line, it prints the contents of the four variables to the screen. It does not print %d %d %c %f, even though it might look as if it does. The "%d %d %c %f" is called a *format string*, which describes the format of what is to follow. The %d means that a decimal integer prints in that location. The %c and %f mean that a character and a floating-point value, respectively, print in those locations. This should make more sense to you later.

For now, you can ignore format strings inside printf lines until Chapter 6, "Input and Output," explains them more fully. The important part of this line is that the four values for i, j, c, and x print on the screen.

The output from this line is

```
4 11 A 40.891499
```

Because this is the only printf in the program, this is the only output the sample program produces. You might think that the program is rather long for such a small output. After you learn more about C, you should be able to write more useful programs.

It's important that you keep in mind that printf() is not a C command. You might recall from the previous chapter that C has no built-in input/output commands. The printf is a built-in function, not an actual command. You have seen one function already, main(), which is one you write the code for. The C programming designers have already written the code for the printf function. At this point, you can think of printf as being a command that outputs values to the screen, but it is really a built-in function.

To differentiate printf from regular C commands, parentheses are used after the name, as in printf(). All function names have parentheses following them in a C program. Sometimes these parentheses have something between them, and sometimes they are blank.

The last two lines in the program are shown here:

```
    return 0;   /* ALWAYS end programs and functions with return */
}
```

The return command simply tells C that this function is finished. C returns control to whatever was controlling the program before it started running. In this case, because there was only one function, control is returned to DOS or to the C editing environment. A value of 0, the traditional value that the program is terminating correctly, is returned to the operating system as well in case the execution of the next program is dependent on the successful execution of this program. If you do not include a value, C typically returns the 0 anyway. (Many programs in this book do not include the zero.) As you learn more about C, you'll learn more about how to utilize these return values.

Actually, the return statement is optional. C would know when it reached the end of the program without this statement. But it is a good programming practice to put a return statement at the end of every function, including main(). Because some functions require a return statement (if you are returning values), it is better to get in the habit of using them, rather than run the risk of leaving one out when you really need it.

The closing brace after the return does two things in this program. It signals the end of a block (begun earlier with the opening brace), which is the end of the main() function, and it signals the end of the program.

What's Next

Although this chapter only skimmed the surface of C, you should have a better understanding of C's nature. This understanding will launch well into the next chapter that explains in more detail about variables and literal constants. Only after you can successfully specify data in a program can you properly write code that acts upon that data and processes the data appropriately.

Variables and Constants

Now that you have seen an overview of the C programming language, you can start writing C programs. In this chapter, you begin to write your own programs from scratch. To understand data processing with C, you must understand how C creates, stores, and manipulates data. This chapter teaches you how C handles data.

This chapter teaches you the following topics:

- Variables and literal constants
- Types of variables and constants
- Special constants
- How to name variables
- How to declare variables
- Assigning values to variables

C Variables

Variables have characteristics. When you decide your program needs another variable, you simply declare (or define) a new variable and C makes sure you get it. You declare all C variables at the top of whatever block of code needs them. Variable declaration requires that you inform C of the variable's name and data type. Other information you might want to include is optional depending on the goals of your program. To declare a variable, you must understand the following characteristics:

- Each variable has a name.

- Each variable has a type.

- Each variable holds a value you put there, when you assign that value to that variable.

Naming Variables

Because you can have many variables in a single program, you must assign names to them so you can keep track of them. Variable names are unique, just as house addresses are unique. If two variables have the same name, C does not know which variable to use when you request one.

Variable names can be as short as a single letter or as long as 31 characters. Their names must begin with a letter of the alphabet, but after the first letter, they can contain letters, numbers, and underscore (_) characters.

TIP

Spaces are not allowed in a variable name, so use the underscore character and combine upper- and lowercase characters to help separate parts of the name.

EXAMPLE

1. The following list of variable names are all valid:

   salary   aug99_Sales   i   indexAge   amount

2. C treats uppercase letters in variable names differently than lowercase letters. For example, each of the following four variables are viewed differently by your C compiler:

   sales   Sales   SALES   sALES

3. Do not give variables the same name as a command or built-in function, and do not begin a name with a number. Use meaningful variable names, so that later you can look at your program and know for what each variable is used.

4. Along with not using spaces or other non-alpha numeric characters (except the underscore), do not use other C functions and code as variable names, either. The following are invalid variable names:

   2001_sales   Aug99+Sales   MY AGE   printf

Variable Types

Variables can hold different types of data. Table 3.1 lists the different types of C variables. For instance, if a variable holds an integer, C assumes no decimal point or fractional part (the part to the right of the decimal point) exists for the variable's value. A very large number of types are possible in C. For now, the most important types you should concentrate on are char, int, and float. You can append the prefix long to make some of them hold larger values than they would otherwise hold. Using the unsigned prefix enables them to hold positive numbers only.

Table 3.1: Some C variable types.

Declaration Name	Type
char	Character
unsigned char	Unsigned character
signed char	Signed character (same as char)
int	Integer
unsigned int	Unsigned integer
signed int	Signed integer (same as int)
short int	Short integer
unsigned short int	Unsigned short integer
signed short int	Signed short integer (same as short int)
long	Long integer
long int	Long integer (same as long)
signed long int	Signed long integer (same as long int)
unsigned long int	Unsigned long integer
float	Floating-point
double	Double floating-point
long double	Long double floating-point

The next section more fully describes each of these types. For now, you need to concentrate on the importance of declaring them before using them.

Declaring Variables

There are two places where you can declare a variable:

- After the opening brace of a block of code (usually at the top of a function)

- Before a function name (such as before main() in the program)

The first of these is the most common, and is used throughout much of this book. (If you declare a variable before a function name, it is called a global variable. Later chapters address the pros and cons of global variables.) To declare a variable, you must state its type, followed by its name. In the previous chapter, you saw a program that declared four variables in the following way:

```
main()
{
    int i, j;     // These 3 lines declare 4 variables
    char c;
    float x;
    // Rest of program follows
```

This declares two integer variables named i and j. You have no idea what is inside those variables, however. You generally cannot assume that a variable holds zero—or any other number—until you assign it a value. The first line basically tells C the following:

"I am going to use two integer variables somewhere in this program. Be expecting them. I want them named i and j. When I put a value into i or j, I ensure that the value is an integer."

Without such a declaration, you could not assign i or j a value later. You must declare all variables before you use them. You could declare each of these two variables on lines by themselves, as in the following code:

```
main()
{
    int i;
    int j;
    // Rest of program follows
```

You do not gain any readability by doing this, however. Most C programmers prefer to declare variables of the same type on the same line.

The second line from the program excerpt declares a character variable called c. Only single characters should be placed there. Next, a floating-point variable called x is declared.

EXAMPLE

1. Suppose you had to keep track of a person's first, middle, and last initials. Because an initial is obviously a character, it would be prudent to declare three character variables to hold the three initials. In C, you could do that with the following statement:

```
main()
{
```

```
    char first, middle, last;
    // Rest of program follows
```

This statement could go after the opening brace of main(). It lets the rest of the program know that you require these three character variables.

2. You could also declare these three variables on three separate lines, although it does not necessarily improve readability to do so. This could be accomplished with the following code:

```
main()
{
    char first;
    char middle;
    char last;
    // Rest of program follows
```

3. Suppose you want to keep track of a person's age and weight. If you want to store these values as whole numbers, they would probably go in integer variables. The following statement would declare those variables:

```
main()
{
    int age, weight;
    /* Rest of program follows */
```

Understanding Data Types

You might wonder why it is important to have so many variable types. After all, a number is just a number. But C has more data types than almost all other programming languages. The variable's type is critical, but choosing the type among the many offerings is not as difficult as it may first appear.

The character variable is easy to understand. A character variable can hold only a single character. You cannot put more than a single character into a character variable.

NOTE

Unlike many other programming languages, C does not have a string variable. Also, you cannot hold more than a single character in a C character variable. To store a string of characters, you must use an *aggregate* variable type that combines other fundamental types, such as an array. Chapter 5, "Preprocessor Directives," explains this more fully.

Integers hold whole numbers. Although mathematicians may cringe at this definition, an integer is really just any number that does not contain a decimal point. All of the following expressions are integers:

45   -932   0   12   5421

Floating-point numbers contain decimal points. They are known as *real* numbers to mathematicians. Any time you need to store a salary, a temperature, or any other number that may have a fractional part (a decimal portion), you must store it in a floating-point variable. All of the following expressions are floating-point numbers, and any floating-point variable can hold them:

```
45.12    -2344.5432    0.00    .04594
```

Sometimes you need to keep track of very large numbers, and sometimes you need to keep track of smaller numbers. Table 3.2 shows a list of ranges that each C variable type might hold.

CAUTION

These ranges are typical, but they may differ from computer to computer. The computer's *word* size determines the range of values (see Appendix A, "Memory Addressing, Binary, and Hexadecimal," for more information on word sizes). Your C compiler's manual will include the exact ranges you can use. Table 3.2's ranges are the minimum that are in use because they adhere to the ANSI C standard, set up by the American National Standards Institute.

Table 3.2: Typical ranges C variables might hold.

Type	Range*
char	−128 to 127
unsigned_char	0 to 255
signed_char	−128 to 127
int	−32768 to 32767
unsigned_int	0 to 65535
signed_int	−32768 to 32767
short_int	−32768 to 32767
unsigned_short_int	0 to 65535
signed_short_int	−32768 to 32767
long_int	−2147483648 to 2147483647
signed_long_int	−2147483648 to 2147483647
float	−3.4E+38 to 3.4E+38
double	−1.7E+308 to 1.7E+308
long_double	−1.7E+308 to 1.7E+308

*Use this table only as a guide; different compilers and different computers may allow different ranges.

The floating-point ranges in Table 3.2 are shown in scientific notation. To determine the actual range, take the number before the E (meaning

Exponent) and multiply it by 10 raised to the power after the plus sign. For instance, a floating-point number (type `float`) can contain a number as small as -3.4×10^{38}.

Notice that long integers and long doubles tend to hold larger numbers (and therefore, have a higher precision) than regular integers and regular double floating-point variables. This is due to the larger number of memory locations used by many of the C compilers for these data types. Again, this is usually—but not always—the case.

LIMIT EXCESSIVE DATA TYPING

If the long variable types hold larger numbers than the regular ones, you might initially want to use long variables for all your data. This would not be required in most cases, and would probably slow your program's execution.

As Appendix A describes, the more memory locations used by data, the larger that data can be. However, every time your computer has to access more storage for a single variable (as is usually the case for long variables), it takes the CPU much longer to access it, calculate with it, and store it.

Use the long variables only if you suspect your data overflows the typical data type ranges. Although the ranges differ among computers, you should have an idea of whether your numbers might exceed the computer's storage ranges. If you are working with extremely large (or extremely small and fractional) numbers, you should consider using the long variables.

Generally, all numeric variables should be signed (the default) unless you know for sure that your data contains only positive numbers. (Some values, such as age and distance, are always positive.) By making a variable an unsigned variable, you gain a little extra storage range (as explained in Appendix A), but that extra range of values must always be positive.

Obviously, you must be aware of what kinds of data your variables hold. You certainly do not always know exactly what all variables are holding, but you can have a general idea. For example, in storing a person's age, you should realize that a long integer variable would be a waste of space, because nobody can live to an age that can't be stored by a regular integer.

At first, it might seem strange for Table 3.2 to state that character variables can hold numeric values. In C, integers and character variables frequently can be used interchangeably. As explained in Appendix A, each ASCII table character has a unique number that corresponds to its location in the table. If you store a number in a character variable, C treats the data as if it were the ASCII character that matched that number in the table. Conversely, you can store character data in an integer variable. C finds that character's ASCII number, and stores that number instead of the character. Examples that help illustrate this follow a little later in the chapter.

DESIGNATING LONG, UNSIGNED, AND FLOATING-POINT LITERAL CONSTANTS

When you type a number, C interprets its type as the smallest type that can hold that number. For example, if you print 63, C knows that this number fits into a signed integer memory location. It does not treat the number as a long integer, because 63 is not large enough to warrant a long integer constant size.

However, you can append a suffix character to numeric constants to override the default type. If you put an L at the end of an integer, C interprets that integer as a long integer. The number 63 is an integer constant, but the number 63L is a long integer constant.

Assign the U suffix to designate an unsigned integer constant. The number 63 is, by default, a signed integer constant. If you type 63U, C treats it as an unsigned integer. The suffix UL indicates an unsigned long constant.

C interprets all floating-point constants (numbers that contain decimal points) as double floating-point constants. This ensures the maximum accuracy for such numbers. If you use the constant 6.82, C treats it as a double floating-point data type, even though it would fit in a regular float. You can append the floating-point suffix (F) or the long double floating-point suffix (L) to constants that contain decimal points to represent a floating-point constant or a long double floating-point constant, respectively, instead of the default double constant value.

You might rarely use these suffixes, but if you need to assign a constant value to an extended or unsigned variable, you may gain a little more accuracy if you add U, L, UL, or F (their lowercase equivalents work, too) to the end of the constant. For example, if you are making changes to someone else's C program, you may want to specify the exact data type of a constant you assign to one of the program's variables. Without the suffix, the program might assume a data value with less precision. By specifying the suffix, you don't have to change the data type of the variable throughout the entire program.

Assigning Values to Variables

Now that you know about the C variable types, you are ready to learn the specifics of putting values into those variables. You do this with the *assignment* statement. The equal sign (=) is used for assigning values to variables. The format of the assignment statement is the following:

```
variable=expression;
```

The variable is any variable that you declared earlier. The expression is any variable, constant, expression, or combination that produces a resulting data type that is the same as the variable's data type.

EXAMPLE

1. If you want to keep track of your current age, salary, and dependents, you could store these values as three C variables. You first declare the variables by deciding on correct types and good names for them. You then assign values to them. Later in the program, these values might change (for example, if the program calculates a new pay increase for you).

Good variable names might be age, salary, and dependents. To declare these three variables, the first part of the main() function might look like this:

```
/* Declare and store three values */
main()
{
    int age;
    float salary;
    int dependents;
```

Notice that you do not need to declare all integer variables together on the same line. After these variables are declared, the next three statements could assign them values, such as

```
    age=32;
    salary=25000.00;
    dependents=2;
/* Rest of program follows */
```

2. Do not put commas in values that you assign to variables. Numeric constants should never contain commas. The following statement is invalid:

```
salary=25,000.00;
```

3. You can assign variables or mathematical expressions to other variables. Suppose you stored your tax rate in a variable called taxRate earlier in a program, then decided to use your tax rate for your spouse's rate as well. At the proper point in the program, you could code the following:

```
spouseTaxRate = taxRate;
```

(The spaces around the equal sign are optional and serve to help make the statement more readable.) At this point in the program, the value in taxRate would be copied to a new variable named spouseTaxRate. The value in taxRate would still be there after this line finishes. This assumes that the variables were declared earlier in the program.

If your spouse's tax rate is going to be 40% of yours, you can assign an expression to the spouse's variable, as in

```
spouseTaxRate = taxRate * .40;
```

Any of the four mathematical symbols you learned in the last chapter, as well as the additional ones you learn about later in the book, can be part of the expression you assign to a variable.

4. If you want to assign character data to a character variable, you must enclose the character in single quotation marks. Enclose all C character constants in single quotation marks.

The following section of a program declares three variables, and then assigns three initials to them. The initials are character constants because they are enclosed in single quotation marks.

```
main()
{
    char first, middle, last;
    first = 'G';
    middle = 'M';
    last = 'P';
    /* Rest of program follows */
```

Because these are variables, you can put other values into them later if the program warrants it.

CAUTION

Do not mix types between variables and values when using assignment statements. In most cases, C lets you do this, but the results are unpredictable. For instance, in the `middle` variable presented in the last example, you could have stored a floating-point constant:

```
middle = 345.43244;    /* Do not do this! */
```

If you did so, `middle` would hold a strange value that would seem to be meaningless. Make sure that values you assign to variables match the variable's type. The only major exception to this occurs when you assign an integer to a character variable, or a character to an integer variable, as you will learn shortly.

Literal Constants

As with variables, there are several types of C constants. Remember that a constant does not change. Integer constants are whole numbers that do not contain decimal points. Floating-point constants are numbers that contain a fractional portion (a decimal point with an optional value to the right of the decimal point).

Integer Constants

You already know that an integer is any whole number without a decimal point. C lets you assign integer constants to variables, use integer constants for calculations, and print integer constants in the `printf()` function.

A regular integer constant cannot begin with a leading 0. To C, the number 012 is not the number twelve. If you precede an integer constant with a 0, C thinks it is an *octal* constant. An octal constant is a base-8 number. The octal numbering system is not used much in today's computer systems. The newer versions of C retain octal capabilities for compatibility with previous versions.

An octal integer constant contains a leading 0, and a hexadecimal constant contains a leading 0x.

A special integer in C that is still greatly used today is the base-16 (or *hexadecimal*) constant. Appendix A describes the hexadecimal numbering system. If you want to represent a hexadecimal integer constant, add the 0x prefix to it. All of the following numbers are hexadecimal numbers:

```
0x10      0x2C4      0xFFFF      0X9
```

Notice that it does not matter if you use a lowercase or uppercase letter x after the leading zero, or an uppercase or lowercase hexadecimal digit (for hex numbers A through F). If you write business application programs in C, you might think you never have the need for using hexadecimal, and you might be correct. For a complete understanding of C and your computer in general, however, you should become a little familiar with the fundamentals of hexadecimal numbers.

Table 3.3 shows a few integer constants represented in their regular decimal, hexadecimal, and octal notations. Each row contains the same number in all three bases.

Table 3.3: Integer constants represented in three different bases.

Decimal	Hexadecimal	Octal
(Base 10)	(Base 16)	(Base 8)
16	0x10	020
65535	0xFFFF	177777
25	0x19	031

NOTE

Floating-point constants might begin with a leading zero, for example, 0.7. They will be properly interpreted by C. Only integers are hexadecimal or octal constants if preceded by a zero.

YOUR COMPUTER'S WORD SIZE IS IMPORTANT

If you write a lot of system programs that use hexadecimal numbers, you probably want to store those numbers in unsigned variables. This keeps C from improperly interpreting positive numbers as negative numbers.

For example, if your computer stores integers in 2-byte words (as most PCs do), the hexadecimal constant 0xFFFF represents either –1 or 65535, depending on how the sign bit is interpreted. If you declared an unsigned integer, such as

```
unsigned int i_num = 0xFFFF;
```

C knows you want it to use the sign bit as data and not as the sign. If you declared the same value as a signed integer, however, as in

```
int i_num = 0xFFFF;    // The word "signed" is optional
```

C thinks this is a negative number (–1) because the sign bit is turned on. (If you were to convert 0xFFFF to binary, you would get sixteen number 1s.) Appendix A describes these concepts in more detail.

String Constants

A string constant is always enclosed in double quotation marks.

One type of C constant, called the string constant, does not have a matching variable. A string constant is always enclosed in double quotation marks. Here are examples of string constants:

```
"C Programming"    "123"    " "    "4323 E. Oak Road"    "x"
```

Any string of characters between double quotation marks—even a single character between double quotation marks—is considered to be a string constant. A single space, a word, or a group of words between double quotation marks are all C string constants. If the string constant contains only numeric digits, it is not a number; it is a string of numeric digits that you cannot use to perform mathematics. You can perform math only on numbers, not on string constants that contain numbers or even on a character constant that might contain a number (enclosed in single quotation marks).

NOTE

A *string constant* is any character, digit, or group of characters enclosed in double quotation marks. A *character constant* is any character enclosed in single quotation marks.

The double quotation marks are never considered part of the string constant. The double quotation marks surround the string and simply inform your C compiler that it is a string constant and not another type of constant.

It is easy to print string constants. Simply put the string constants in a printf() function. No other printf() characters you have seen, such as "%d" or "%c", are needed. Here is an example of what you need to type to print a string constant to the screen:

```
printf("C By Example");
```

1. The following program displays a simple message onscreen. No variables are needed because no data is stored or calculated.

```
/* Filename: C3ST1.C
   Display a string on-screen */
#include <stdio.h>
main()
{
    printf("C programming is fun!");
    return;
}
```

Remember to make the last line in your C program (before the closing brace) a return statement.

2. You probably want to label the output from your programs. Do not print the value of a variable unless you also print a string constant describing that variable. The following program computes sales tax for a sale and prints the tax. Notice a message is printed first that tells the program user what the next number means:

```
/* Filename: C3ST2.C
   Compute sales tax and display it with an appropriate message */

#include <stdio.h>

main()
{
    float sale, tax;
    float tax_rate = .08;     /* Sales tax percentage */

    /* Determine the amount of the sale */
    sale = 22.54;

    /* Compute the sales tax */
    tax = sale * tax_rate;

    /* Print the results */
    printf("The sales tax is:");
    printf("%f", tax);

    return 0;
}
```

STRING-CONSTANT ENDINGS

An additional aspect of string constants sometimes confuses beginning C
programmers. All string constants end with a zero. You do not see the zero,
but C makes sure it stores the zero at the end of the string in memory.
Figure 3.1 shows what the string "C Program" looks like in memory.

Figure 3.1: *In memory, a string constant always ends with 0.*

You do not put the zero at the end of a string constant; C does it for you
every time it stores a string. If your program contained the string "C
Program", for example, the compiler recognizes it as a string constant (from
the double quotation marks) and stores the zero at the end.

The zero is important to C and is called the *string delimiter*. Without the
string delimiter, C would not know where the string constant ended in
memory. (Remember that the double quotation marks are not stored as part
of the string, so C cannot use them to determine where the string ends.)

The string-delimiting zero is not the same as the character zero. If you look
at the ASCII table in Appendix C, "ASCII Table," you can see that the first
entry, ASCII number 0, is the *null* character. (If you are unfamiliar with the
ASCII table, you should read Appendix A for a review.) This differentiates
the string-delimiting zero from the character '0', whose ASCII value is 48.

As explained in Appendix A, all memory locations in your computer actually
hold bit patterns for characters. If the letter A is stored in memory, an A is
not really there; the binary bit pattern for the ASCII A (01000001) is stored
there. Because the binary bit pattern for the null zero is 00000000, the
string-delimiting zero is also called a *binary zero*.

To illustrate this further, Figure 3.2 shows the bit patterns for the following
string constant when stored in memory:

"I am 30"

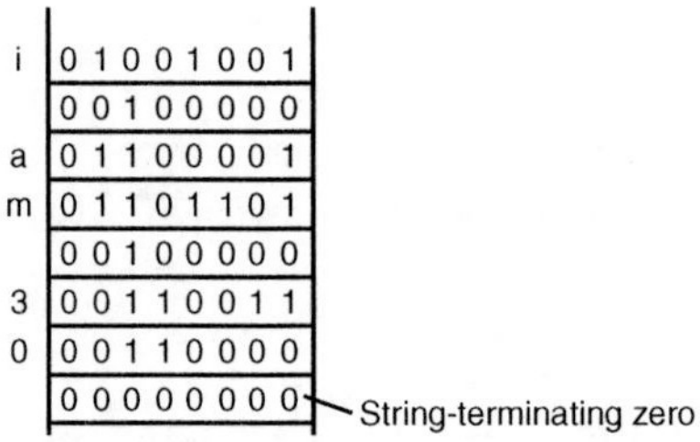

```
i  01001001
   00100000
a  01100001
m  01101101
   00100000
3  00110011
0  00110000
   00000000 ── String-terminating zero
```

Figure 3.2: *The bit pattern showing that a null zero and a character zero are different.*

Figure 3.2 shows how a string is stored in your computer's memory at the binary level. It is important for you to recognize that the character 0, inside the number 30, is not the same zero (at the bit level) as the string-terminating null zero. If it were, C would think this string ended after the 3, which would be incorrect.

C's method of storing strings is a fairly advanced concept, but you truly need to understand it before continuing. If you are new to computers, reviewing the material in Appendix A will help you understand this concept.

STRING LENGTHS

Many times, your program needs to know the length of a string. This becomes critical when you learn how to accept string input from the keyboard. The length of a string is the number of characters up to, but not including, the delimiting null zero. Do not include the null character in that count, even though you know C adds it to the end of the string.

EXAMPLE

1. The following are all string constants:

   `"0"`   `"C"`   `"A much longer string constant"`

2. The following shows some string constants and their corresponding string lengths. All string constants have a specified length.

String	Length
`"C"`	1
`"0"`	1
`"Hello"`	5
`" "`	0
`"30 oranges"`	10

Character Constants

All C character literal constants should be enclosed within single quotation marks. The single quotation marks are not part of the character, but they serve to delimit the character. The following are valid C character constants:

```
'w'   'W'   'C'   '7'   '*'   '='   '.'   'K'
```

C does not append a null zero to the end of character constants. You should know that the following are very different to C:

```
'R'     and     "R"
```

`'R'` is a single character constant. It is one character long, because all character constants (and variables) are one character long. `"R"` is a string constant because it is delimited by double quotation marks. Its length is also one, but it includes a null zero in memory so C knows where the string ends. Because of this difference, you cannot mix character constants and character strings. Figure 3.3 shows how these two constants are stored in memory.

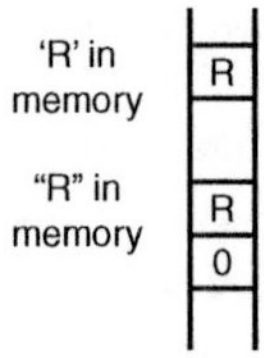

Figure 3.3: *This figure shows the difference in memory between* `'R'` *as a character constant and* `"R"` *as a string constant.*

All of the alphabetic, numeric, and special characters on your keyboard can be character constants. Some characters, however, cannot be represented with your keyboard. They include some of the higher ASCII characters (such as the Spanish Ñ). Because you do not have keys for every character in the ASCII table, C lets you represent these characters by typing their ASCII hexadecimal number inside single quotation marks.

For example, to store the Spanish Ñ in a variable, look up its hexadecimal ASCII number from Appendix C. You find that it is A5. Add the prefix \x to it and enclose it in single quotation marks, so C will know to use the special character. You could do that with the following code:

```
char sn='\xA5';   // Puts the Spanish N into the variable called sn
```

This is the way to store (or print) any character from the ASCII table, even if that character does not have a key on your keyboard.

The single quotation marks still tell C that a single character is inside the quotation marks. Even though `'\xA5'` contains four characters inside the quotation marks, those four characters represent a single character, not a character string. However, if you were to include those four characters inside a string constant, C would treat `\xA5` as a single character within the string. The following string constant

`"An accented a is \xA0"`

is a C string that is 18 characters long, not 21 characters. C interprets the `\xA0` character as the á, just as it should.

Any character preceded by a backslash, \, (such as these have been) is called an *escape sequence*, or *escape character*. Table 3.4 shows some additional escape sequences that come in handy when you want to print special characters.

TIP

Include `\n` in a `printf()` when you want to skip to the next line.

Table 3.4: Special C escape sequence characters.

Escape Sequence	Meaning
\a	Alarm (the terminal's bell)
\b	Backspace
\f	Form feed (for the printer)
\n	Newline (carriage return and line feed)
\r	Carriage return
\t	Tab
\v	Vertical tab
\\	Backslash (\)
\?	Question mark
\'	Single quotation mark
\"	Double quotation mark
\ooo	Octal number
\xhh	Hexadecimal number
\0	Null zero (or binary zero)

MATH WITH C CHARACTERS

Because C links characters so closely with their ASCII numbers, you can perform arithmetic on character data. The following section of code

```
char c;
c = 'T' + 5;        /* Add 5 to the ASCII character */
```

actually stores a value Y in variable type c. The ASCII value of the letter T is 84. Adding 5 to 84 produces 89. Because the variable c is not an integer variable, but is a character variable, C knows to put in c the ASCII character for 89, not the number itself.

Conversely, you can store character constants in integer variables. If you do, C interprets and stores the matching ASCII number (an integer) instead of the character. The following section of code

```
int i='P';
```

does not put a letter P in i because i is not a character variable. C assigns the number 80 in the variable because 80 is the ASCII number for the letter P.

EXAMPLE

1. To print two names on two different lines, include the \n between them:

```
printf("Harry\nJerry");
```

When the program gets to this line, it prints the following:

```
Harry
Jerry
```

2. The following short program rings the bell on your computer by assigning the \a escape sequence to a variable and then printing that variable:

```
/* Filename: C3BELL.C
   Rings the bell */
#include <stdio.h>

main()
{
    char bell='\a';
    printf("%c", bell);   /* "%c" means print a character value */
    return;
}
```

What's Next

You've learned about C's variable and literal constant types, how to name variables, and how to assign variable values, but you have not yet seen string variables. C supports no string variables, so you cannot store string data in string variables (as you can in other programming languages). However, you can "fool" C into thinking it has a string variable by using a character array to hold strings. You learn this important concept in the next chapter.

4

Introduction to Arrays

Even though C does not support string variables, you can make C think it supports string variables with character arrays. The concept of arrays might be new to you, but this chapter explains how easy they are to declare and use. After you declare these arrays, they can hold character strings— just as if they were real string variables. Manipulating characters and words is one thing that separates your computer from a powerful calculator; this capability gives computers true data processing capabilities.

This chapter teaches you the following topics:

- Character arrays
- How character arrays and strings are alike and how they differ
- Declaring character arrays as strings

Introducing Arrays

Almost every type of data in C has a corresponding variable type, but there is no variable for holding character strings. The authors of C realized that you need some way to store strings in variables, but instead of storing them in a string variable (as in some languages such as BASIC or Pascal) you must store them in an *array* of characters.

If you have only programmed a little before, arrays might be new to you. An array is a list (sometimes called a *table*) of variables, and most programming languages enable the use of such lists. Suppose you had to keep track of the sales records of 100 salespeople. You could make up 100 variable names and assign to each one a different salesperson's sales record.

All those different variable names, however, are difficult to track. If you were to put them in an array of floating-point variables, you would need to keep track of only a single name (the array name) and could reference each of the 100 values by a numeric subscript.

Part VI, "Building Blocks," covers array processing in more detail. However, to work with character string data in your early programs, you need to become familiar with the concept of an array of characters (called a *character array*).

Because a string is simply a list of one or more characters, a character array is the perfect place to hold strings of information. Suppose you want to keep track of a person's full name, age, and salary in variables. The age and salary are easy because there are variable types that can hold such data. You would write the following code to declare those two variables:

```
int age;
float salary;
```

You have no string variable to hold the name, but you can create an appropriate array of characters (which is really one or more character variables next to each other in memory) with the following declaration:

```
char name[15];
```

This reserves a character array. An array declaration always includes brackets ([ ]) that declare the storage C needs to reserve for the array. This array is 15 characters long. The array name is name. You can also assign to the character array a value at the time you declare it. The following declaration statement not only declares the character array, but also assigns the name "Michael Jones" at the same time:

```
char name[15]="Michael Jones";
```

Figure 4.1 shows what this array looks like in memory. Each of the 15 boxes of the array is called an *element*. Notice the null zero (the string-terminating character) at the end of the string. Notice also that the last character of the array contains no data. You filled only the first 14 elements of the array with the data and the data's null zero. The fifteenth element actually has a value in it—but we are not concerned with whatever follows the string's null zero.

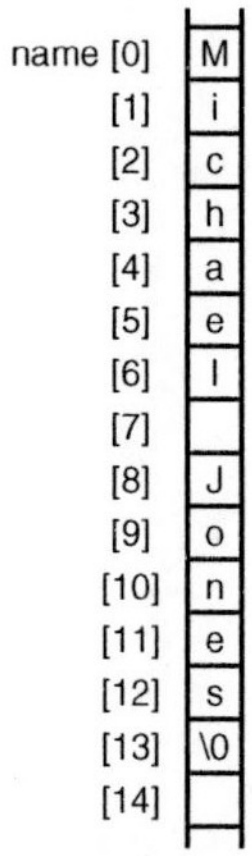

```
name [0]   M
    [1]    i
    [2]    c
    [3]    h
    [4]    a
    [5]    e
    [6]    l
    [7]
    [8]    J
    [9]    o
   [10]    n
   [11]    e
   [12]    s
   [13]    \0
   [14]
```

Figure 4.1: *Here is a character array after being declared and assigned a string value.*

You can access individual elements within an array, or you can access the array as a whole. This is the primary advantage of an array over the use of many differently named variables. You can assign values to the individual array elements by putting the elements' location, called a *subscript*, in brackets, as follows:

```
name[3]='k';
```

This overwrites the h in the name Michael with a k. The string now looks like the one in Figure 4.2.

All array subscripts start at zero. Therefore, to overwrite the first element, you must use 0 as the subscript. Assigning name[3] (as is done in Figure 4.2) changes the value of the fourth element in the array.

You can print the entire string—or, more accurately, the entire array—with a single printf() function, as follows:

```
printf(name);
```

or

```
printf("%s", name);
```

Notice that when you print an array, you do not put the brackets after the array name. Also, as long as a character array holds a string—and it does as long as you put in a string, or ensure that a null zero is at the end of its character data—you can print it with or without the "%s" (string) format code.

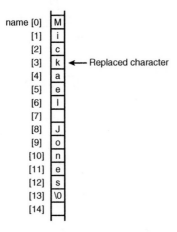

Figure 4.2: The array contents (refer to Figure 4.1) after changing one of the elements.

But you must be sure to reserve enough characters in the array to hold the entire string. The following

```
char name[5]="Michael Jones";  /* Not valid! */
```

would be incorrect because it reserves only five characters for the array, while the name and its null zero require 14 characters. However, C does not give you an error message if you try to do this; instead, it overwrites whatever follows the name array in memory. This can cause unpredictable results and is never correct.

Always reserve enough array elements to hold the string, plus its null-terminating character. It is easy to forget the null character, but don't do it. If your string contains 13 characters, it also must have a 14th for the null zero—or it will never be treated like a string. To help eliminate this error, C gives you a shortcut. The following two character array statements are the same:

```
char horse[9]="Stallion";
```

and

```
char horse[]="Stallion";
```

Even without entering the specific value in the brackets (as in statement two), if you at least assign a value to a character array at the same time you declare the array, C counts the string's length, adds one for the null zero, and reserves that much array space for you automatically.

Never declare a character array (or any other type of array) with empty brackets, if you also do not assign values to that array at the same time. The following statement

```
char people[];   /* Not recommended! */
```

does not reserve any space for the array called people. Because you did not assign the array a value when you declared it, C assumes this array contains zero elements. Therefore, you have no room to put values into this array later. Most compilers generate an error if you attempt this.

Character Arrays Versus Strings

In the previous section, you saw how to put a string into a character array. Strings can exist in C only as string constants, or stored in character arrays. At this point, you need to understand only that strings must be stored in character arrays. As you read through this book and become more familiar with arrays and strings, however, you should become more comfortable with their use.

NOTE

Strings must be stored in character arrays, but not all character arrays contain strings.

Look at the two arrays shown in Figure 4.3. The first one, called cara1, is a character array, but it does not contain a string. Instead of a string, it contains a list of several characters. The second array, called cara2, contains a string because it has a null zero at the end.

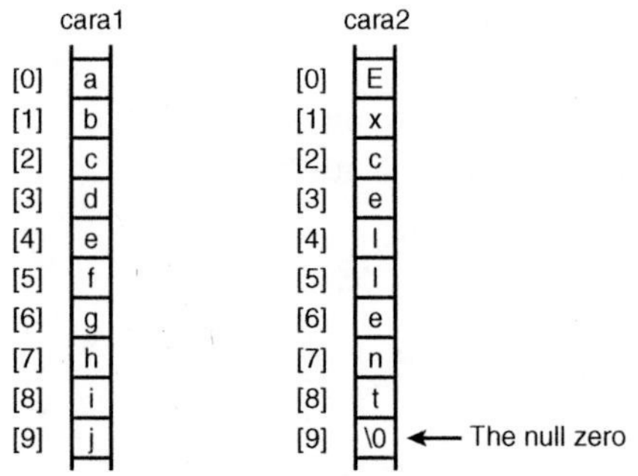

	cara1		cara2
[0]	a	[0]	E
[1]	b	[1]	x
[2]	c	[2]	c
[3]	d	[3]	e
[4]	e	[4]	l
[5]	f	[5]	l
[6]	g	[6]	e
[7]	h	[7]	n
[8]	i	[8]	t
[9]	j	[9]	\0 ← The null zero

Figure 4.3: *Two character arrays: The one to the left contains characters, and the one to the right contains a character string.*

These arrays could be initialized with the following declaration statements:

```
char cara1[10]={'a', 'b', 'c', 'd', 'e', 'f', 'g', 'h', 'i', 'j'};
char cara2[10]="Excellent";   // C supplies the null zero
```

If you want to put only individual characters into an array, you must enclose the list of characters in braces, as shown. You could also initialize cara1 later in the program, using assignment statements, as the following code section does:

```
char cara1[10];
cara1[0]='a';
cara1[1]='b';
cara1[2]='c';
cara1[3]='d';
cara1[4]='e';
cara1[5]='f';
cara1[6]='g';
cara1[7]='h';
cara1[8]='i';
cara1[9]='j';    // Last element possible with subscript of 9
```

Because the cara1 character array does not contain a null zero, it does not contain a string of characters. It does contain characters that can be stored in the array—and used individually—but you cannot treat the array in a program as if the array were a string variable.

CAUTION

You cannot assign string values to character arrays in a regular assignment statement, except when you first declare them, as shown. After you declare a string array, you must assign the string to the array one character at a time or by using one of several functions.

Because a character array is not a string variable (it can be used only to hold a string), it cannot go on the left side of an equal (=) sign. The program that follows is invalid:

```
// Filename: C4ALF.C
#include <stdio.h>
main()
{
    char petname[20];      /*  Reserve space for the pet's name */
    petname = "Alfalfa";  /* INVALID! */
    printf(petname);
    return 0;
}
```

Because the pet's name was not assigned at the time the character array was declared (line 5), it cannot be assigned a value later. But the following is allowed, because you can assign values individually to a character array:

```
// Filename: C4PETSTR.C
#include <stdio.h>
main()
{
    char petname[20]; // Reserve space for the pet's name
    petname[0]='A';   // Assign values one element at a time
    petname[1]='l';
    petname[2]='f';
    petname[3]='a';
    petname[4]='l';
    petname[5]='f';
    petname[6]='a';
    petname[7]='\0';  // Needed to ensure this is a string!
    printf(petname);  // Now the pet's name prints properly
    return 0;
}
```

The petname character array now holds a string because the last character is a null zero. How long is the string in petname? It is seven characters long because the length of a string never includes the null zero.

You cannot assign more than 20 characters to this array because its reserved space is only 20 characters. However, you can store any string of 19 (leaving one for the null zero) or fewer characters to the array. If you put the "Alfalfa" string into the array as shown, then assign a null zero to petname[3] as in

```
petname[3]='\0';
```

The string in petname is now just three characters long. You have, in effect, shortened the string. There are still 20 characters reserved for petname, but the data inside it is the string "Alf" ending with a null zero.

There are many other ways to assign a value to a string. You can use the strcpy() function, for example. This is a built-in function—like printf()— enabling you to copy a string constant into a string. To copy the "Alfalfa" pet name into the petname array, you could type:

```
strcpy(petname, "Alfalfa");  // Copies Alfalfa into the array
```

The strcpy() function puts string constants into string arrays.

The strcpy() ("string copy") function assumes that the first value in the parentheses is a character array name, and that the second value is a valid string constant or another character array that holds a string. You must be sure that the first character array in the parentheses is long enough (in number of reserved elements) to hold whatever string you copy into it.

Other methods of initializing arrays are explored throughout the rest of this book.

EXAMPLE

1. Suppose you want to keep track of your aunt's name in a program so you can print it. If your aunt's name is Ruth Ann Cooper, you need to reserve at least 16 elements—15 to hold the name and one to hold the null character. The following statement properly reserves a character array to hold the name:

```
char aunt_name[16];
```

2. If you want to put your aunt's name in the array at the same time you reserve the array storage, you could do it like this:

```
char aunt_name[16]="Ruth Ann Cooper";
```

You also could leave out the array size and let C count the number needed:

```
char aunt_name[]="Ruth Ann Cooper";
```

3. Suppose you want to keep track of the names of three friends. The longest name is 20 characters (including the null zero). You simply need to reserve enough character-array space to hold each friend's name. The following would do it:

```
char friend1[20];
char friend2[20];
char friend3[20];
```

These array declarations should go towards the top of the block, along with any integer, floating-point, or character variables you need to declare.

4. The next example asks the user for a first and last name. It then prints the user's initials onscreen by printing the first character of each name in the array. The program must print each array's 0 subscript because the first subscript of any array begins at 0, not 1.

```
/* Filename: C4INIT.C
    Print the user's initials */
#include <stdio.h>
main()
```

```
    {
        char first[20];    // Holds the first name
        char last[20];     // Holds the last name

        printf("What is your first name? ");
        scanf(" %s", first);
        printf("What is your last name? ");
        scanf(" %s", last);

        /* Print the initials */
        printf("Your initials are %c.%c.", first[0], last[0]);
        return 0;
    }
```

5. The following program takes your three friends' character arrays and assigns them string values, by using the three methods shown in this chapter:

```
/* Filename: C4STR.C
   Store and initialize 3 character arrays for 3 friends */
#include <stdio.h>
#include <string.h>
main()
{
    // Declare all arrays, and initialize the first one
    char friend1[20] = "Jackie Paul Johnson";
    char friend2[20];
    char friend3[20];

// Use a function to initialize the second array
    strcpy(friend2, "Julie L. Roberts");

    friend3[0]='A';    // Initialize the last, an element at a time
    friend3[1]='d';
    friend3[2]='a';
    friend3[3]='m';
    friend3[4]=' ';
    friend3[5]='G';
    friend3[6]='.';
    friend3[7]=' ';
    friend3[8]='S';
    friend3[9]='m';
    friend3[10]='i';
    friend3[11]='t';
```

```
        friend3[12]='h';
        friend3[13]='\0';

        /* Print all three names */
        printf("%s\n", friend1);
        printf("%s\n", friend2);
        printf("%s\n", friend3);
        return 0;
}
```

The last method of initializing a character array with a string—one element at a time—is not used as often as the other methods.

What's Next

Even though C has no string variables, character arrays can hold string constants. After you put a string into a character array, you can print or manipulate it as if it were a string. Now that you know how to store all kinds of data in your C programs, the next chapter explains how to utilize preprocessor directives that work on your program's source code. Pre-processor directives can save you programming time by working on your source code so you don't have to as you'll learn in the next chapter.

5

Preprocessor Directives

The C compiler routes your programs through a preprocessor before it compiles them. C's preprocessor might be called a "pre-compiler" because it pre-processes and prepares your source code for compiling before your compiler receives it.

Because this *preprocess* is so important to C, you should familiarize yourself with it before learning more specialized commands in the language itself. Regular C commands do not affect the preprocessor. You must supply special non-C commands, called preprocessor directives, to control the preprocessor. These directives enable you, for example, to effect changes to your source code before it reaches the compiler.

This chapter teaches you the following topics:

- What preprocessor directives are
- The #include preprocessor directive
- The #define preprocessor directive
- How to use the preprocessor directives

Understanding Preprocessor Directives

Preprocessor directives are commands that you supply to the preprocessor. All preprocessor directives begin with a pound sign (#). Never put a semicolon at the end of preprocessor directives, because they are preprocessor commands and not C commands. Preprocessor directives typically begin in column 1 of your source program. They could begin in any column, of course, but you should stay with tradition and start them in the first column wherever they appear. Listing 5.1 contains a program containing three preprocessor directives.

Listing 5.1: Three preprocessor directives control calculations and output.

```
/* Filename: C5PRE.C

    C program that demonstrates preprocessor directives */


#include <stdio.h>
#define AGE 28
#define MESSAGE "Welcome to C."


main()
{
    int i = 10, age;    // i is assigned a value at declaration
                        // age is still UNDEFINED

    age = 5;            // Puts 5 in the variable age

    i = i * AGE;        // AGE is not the same as the variable age

    printf("%d %d %d", i, age, AGE);  // Prints 280 5 28
    printf(MESSAGE);    // "Welcome to C" gets printed on screen

    return 0;
}
```

Preprocessor directives cause your C preprocessor to change your source code, but these changes last only as long as the compilation takes. When you look at your source code again, the preprocessor is finished with your file and its changes are no longer in the file. Your preprocessor does not in any way compile your program or look at your actual C commands. Some beginning C students tend to get confused by this, but you shouldn't as long as you realize your program has yet to be compiled when your preprocessor directives execute.

It has been said that a preprocessor does nothing more than text-editing to your program. This analogy holds true throughout this chapter.

The #include Directive

The #include preprocessor directive *merges* a disk file into your source program. Remember that a preprocessor directive does nothing more than a word processing command might do to your program; word processors also are capable of file merging. The format of the #include preprocessor directive follows:

```
#include <filename>
```

or

```
#include "filename"
```

In the #include directive, the *filename* must be an ASCII text file (just as your source file must be) that resides on your disk. To better illustrate this, it might help to leave C for just a moment. The following example shows the contents of two files on disk. One is called OUTSIDE and the other is called INSIDE.

The OUTSIDE file contains the following lines:

```
Now is the time for all good men
#include <INSIDE>
to come to the aid of their country.
```

The INSIDE file consists of the following:

```
A quick brown fox jumped
over the lazy dog.
```

Assume you can run the OUTSIDE file through the C preprocessor, which would find the #include directive and replace it with the entire file called INSIDE. In other words, the C preprocessor directive would merge the INSIDE file into the OUTSIDE file—at the #include location—and OUTSIDE would expand to include the merged text. After the preprocessing ends, OUTSIDE would look like this:

```
Now is the time for all good men
A quick brown fox jumped
over the lazy dog.
to come to the aid of their country.
```

The INSIDE file remains on disk in its original form. Only the file containing the #include directive is changed. But note that this change is only temporary; that is, OUTSIDE is expanded by the included file only for as long as it takes to compile the program.

A few examples that are more usable with C might help, because the OUTSIDE and INSIDE files are not C programs. You might want to #include a file containing common code that you frequently use. Suppose you print your name and address often in your C programs. You could always type the following few lines of code in every program that prints your name and address:

```
printf("Kelly Jane Peterson\n");
printf("Apartment #217\n");
printf("4323 East Skelly Drive\n");
printf("New York, New York\n");
printf("               10012\n");
```

Instead of having to retype the same five lines everywhere you want your name and address to print, you could just type them once and save them in a file called myadd.c. From then on, you would only need to type the single line:

```
#include <myadd.c>
```

This not only saves typing, but it also maintains consistency and accuracy. (Sometimes this kind of repeated text is known as *boilerplate*.)

You usually can use angled brackets (<>) or double quotation marks (" ") around the included filename with the same results. The angled brackets tell the preprocessor to look for the include file in a default include directory, set up by your compiler. The double quotes tell the preprocessor first to look for the include file in the directory where the source code is stored and, if missing, then to look for it in the system's include directory.

Most of the time, you do see angled brackets around the included filename. If you want to include sections of code in other programs, be sure to store that code in the system's include directory (if you use angled brackets).

Even though #include works well for inserted source code, there are other ways to include common source code that are more efficient. You learn about these methods, called external functions, in Chapter 13, "Introduction to C Functions."

This source code #include example serves well to explain what the #include preprocessor directive does. Despite this fact, #include seldom is used to include source code text, but is more often used to include special system files called *header* files. These system files inform C how to interpret the many built-in functions that you use. Your C compiler comes with its own header files. When you (or your system administrator) installed your C compiler, these header files were automatically stored on your disk in the system's include directory. Their filenames always end in .h to differentiate them from regular C source code.

The most common header file is named stdio.h. This gives your C compiler needed information about the built-in printf() function, as well as other very useful and common built-in routines that perform input and output. The name "stdio.h" stands for *standard input/output header*.

At this point, you don't really need to understand the stdio.h file. You should, however, place this file before main() in every program you write. It is rare that a C program does not need stdio.h included, but if it isn't needed, including it does no harm. Your programs can work without stdio.h (you've already seen it happen in this book); nevertheless, your programs are more accurate and hidden errors come to the surface much faster if you include this file.

Throughout this book, whenever a new built-in function is described, the function's matching header file also is given. Because almost every C program you write includes a printf() to print to the screen, almost every program contains the following line:

```
#include <stdio.h>
```

In the previous chapter, you saw the strcpy() function. Its header file is called string.h. Therefore, if you write a program that contains strcpy(), you should also include its matching header file at the same time you include <stdio.h>. These go on separate lines, such as

```
#include <stdio.h>
#include <string.h>
```

The order of your included files does not matter as long as you include them before the functions that need them. Most C programmers include all of their needed header files before main().

These header files are nothing more than text files. If you like, search your disk with your C editor and find one, such as stdio.h, and look at it. The file might seem very complex at this point, but there is nothing "hidden" about it. If you do look at a header file, however, do not change it in any way. If you do, you might have to reload your compiler from scratch to restore the file.

EXAMPLE

1. The following program is very short. It includes the name-and-address printing routine described earlier. After printing the name and address, it ends.

```
/* Filename: C5INC1.C
   Illustrates the #include preprocessor directive */
main()
{
  #include "myadd.c"
  return 0;
}
```

The double quotes are used because the file named myadd.c is stored in the same directory as the source file. Remember that if you type this program into your computer (after typing and saving the myadd.c file) and then compile your program, the myadd.c file is included only as long as it takes to compile the program. Your compiler does not see this file. Your compiler sees—and "thinks" you typed—the following:

```
/* Filename: C5INCL1.C
    Illustrates the #include preprocessor directive */
main()
{
printf("Kelly Jane Peterson\n");
printf("Apartment #217\n");
printf("4323 East Skelly Drive\n");
printf("New York, New York\n");
printf("                10012\n");
    return 0;
}
```

This explains what is meant by a preprocessor: The changes are made to your source code before it is ever compiled. Your original source code is restored as soon as the compile is finished. When you look at your program again, it is back in its original form, as originally typed, with the #include statement.

2. Because this program uses printf(), it also should include the standard input/output header file as follows:

```
/* Filename: C5INCL2.C
    Illustrates the #include preprocessor directive */

#include <stdio.h>

main()
{
#include "myadd.c"
    return 0;
}
```

3. The following program copies a message into a character array and prints it to the screen. Because the printf() and strcpy() built-in functions are used, both of their header files also should be included.

```
/* Filename: C5INCL3.C
    Uses two header files */

#include <stdio.h>
```

```
#include <string.h>

main()
{
    char message[20];
    strcpy(message, "This is fun!");
    printf(message);
    return 0;
}
```

The #define Directive

The #define preprocessor directive also commonly is used in many C programs. This directive might seem strange at first, but it really does nothing more than a search-and-replace command does on a word processor. The format of #define is

#define *ARGUMENT1 argument2*

where *ARGUMENT1* is a single word containing no spaces. Use the same naming rules for the #define statement's first argument as for variables (refer to Chapter 4, "Introduction to Arrays"). For the first argument, it is traditional to use uppercase letters—one of the only uses of uppercase in the entire C language. At least one space separates *ARGUMENT1* from *argument2*. The *argument2* can be any character, word, or phrase; it also can contain spaces or anything else you can type on the keyboard. Because #define is a preprocessor directive and not a C executable command, do not put a semicolon at the end of its expression.

The #define preprocessor directive replaces the occurrence of *ARGUMENT1* everywhere in your program with the contents of *argument2*. In most cases, the #define directive should go before main() (along with any #include directives). Look at the following #define directive:

#define AGELIMIT 21

If your program includes one or more occurrences of the term AGELIMIT, the preprocessor replaces every one of them with the number 21. The compiler then reacts as if you actually had typed 21 instead of AGELIMIT, because the preprocessor changes all occurrences of AGELIMIT to 21 before your compiler sees the source code. But, again, the change is only temporary. After your program is compiled, you see it as you originally typed it, with #define and AGELIMIT still intact.

AGELIMIT is not a variable, because variables are declared and assigned values only at the time when your program is compiled and run. The preprocessor changes your source file before the time it is compiled.

You might wonder why you would ever need to go to this much trouble. If you want 21 everywhere AGELIMIT occurs, you could type 21 to begin with. But the advantage of using #define over constants is that if the age limit ever changes (perhaps down to 18), you need to change only one line in the program—and not every single occurrence of the constant 21.

Because #define enables you to easily define and change constants, the replaced arguments of the #define directive are sometimes called *defined constants*. You can define any type of constant, including string constants. The following program contains a defined string constant that replaces a string in two places:

```
/* Filename: C5DEF1.C

   Defines a string constant and uses it twice */


#include <stdio.h>
#define MYNAME "Phil Ward"


main()
{
   char name[]=MYNAME;
   printf("My name is %s \n", name);    // Prints the array
   printf("My name is %s \n", MYNAME); // Prints the defined constant
   return 0;
}
```

The first argument of #define is in uppercase to distinguish it from variable names in the program. Variables are usually entered in lowercase. Although your preprocessor and compiler would not get confused, people who look at your program can more quickly scan through and tell which items are defined constants and which are not. They know when they see an uppercase word (if you follow the recommended standard for this first #define argument) to look at the top of the program for its actual defined value.

The fact that defined constants are not variables is made even clearer in the following program. This program prints five values. The printed values appear following the program and you should study the program thoroughly to understand how the #define preprocessor directives expanded to produce the output.

```
/* Filename: C5DEF2.C

   Illustrates that #define constants are not variables */


#include <stdio.h>
```

```
#define X1 b+c
#define X2 X1 + X1
#define X3 X2 * c + X1 - d
#define X4 2 * X1 + 3 * X2 + 4 * X3

main()
{
   int b = 2;        /* Declares and initializes four variables */
   int c = 3;
   int d = 4;
   int e = X4;

   printf("%d  %d  %d  %d  %d", e, X1, X2, X3, X4);
   return 0;
}
```

The output from this program is

44   5   10   17   44

If you had treated X1, X2, X3, and X4 as variables, you would not get the correct answers. X1 through X4 are not variables; they are defined constants. Before your program is compiled, the preprocessor looks at the first line and knows to change every occurrence of X1 to b+c. This occurs before the next #define is processed. Therefore, after the first #define, the source code looks like this:

```
/* Filename: C5DEF2.C
   Illustrates that #define constants are not variables */

#include <stdio.h>

#define X2 b+c + b+c
#define X3 X2 * c + b+c - d
#define X4 2 * b+c + 3 * X2 + 4 * X3

main()
{
   int b=2;        /* Declares and initializes four variables */
   int c=3;
   int d=4;
   int e=X4;
```

```
      printf("%d  %d  %d  %d  %d", e, b+c, X2, X3, X4);
      return 0;
}
```

After the first #define finishes, the second one takes over and changes every occurrence of X2 to b+c + b+c. Your source code at that point becomes

```
/* Filename: C5DEF2.C
   Illustrates that #define constants are not variables */


#include <stdio.h>


#define X3 b+c + b+c * c + b+c - d
#define X4 2 * b+c + 3 * b+c + b+c + 4 * X3


main()
{
   int b=2;       /* Declares and initializes four variables */
   int c=3;
   int d=4;
   int e=X4;


   printf("%d  %d  %d  %d  %d", e, b+c, b+c + b+c, X3, X4);
   return 0;
}
```

After the second #define finishes, the third one takes over and changes every occurrence of X3 to b+c + b+c * c + b+c - d. Your source code then becomes

```
/* Filename: C5DEF2.C
   Illustrates that #define constants are not variables */


#include <stdio.h>


#define X4 2 * b+c + 3 * b+c + b+c + 4 * b+c + b+c * c + b+c - d


main()
{
   int b=2;       /* Declares and initializes four variables */
   int c=3;
```

```
    int d=4;
    int e=X4;


    printf("%d  %d  %d  %d  %d", e, b+c, b+c + b+c, b+c + b+c * c + b+c - d, X4);
    return 0;
}
```

The source code is growing rapidly. After the third #define finishes, the fourth and last one takes over and changes every occurrence of X4 to 2 * b+c + 3 * b+c + b+c + 4 * b+c + b+c * c + b+c - d. Your source code at this last point becomes

```
/* Filename: C5DEF2.C
    Illustrates that #define constants are not variables */


#include <stdio.h>


main()
{
    int b=2;       /* Declares and initializes four variables */
    int c=3;
    int d=4;
    int e=2 * b+c + 3 * b+c + b+c + 4 * b+c + b+c * c + b+c - d;


    printf("%d  %d  %d  %d  %d", e, b+c, b+c + b+c, b+c +
            b+c * c + b+c - d, 2 * b+c + 3 * b+c + b+c +
            4 * b+c + b+c * c + b+c - d);
    return 0;
}
```

This is what your compiler actually sees. You did not type this complete listing; you typed the original listing that was shown first. The preprocessor expanded your source code into this longer form, just as if you had typed it this way.

NOTE

C performs multiplication before addition and subtraction when performing calculations. Chapter 7, "Operators and Precedence," explains this calculation order in more detail.

This might be an extreme example, but it serves to illustrate how #define works on your source code and doesn't define any variables. The #define really behaves like a word processor's search-and-replace command. Because of this, you can even rewrite the C language itself.

If you are used to BASIC, you might be more comfortable using PRINT instead of C's printf() when you want to print onscreen. If so, the #define statement

```
#define PRINT printf
```

enables you to print in C with these statements:

```
PRINT("This is a new printing technique\n");
PRINT("I could have used printf() instead."\n);
```

This works because by the time your compiler sees the program, it sees only the following:

```
printf("This is a new printing technique\n");
printf("I could have used printf() instead."\n);
```

Also, you cannot replace a defined constant if it resides in another string constant. For example, you could not use the #define statement

```
#define AGE
```

to replace information in this printf()

```
printf("AGE");
```

because AGE is a string constant, and it prints literally just as it appears inside the double quotes. The preprocessor can replace only defined constants that do not appear within quotation marks.

DO NOT OVERDO #define

Many early C programmers enjoyed redefining parts of the language to suit whatever they were used to in another language. The printf() to PRINT example is one example of this. You can redefine virtually any C statement or function to "look" any way you like.

But there is a danger to this, and you should be very wary of using #define for this purpose. Redefining the language becomes very confusing to others who might need to modify your program later. Also, as you become more familiar with C, you should naturally start using the true C language more and more. When you are comfortable with C, older programs that you redefined will be confusing even to you.

So if you are going to program in C, use the language conventions that C provides. Avoid trying to redefine commands in the language. Think of the #define directive as a great way to define numeric and string constants. If those constants ever change, you only need to change one line in your program. "Just say NO" to any temptation to redefine commands and built-in functions.

EXAMPLE

1. Suppose you want to keep track of your company's target sales amount of $55,000.00. That target amount has not changed for the last two years. Because it probably will not change soon (sales are flat), you decide to start using a defined constant to represent this target amount. However, if target sales do change, you just have to change the amount on the #define line. It would look like

```
#define TARGETSALES 55000.00
```

which defines a floating-point constant. You can then assign TARGETSALES to floating-point variables and print it, just as if you had typed 55000.00 throughout your program, as these lines show:

```
amt = TARGETSALES
printf("%f",TARGETSALES);
```

2. If you find yourself defining the same constants in many programs, you might consider putting them in their own file on disk and then #include them. This saves typing your defined constants at the top of every program. If you store these constants in a file, called mydefs.c, in your program's directory, you could include it with the following #include statement:

```
#include "mydefs.c"
```

(To use angled brackets, you would have to store the file in your system's include directory.)

3. Defined constants are good for array sizes. For example, suppose you declare an array for a customer's name. When you write the program, you know you don't have a customer whose name is longer than 22 characters (including the null). Therefore, you can do this:

```
#define CNMLENGTH 22
```

When you define the array, you can use this:

```
char cust_name[CNMLENGTH]
```

Other statements that need to know the array size can also use CNMLENGTH. If the array size changes, you only need to change the single #define directive and not the array size value every where else the constant 22 would appear without the #define.

4. Many C programmers define a list of error messages. After they define the messages with an easy-to-remember name, they can print those constants if an error occurs—while still maintaining consistency throughout their programs. Often, you might see something like the following towards the top of C programs.

```
#define DISKERR "Your disk drive seems not to be working"
#define PRNTERR "Your printer is not responding"
#define AGEERR  "You cannot enter an age that small"
#define NAMEERR "You must enter a full name"
```

What's Next

Although #define and #include are the only two preprocessor directives you know so far, they are the two used in most C programs. Despite the fact that these directives are not executed, they temporarily change your source code by merging and defining constants into your program.

The next chapter explains printf() in more detail. Although you now know that printf() sends output to the screen, many printf() options exist. You need to understand printf() better to produce better output. In addition to printf(), you also learn how to get keyboard input into your C programs.

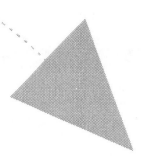

6

Input and Output

You have already seen the printf() function, which prints values to the screen. In this chapter, you'll learn many of the options available with printf(). In addition to output, your programs become much more powerful if you learn how to get input from the keyboard. The scanf() is a function that mirrors printf(). Instead of sending output values to the screen, scanf() accepts values that the user types at the keyboard.

printf() is your basic screen output function, and scanf() is your basic keyboard input function. printf() and scanf() offer beginning C programmers output and input functions they can use with relative ease. Both of these functions are limited—especially scanf()—but they do enable your programs to send output and to receive input.

This chapter teaches you the following topics:

- The printf() function and its optional arguments

- Control strings

- Conversion characters

- Modifying conversion characters

- The scanf() function

Understanding `printf()`

`printf()` sends data to the standard output device, which is generally the screen—unless you redirect the standard output to a different device. If you do nothing special, `printf()` sends all output to the text window that your compiler sets up for C programs.

CAUTION

`printf()` does not take advantage of windowed output. To output to windows, you must learn more about Windows programming using C. Better tools and languages are now available for writing Windows programs than C, but most of them rely on a heavy foundation of C. Therefore, what you learn here will come in handy even if you don't work in textual computing environments.

The format of `printf()` is a little different from that of regular C commands. The values that go inside the parentheses vary, depending upon the data you are printing. However, as a general rule, the following `printf()` format holds true:

```
printf(control_string [, one or more values]);
```

Notice that `printf()` always requires a *control_string*. This is a string, or a character array containing a string, that determines how the rest of the values (if any are listed) print. These values can be variables, constants, expressions, or a combination of all three.

Printing Strings

The easiest data to print with `printf()` are strings. To print a string constant, you simply put that string constant inside the `printf()` function. For example, to print the string The rain in Spain, you would simply type the following:

```
printf("The rain in Spain");
```

Remember, though, that `printf()` does not perform an automatic carriage return. This means that the screen's cursor remains after the last character printed. Subsequent `printf()`s begin right next to that last-printed character.

To better understand this, try to predict the output from these three `printf()` functions:

```
printf("Line 1");
printf("Line 2");
printf("Line 3");
```

This produces

```
Line 1Line 2Line 3
```

which is probably not what is intended. Therefore, you must include the newline character, \n, whenever you want to move the cursor to the next line. The following three printf() functions produce a three-line output:

```
printf("Line 1\n");
printf("Line 2\n");
printf("Line 3\n");
```

The output from these printf() functions is

```
Line 1
Line 2
Line 3
```

The \n character sends the cursor to the next line—no matter where you insert it. The following three printf() functions also produce the correct three-line output:

```
printf("Line 1");
printf("\nLine 2\n");
printf("Line 3");
```

The second printf() prints a new line before it prints anything else. It then prints its string followed by another new line. The third string prints on that new line.

You also can print strings stored in character arrays by putting the array name inside the printf(). For example, if you were to store your name in an array defined as

```
char my_name[] = "Lyndon Harris";
```

you could print the name with this printf():

```
printf(my_name);
```

1. The following section of code prints three string constants on three different lines:

```
printf("Nancy Carson\n");
printf("1213 Oak Street\n");
printf("Fairbanks, Alaska\n");
```

2. Programmers often use printf() to label output. Before printing an age, amount, salary, or any other numeric data, you should always print a string constant that tells the user what the number means. The following printf() lets the user know that the next number to be printed is an age. Without this printf(), the user might not recognize that the number is an age.

```
printf("Here is the age that was found in our files:");
```

3. All four of these printf()s produce different output, because all four string constants are different:

```
printf("Come back tomorrow\n");
printf("Come   back   tomorrow\n");
printf("cOME BACK TOMORROW\n");
printf("C o m e   b a c k   t o m o r r o w\n");
```

4. You can print a blank line by printing two newline characters (\n) next to each other after your string, as in

```
printf("Prepare the invoices...\n\n");
```

5. The following program assigns a message in a character array, and then prints that message:

```
/* Filename: C6PS.C
    Prints a string stored in a character array */
#include <stdio.h>
main()
{
    char_message[] = "Please turn on your printer";
    printf(message);
    return 0;
}
```

This prints the string stored in message—and keeps printing until the null zero is reached. This is why the null zero is so important; it tells C where your string in the array ends.

Defining Conversion Characters

Inside many of the printf()s that you have seen in the last few chapters were several *conversion characters*. These special characters tell printf() exactly how the data (following the characters) are to be interpreted. Table 6.1 shows a list of several conversion characters. Because any type of data can go inside the printf()'s parentheses, these conversion characters are needed any time you print more than a string constant. If you don't want to print a string, then the string constant must contain at least one of the conversion characters.

Table 6.1: The `printf()` *conversion characters.*

Conversion Character	Output
%s	String of characters (until null zero is reached)
%c	Character
%d	Decimal integer
%f	Floating-point numbers
%e	Exponential notation floating-point numbers
%g	Use the shorter of %f or %e
%u	Unsigned integer
%o	Octal integer
%x	Hexadecimal integer
%%	Prints a percent sign (%)

NOTE

You can insert an l (lowercase *L*) or L before the integer and floating-point conversion characters (such as %ld and %lf) to indicate that a long integer or long double floating-point is to be printed.

The first four conversion characters are used much more often than the others. Any character that is not shown in Table 6.1 prints exactly as it appears in the control string. Each of the following sections describe these conversion characters and their uses in `printf()`.

String Conversion Character %s

If you print a string constant, the string conversion character is not required. The following two `printf()`s are identical:

```
printf("C is fun!\n");
printf("%s", "C is fun!\n");
```

The %s informs the `printf()` function that a string follows. Because C does not need the %s to print strings, the %s is redundant. You also can include the %s if you print strings stored in character arrays but, again, the %s is not needed. If cary was a character array containing a valid string, both of the following `printf()`s would work:

```
printf("%s", cary);   // Prints the string in cary
printf(cary);     // Works as long as cary is an array
                  //    that holds a valid string
```

The reason C does not need the %s conversion character is because anything *not* a conversion character prints exactly as it appears in the control string.

Character Conversion Character %c

You must, however, use the %c conversion character any time you print single characters, whether they are character constants or character variables. You would use the following printf() to print three character constants:

```
printf("%c %c %c", 'A','B','C');
```

These three character constants print with one blank between them. Figure 6.1 shows why this is the case. Each %c informs C that a character appears in its place, and the blank that follows the first two %c conversion characters prints as blank.

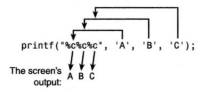

Figure 6.1: *This illustrates the correlation between the conversion characters and their values.*

You must also use the %c conversion character when you print character variables. This includes single elements (such as c[3]) from a character array.

EXAMPLE

The following program stores the three letters into three character variables, and then prints them:

```
/* Filename: C6PC.C
   Stores and prints the contents of 3 variables */
#include <stdio.h>
main()
{
    char first, second, last;
    first='A';
    second='B';
    last='C';

    printf("%c %c %c", first, second, last);
    return 0;
}
```

Integer and Floating-Point Conversion Characters %d and %f

When you want to print a numeric constant or variable, you must include the proper conversion character inside the printf() control string. If i, j, and k are integer variables, you cannot print them with the printf() that follows:

```
printf(i,j,k);
```

Because printf() is a function and not a command, this printf() function has no way of knowing what type the variables are. The results are unpredictable, and you might see garbage on your screen—if anything appears at all.

When you print numbers, you must first print a control string that includes the format of those numbers. The following printf() prints a string. In the output from this line, a string appears with an integer (%d) and a floating-point number (%f) printed inside that string.

```
printf("I am Betty, I am %d years old, and I make %f\n", 35, 34050.25);
```

This produces the following output:

```
I am Betty, I am 35 years old, and I make $34050.25
```

Figure 6.2 shows how C interprets the control string and the variables that follow. Be sure you understand this example before moving on. It is the foundation of the printf() function.

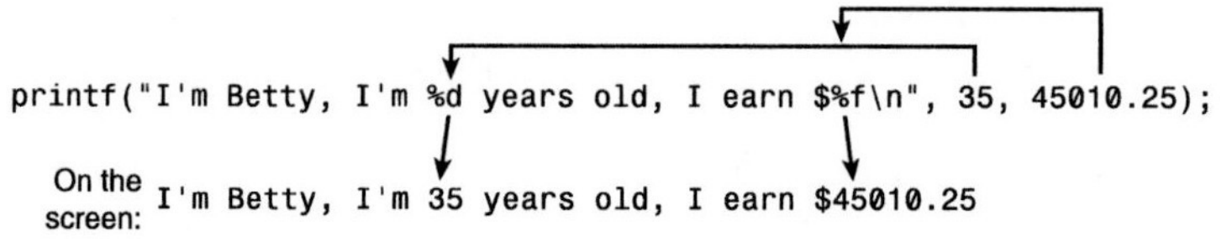

```
printf("I'm Betty, I'm %d years old, I earn $%f\n", 35, 45010.25);

On the
screen:   I'm Betty, I'm 35 years old, I earn $45010.25
```

Figure 6.2: *Here, the print command converts values of a control string.*

You also can print integer and floating-point variables in the same manner.

NOTE

The %i also works as an integer printf() conversion character. This is easier to remember (%i for integer), but it is rarely used by C programmers. Follow the general standard and use %d for printing integers.

EXAMPLE

1. The following program stores a few values in three variables, and then prints the results:

```
/* Filename: C6PRNT1.C
   Print values in variables */
#include <stdio.h>
```

```
main()
{
    char first='E';            // Store some character, integer,
    char middle='W';           // and floating-point variables
    char last='C';
    int age=32;
    int dependents=2;
    float salary=25000.00;
    float bonus=575.25;

    /* Print the results */
    printf("%c%c%c", first, middle, last);
    printf("%d%d", age, dependents);
    printf("%f%f", salary, bonus);
    return 0;
}
```

OUTPUT

```
EWC 32 2 25000.000000 575.250000
```

Given this misleading and unlabeled output, something needs to be done to add description to the data the program produces.

2. As you saw from the output, the previous program doesn't help the user at all. The output is not labeled, and it all prints on a single line. Here is the same program with a few messages printed before the numbers, and some newline characters placed where they are needed:

```
/* Filename: C6PRNT2.C
   Print values in variables with appropriate labels */
#include <stdio.h>

main()
{
    char first='E';            // Store some character, integer,
    char middle='W';           // and floating-point variables
    char last='C';
    int age=32;
    int dependents=2;
    float salary=25000.00;
    float bonus=575.25;

    /* Print the results */
    printf("Here are the initials:\n");
    printf("%c%c%c\n\n", first, middle, last);
    printf("The age and number of dependents are:\n");
```

```
    printf("%d   %d\n\n", age, dependents);
    printf("The salary and bonus are:\n");
    printf("%f %f", salary, bonus);
    return 0;
}
```

The output from this program is

```
Here are the initials:
EWC
The age and number of dependents are:
32    2
The salary and bonus are:
25000.000000 575.250000
```

The floating-point values print with too many zeros, of course, but the numbers are correct. The next section shows you how to limit the number of leading and trailing zeros that are printed.

3. If you need to print a table of numbers, you can use the \t tab charac- ter. Place the tab character between each of the numbers that print. The following program prints a list of baseball team names and the number of hits for each during the first three weeks of the season:

```
/* Filename: C6TEAM.C
    Prints a table of team names and hits for three weeks */
#include <stdio.h>

main()
{
    printf("Parrots\tRams\tKings\tTitans\tChargers\n");
    printf("%d\t%d\t%d\t%d\t%d\n", 3,5,2,1,0);
    printf("%d\t%d\t%d\t%d\t%d\n", 2,5,1,0,1);
    printf("%d\t%d\t%d\t%d\t%d\n", 2,6,4,3,0);

    return 0;
}
```

This program produces the following table. You can see that, even though the names are of different widths, the numbers print correctly beneath them. The \t character forces the next name or value into the next tab position (every 8 characters for most C compilers).

Parrots	Rams	Kings	Titans	Chargers
3	5	2	1	0
2	5	1	0	1
2	6	4	3	0

NOTE

The %x and %o are used to print hexadecimal and octal numbers. Even if you store a hexadecimal number in an integer variable (with the leading 0x characters, such as 0x3C1), that variable prints as a decimal value if you use the %d conversion character.

Conversion Character Modifiers

You already have seen the need for additional program output control. All floating-point numbers print (using %f) with too many decimal places for most applications. What if you want to print only dollars and cents (two decimal places), or print an average with a single decimal place? If you want to control the way these conversion characters produce output, you have to include a modified conversion character.

You can insert a modifying number inside many of the numeric conversion characters. This number tells C how many print positions to use. For example, the following printf() prints the number 456, using three positions (the length of the data):

```
printf("%d", 456);
```

If the 456 were stored in an integer variable, it would still use three positions to print because the number of digits printed is three. However, if you insert a number before the d in the conversion character, you can control exactly how many positions print. The following printf() prints the number 456 in five positions (with two leading spaces):

```
printf("%5d", 456);
```

You typically use the width number when you want to print data in uniform columns. The following program shows you the importance of the width number. Each printf() output is described in the adjacent comment.

```
/* Filename: C6MOD1.C
    Illustrates various integer width printf() modifiers */
#include <stdio.h>
main()
{               // The output appears below
    printf("%d%d%d \n", 456, 456, 456);     //456456456
    printf("%5d%5d%5d \n", 456, 456, 456);  //  456  456  456
    printf("%7d%7d%7d \n", 456, 456, 456);  //    456    456    456
    return 0;
}
```

When you put a width number inside a conversion character, C right-justifies the number in the width you specify. In other words, when you specify an 8-digit width, C prints a value inside those 8 digits, padding the number with leading blanks if the number does not fill the full width. If you do not specify a width large enough to hold the number, C ignores your width request and prints the number in its entirety.

If you put a minus sign before the width specifier, C left-justifies the number inside the width. For example, the following program prints its numbers to the left of its fields, as shown especially in the final two comments:

```
/* Filename: C6MOD2.C
    Illustrates various integer width printf() modifiers */
#include <stdio.h>
main()
{               // The output appears below
    printf("%d%d%d \n", 456, 456, 456);      //456456456
    printf("%-5d%-5d%-5d \n", 456, 456, 456);  //456  456  456
    printf("%-7d%-7d%-7d \n", 456, 456, 456);  //456    456    456
    return 0;
}
```

You can control the width of strings in the same manner, by using the width modifier in the %s string conversion character. If you do not specify enough width to output the full string, C ignores your width. The mailing list application at the back of this book uses the same technique to print names on mailing labels.

The width specifiers become more important when you want to print floating-point numbers. The format of the floating-point width specifier is

%width.decimalsf

The floating-point conversion character, %6.2f, tells C to print a floating-point number within six positions, including the decimal point and the fractional part. It also informs C to print two decimal places. If C has to round the fractional part, it does so. The printf()

printf("%6.2f", 134.568767);

produces this output:

134.57

Without the format modifier, C would print

134.568767

TIP

When printing floating-point numbers, C always prints the entire portion to the left of the decimal (to maintain as much accuracy as possible) no matter how many positions wide you specify. Therefore, many C programmers ignore the width specifier for floating-point numbers and specify only the decimal part, as in %.2f.

---

1. Earlier, you saw how the \t tab character can be used to print columns of data. The tab character is limited to eight columns. If you want more control over the width of your data, use a modifying width in the output conversion characters. The following program is a modified version of C6TEAM.C that uses the width specifier instead of the tab character. It ensures that each column is 10 characters wide.

```c
/* Filename: C6TEAMMD.C
   Prints a table of team names and hits for three weeks
   using width modifying conversion characters */
#include <stdio.h>

main()
{
    // This long statement line spans two lines
    printf("%10s%10s%10s%10s%10s\n",
            "Parrots","Rams","Kings","Titans","Chargers");
    printf("%10d%10d%10d%10d%10d\n", 3,5,2,1,0);
    printf("%10d%10d%10d%10d%10d\n", 2,5,1,0,1);
    printf("%10d%10d%10d%10d%10d\n", 2,6,4,3,0);

    return 0;
}
```

2. The following program is a payroll program. The output prints dollar amounts (to two decimal places).

```c
/* Filename: C6PAY1.C
   Computes and prints payroll data
   properly in dollars and cents */
#include <stdio.h>

main()
{
    char emp_name[] = "Larry Payton";
    char pay_date[] = "03/09/2000";
    int hours_worked = 40;
    float rate=7.50;              // Pay per hour
    float tax_rate=.40;           // Tax percentage rate
    float gross_pay, taxes, net_pay;

    /* Compute the pay amount */
    gross_pay = hours_worked * rate;
    taxes = tax_rate * gross_pay;
    net_pay = gross_pay - taxes;
```

```
    /* Print the results */
    printf("As of %s\n", pay_date);
    printf("%s worked %d hours\n", emp_name, hours_worked);
    printf("and got paid %6.2f\n", gross_pay);
    printf("After taxes of %5.2f\n", taxes);
    printf("his take-home pay was $%6.2f\n", net_pay);

    return 0;
}
```

OUTPUT

The following is the output from this program. Remember that the floating-point variables still hold their full precision (to six decimal places). The modifying width numbers affect only how the variables are output, not what is stored in them.

```
As of 03/09/2000
Larry Payton worked 40 hours
and got paid 300.00
After taxes of 120.000000
his take-home pay was $180.00
```

3. Most C programmers do not use the width specifier to the left of the decimal point when printing dollars and cents. Here again is the payroll program that uses the shortcut floating-point width method. Notice the last three printf() statements include the %.2f modifier. C knows to print the full number to the left of the decimal, but only two places to the right.

```
/* Filename: C6PAY2.C
    Computes and prints payroll data properly using the shortcut
    modifier */
#include <stdio.h>

main()
{
    char emp_name[]="Larry Payton";
    char pay_date[]="03/09/2000";
    int hours_worked=40;
    float rate=7.50;              /* Pay per hour */
    float tax_rate=.40;           /* Tax percentage rate */
    float gross_pay, taxes, net_pay;

    /* Compute the pay amount */
    gross_pay = hours_worked * rate;
    taxes = tax_rate * gross_pay;
    net_pay = gross_pay - taxes;
```

```
            /* Print the results */
            printf("As of %s\n", pay_date);
            printf("%s worked %d hours\n", emp_name, hours_worked);
            printf("and got paid %.2f\n", gross_pay);
            printf("After taxes of %.2f\n", taxes);
            printf("his take-home pay was $%.2f\n", net_pay);

            return 0;
        }
```

This program's output is the same as that of the last one.

Keeping Count of Output

Make sure your printed values match the control string supplied with
them. The printf() function cannot fix problems resulting from mismatched values and control strings. Don't try to print floating-point values
with character string control codes. If you list five integer variables in a
printf(), be sure to include five %d conversion characters in the printf()
as well.

PRINTING ASCII VALUES

There is one exception to the rule of printing with matching conversion characters. If
you want to print the ASCII value of a character, you can print that character (whether it
is a constant or a variable) with the integer %d conversion character. Instead of printing
the character, C prints the matching ASCII number for that character.

Conversely, if you print an integer with a %c conversion character, you see the character
that matches that integer's value from the ASCII table.

The following printf()s illustrate this:

```
printf("%c", 65);  // Prints letter A
printf("%d", 'A'); // Prints number 65
```

EXAMPLE

Depending on your C compiler, your output may be empty—or produce
garbage on the screen—if you mismatch your parameters. The following
example illustrates some of the problems that can occur. Because these
printf()s are mismatched (the control strings don't always match the variables and constants being printed), you should check the comment to the
right for the probable output or error that might occur.

```
/* Filename: C6PROB.C

   Program to demonstrate possible printf() problems */
```

```
main()
{
    int i, j, k;
    char a, b, c;

    i = 4;
    j = 5;
    k = 6;

    a = 'I';
    b = 'B';                                    /*****************************/
    c = 'M';                                    /* Output is shown below:    */
                                                /*                           */
    printf("This is a message\n");              /* This is a message         */
    printf("%d %d %d\n", i, j, k);              /* 4 5 6                     */
    printf(i, j, k);                            /*         (unpredictable)   */
    printf("\n%c %d  %c %d", a, i, c, j);       /* I 4  M 5                  */
    printf("\nB%cB%cB%c\n", a, a, a);           /* BIBIBI                    */
    printf(a, b, c);                            /*         (unpredictable)   */
    printf("\nHi.\n", a, b, c);                 /* Hi.                       */
    printf("%d %d\n", i, j, k);                 /* 4 5                       */
    printf("%c %c %c %c\n", a, b, c);           /* I B M  (garbage)          */
    printf("%cc%dd\n", a, i);                   /* Ic4d                      */
    printf("%s\n", "No conv. char. needed");    /* No conv. char. needed     */
    printf("No conv. char. needed");            /* No conv. char. needed     */
    printf("\n%s %c", "A", 'A');                /* A A                       */
    printf("\n%s %c", 'A', "A");                /*         (unpredictable)   */
    printf("\nNumber in string %d, see?", i);   /* Number in string 4, see?  */
    printf("\nWatch your types! %d %c", b, j);  /* Watch your types!(garbage)*/
                                                /*****************************/
    return 0;
}
```

The bottom line is this: Avoid these types of problems by making sure every conversion character inside your printf() control string matches the data that follows the control string.

Using `scanf()` for Input

You now understand how C represents data and variables, and how to print that data. However, there is another part of this programming you haven't seen: how a user inputs data into your programs.

Until now, every program has had no input of data. All the data you've worked with have been assigned to variables within the programs. However, this is not always the best way to input data, and also, you rarely know what your data is going to be at the time you write your programs. Most data only becomes known when you run the programs, or another user runs them.

The `scanf()` function is one way to get input from the keyboard. When your programs reach the line with a `scanf()`, the user at the keyboard can enter values directly into variables. With this, your program can process those variables and produce output.

The `scanf()` function has its drawbacks (discussed later in this section), but if you understand the `printf()` function, `scanf()` shouldn't pose too much of a problem. Therefore, the next few chapters make use of `scanf()` until you learn even more powerful (and flexible) input methods.

The `scanf()` function looks very much like `printf()`. It contains a control string and one or more variables to the right of the control string. The control string describes to C exactly what the incoming keyboard values look like, and what their types are. The format of `scanf()` is

```
scanf(control_string, one or more values);
```

The `stdio.h` header file contains the information C needs for `scanf()`, so include it whenever you use `scanf()`.

The `scanf()` *control_string* uses almost the same conversion characters as the `printf()` *control_string*, with two slight differences. You should never include the newline character (`\n`) in a `scanf()` control string. The `scanf()` function "knows" the input is finished when the user presses Enter. If you supply an additional newline code, `scanf()` gets confused and might not terminate properly. Also, always put a beginning space inside every `scanf()` control string. This does not affect the user's input, but `scanf()` sometimes requires it to work properly. Later examples clarify this.

As mentioned earlier, `scanf()` poses a few problems. The `scanf()` function requires that your user type the input exactly the way *control_string* specifies. Because you cannot control your user's typing, this cannot always be ensured. For example, you might want the user to enter an integer value followed by a floating-point value (your `scanf()` control string might expect it too), but your user might decide to enter something else. If this happens, there is not much you can do. The resulting input will be incorrect, but your C program has no reliable method for testing user accuracy—for the user—before your program is run.

For the next few chapters, assume that the user knows to enter the proper values. However, for your own programs used by others, be on the lookout for additional methods to get better input.

CAUTION

The user's keyboard input values must match exactly—in number and type—to the control string contained in each `scanf()`.

Another problem with `scanf()` is not as easy to explain at this point in the book. The `scanf()` function requires that you use pointer variables, not regular variables, in its parentheses. Although this sounds complicated, it doesn't have to be. You should have no problem with `scanf()`'s pointer requirements if you remember the following two simple rules:

- Always put an ampersand (&) before variable names inside a `scanf()`.

- Never put an ampersand (&) before an array name inside a `scanf()`.

Despite these strange `scanf()` rules, you can learn this function very quickly by looking at a few examples.

EXAMPLE

1. If you want a program that computes a 7% sales tax, you can use the `scanf()` function to get the sales, compute the tax, and then print the results, as the following program demonstrates:

```
/* Filename: C6SLTX.C
   Prompt for a sales amount and print the sales tax */
#include <stdio.h>
main()
{
    float total_sale;    // User's sale amount will go here
    float stax;

    /* Display a message for the user */
    printf("What is the total amount of the sale? ");

    /* Get the sales amount from user */
    scanf(" %f", &total_sale);    // Don't forget the beginning space
and &

    /* Calculate sales tax */
    stax = total_sale * .07;

    printf("The sales tax for %.2f is %.2f", total_sale, stax);
```

```
    return 0;
}
```

If you run this program and enter 10.00 for the sale amount, you'll see this output:

```
What is the total amount of the sale? 10.00
The sales tax for 10.00 is 0.70
```

The first `printf()` does not contain a newline character (\n) so the user's response to the prompt appears directly to the right of the question mark.

2. Use the string %s conversion character to input keyboard strings into character arrays with `scanf()`. You are limited, however, to getting one word at a time, because the `scanf()` does not let you type more than one word into a single character array. The following program asks users for their first and last names. It must store these two names in two different character arrays, because `scanf()` cannot get both names at once. The program then prints the names in reverse order:

```
/* Filename: C6PHON1.C
    Program that gets the user's name and prints it
    to the screen as it would appear in a phone book. */
#include <stdio.h>
main()
{
    char first[20], last[20];
    printf("What is your first name? ");
    scanf(" %s", first);
    printf("What is your last name? ");
    scanf(" %s", last);
    printf("\n\n");     /* Print 2 blank lines */
    printf("In a phone book, your name would look like this:\n");
    printf("%s, %s", last, first);
    return 0;
}
```

```
What is your first name? Martha
What is your last name? Roberts

In a phone book, your name would look like this:
Roberts, Martha
```

Notice that you do not include the ampersand before an array name, only before "single" nonarray variables.

3. Suppose you want to write a program, for your 7-year-old daughter, that performs simple addition. The following program prompts her for two numbers. The program then waits for her to type an answer. When she gives her answer, the program displays the correct result so she can see how well she did. (Later, you learn how you can immediately let her know whether her answer is correct.)

```c
/* Filename: C6MATH.C
   Program to help children with simple addition.
   Prompt child for 2 values, after printing a title message */
#include <stdio.h>
main()
{
    int num1, num2, ans;
    int her_ans;

    printf("*** Math Practice ***\n");
    printf("\n\n");      // Print 2 blank lines
    printf("What is the first number? ");
    scanf(" %d", &num1);
    printf("What is the second number? ");
    scanf(" %d", &num2);

    /* Compute answer and give her a chance to wait for it */
    ans=num1+num2;

    printf("\nWhat do you think is the answer? ");
    scanf(" %d", &her_ans);    // Nothing is done with this

    /* Print answer after a blank line */
    printf("\n%d plus %d is: %d\n", num1, num2, ans);
    printf("\nHope you got it right!");
    return 0;
}
```

What's Next

After learning the printf() and scanf() functions in this chapter, you should be able to print almost anything onscreen. You now have the tools you need to begin writing programs that fit the data processing model of "Input-Process-Output." This chapter concludes the preliminaries of the C programming language. The next chapter, "Operators and Precedence," teaches how C's math and relational operators manipulate data, as well as the important table of precedence.

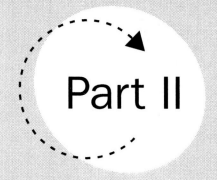

Part II

C's Operators

Operators and Precedence

Relational and Logical Operators

Remaining C Operators

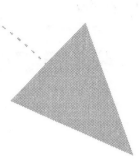

7

Operators and Precedence

You now understand variables and can perform simple input and output. Without the capability to calculate, your computer would be worth little indeed. This chapter begins a new part of the book that introduces you to C's numerous operators. C supports a wide range of operators, and understanding the operators is key to understanding C. Not only must you know how the operators work, you must also understand the proper order that operators execute when they appear together in a single statement.

This chapter teaches you the following topics:

- Primary math operators

- Order of operator precedence

- Assignment statements

- Mixed data-type calculations

- Typecasting

C's Primary Math Operators

A C *math operator* is a symbol used for adding, subtracting, multiplying, dividing, as well as other operations. C operators are not always mathematical in nature, but many are. Table 7.1 explains these operator symbols and their primary meanings.

Table 7.1: C primary operators.

Symbol	Meaning
*	Multiplication
/	Division and Integer Division
%	Modulus or Remainder
+	Addition
–	Subtraction

Most of these operators work in the familiar way you are used to. Multiplication, addition, and subtraction produce the same results (and the division operator usually) as you get when you do these math functions with a calculator. Table 7.2 shows four samples that illustrate four of these simple operators.

Table 7.2: Typical operator results.

Formula	Result
4 * 2	8
64 / 4	16
80 – 15	65
12 + 9	21

Table 7.2 contains examples of *binary operations* performed with the four operators. Don't confuse this term with *binary numbers*. When an operator is used between two constants, variables, or a combination of both, it is called a *binary operator* because it operates using two values. When you use these operators (such as assigning their results to variables), C does not "care" whether you put spaces around the operators or not.

The Unary Operators

A *unary operator* operates on, or affects, a single value. For instance, you can assign a variable a positive or negative number by using a unary + or –. You can also assign a variable another positive or negative number by using a unary + or –.

1. The following section of code assigns four variables a positive or a negative number. The plus and minus signs are all unary because they are not used between two values.

```
a = -25;    // Assign 'a' a negative 25
b = +25;    // Assign 'b' a positive 25 (+ is not needed)
c = -a;     // Assign 'c' the negative of 'a' (-25)
d = +b;     // Assign 'd' the positive of 'b' (+ is not needed)
```

2. You generally do not need to use the unary plus sign. C assumes that a number or variable is positive, even if you don't put a plus in front of it. The following four statements are equivalent to the last, except that they do not contain plus signs.

```
a = -25;    // Assign 'a' a negative 25
b =  25;    // Assign 'b' a positive 25
c = -a;     // Assign 'c' the negative of 'a' (-25)
d =  b;     // Assign 'd' the positive of 'b'
```

3. The unary negative comes in handy when you want to negate a single number or variable. The negative of a negative is positive. Therefore, the following short program assigns a negative number (using the unary –) to a variable, and then prints the negative of that same variable. Because it had a negative number to begin with, the printf() produces a positive result.

```
/* Filename: C7NEG.C
   The negative of a variable that contains a negative value */
#include <stdio.h>
main()
{
    signed int temp=-12;   // 'signed' is not needed because
                           //     that is the default
    printf("%d", -temp);   // Produces a 12 on the screen

    return 0;
}
```

The variable declaration does not need the *signed* prefix, because all integer variables are signed by default.

4. If you want to subtract the negative of a variable, make sure you put a space before the unary minus sign. For example, the following line

```
new_temp = old_temp - -inversion_factor;
```

temporarily negates the `inversion_factor` and then subtracts that negated value from `old_temp`.

Division and Modulus

The division sign (`/`) and the modulus operator (`%`) may behave in ways unfamiliar to you. They're often as easy to use, however, as the other operators you have just seen.

The forward slash (`/`) always divides. However, it produces an integer `divide` if integer values (constants, variables, or a combination of both) appear on both sides of the slash. If there is a remainder, C discards it.

The percent sign (`%`) produces a *modulus*, or a *remainder*, of an integer division. It requires that integers be on both sides of the symbol, or it does not work.

EXAMPLE

1. Suppose you want to compute your weekly pay. The following program asks for your yearly pay, divides it by 52, and prints the results to two decimal places.

```c
/* Filename: C7DIV.C
    Displays user's weekly pay */
#include <stdio.h>
main()
{
    float weekly, yearly;
    printf("What is your annual pay? ");   // Prompt user
    scanf("%f", &yearly);

    weekly = yearly/52;   // Computes the weekly
    printf("\n\nYour weekly pay is $%.2f", weekly);
    return 0;
}
```

OUTPUT

Because a floating-point number is used in the division, C produces a floating-point result. Here is a sample run from such a program:

```
What is your annual pay? 38000.00
Your weekly pay is $730.77
```

2. Integer division does not round its results. If you divide two integers and the answer is not a whole number, C ignores the fractional part. The following `printf()`s help show this. The output that would result from each `printf()` appears in the comment to the right of each line.

```
printf("%d \n", 10/2);        // 5  (no remainder)
printf("%d \n", 300/100);     // 3  (no remainder)
printf("%d \n", 10/3);        // 3  (discarded remainder)
printf("%d \n", 300/165);     // 1  (discarded remainder)
```

The Order of Precedence

Knowing the meaning of the math operators is the first of two steps toward your understanding of C calculations. You must also understand the *order of precedence*. The order of precedence (sometimes called the *math hierarchy*, or *order of operators*) determines exactly how C computes formulas. The precedence of operators is exactly the same as that used in high school algebra courses. (But don't worry, this is the easy part of algebra!) To see how the order of precedence works, try to determine the result of the following simple calculation:

```
2 + 3 * 2
```

If you said 10, you would not be alone; many people would respond with 10. However, 10 is correct only if you interpret the formula from left to right. But what if you calculated the multiplication first? If you took the value of 3 * 2 and got an answer of 6, and then added the 2 to it, you would end up with an answer of 8—which is exactly the same answer that C computes.

C always performs multiplication, division, and modulus first, and then addition and subtraction. Table 7.3 shows the order of the operators you have seen so far. Of course, there are many more levels to C's precedence table of operators than those shown in Table 7.3. Unlike most computer languages, C has 15 levels of precedence. Appendix B, "C's Precedence Table," contains the complete precedence table, and you might notice in that appendix that multiplication, division, and modulus reside on level 3, one level higher than level 4's addition and subtraction. In the next few chapters, you learn how to use the remainder of this precedence table in your C programs.

Table 7.3: Order of precedence for primary operators.

Order	Operator
First	Multiplication, division, modulus remainder (*, /, %)
Second	Addition, subtraction (+, −)

EXAMPLE

1. It is easy to follow C's order of operators if you follow the intermediate results one at a time. The three calculations in Figure 7.1 show you how to do this.

```
6 + 2 * 3 – 4/2          3 * 4/2 + 3 – 1          20/3 + 5 % 2
    \ |                     \ /                      \ /
6 + 6 – 4/2              12 /2 + 3 – 1            6  + 5 % 2
      \ /                   \ /                        \ /
  6 + 6 – 2               6  + 3 – 1              6  +  1
  \ /                     \  /                    \  /
   12  – 2                 9  – 1                   7
     \  /                   \  /
      10                     8
```

Figure 7.1: *Calculations show C's order of operators with lines indicating precedence.*

2. Looking back at the order of precedence table again, you might notice that multiplication, division, and modulus are on the same level. This implies that there is no hierarchy on that level. If more than one of these operators appear in a calculation, C performs the math from left to right. The same is true of addition and subtraction—the leftmost operation is done first.

   Figure 7.2 illustrates this.

```
10 / 5 * 2 – 2 + 1
 \ /
  2  * 2 – 2 + 1
  \ /
   4  – 2 + 1
   \  /
    2  + 1
    \   /
     3
```

Figure 7.2: *Here is C's order of operators from left to right with lines indicating precedence.*

Because the division in Figure 7.2 appears to the left of the multiplication, it is computed first, because division and multiplication are on the same level.

You now should be able to follow the order of these C operators. You really don't need to worry about the math because C does all the actual work. However, you should understand this order of operators so you know how to structure your calculations. Now that you have mastered this order, it's already time to see how you can override it with parentheses.

Using Parentheses

If you want to override the order of precedence, you can put parentheses in the calculation. The parentheses actually reside on a level above the multiplication, division, and modulus in the precedence table. In other words, any calculation in parentheses—whether it is addition, subtraction, division, or whatever—is always calculated before the rest of the line. The other calculations are then performed in their normal operator order.

The first formula in this chapter, 2 + 3 * 2, produced an 8 because the multiplication was performed before addition. However, by adding parentheses around the addition, as in (2 + 3) * 2, the answer becomes 10.

In the precedence table shown in Appendix B, the parentheses reside on level 1 (the highest level in the table). Being higher than the other levels makes parentheses take precedence over multiplication, division, and all other operators.

EXAMPLE

1. The calculations shown in Figure 7.3 illustrate how parentheses override the regular order of operators. These are the same three formulas shown in the last section, but their results are calculated differently because the parentheses override the normal order of operators.

```
6 + 2 * (3 – 4) / 2        3 * 4 / 2 + (3 – 1)       20 / (3 + 5) % 2
       \  /                      \  /                      \  /
6 + 2 * – 1 / 2            3 * 4 / 2 +  2            20 / 8 % 2
    \  /                      \  /                       \  /
6 +  – 2 / 2               12 / 2 +  2                2   % 2
       \  /                    \  /                     \   /
    6 +  – 1                  6 +  2                      0
       \  /                    \  /
        5                       8
```

Figure 7.3: *The use of parentheses as the highest precedence level with lines indicating precedence determines the operator order.*

2. If an expression contains parentheses-within-parentheses, C evaluates the innermost parentheses first. The expressions in Figure 7.4 illustrate this.

```
5 * [5 + (6 – 2) + 1]
         \  /
5 * (5 +  4  + 1)
       \  /
5 *   (9   + 1 )
         \  /
    5 *   10
       \  /
        50
```

Figure 7.4: *This is a precedence example of parentheses-within-parentheses with lines indicating precedence.*

3. The following program produces an incorrect result, even though it looks as if it should work. See if you can spot the error.

```
/* Filename: C7AVG1.C
   Compute the average of three grades */
#include <stdio.h>
main()
{
   float avg, grade1, grade2, grade3;

   grade1 = 87.5;
   grade2 = 92.4;
   grade3 = 79.6;

   avg = grade1 + grade2 + grade3 / 3.0;
   printf("The average is %.1f", avg);
   return 0;
}
```

The problem is that division is performed first. Therefore, the third grade is first divided by 3.0, and then the other two grades are added to that result. To correct this problem, you would simply have to add one set of parentheses, as shown in the following:

```
/* Filename: C7AVG2.C
   Compute the average of three grades */
#include <stdio.h>
main()
{
   float avg, grade1, grade2, grade3;

   grade1 = 87.5;
   grade2 = 92.4;
   grade3 = 79.6;

   avg = (grade1 + grade2 + grade3) / 3.0;
   printf("The average is %.1f", avg);
   return 0;
}
```

TIP

Use plenty of parentheses in your C programs to make the order of operators clearer, even when you don't have to override their default order. It sometimes makes the calculations easier to understand later, when you might need to modify the program.

SHORTER IS NOT ALWAYS BETTER

When you program computers for a living, it is much more important to write programs that are easy to understand than programs that are short, or that include tricky calculations.

Maintainability is the computer industry's word for changing and updating programs that were written in a simple style earlier. The business world is changing rapidly, and the programs companies have used for years must be updated often to reflect this changing environment. Businesses do not always have the resources to write programs from scratch, so they usually make do by modifying the ones they have.

Years ago when computer hardware was much more expensive, and when computer memories were much smaller, it was important to write small programs, which often relied on clever, individualized tricks and shortcuts. Unfortunately, such programs are often difficult to revise, especially if the original programmers leave and someone else (you!) must step in and modify all their original code.

Companies are realizing the importance of spending time to write programs that are easy to modify and that do not rely on tricks, or "quick and dirty" routines that are hard to follow. You can be a much more valuable programmer if you write clean programs, with lots of white space, lots of remarks, and very straightforward code. Put parentheses around formulas if it makes them clearer, and use variables for storing results in case you need the same answer later in the program. Break long calculations into several smaller ones.

Throughout the rest of this book, you can read tips on writing maintainable programs. You and your colleagues might appreciate these tips when you incorporate them into your own C programs.

The Assignment Statements

In C, the assignment operator (=) behaves differently from what you might be used to in other languages. So far, you have seen it used for simple assignment of values to variables, which is consistent with its use in most other programming languages.

However, the assignment operator also can be used in other ways, such as multiple assignment statements and compound assignments, as the following sections illustrate.

Multiple Assignments

If two or more equals signs appear in an expression, each of them performs an assignment. This introduces a new aspect of the precedence order you should understand. Consider the following expression:

```
a=b=c=d=e=100;
```

This may seem confusing at first, especially if you know other computer languages. To C, the equals sign always means: Assign the value on the right to the variable on the left. This right-to-left order is described in Appendix B's precedence table. The fourth column in the table is labeled

Associativity, which describes the direction of the operation. The assignment operator associates from right to left, whereas some of the other C operators associate from left to right.

Because the assignment associates from right to left, the previous expression first assigns the 100 to the variable named e. This produces a value, 100, of the expression. In C, all expressions produce values, typically the result of assignments. Therefore, this value, 100, is then assigned to the variable d. The value of that, 100, is assigned to c, then to b, and finally to a. Whatever values were in the five variables previous to this statement would be replaced by 100 after the statement finishes.

Because C does not automatically set variables to zero before you use them, you might want to zero them out before with a single assignment statement. The following section of variable declarations and initializations is performed using multiple assignment statements:

```c
#include <stdio.h>

main()
{
    int ctr, num_emp, num_dep;
    float sales, salary, amount;

    ctr=num_emp=num_dep=0;
    sales=salary=amount=0;
    /* Rest of program follows */
```

In C, you can include the assignment statement almost anywhere in a program, even within another calculation. For example, consider the statement

```c
value = 5 + (r = 9 - c);
```

which is a perfectly legal C statement. The assignment operator resides on the first level of the precedence table, and always produces a value. Because its associativity is right to left, the r is first assigned 9 − c because the rightmost equal sign is evaluated first. The subexpression (r = 9 − c) produces a value (whatever is placed into r) that is added to 5 before storing that result in value.

EXAMPLE

Because C does not initialize variables to zero before you use them, you might want to include a multiple assignment operator to zero them out before using them. The following section of code ensures that all variables are initialized before the rest of the program uses them:

```c
#include <stdio.h>

main()
(
```

```
int num_emp, dependents, age, hours;
float salary, hr_rate, taxrate;

/* Initialize all variables to zero */
num_emp=dependents=age=hours=0;
salary=hr_rate=taxrate=0.0;


/* Rest of program follows */
```

Compound Assignments

Many times in programming, you might want to update the value of a variable. That is, you need to take a variable's current value, add or multiply that value by an expression, and then assign it back into the original variable. The following assignment statement demonstrates this:

```
salary=salary*1.2;
```

This expression multiplies the old value of salary by 1.2 (in effect, raising the value in salary by 20%), then assigns it back into salary. C provides several operators, called *compound operators*, which you can use any time the same variable appears on both sides of the equals sign. The compound operators are shown in Table 7.4.

Table 7.4: C's compound operators.

Operator	Example	Equivalent
+=	bonus+=500;	bonus=bonus+500;
–=	budget-=50;	budget=budget–50;
*=	salary*=1.2;	salary=salary*1.2;
/=	factor/=.50;	factor=factor/.50;
%=	daynum%=7;	daynum=daynum%7;

The compound operators are low in the precedence table. They typically are evaluated very late in equations that use them.

EXAMPLE

1. You have been storing your factory's production amount in a variable called prod_amt, and your supervisor has just informed you of a new addition that needs to be applied to that production value. You could code this update in a statement that looks like this:

```
prod_amt = prod_amt + 2.6;   /* Add 2.6 to current production */
```

Instead of this formula, you should use C's compound addition operator by coding it like this:

```
prod_amt += 2.6;   /* Add 2.6 to current production */
```

2. Suppose you are a high school teacher who wants to adjust your students' grades upward. You gave a test that seemed too difficult, and the grades were not up to your expectations. If you had stored each of the student's grades in variables named grade1, grade2, grade3, and so on, you could update the grades from within a program with the following section of compound assignments:

```
grade1*=1.1;       // Increase each student's grade by 10 percent
grade2*=1.1;
grade3*=1.1;
/* Rest of grade changes follow */
```

3. The precedence of the compound operators requires important consideration when you decide how to code compound assignments. Notice from Appendix B that the compound operators are on level 14, much lower than the regular math operators. This means you must be careful how you interpret them.

   For example, suppose you want to update the value of a sales variable with this formula:

   ```
   4-factor+bonus
   ```

   You could update the sales variable with the following statement:

   ```
   sales += 4 - factor + bonus;
   ```

   This adds the quantity 4−factor+bonus to sales. Because of precedence, this is not the same as the following:

   ```
   sales = sales + 4 - factor + bonus;
   ```

   Because the += operator is much lower in the precedence table than + or −, it is performed last, and from right-to-left associativity. Therefore, the following are equivalent, from a precedence viewpoint:

   ```
   sales += 4 - factor + bonus;
   ```

   and

   ```
   sales = sales + (4 - factor + bonus);
   ```

Mixing Data Types in Calculations

You can mix data types in C, such as adding together an integer and a floating-point value. C generally converts the smaller of the two types into the other. For instance, if you add a double to an integer, C first converts the integer into a double value, then performs the calculation. This produces the most accurate result possible. The automatic conversion of data types is only temporary; the converted value is back in its original data type as soon as the expression is finished.

If C converted two different data types to the smaller value's type, the higher-precision value would be truncated, or shortened too much, and accuracy would be lost. For example, in the following short program, the floating-point value of sales is added to an integer called bonus. Before C computes the answer, it converts bonus to floating-point which results in a floating-point answer:

```
/* Filename: C7DATA.C

   Demonstrate mixed data type in an expression */

#include <stdio.h>

main()

{

    int bonus=50;

    float salary=1400.50;

    float total;


    total=salary+bonus;   /* bonus becomes floating-point temporarily */

    printf("The total is %.2f", total);

    return 0;

}
```

Type Casting

Most of the time, you don't have to worry about C's automatic conversion of data types. However, problems can occur if you mix unsigned variables with variables of other data types. Because of differences in computer architecture, unsigned variables do not always convert to the larger data type. This can result in loss of accuracy, and even incorrect results.

You can override C's default conversions by specifying your own temporary type change. This is called *type casting*. When you type cast, you temporarily change a variable's data type from its declared data type to a new one. The format of a type cast is

(*data type*) *expression*

where *data type* can be any valid C data type, and the *expression* can be a variable, constant, or an expression that combines both. The following code type casts the integer variable age into a double floating-point variable, temporarily, so it can be multiplied by the double floating-point factor:

```
age_factor = (double)age * factor;    /* Temporarily change age */
                                      /*      to double          */
```

EXAMPLE

1. Suppose you want to verify the interest calculation used by your bank on a loan. The interest rate is 15.5%, stored as .155 in a floating-point variable. The amount of interest you owe is computed by multiplying the interest rate by the amount of the loan balance, and then multiplying that by the number of days in the year since the loan originated. The following program finds the daily interest rate by dividing the annual interest rate by 365, the number of days in a year. C must convert the integer 365 to a floating-point constant automatically, because it is used in combination with a floating-point variable.

```
/* C7INT1.C
   Calculate interest on a loan */
#include <stdio.h>
main()
{
    int days=45;  // Days since loan origination
    float principle = 3500.00; // Original loan amount
    float interest_rate=0.155;   // Annual interest rate
    float daily_interest;   // Daily interest rate

    daily_interest=interest_rate/365;  // Compute floating-point value

    // Because days is integer, it too will be converted to float next
    daily_interest = principle * daily_interest * days;
    principle+=daily_interest;  // Update the principle with interest
    printf("The balance you owe is %.2f", principle);
    return 0;
}
```

OUTPUT

The output of this program follows:

```
The balance you owe is 3566.88
```

2. Instead of letting C perform the conversion, you may want to type cast all mixed expressions to ensure they convert to your liking. Here is the same program as in the first example, except type casts are used to convert the integer constants to floating-points before they are used:

```
/* C7INT2.C
   Calculate interest on a loan using type casting */
#include <stdio.h>
main()
{
    int days=45;   // Days since loan origination
    float principle = 3500.00;   // Original loan amount
    float interest_rate=0.155;   // Annual interest rate
    float daily_interest;        // Daily interest rate

    daily_interest=interest_rate/(float)365;   // Type cast days to
➥float

    /* Since days is integer, convert it to float too */
    daily_interest = principle * daily_interest * (float)days;
    principle+=daily_interest;   // Update the principle with
➥interest
    printf("The balance you owe is %.2f", principle);
    return 0;
}
```

The output from this program is exactly the same as from the previous
one.

What's Next

You now should understand C's primary math operators and the importance of the precedence table. Parentheses group operations together so
they can override the default precedence levels. Unlike in some other programming languages, every operator in C has a meaning, no matter where
it appears in an expression. This enables you to use the assignment operator (the equals sign) in the middle of other expressions. The following two
chapters extend this operator introduction to include relational, logical,
and other operators. These operators enable you to compare data and then
compute accordingly.

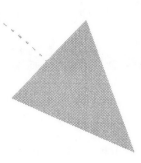

Relational and Logical Operators

This chapter shows you how to create data-driven programs. These programs do not execute the same way every time they are run. This is possible through the use of *relational* operators that conditionally control other statements. Relational operators first "look" at the constants and variables in the program, and then operate according to what they "find." This may sound like difficult programming, but it is actually quite straightforward and intuitive.

This chapter teaches you the following topics:

- Relational operators
- The `if` statement
- The `else` statement

Defining Relational Operators

In addition to the math operators you learned in Chapter 7, "Operators and Precedence," there are also operators that you use for data comparisons. They are called *relational operators*, and their task is to compare data. They enable you to know whether two variables are equal, not equal, or which one is less or more than the other. Table 8.1 lists each relational operator and its meaning.

Table 8.1: The relational operators.

Operator	Description
==	Equal to
>	Greater than
<	Less than
>=	Greater than or equal to
<=	Less than or equal to
!=	Not equal to

The six relational operators form the foundation of comparing data in C programming. They always appear with two constants, variables, expressions (or some combination of these), with one on each side of the operator. These relational operators are so useful that you should learn them as well as you know the +, -, *, /, and % mathematical operators.

NOTE

Unlike many programming languages, C uses a double equal sign (==) as a test for equality. The single equal sign (=) is reserved for assignment of values only.

---

1. Assume that a program initializes four variables as follows:

```
int a=5;
int b=10;
int c=15;
int d=5;
```

The following statements are then True:

a is equal to d, so a == d

b is less than c, so b < c

c is greater than a, so c > a

b is greater than or equal to a, so b >= a

d is less than or equal to b, so d <= b

b is not equal to c, so b != c

These are not C statements; they are statements of comparison (*relational logic*) between values in the variables. Relational logic is easy, and you've probably seen relational logic in other programming languages.

Relational logic always produces a *True* or *False* result. In C, unlike some other programming languages, you can directly use the True or False result of relational operators inside other expressions. You will soon learn how to do this; but for now, you need only understand that the following True and False evaluations are correct:

- A True relational result evaluates to 1.

- A False relational result evaluates to 0.

Each of the statements presented earlier in this example evaluate to a 1, or True, result.

2. If you assume the same values as stated for the previous example's four variables, then each of these statements about those values is False (0):

```
a == b
b > c
d < a
d > a
a != d
b >= c
c <= b
```

You should study these statements to see why each is False and evaluates to 0. The variables a and d, for example, are exactly equal to the same value (5), so neither is greater or lesser than the other.

The if Statement

You incorporate relational operators in C programs with the if statement. Such an expression is called a *decision statement* because it tests a relationship—using the relational operators—and, based on the test's result, makes a decision about which statement to execute next.

The if statement is formatted as follows:

```
if (condition)
   { block of 1 or more C statements }
```

The *condition* includes any relational comparison, and it must be enclosed in parentheses. You saw several relational comparisons earlier, such as a==d, c<d, and so on. The *block of 1 or more C statements* is any C statement, such as an assignment or printf(), enclosed in braces. The block of the if, sometimes called the *body* of the if statement, is usually indented a few spaces for readability. This enables you to see, at a glance, exactly what executes if the *condition* is True.

If only one statement follows the if, the braces are not required (but it is always good to include them). The block executes only if the *condition* is True. If the *condition* is False, C ignores the block and simply executes the next appropriate statement in the program that follows the if statement.

Basically, you can read an if statement in the following way: "If the condition is True, perform the block of statements inside the braces. Otherwise, the condition must be False; so do not execute that block, but continue executing the rest of the program as though this if did not exist."

CAUTION

Do not put a semicolon after the parentheses of the relational test. Semicolons go after each statement inside the block.

EXPRESSIONS AS THE CONDITION

C interprets any nonzero value as True, and zero always as False. This enables you to insert regular non-conditional expressions within the if logic. To see this, consider the following section of code:

```c
#include <stdio.h>
main()
{
    int age = 21;    // Declares and assigns age as 21

    if (age=85)
    {  printf("You have lived through a lot!"); }
    // Rest of program goes here
```

At first, it may seem as though the printf() does not execute, but it does. Because a regular assignment operator (=) is used (and not a relational operator, ==), C performs the assignment of 85 to age. This, as with all assignments you saw in Chapter 7, produces a value for the expression of 85. Because 85 is nonzero, C interprets the if condition as True and then performs the body of the if statement.

Mixing up the relational equality test (==) and the regular assignment operator (=) is a common error made in C programs, and the nonzero True test makes this bug even more difficult to find.

The designers of C intended that you take advantage of this feature whenever you could. Instead of putting an assignment before an if, and then testing the result of that assignment, you can combine the assignment and if into a single statement.

Test your understanding of this by considering: Would C interpret the following condition as True or False?

```
if (10 == 10 == 10)...
```

Be careful. At first glance, it seems True; but C "thinks" the expression is False. Because the == operator associates from left to right, the first 10 is compared to the second. Because they are equal, the result is 1 (for True) and the 1 is then compared to the third 10—which results in a 0 (for False)!

EXAMPLE

1. The following are examples of valid C if statements:

```
if (sales > 5000)
    { bonus = 500; }
```

If the preceding code is part of a C program, the value inside the variable sales determines what happens next. If sales contains more than 5,000, the next statement that executes is the one inside the block which initializes bonus. If, however, sales contains 5,000 or less, the block does not execute, and the line following the if's block executes:

```
if (age <= 21)
    { printf("You are a minor.\n");
      printf("What is your grade?");
      scanf(" %d", &grade); }
```

If the value in age is less than or equal to 21, the lines of code within the block execute next. Otherwise, C skips the entire block and continues with the remaining program:

```
if (balance > low_balance)
    { printf("Past due!\n"); }
```

If the value in balance is more than that in low_balance, execution of the program continues at the block and the message Past due! prints onscreen. You can compare two variables to each other (as in this example) or a variable to a constant (as in the previous examples) or a constant to a constant (although this is rarely done) or a constant to any expression in place of any variable or constant. The following if statement shows an expression included within the if:

```
If (pay * tax_rate == minimum)
    { low_salary = 1400.60; }
```

The precedence table of operators in Appendix B, "C's Precedence Table," includes the relational operators. They are at levels 6 and 7, lower than the other primary math operators. When you use expressions such as the one shown in this example, you can make these expressions much more readable by enclosing them in parentheses (even though this is not required). Here is a rewrite of this if statement with ample parentheses:

```
If ((pay * tax_rate) == minimum)
   { low_salary = 1400.60; }
```

2. The following is a simple program that computes a salesperson's pay. The salesperson gets a basic flat rate of $4.10 per hour. In addition, if the sales are more than $8,500, the salesperson also receives an additional $500 as a bonus. This is a good introductory example of conditional logic that depends on a relation between two values, sales and $8500.

```c
/* Filename: C8PAY1.C
   Calculates a salesperson's pay based on his or her sales */
#include <stdio.h>
main()
{
    char sal_name[20];
    int hours;
    float total_sales, bonus, pay;

    printf("\n\n");          // Print 2 blank lines
    printf("Payroll Calculation\n");
    printf("------------------\n");

    /* Ask the user for needed values */
    printf("What is salesperson's last name? ");
    scanf(" %s", sal_name);    // No & because it's an array
    // scanf() produces automatic newline
    //            when user presses Enter
    printf("How many hours did the salesperson work? ");
    scanf(" %d", &hours);
    printf("What were the total sales? ");
    scanf(" %f", &total_sales);

    bonus = 0;       // Initially, there is no bonus

    /* Compute the base pay */
    pay = 4.10 * (float)hours;   // Type cast the hours

    /* Add bonus only if sales were high */
```

```
if (total_sales > 8500.00)
    { bonus = 500.00; }

printf("%s made $%.2f \n", sal_name, pay);
printf("and got a bonus of $%.2f", bonus);

return 0;
}
```

OUTPUT

The following output shows the result of running this program twice, each time with different input values. Notice that the program does two different things: It computes a bonus for one employee, but doesn't for the other. The $500 bonus is a direct result of the if statement. The assignment of $500 to bonus is executed only if the value in total_sales is more than $8500.

```
Payroll Calculation
- - - - - - - - - - - - - - - - - -
What is salesperson's last name? Harrison
How many hours did the salesperson work? 40
What were the total sales? 6050.64
Harrison made $164.00
and got a bonus of $0.00

Payroll Calculation
- - - - - - - - - - - - - - - - - -
What is salesperson's last name? Robertson
How many hours did the salesperson work? 40
What were the total sales? 9800
Robertson made $164.00
and got a bonus of $500.00
```

3. While programming the way users will input data, you are often wise to program *data validation* on the values they type. If they enter a bad value (for instance, a negative number when you know the input cannot be negative), you can inform them of the problem and ask them to re-enter the data.

Not all data can be validated, of course, but most of it can be checked for reasonableness. For example, if you write a student record-keeping program, in order to track each student's name, address, age, and other pertinent data, you could check to see whether the age falls within a reasonable range. If the user enters **213** for the age, you know the value is incorrect. If the user enters **-4** for the age, you know this value is also incorrect. Not all erroneous input for age can be checked, however. If the user is 21, for instance, and types **22**, your program would have no way of knowing whether this is correct, because 22 falls within a reasonable age range for students.

The following program is a routine that requests an age, and checks to make sure it is more than 10. This is certainly not a foolproof test (because the user can still enter incorrect ages), but it takes care of extremely low values. If the user enters a bad age, the program asks for it again inside the if statement:

```c
/* Filename: C8AGE.C
   Program that helps ensure age values are reasonable */
#include <stdio.h>
main()
{
    int age;

    printf("\nWhat is the student's age? ");
    scanf(" %d", &age);

    if (age < 10)
      { printf("%c", '\x07');    // BEEP
        printf("*** The age cannot be less than 10 ***\n");
        printf("Try again...\n\n");
        printf("What is the student's age? ");
        scanf(" %d", &age);
      }

    printf("Thank you. You entered a valid age.");
    return 0;
}
```

The preceding routine could also be a section of a longer program. You learn later how to prompt repeatedly for a value until a valid input is given. This program takes advantage of the bell (ASCII 7) to warn the user that a bad age was entered.

If the entered age is less than 10, the user receives an error message. The program beeps and warns the user about the bad age before asking for it again.

The following shows the result of running this program. Notice that the program "knows," due to the if statement, whether age is more than 10:

OUTPUT

```
What is the student's age? 3
*** The age cannot be less than 10 ***
```

```
Try again...

What is the student's age? 21
Thank you.   You entered a valid age.
```

4. Unlike many languages, C does not include a square math operator. Remember that you "square" a number by multiplying it by itself (3*3, for example). Because many computers do not allow for integers to hold more than the square of 180, the following program uses if statements to make sure the number fits as an integer answer when it is computed.

   The program takes a value from the user and prints its square—unless it is more than 180. The message Square is not allowed for numbers over 180 appears onscreen if the user types an overly large number.

```
/* Filename: C8SQR1.C
   Print the square of the input value
   if the input value is less than 180 */
#include <stdio.h>
main()
{
    int num, square;

    printf("\n\n");   /* Print 2 blank lines */
    printf("What number do you want to see the square of? ");
    scanf(" %d", &num);

    if (num <= 180)
    { square = num * num;
      printf("The square of %d is %d", num, square);
    }

    if (num > 180)
    { printf("%c", '\x07');    /* BEEP */
      printf("\n*** Square is not allowed for numbers over 180 ***");
      printf("\nRun this program again and try a smaller value.");
    }

    printf("\nThank you for requesting square roots.\n");
    return 0;
}
```

The following output shows a couple of sample runs with this program. Notice that both conditions work: If the user enters a number less than 180, the calculated square appears, but if the user enters a larger number, an error message appears.

```
What number do you want to see the square of? 45
The square of 45 is 2025
Thank you for requesting square roots.


What number do you want to see the square of? 212

*** Square is not allowed for numbers over 180 ***
Run this program again and try a smaller value.
Thank you for requesting square roots.
```

This program is improved when you learn the else statement later in this chapter. This code includes a redundant check of the user's input. The variable num must be checked once to print the square if the input number is less than or equal to 180, and checked again for the error message if it is greater than 180.

5. The value of 1 and 0 for True and False, respectively, can help save you an extra programming step, which you are not necessarily able to save in other languages. To understand this, examine the following section of code:

```
commission = 0;    /* Initialize commission */

if (sales > 10000)
    { commission = 500.00; }

pay = net_pay + commission;    /* Commission is 0 unless high sales
➥*/
```

This program can be streamlined and made more efficient by combining the if's relational test because you know that if returns 1 or 0:

```
pay = net_pay + (commission = (sales > 10000) * 500.00);
```

This single line does what it took the previous four lines to do. Because the rightmost assignment has precedence, it gets computed first. The variable sales is compared to 10000. If it is more than 10000, a True result of 1 is returned. That 1 is multiplied by 500.00 and stored in commission. If, however, the sales were not more than 10000, a 0 would result, and 0 multiplied by 500.00 still returns 0.

Whichever value (500.00 or 0) is assigned to commission also becomes the value of that expression. That value is then added to net_pay and stored in pay.

The else Statement

The else statement never appears in a program without an if statement. This section introduces the else statement by showing you the popular if-else combination statement. Its format is

```
if (condition)
  { A block of 1 or more C statements }
else
  { A block of 1 or more C statements }
```

The first part of the if-else is identical to the if statement. If the *condition* is True, then the block of C statements following the if executes. However, if the *condition* is False, the block of C statements following the else executes instead. Whereas the simple if statement determines what happens only when the *condition* is True, the if-else also determines what happens if the *condition* is False. No matter what the outcome is, the statement following the if-else executes next.

The following describes the nature of the if-else:

- If the *condition* test is True, the entire block of statements following the if is performed.

- If the *condition* test is False, the entire block of statements following the else is performed.

NOTE

You can also compare characters, in addition to numbers. When you compare characters, C uses the ASCII table to determine which character is "less than" (lower in the ASCII table than) the other. But you cannot compare character strings or arrays of character strings directly with relational operators.

EXAMPLE

1. The following program asks the user for a number. It then prints whether or not the number is greater than zero, by using the if-else statement:

```
/* Filename: C8IFEL1.C
   Demonstrates if-else by printing whether an
   input value is greater than zero or not */
#include <stdio.h>
main()
```

```
{
    int num;

    printf("What is your number? ");
    scanf(" %d", &num);    // Get the user's number

    if (num > 0)
        { printf("More than 0\n"); }
    else
        { printf("Less or equal to 0\n"); }

    /* No matter what the number was, the following executes */
    printf("\n\nThanks for your time!");
    return 0;
}
```

There is no need to test for both possibilities when you use an else. The if tests to see whether the number is greater than zero, and the else automatically takes care of all other possibilities.

2. The following program asks the user for his or her first name, and then stores it in a character array. The first character of the array is checked to see whether it falls in the first half of the alphabet. If it does, an appropriate message is displayed:

```
/* Filename: C8IFEL2.C
   Tests the user's first initial and prints a message */
#include <stdio.h>
main()
{
    char last[20];    // Holds the last name
    printf("What is your last name? ");
    scanf(" %s", last);

    /* Test the initial */
    if (last[0] <= 'P')
        { printf("Your name is early in the alphabet.\n");}
    else
        { printf("You have to wait a while for YOUR name to be
  ➥called!");}
    return 0;
}
```

Notice that because a character array element is being compared to a character constant, you must enclose the character constant inside single quotes. The data type on each side of each relational operator must also match.

3. The following program is a more complete payroll routine than you have seen. It uses the `if` to illustrate how to compute overtime pay. The logic goes something like this:

If employees work 40 hours or fewer, they get paid regular pay (their hourly rate times the number of hours worked). If employees work between 40 and 50 hours, they get one-and-a-half times their hourly rate for those hours over 40, in addition to their regular pay for the first 40. All hours over 50 are paid at double the regular rate.

```c
/* Filename: C8PAY2.C
   Compute the full overtime pay possibilities */
#include <stdio.h>
main()
{
    int hours;
    float dt, ht, rp, rate, pay;

    printf("\n\nHow many hours were worked? ");
    // Enter whole numbers only
    scanf(" %d", &hours);
    printf("\nWhat is the regular hourly pay?");
    scanf(" %f", &rate);

    /* Compute pay here */
    /* Double-time possibility */
    if (hours > 50)
      { dt = 2.0 * rate * (float)(hours - 50);
        ht = 1.5 * rate * 10.0; } // Time + 1/2 for 10 hours
    else
      { dt = 0.0; }  // Either none or double for those hours over 50

    /* Time and a half */
    if ((hours > 40) && (hours <= 50))
      { ht = 1.5 * rate * (float)(hours - 40); }

    /* Regular Pay */
    if (hours >= 40)
      { rp = 40 * rate; }
    else
      { rp = (float)hours * rate; }
```

```
    pay = dt + ht + rp;    // Add up 3 components of payroll

    printf("\nThe pay is %.2f", pay);
    return 0;
}
```

4. The block of statements following the if can contain any valid C statement—even another if statement! This sometimes comes in handy, as the following example shows.

This program could be run to give an award to employees based on their years of service to your company. In this example, you are giving a gold watch to those with more than 20 years of service, a paper-weight to those with more than 10 years, and a pat on the back to everyone else.

```
/* Filename: C8SERV.C
   Prints a message depending on years of service */
#include <stdio.h>
main()
{
    int yrs;
    printf("How many years of service? ");
    scanf(" %d", &yrs);    // Get the years they have worked

    if (yrs > 20)
        { printf("Give a gold watch\n"); }
    else
        { if (yrs > 10)
          { printf("Give a paper weight\n"); }
          else
              { printf("Give a pat on the back\n"); }
        }
    return 0;
}
```

You should probably not rely on the if within an if to take care of too many conditions, because more than three or four conditions can add confusion. You might get into some messy logic, such as: "If this is True, and then if this is also True, then do something; but if not that, but something else is True, then…" (and so on). The switch statement that you learn about in Chapter 12, "Controlling Flow," handles these types of multiple if selections much better than a long if-within-an-if statement does.

What's Next

You now have the tools to write powerful data-checking programs. This chapter showed you how to compare constants, variables, and combinations of both by using the relational operators. You can now *conditionally execute* statements within your programs.

The next chapter takes conditional logic one step further by combining relational operators in order to create logical operators (sometimes called *compound conditions*). These logical operators further improve your program's ability to make selections based on data comparisons.

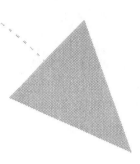

Remaining C Operators

C's *logical operators* enable you to combine relational operators into more powerful data-testing statements. The logical operators are sometimes called *compound relational operators*. As C's precedence table shows (see Appendix B, "C's Precedence Table"), relational operators take precedence over logical operators when you combine them. The precedence table plays an important role in these types of operators, as this chapter stresses.

To conclude your study of C operators, this chapter also describes many of the unusual operators found only in C and languages designed from C. Even if you have programmed in other languages for many years, you still may be surprised by the power of these C operators.

This chapter teaches you the following topics:

- How logical operators are used

- The ?: conditional operator

- The increment and decrement operators

- The sizeof and comma operators

Defining Logical Operators

There may be times when you need to test more than one set of variables. You can combine more than one relational test into a *compound relational test* by using C's logical operators, as shown in Table 9.1.

Table 9.1: Logical operators.

Operator	Meaning
&&	AND
¦¦	OR
!	NOT

The first two logical operators, && and ¦¦, never appear by themselves. They typically go between two or more relational tests.

Tables 9.2, 9.3, and 9.4 illustrate how each logical operator works. These tables are called *truth tables* because they show you how to achieve True results from an if statement that uses these operators.

*Table 9.2: The AND (**&&**) truth table—both sides of the operator must be True.*

True AND True = True

True AND False = False

False AND True = False

False AND False = False

Table 9.3: The OR (¦¦) truth table—one or the other side of the operator must be True.

True OR True = True

True OR False = True

False OR True = True

False OR False = False

Table 9.4: The NOT (!) truth table—causes an opposite relation.

NOT True = False

NOT False = True

Logical Operators and Their Use

The True and False on each side of the operators represent a relational if test. The following statements, for example, are valid if tests that use logical operators (sometimes called compound relational operators).

```
if ((a < b) && (c > d))
    { printf("Results are invalid."); }
```

The variable a must be less than b and, at the same time, c must be greater than d in order for the printf() to execute. The if statement still requires parentheses around its complete conditional test. Consider this portion of a program:

```
if ((sales > 5000) || (hrs_worked > 81))
    { bonus=500; }
```

The sales must be more than 5,000, or the hrs_worked must be more than 81, before the assignment executes.

```
IF (!(sales < 2500))
    { bonus = 500; }
```

If sales is greater than or equal to 2,500, bonus is initialized. This illustrates an important programming tip: Use ! sparingly. Or, as some professionals so wisely put it: "Do *not* use ! or your programs will *not* be !(unclear)." It would be much clearer to rewrite this last example by turning it into a positive relational test:

```
if (sales >= 2500)
  { bonus 500; }
```

But the ! operator is sometimes helpful, especially when testing for end-of-file conditions. Most of the time you can avoid using ! by using the reverse logic shown in the following:

!(var1 == var2) is the same as (var1 != var2)

!(var1 <= var2) is the same as (var1 > var2)

!(var1 >= var2) is the same as (var1 < var2)

!(var1 != var2) is the same as (var1 == var2)

!(var1 > var2) is the same as (var1 <= var2)

!(var1 < var2) is the same as (var1 >= var2)

Notice that the overall format of the if statement is retained when you use logical operators, but the relational test is expanded to include more than one relation. You even can have three or more, as in the following statement:

```
if ((a == B) && (d == f) || (l = m) || !(k <> 2)) …
```

This is a little too much, however, and good programming practice dictates using at most two relational tests inside a single if statement. If you need to combine more than two, use more than one if statement to do so.

INTERNAL TRUTHS

The True or False results of relational tests occur internally at the bit level. For example, take the if test

```
if (a == 6) …
```

to determine the truth of the relation, (a==6). The computer takes a binary 6, or 00000110, and compares it, bit by bit, to the variable a. If a contains 7, a binary 00000111, the result of this equal test would be False, because the right bit (called the *least-significant bit*) is different.

C's Logical Efficiency

C attempts to be more efficient than other languages. If you combine multiple relational tests with one of the logical operators, C does not always interpret the full expression. This ultimately makes your programs run faster, but there are dangers. For example, if your program is given the conditional test

```
if ((5 > 4) ¦¦ (sales < 15) && (15 != 15)) …
```

then C only "looks at" the first condition, (5 > 4), and realizes it does not need to look further. Because (5 > 4) is True and because ¦¦ (OR) anything that follows it is still True, C does not bother with the rest of the expression. The same holds true for the following statement:

```
if ((7 < 3) && (age > 15) && (initial == 'D')) …
```

C looks only at the first condition, which is False. Because the && (AND) anything else that follows it is also going to be False, C does not interpret the expression to the right of (7 < 3). Most of the time, this doesn't pose any problem, but you should be aware that the following expression may not fulfill your expectations:

```
if ((5 > 4) ¦¦ (num = 0)) …
```

The (num = 0) assignment never executes, because C only needs to interpret (5 > 4) to see whether the entire expression is True or False. Because of this danger, do *not* include assignment expressions in the same condition as a logical test. The following single if condition

```
if ((sales > old_sales) ¦¦ (inventory_flag = 'Y')) …
```

should be broken into two statements, such as

```
inventory_flag = 'Y';
if ((sales > old_sales) ¦¦ (inventory_flag)) …
```

so that the inventory_flag is always assigned the 'Y' value, no matter how the (sales > old_sales) expression tests.

EXAMPLE

1. The summer Olympics are held every four years during each year that is divisible evenly by 4. The U.S. Census is taken every 10 years, in each year that is evenly divisible by 10. The following short program asks for a year, and then tells the user if it is a year of the summer Olympics, a year of the census, or both. It uses relational operators, logical operators, and the modulus operator to determine this output.

```c
/* Filename: C9YEAR.C
   Determines if it is Summer Olympics year,
   U.S. Census year, or both                    */
#include <stdio.h>
main()
{
    int year;
    /* Ask for a year */
    printf("What is a year for the test? ");
    scanf(" %d", &year);

    /* Test the year */
    if (((year % 4)==0) && ((year % 10)==0))
      { printf("Both Olympics and U.S. Census!");
        return 0; }
    if ((year % 4)==0)
      { printf("Summer Olympics only"); }
    else
        { if ((year % 10)==0)
            { printf("U.S. Census only"); }
        }
    return 0;
}
```

2. Now that you know about compound relations, you can write an age-checking program like the one presented in Chapter 8, "Relational and Logical Operators," C8AGE.C. That example ensured the age would be above 10. This is another way you can validate input for reasonableness. The following program includes a logical operator in its if, to see whether the age is greater than 10 and less than 100. If either of these is the case, the program knows that the user did not enter a valid age.

```c
/* Filename: C9AGE.C
   Program that helps ensure age values are reasonable */
#include <stdio.h>
main()
{
    int age;
```

```
        printf("What is your age? ");
        scanf(" %d", &age);
        if ((age < 10) || (age > 100))
          { printf(" \x07 \x07 \n");    // Beep twice
            printf("*** The age must be between 10 and 100 ***\n"); }
        else
          { printf("You entered a valid age."); }
        return 0;
}
```

3. The following program might be used by a video store to calculate a discount, based on the number of rentals people transact as well as their customer status. Customers are classified either R for Regular or S for Special. Special customers have been members of the rental club for more than one year. They automatically receive a 50-cent discount on all rentals. The store also holds "value days" several times a year. On value days, all customers get the 50-cent discount. Special customers do not receive an additional 50 cents off during value days, because every day is a discount for them.

The program asks for each customer's status and whether or not it is a value day. It then uses the || relation to test for the discount. You might look at this problem with the following idea in mind:

"If a customer is Special or if it is a value day, deduct 50 cents from the rental."

That's basically the idea of the if decision in the following program. Even though Special customers do not get an additional discount on value days, there is one final if test for them that prints an extra message at the bottom of the screen's indicated billing.

```
/* Filename: C9VIDEO.C
    Program to compute video rental amounts and gives
    appropriate discounts based on the day or customer status. */
#include <stdio.h>
main()
{
    float tapeCharge, discount, rentalAmt;
    char firstName[15];
    char lastName[15];
    int numTapes;
    char valDay, spStat;
```

```
printf("\n\n *** Video Rental Computation ***\n");
printf("          ----------------------\n"); // Underline

tapeCharge = 2.00;    // The before-discount tape
                      // fee per tape
/* Get input data */
printf("\nWhat is customer's first name? ");
scanf(" %s", firstName);
printf("What is customer's last name? ");
scanf(" %s", lastName);

printf("\nHow many tapes are being rented? ");
scanf(" %d", &numTapes);

printf("Is this a Value day (Y/N)? ");
scanf(" %c", &valDay);

printf("Is this a Special Status customer (Y/N)? ");
scanf(" %c", &spStat);

/* Calculate rental amount */
discount = 0.0;    // Increase the discount IF
                   // they are eligible
if ((valDay == 'Y') || (spStat == 'Y'))
   { discount = 0.5;
      rentalAmt = (numTapes * tapeCharge) -
                  (discount * numTapes); }

/* Print the bill */
printf("\n\n** Rental Club **\n\n");
printf("%s %s rented %d tapes\n", firstName,
        lastName, numTapes);
printf("The total was %.2f\n", rentalAmt);
printf("The discount was %.2f per tape\n", discount);

/* Print extra message for Special Status customers */
if (spStat == 'Y')
   { printf("\nThank them for being a Special Status customer");}
return 0;
}
```

OUTPUT

Notice from the output that Special customers have the extra message at the bottom of the screen. This program, due to its if statements, performs differently depending on the data entered. No discount is applied for Regular customers on non-value days.

```
        *** Video Rental Computation ***
        ------------------------

        What is customer's first name? Diane
        What is customer's last name? Moore

        How many tapes are being rented? 3
        Is this a Value day (Y/N)? N
        Is this a Special Status customer (Y/N)? Y

        ** Rental Club **

        Diane Moore rented 3 tapes
        The total was 4.50
        The discount was 0.50 per tape

        Thank them for being a Special Status customer
```

Logical Operators and Their Precedence

The math precedence order you read about in Chapter 7, "Operators and Precedence," did not include the logical operators. To be complete, you should be familiar with the entire order of precedence, as presented in Appendix B. As you can see, the math operators take precedence over the relational operators, and the relational operators take precedence over the logical operators.

You might wonder why the relational and logical operators are included in a precedence table. The following statement helps show you why:

```
if ((sales < min_sal * 2 && yrs_emp > 10 * sub) …
```

Without the complete order of operators, it would be impossible to determine how such a statement would execute. According to the precedence order, this `if` statement would execute as follows:

```
if ((sales < (min_sal * 2)) && (yrs_emp > (10 * sub))) …
```

This still may be confusing, but it is less so. The two multiplications would be performed first, followed by the relations < and >. The && is performed last because it is lowest in the precedence order of operators.

To avoid such ambiguous problems, be sure to use ample parentheses—even if the default precedence order is still your intention. It is also wise to resist combining too many expressions inside a single `if` relational test.

Notice that || (OR) has lower precedence than && (AND). Therefore, the following `if` tests are equivalent:

```
if ((first_initial == 'A') && (last_initial == 'G') ¦¦
    (id == 321)) …
if (((first_initial == 'A') && (last_initial == 'G')) ¦¦
    (id == 321)) …
```

The second is clearer, due to the parentheses, but the precedence table makes them identical.

The Conditional Operator

The *conditional operator* is C's only *ternary* operator, which requires three operands (as opposed to the unary's single and the binary's double operand requirements). The conditional operator is used to replace if-else logic in some situations. The conditional operator is a two-part symbol, ?:, whose format follows:

conditional_expression ? expression1 : expression2;

The *conditional_expression* is any expression in C that results in a True (nonzero) or False (zero) answer. If the result of the *conditional_expression* is True, *expression1* executes. Otherwise, if the result of the *conditional_expression* is False, *expression2* executes. Only one of the expressions following the question mark ever executes. Put a single semicolon at the end of *expression2*. The internal expressions, such as *expression1*, should not have a semicolon.

Figure 9.1 illustrates the conditional operator a little more clearly.

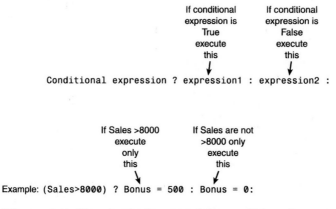

Figure 9.1: Here is the format of the conditional operator.

If you require simple if-else logic, the conditional operator usually provides a more direct and succinct method, although you should always prefer readability over compact code.

To get a glimpse of the conditional operator at work, consider the section of code that follows:

```
if (a > b)
    { ans = 10; }
else
    { ans = 25; }
```

You can easily rewrite this kind of if-else code by using a single conditional operator:

```
a > b ? (ans = 10) : (ans = 25);
```

Although parentheses are not required around the *conditional_expression* to make it work, they usually improve readability. This statement's readability could be improved by using parentheses, as follows:

```
(a > b) ? (ans = 10) : (ans = 25);
```

Because each C expression has a value—in this case, the value being assigned—this statement could be made even more succinct, without loss of readability, by assigning ans the answer to the left of the conditional:

```
ans = (a > b) ? (10) : (25);
```

This expression says: If a is greater than b, assign 10 to ans; otherwise, assign 25 to ans. Almost any if-else statement can be rewritten as a conditional, and vice versa. You should practice converting one to the other, in order to acquaint yourself with the conditional operator's purpose.

NOTE

Any valid if C statement can be a *conditional_expression*, including all relational and logical operators as well as any of their possible combinations.

EXAMPLE

1. Suppose you are looking over your early C programs, and you notice the following section of code:

```
if (production > target)
    { target *= 1.10; }
else
    { target *= .90; }
```

You realize that such a simple if-else statement can be rewritten, using a conditional operator, and that more efficient code would result. So you could therefore change it to the following single statement:

```
(production > target) ? (target *= 1.10) : (target *= .90);
```

2. Using a conditional operator, you can write a routine to find the minimum value between two variables. This is sometimes called a *minimum routine*. The statement to do this is

```
minimum = (var1 < var2) ? var1 : var2;
```

If var1 is less than var2, the value of var1 is assigned to minimum. If var2 is less, the value of var2 is assigned to minimum. If the variables are equal, the value of var2 is assigned to minimum, because it does not matter which is assigned.

3. A *maximum routine* can be written just as easily:

```
maximum = (var1 > var2) ? var1 : var2;
```

4. Taking the previous examples a step further, you can also test for the sign of a variable. The following conditional expression assigns –1 to the variable called sign if testvar is less than 0; 0 to sign if testvar is zero; and +1 to sign if testvar is 1 or more.

```
sign = (testvar < 0) ? -1 : (testvar > 0);
```

It might be easy to spot why the less-than test results in a –1, but the second part of the expression might be confusing. This works well because of C's 1 and 0 (for True and False, respectively) return values from a relational test. If testvar is 0 or greater, sign is assigned the answer of (testvar > 0). The value of (testvar > 0) is 1 if True (therefore, testvar is more than 0) or 0 if testvar is equal to 0.

The preceding statement shows C's efficient conditional operator very well. It may also help you to write this using typical if-else logic. Here is the same problem written with a typical if-else statement:

```
if (testvar < 0)
    { sign = -1; }
else
    { sign = (testvar > 0); }    // testvar can only be
                                 // 0 or more here
```

The Increment and Decrement Operators

C offers two unique operators that add or subtract 1 to or from variables. These are the *increment* and *decrement* operators, ++ and – –. Table 9.5 shows how these operators relate to other types of expressions you have seen. Notice that the ++ and – – can go on either side of the modified variable. If the ++ or – – appears on the left, it is known as a *prefix* operator. If it appears on the right, it is a *postfix* operator.

Table 9.5: The ++ and −− operators.

Operator	Example	Description	Equivalent Statements
++	i++;	postfix	i = i + 1; i += 1;
++	++i;	prefix	i = i + 1; i += 1;
−−	i−−;	postfix	i = i − 1; i −= 1;
−−	−−i;	prefix	i = i − 1; i −= 1;

Any time you need to add 1 to a variable, or subtract 1 from a variable, you can use these two operators. As Table 9.5 shows, if you need to increment or decrement only a single variable, these operators enable you to do so.

INCREMENT AND DECREMENT EFFICIENCY

The increment and decrement operators are straightforward, efficient methods for adding 1 to a variable and subtracting 1 from a variable. You often need to do this during counting or processing loops, as shown in Part III of this book, "Controlling Your Program's Execution."

These two operators compile directly into their assembly language equivalents. Almost all computers include, at their lowest binary machine-language commands, increment and decrement instructions. If you use C's increment and decrement operators, you ensure that they compile down into these low-level equivalents.

If, however, you code expressions to add or subtract 1 (as you would do in other programming languages), such as the expression i = i − 1, you do not actually ensure that C compiles this instruction into its efficient machine-language equivalent.

Whether you use prefix or postfix does not matter—if you are incrementing or decrementing single variables on lines by themselves. However, when you combine these two operators with other operators in a single expression, you must be aware of their differences. Consider the following program section. Here, all variables are integers because the increment and decrement operators work only on integer variables:

```
a = 6;
b = ++a - 1;
```

What are the values of a and b after these two statements finish? The value of a is easy to determine: it is incremented in the second statement, and so it is 7 due to the ++ operator. However, b is either 5 or 6 depending upon when the variable a increments. To determine when a increments, consider the following rule:

- If a variable is incremented or decremented with a prefix operator, the increment or decrement occurs before the variable's value is used in the rest of the expression.

- If a variable is incremented or decremented with a postfix operator, the increment or decrement occurs after the variable's value is used in the rest of the expression.

In the previous code, a contains a prefix increment. Therefore, its value is first incremented to 7, then 1 is subtracted from 7, and the result (6) is assigned to b. But if a postfix increment is used, as in

```
a = 6;
b = a++ - 1;
```

a is 6; therefore, 5 is assigned to b because a does not increment to 7 until after its value is used in the expression. The precedence table in Appendix B shows that prefix operators contain much higher precedence than almost every other operator, especially low-precedence postfix increments and decrements.

TIP

If the order of prefix and postfix confuses you, break your expressions into two lines of code, putting the increment or decrement before or after the expression that uses it.

By taking advantage of this tip, you can now rewrite the previous example as follows:

```
a = 6;
b = a - 1;
a++;
```

There is now no doubt as to when a gets incremented: a increments after b is assigned to a–1.

Even parentheses cannot override the postfix rule. Consider the following statement:

```
x = p + (((amt++)));
```

There are too many unneeded parentheses here, but even the redundant parentheses are not enough to increment amt before adding its value to p. Postfix increments and decrements always occur after their variables are used in the surrounding expression.

CAUTION

Do not attempt to increment or decrement an expression. You can apply these operators only to variables. The following expression is invalid:

```
sales = ++(rate * hours);   /* Not allowed! */
```

---

1. As you should with all other C operators, keep the precedence table in mind when you evaluate expressions that increment and decrement. Figures 9.2 and 9.3 show you some examples that illustrate these operators. Notice how the precedence table takes on new meaning when you study the order of operators that takes place in Figure 9.3.

```
int i=1;
int j=2;
int k=3;
ans = i++*j - --k;

  i++* j - 2
    \ /
     2  -  2
      \   /
        0
```

ans = 0, then i increments by 1 to its final value of 2.

```
int i=1;
int j=2;
int k=3;
ans = i++*j - k--;

  2 *j - k--
   \ /
    4  - k--
     \   /
       1
```

ans = 1, then k decrements by 1 to its final value of 2.

Figure 9.2: *C operators incrementing (above) and decrementing (below) by order of precedence.*

```
int i=0;
int j=1;
int k=0;
int m=1
ans = i++ && ++j||m++;
          |
   i++ && 0 || k || m++
    \  /
      0  || k || m++
       \   /
         0  || m++
          \   /
            1
```

ans = 1, then i increments by 1 to its final value of 1,
and m increments by 1 to its final value of 2.

Figure 9.3: *Another example of C operators and their precedence.*

2. Considering the precedence table—and, more importantly, what you know about C's relational efficiencies—what is the value of the ans in the following section of code?

```
int i=1, j=20, k=-1, l=0, m=1, n=0, o=2, p=1;
ans = i || j-- && k++ || ++l && ++m || n-- & !o || p--;
```

This, at first, seems to be extremely complicated. Nevertheless, you can simply glance at it and determine the value of ans, as well as the ending value of the rest of the variables.

Recall that when C performs a relation || (OR), it ignores the right side of the || if the left value is True (any nonzero value is True). Because True or any other value is still True, C does not "think" it needs to look at the values on the right. Therefore, C performs this expression by seeing that i is True and then continues to the next statement; the right side has no bearing on the result since only one of the two sides have to be True for the entire expression to be True.

NOTE

Because i is True, C "knows" the entire expression is True and ignores the rest of it after the first ||. Therefore, it is important to realize that every other increment and decrement expression is ignored. The result is that only ans is changed by this expression; the rest of the variables, j through p, are never incremented or decremented, even though several of them contain increment and decrement operators. If you use relational operators, be aware of this problem and break out all increment and decrement operators into statements by themselves, placing them on lines before the relational statements that use their values.

The sizeof Operator

There is another operator in C that does not look like an operator at all. It looks like a built-in function, but it is called the sizeof operator. In fact, if you think of sizeof as a function call, you may not get too confused because it works in a very similar way. The format of sizeof is as follows:

sizeof *data*

or

sizeof(*data type*)

The sizeof operator is unary, because it operates on a single value. This operator produces a result that represents the size, in bytes, of the *data* or *data type* specified. Because most data types and variables require different amounts of internal storage on different computers, the sizeof operator is provided to enable programs to maintain consistency on different types of computers.

TIP

Most C programmers use parentheses around the sizeof argument, whether that argument is *data* or *data type*. Because you must use parentheses around *data type* arguments and you can use them around *data* arguments, it doesn't hurt you to always use them for both kinds of arguments.

The sizeof operator is sometimes called a *compile-time operator*. At compile-time, instead of runtime, the compiler replaces each occurrence of sizeof in your program with an unsigned integer value. But because sizeof is used more in advanced C programming, this operator is better utilized later in the book for performing more advanced programming requirements.

If you use an array as the sizeof argument, C returns the number of bytes you originally reserved for that array. Data inside the array have nothing to do with its returned sizeof value—even if it's only a character array containing a very short string.

EXAMPLE

Suppose you want to know the size, in bytes, of floating-point variables for your computer. You can determine this by putting the keyword float in parentheses—after sizeof—as shown in the following program:

```
/* Filename: C9SIZE1.C
    Prints the size of floating-point values */
#include <stdio.h>
main()
{
    printf("The size of floating-point variables \n");
    printf("on this computer is: %d ", (int) sizeof(float));
    return 0;
}
```

This program may produce different results on different computers. You can use any valid data type as the sizeof argument. When you directly print sizeof results, as shown here, you should type cast sizeof to an integer in order to print it properly with %d.

On most computers, this program very probably produces this output:

```
The size of floating-point variables on this computer is: 4
```

OUTPUT

Your output will differ only if your computer uses a different amount of storage for floating-point values.

The Comma Operator

Another C operator, sometimes called a *sequence point*, works a little differently. This is the *comma operator* (,), which does not directly operate on data, but produces a left-to-right evaluation of expressions. This operator enables you to put more than one expression on a single line by separating each one with a comma.

Already you have seen one use of the sequence point comma, when you learned how to declare and initialize variables. In the following section of code, the comma separates statements. Because the comma associates from left to right, the first variable, i, is declared and initialized before the second variable:

```c
main()
{
    int i=10, j=25;
    /* Rest of program follows */
```

However, the comma is not a sequence point when it is used inside function parentheses. Then it is said to separate arguments, but it is not a sequence point. Consider the printf() that follows:

```c
printf("%d %d %d", i, i++, ++i);
```

You may get one of many results from such a statement. The commas serve only to separate arguments of the printf(), and do not generate the left-to-right sequence that they would otherwise when they aren't used in functions. With the statement shown here, you are not ensured of any order. The postfix i++ might possibly be performed before the prefix ++i, even though the precedence table does not explain this. Here, the order of evaluation depends on how your compiler sends these arguments to the printf() function.

TIP

Do not put increment operators or decrement operators in function calls.

EXAMPLE

1. You can put more than one expression on a line, using the comma as a sequence point. The following program does this:

```c
/* Filename: C9COM1.C
    Illustrates the sequence point */
#include <stdio.h>
main()
{
    int num, sq, cube;
    num = 5;
```

```
        /* Calculate the square and cube of the number */
        sq = (num * num), cube = (num * num * num);

        printf("The square of %d is %d, and the cube is %d",
                num, sq, cube);
        return 0;
}
```

This is not necessarily recommended, however, because it doesn't add anything to the program and actually decreases its readability. In this example, the square and cube are probably better computed on two separate lines.

2. The comma enables some interesting statements. Consider the following section of code:

```
i = 10
j = (i = 12, i + 8);
```

When this code finishes executing, j has the value of 20—even though this is not necessarily clear. In the first statement, i is assigned 10. In the second statement, the comma causes i to be assigned a value of 12, then j is assigned the value of i + 8, or 20.

3. In the following section of code, ans is assigned the value of 12, because the assignment before the comma is performed first. Despite this right-to-left associativity of the assignment operator, the comma's sequence point lastly forces the assignment of 12 into x, before x is assigned to ans.

```
ans = (y = 8, x = 12);
```

When this finishes, y contains 8, x contains 12, and ans also contains 12.

NOTE

C and other languages based on C support a set of operators known as *bitwise operators*. The bitwise operators work on data values differently from the way the other operators do. The bitwise operators work on data's internal binary representation (see Appendix A, "Memory Addressing, Binary, and Hexadecimal," for a review of binary representation).

What's Next

This chapter extended the `if` statement to include the logical operators so that you can now build complex relationships between your data values. The remaining regular C operators such as the conditional and `sizeof` operators enable you to work with data that would require extra programming effort in most major programming languages that do not support such operators. You now have the tools needed to write conditional executing programs using the new commands that you will learn beginning in the next chapter. The next chapter begins a new part in this book, "Controlling Your Program's Execution," and explains how to combine the operators with controlling commands to make your C programs respond to data and execute according to that data.

Part III

Controlling Your Program's Execution

The while Loop

The for Loop

Controlling Flow

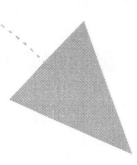

10

The while Loop

This and the next two chapters introduce you to C constructs, the control and looping commands in programming languages. C constructs include powerful, succinct, efficient looping commands similar to those of other languages you may already know. The while loops, taught here, enable your programs to repeat a series of statements, over and over, as long as a certain condition is always met.

This chapter teaches you the following topics:

- The while statement
- Looping in C
- The do-while loop
- The exit() function
- The break statement
- Using counters and totals in C programs

The while Statement

The while statement is one of several C construct statements. Each construct is a programming language statement—or a series of statements—that controls looping. The while statement, like other such statements, is a *looping statement* that controls the execution of a series of other statements. Looping statements cause parts of a program to execute repeatedly, as long as a certain condition is being met.

The format of the while statement is this:

```
while (test expression)
   { block of one or more C statements; }
```

The parentheses around *test expression* are required. As long as the *test expression* is True (nonzero), the block of one or more C statements executes, repeatedly, until the *test expression* becomes False (evaluates to zero). Braces are required before and after the body of the while loop, unless you want to execute only one statement. Each statement in the body of the while loop requires a semicolon at the end.

The *test expression* usually contains relational, and possibly logical, operators. These operators provide the True-False condition checked in the *test expression*. If the *test expression* is False when the program reaches the while loop for the first time, the body of the while loop does not execute at all. Regardless of whether the body of the while loop executes no times, one time, or many times, the statements following the while loop's closing brace execute if and when the *test expression* becomes False.

Because the *test expression* determines when the loop finishes, the body of the while loop must change the variables used in the *test expression*. Otherwise, the *test expression* never changes and the while loop repeats forever. This is known as an *infinite loop*, and you should avoid it.

TIP

If the body of the while loop contains only one statement, you need not enclose the loop in braces. Nevertheless, good programming practices dictate that you should enclose all while loop statements in braces because if you must add more statements to the body of the while loop later, your braces are already there.

EXAMPLE

1. Some programs presented earlier in the book require user input with scanf(). If users do not enter appropriate values, these programs display an error message and ask the user to enter another value. This approach is fine, but now that you understand the while loop construct, you should put the error message inside a loop. In this way, users see the message continually until they type proper input values, rather than once.

The following program is short, but it demonstrates a while loop being used to ensure valid user keyboard input. It asks users if they want to continue. You might want to incorporate this program into a larger one that requires user permission to continue. Put a prompt, such as the one presented here, at the bottom of a screen full of text. The text remains onscreen until the user tells the program to continue executing.

```c
/* Filename: C10WHIL1.C
   Input routine to ensure that user types a
   correct response. This routine might be part
   of a larger program. */
#include <stdio.h>
main()
{
    char ans;

    printf("Do you want to continue (Y/N)? ");
    scanf(" %c", &ans);                    // Get user's answer

    while ((ans != 'Y') && (ans != 'N'))
        { printf("\nYou must type a Y or an N\n");   // Warn
                                                     //   and ask
            printf("Do you want to continue (Y/N)?"); // again
            scanf(" %c", &ans); }          /* Body of while loop
                                              ends here */

    return 0;
}
```

Notice that the two scanf() functions do the same thing. An initial scanf(), outside the while loop, must be done to get an answer that the while loop can check. If users type something other than Y or N, the program prints an error message, asks for another answer, and then loops back to check the answer again. This is a more preferred method of data-entry validation than giving users only one additional chance to get it right.

OUTPUT

The while loop tests the test expression at the top of the loop. This is why the loop may never execute. If the test is initially False, the loop does not execute even once. The output from this program is shown as follows. The program repeats indefinitely, until the relational test is True (that is, as soon as the user types either Y or N).

```
Do you want to continue (Y/N)? k

You must type a Y or an N
Do you want to continue (Y/N)? c

You must type a Y or an N
Do you want to continue (Y/N)? s

You must type a Y or an N
Do you want to continue (Y/N)? 5

You must type a Y or an N
Do you want to continue (Y/N)? Y
```

2. The following program is an example of an *invalid* while loop. See if you can find the problem.

```c
/* Filename: C10WHBAD.C
   Bad use of a while loop */
#include <stdio.h>
main()
{
    int a=10, b=20;
    while (a > 5)
        { printf("a is %d, and b is %d \n", a, b);
          b = 20 + a; }
    return 0;
}
```

This while loop is an example of an infinite loop. It is vital that at least one statement inside the while changes a variable in the test expression (in this example, the variable a); otherwise, the condition is always True. Because the variable a does not change inside the while loop, this program will never end without the user's intervention.

TIP

If you inadvertently write an infinite loop, you must stop the program yourself. If you use a PC, this typically means pressing Ctrl+Break. If you are using a UNIX-based system or a mainframe, your system administrator might have to stop your program's execution.

---

3. The following program asks users for a first name, then uses a while loop to count the number of characters in the name. This is a *string length program*; that is, it counts characters until it reaches the null zero. Remember that the length of a string equals the number of characters in the string up to—but not including—the null zero.

```
/* Filename: C10WHIL2.C
   Counts the number of letters in the user's first name */
#include <stdio.h>
main()
{
    char name[15];            // Will hold user's first name
    int count=0;        // Will hold total characters in name

    /* Get the user's first name */
    printf("What is your first name? ");
    scanf(" %s", name);

    while (name[count] > 0) // Loop until null zero reached
        {  count++; }                      // Add 1 to the count

    printf("Your name has %d characters", count);
    return 0;
}
```

The loop continues as long as the value of the next character in the name array is more than zero. Because the last character in the array is a null zero, the test is False on the name's last character and the statement following the body of the loop continues.

NOTE

A built-in string function called strlen() determines the length of strings. You learn about this function in Chapter 18, "String and Numeric Functions."

---

4. The previous string length program's while loop is not as efficient as it could be. Because a while loop fails when its test expression is zero, there is no need for the greater-than test. By changing the test expression as the following program shows, you can improve the efficiency of the string length count.

```
/* Filename: C10WHIL3.C
   Counts the number of letters in the user's first name */
#include <stdio.h>
main()
{
    char name[15];              // Will hold user's first name
    int count=0;        // Will hold total characters in name
```

```
      /* Get the user's first name */
      printf("What is your first name? ");
      scanf(" %s", name);

      while (name[count])   /* Loop until null zero is reached
         {  count++; }                    // Add 1 to the count

      printf("Your name has %d characters", count);
      return 0;
   }
```

The do-while Loop

The body of the do-while executes at least once.

The do-while statement controls the do-while loop, which is similar to the while loop except the relational test occurs at the bottom (rather than top) of the loop. This ensures that the body of the loop executes at least once. The do-while tests for a positive relational test; that is, as long as the test is True, the body of the loop continues to execute.

The format of the do-while is

```
do
    { block of one or more C statements; }
while (test expression)
```

The *test expression* must be enclosed within parentheses, just as it does with a while statement.

EXAMPLE

1. The following program is just like the first one you saw with the while loop (C10WHIL1.C), except the do-while is used instead. Notice the placement of the *test expression*. Because this expression concludes the loop, user input does not need to appear before the loop and then again in its body.

```
/* Filename: C10WHIL4.C
   Input routine to ensure that user types a
   correct response. This routine might be part
   of a larger program. */
#include <stdio.h>
main()
```

```
{
    char ans;

    do
      { printf("\nYou must type a Y or an N\n");    // Warn
                                                    // and ask
          printf("Do you want to continue (Y/N) ?"); // again
          scanf(" %c", &ans); }            /* Body of while loop
                                               ends here */
    while ((ans != 'Y') && (ans != 'N'));

    return 0;
}
```

2. Suppose you are entering sales amounts into the computer in order to calculate extended totals. You want the computer to print the quantity sold, part number, and extended total (quantity times the price per unit). The following program does that:

```
/* Filename: C10INV1.C
   Gets inventory information from user and prints
   an inventory detail listing with extended totals */
#include <stdio.h>
main()
{
    int partNo, quantity;
    float cost, extCost;

    printf("*** Inventory Computation ***\n\n");    // Title

    /* Get inventory information */
    do
      { printf("What is the next part number (-999 to end)? ");
        scanf(" %d", &partNo);
        if (partNo != -999)
            { printf("How many were bought? ");
              scanf(" %d", &quantity);
              printf("What is the unit price of this item? ");
              scanf(" %f", &cost);
              extCost = cost * quantity;
              printf("\n%d of # %d will cost %.2f", quantity,
                        partNo, extCost);
              printf("\n\n\n");       // Print two blank lines
            }
```

```
        } while (partNo != -999);          // Loop only if part
                                           // number is not -999


        printf("End of inventory computation\n");
        return 0;
    }
```

Here is the program's output:

```
*** Inventory Computation ***

What is the next part number (-999 to end)? 123
How many were bought? 4
What is the unit price of this item? 5.43


4 of # 123 will cost 21.72

What is the next part number (-999 to end)? 526
How many were bought? 25
What is the unit price of this item? 1.25


4 of # 526 will cost 32.50

What is the next part number (-999 to end)? -999
End of inventory computation
```

The do-while loop controls the entry of the customer sales informa-tion. Notice the "trigger" that ends the loop. If the user enters –999 for the part number, the do-while loop quits because no part numbered –999 exists in the inventory.

However, this program could be improved in several ways. The invoice could be printed to the printer instead of the screen. Your compiler and operating system determine how you direct output to the printer. In addition, the inventory total (the total amount of the entire order) could be computed. You learn how to total such data in the "Counters and Totals" section, later in this chapter.

The if Statement Versus the while Loop

Some beginning programmers confuse the if statement with loop constructs. The while and do-while loops repeat a section of code multiple times, depending on the condition being tested. The if statement may or may not execute a section of code; if it does, it executes that section only once.

Use an if statement when you conditionally want to execute a section of code once, and use a while or do-while loop if you want it to execute more than once. Figure 10.1 shows differences between the if statement and the two while loops.

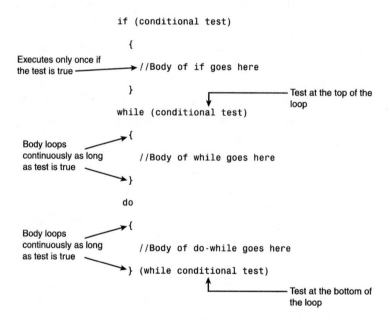

Figure 10.1: *Here are the differences between the* if *statement and the two* while *loops.*

The exit() Function and break Statement

C provides the exit() function as a way to leave a program early (before its natural finish). The format of exit() is

```
exit(status);
```

where *status* is an optional integer variable or constant. If you are familiar with your operating system's return codes, *status* enables you to test the results of C programs. In MS-DOS, for example, *status* is sent to the operating system's errorlevel *environment variable*, where it can be tested by batch files. Windows programs can send their return value to the controlling Windows operating system as well. The following statement returns a 1 to the operating system. It is up to the programmer to test this return value using the operating system's coding or batch language for the value to be further used.

```
exit(1)
```

Many times, something happens in a program that requires the program's termination. It may be a major problem, such as a disk drive error. Perhaps users indicate that they want to quit the program—you can tell this by giving your users a special value to type in scanf(). The exit() function can be put on a line by itself, or anywhere else that a C statement or function can appear. Typically, exit() is placed in the body of an if statement to end the program early, depending on the result of some relational test.

You should include the stdlib.h header file when you use exit(). This file describes the operation of exit() to your program. Whenever you use a function in a program, you should know its corresponding #include header file, which is usually listed in the compiler's reference manual.

Instead of exiting an entire program, however, you can use the break statement to exit the current loop. The format of break is

```
break;
```

The break statement can go anywhere in a C program that any other statement can go, but it typically appears in the body of a while or do-while loop in order to leave the loop early. The following examples illustrate the exit() function and the break statement.

NOTE

The break statement exits only the most current loop. If you have a while loop in another while loop, break exits only the internal loop. If you want to break out of the outer loop, you will have to add one in the outer loop.

EXAMPLE

1. Here is a simple program that shows you how the exit() function works. This program looks as though it prints several messages onscreen, but that is misleading. Because exit() appears early in the code, this program quits immediately after main()'s opening brace:

```
/* C10EXIT1.C
   Quits very early due to exit() function */
#include <stdio.h>
#include <stdlib.h>                 // Required for exit()
main()
{
   exit(1);                         // Forces program to end here
```

```
printf("C programming is fun.\n");
printf("I like learning C by example!\n");
printf("C is a powerful language that is
        not difficult to learn.");

return 0;
}
```

2. The break statement is not intended to be as strong a program exit as the exit() function. Whereas exit() ends the entire program, break quits only the loop that is currently active. In other words, break is usually placed inside a while or do-while loop to make the program think the loop is finished. The statement following the loop executes after a break occurs, but the program does not quit as it does with exit().

The following program appears to print C is fun! until the user enters **N** to stop it. The message prints only once, however, because the break statement forces an early exit from the loop.

```
/* Filename: C10BRK.C
   Demonstrates the break statement */
#include <stdio.h>
main()
{
    char userAns;

    do
      { printf("C is fun! \n");
        break;                         /* Causes early exit */
        printf("Do you want to see the message again (N/Y)? ");
        scanf(" %c", &userAns);
      } while (userAns == 'Y');

    printf("That's all for now\n");
    return 0;
}
```

OUTPUT

This program always produces the following output:

```
C is fun!
That's all for now
```

You can tell from this program's output that the break statement does not let the do-while loop reach its natural conclusion, but causes it to finish early. The final `printf()` prints because only the current loop—and not the entire program—exits with the `break` statement.

3. Unlike the previous program, `break` is usually placed after an `if` statement. This makes it a *conditional* break, which occurs only if the relational test of the `if` statement is True.

A good illustration of this is the inventory program you saw earlier (`C10INV1.C`). Even though the users enter –999 when they want to quit the program, an additional `if` test is needed inside the `do-while`. The –999 ends the `do-while` loop, but the body of the `do-while` still needs an `if` test, so the remaining quantity and cost prompts are not given.

By inserting a `break` after testing for the end of the user's input, as shown in the following program, the `do-while` does not need the `if` test. The `break` quits the `do-while` as soon as the user signals the end of the inventory by entering –999 as the part number.

```c
/* Filename: C10INV2.C
    Gets inventory information from user and prints
    an inventory detail listing with extended totals */
#include <stdio.h>
main()
{
    int partNo, quantity;
    float cost, extCost;

    printf("*** Inventory Computation ***\n\n");    // Title

    /* Get inventory information */
    do
     { printf("What is the next part number (-999 to end)? ");
        scanf(" %d", &partNo);
        if (partNo == -999)
          { break; }                          // Exit the loop if
                                              // no more part numbers
        printf("How many were bought? ");
        scanf(" %d", &quantity);
        printf("What is the unit price of this item? ");
        scanf(" %f", &cost);
        printf("\n%d of # %d will cost %.2f",
                quantity, partNo, cost);
        printf("\n\n\n");                     // Print two blank lines
     } while (partNo != -999);                // Loop only if part
                                              // number is not -999
```

```
    printf("End of inventory computation\n");
    return 0;
}
```

4. The following program might be used to control two other programs. It illustrates how C can pass information to DOS with exit(). This is your first example of a menu program. Similar to a restaurant menu, a C menu program lists possible user choices. The users decide what they want the computer to do from the menu's available options. The mailing list application in Chapter 25, "Putting It All Together," uses a menu for its user options.

This program returns either a 1 or a 2 to its operating system, depending on the user's selection. It is then up to the operating system to test the exit value and run the proper program.

```
/* Filename: C10EXIT2.C
   Asks user for his or her selection and returns
   that selection to the operating system with exit() */
#include <stdio.h>
#include <stdlib.h>
main()
{
    int ans;

    do
      { printf("Do you want to:\n\n");
        printf("\t1. Run the word processor \n\n");
        printf("\t2. Run the database program \n\n");
        printf("What is your selection? ");
        scanf(" %d", &ans);
      } while ((ans != 1) && (ans != 2));   // Ensures user
                                            // enters 1 or 2
    exit(ans);   // Return value to operating system
    return 0;
}
```

Counters and Totals

Counting is important for many applications. You might need to know how many customers you have or how many people scored over a certain average in your class. You might want to count how many checks you wrote last month with your computerized checkbook system.

Before you develop C routines to count occurrences, think of how you count in your own mind. If you were adding a total number of something, such as the stamps in your stamp collection or the number of wedding invitations you sent out, you would probably do the following.

Begin with a total of zero stamps. After purchasing a stamp, you would add one to the total, bringing it to one. Buy another stamp, add another one, bringing the total to two. You continue counting upward as you add stamps to the collection.

This is all you do when you count with C: Assign 0 to a variable and add 1 to it every time you process another data value. The increment operator (++) is especially useful for counting.

EXAMPLE

1. To illustrate using a counter, the following program prints "Computers are fun!" 10 times on the screen. You could write a program that has 10 printf() functions, but that would not be very elegant. It would also be too cumbersome to have 5000 printf() functions, if you wanted to print that same message 5,000 times.

   By adding a while loop and a counter that stops after a certain total is reached, you can control this printing, as the following program shows:

```c
/* Filename: C10CNT1.C
   Program to print a message 10 times */
#include <stdio.h>
main()
{
    int ctr = 0;    // Holds the number of times printed

    do
      { printf("Computers are fun!\n");
        ctr++;                          // Add one to the count,
                                        // after each printf()
      } while (ctr < 10);               // Print again if fewer
                                        // than 10 times

    return 0;
}
```

OUTPUT

The output from this program is shown as follows. Notice that the message prints exactly 10 times:

```
Computers are fun!
Computers are fun!
Computers are fun!
Computers are fun!
Computers are fun!
Computers are fun!
```

```
Computers are fun!
Computers are fun!
Computers are fun!
Computers are fun!
```

The heart of the counting process in this program is the statement that follows:

```
ctr++;
```

You learned in Chapter 9, "Remaining C Operators," that the increment operator adds 1 to a variable. In this program, the counter variable is incremented each time the do-while loops. Because the only operation performed on this line is the increment of ctr, the prefix increment (++ctr) would produce the same results.

2. The previous program not only added to the counter variable, but also performed the loop a specific number of times. This is a common method of conditionally executing parts of a program for a fixed number of times.

The following program is a password program. A password is stored in an integer variable. The user must correctly enter the matching password within three attempts. If the user does not type the correct password in that time, the program ends. This is a common method that dial-up computers use. They enable a caller to try the password a fixed number of times, and then hang up the phone if that limit is exceeded. This helps deter people from trying hundreds of different passwords at any one sitting.

If users guess the correct password in three tries, they see the secret message:

```
/* Filename: C10PASS1.C
   Program to prompt for a password and
   check it against an internal one */
#include <stdio.h>
main()
{
    int storedPass = 11862;
    int numTries = 0;       // Counter for password attempts
    int userPass;

    while (numTries < 3)                 // Loop only 3 times
        { printf("\nWhat is the password (You get \
➥3 tries...)? ");
            scanf(" %d", &userPass);
            numTries++;                  // Add 1 to counter
```

```
                     if (userPass == storedPass)
                        { printf("You entered the correct password.\n");
                           printf("The cash safe is behind the picture \
   ➥of the ship.\n");
                           exit();
                        }
                     else
                        { printf("You entered the wrong password.\n");
                        if (numTries == 3)
                        { printf("Sorry, you get no more chances"); }
                        else
                        { printf("You get %d more tries...\n",
                                   (3-numTries) ); }
                     }
                  }                                    // End of while loop
            return 0;
         }
```

This program gives users three chances—in case they make one or two typing mistakes. But after three unsuccessful attempts, the program quits without displaying the secret message.

3. The following program is a letter guessing game. It includes a message telling users how many tries they made before guessing the correct letter. A counter counts the number of these tries:

```
/* Filename: C10GUES.C
   Letter guessing game */
#include <stdio.h>
main()
{
   int tries = 0;
   char compAns, userGuess;

   // Save the computer's letter
   compAns = 'T';                      // Change to a different
                                       //   letter if desired

   printf("I am thinking of a letter... ");
   do
      { printf("What is your guess? ");
        scanf(" %c", &userGuess);
        tries++;    /* Add 1 to the guess counting variable */
        if (userGuess > compAns)
           { printf("Your guess was too high\n");
             printf("\nTry again...");
```

```
            }
        if (userGuess < compAns)
            { printf("Your guess was too low\n");
              printf("\nTry again... ");
            }
    } while (userGuess != compAns);   // Quit when a
                                      // match is found

    /* They got it right, let them know */
    printf("*** Congratulations!  You got it right! \n");
    printf("It took you only %d tries to guess.", tries);
    return 0;
}
```

OUTPUT

Here is the output from one sample execution of this program:

```
I am thinking of a letter... What is your guess? A
Your guess was too low

Try again... What is your guess? Z
Your guess was too high

Try again... What is your guess? M
Your guess was too low

Try again... What is your guess? W
Your guess was too high

Try again... What is your guess? S
Your guess was too high

Try again... What is your guess? T
*** Congratulations!  You got it right!
It took you only 6 tries to guess.
```

Producing Totals

Writing a routine to add values is as easy as counting. Instead of adding 1 to the counter variable, you add a value to the total variable. For instance, if you want to find the total dollar amount of checks you wrote during December, you could start at nothing (0) and add to that the amount of every check written in December. Instead of building a count, you are building a total.

When you want C to add values, just initialize a total variable to zero,

EXAMPLE

then add each value to the total until you have included all the values.

1. Suppose you want to write a program that adds your grades for a class you are taking. The teacher has informed you that you earn an A if you can accumulate over 450 points.

The following program keeps asking you for values until you type –1. The –1 is a signal that you are finished entering grades and now want to see the total. This program also prints a congratulatory message if you have enough points for an A.

```c
/* Filename: C10GRAD1.C
   Adds up grades and determines if an A was made */
#include <stdio.h>
main()
{
    float totalGrade=0.0;
    float grade;                    /* Holds individual grades */

    do
    { printf("What is your grade? (-1 to end) ");
      scanf(" %f", &grade);
      if (grade >= 0.0)
        { totalGrade += grade; }          /* Add to total */
    } while (grade >= 0.0);      /* Quit when -1 entered */

    /* Control begins here if no more grades */
    printf("\n\nYou made a total of %.1f points\n",
            totalGrade);
    if (totalGrade >= 450.00)
        { printf("** You made an A!!"); }

    return 0;
}
```

OUTPUT

Notice that the –1 response does not get added to the total number of points. This program checks for the –1 before adding to totalGrade.

Here is the output from this program:

```
What is your grade? (-1 to end) 87
What is your grade? (-1 to end) 89
What is your grade? (-1 to end) 96
What is your grade? (-1 to end) 78
What is your grade? (-1 to end) 99
What is your grade? (-1 to end) 87
What is your grade? (-1 to end) 89
What is your grade? (-1 to end) -1
```

```
You made a total of 625.0 points
** You made an A!!
```

2. The following program is an extension of the grade calculating program. It not only totals the points, but also computes their average.

   The average calculation must know how many grades were entered before it will work. This is a subtle problem because the number of grades to be entered is unknown in advance. Therefore, every time the user enters a valid grade (not –1), the program must add 1 to a counter as well as add that grade to the total variable. This is a combination counting and totaling routine, which is common in many programs.

```c
/* Filename: C10GRAD2.C
   Adds up grades, computes average,
   and determines if an A was made. */
#include <stdio.h>
main()
{
   float totalGrade=0.0;
   float gradeAvg = 0.0;
   float grade;
   int gradeCtr = 0;

   do
   { printf("What is your grade? (-1 to end) ");
     scanf(" %f", &grade);
     if (grade >= 0.0)
       { totalGrade += grade;              // Add to total
         gradeCtr ++; }                     // Add to count
   } while (grade >= 0.0);           // Quit when -1 entered

   /* Control begins here if no more grades */
   gradeAvg = (totalGrade / gradeCtr);        // Compute
                                              //    average
   printf("\nYou made a total of %.1f points.\n",
           totalGrade);
   printf("Your average was %.1f \n", gradeAvg);
   if (totalGrade >= 450.0)
      { printf("** You made an A!!"); }
   return 0;
```

}

Here is the output of this program. Congratulations! You are on your way to becoming a master C programmer.

```
What is your grade? (-1 to end) 88
What is your grade? (-1 to end) 98
What is your grade? (-1 to end) 97
What is your grade? (-1 to end) 87
What is your grade? (-1 to end) 94
What is your grade? (-1 to end) 96
What is your grade? (-1 to end) -1

You made a total of 560.0 points
Your average was 93.3
** You made an A!!
```

What's Next

This chapter showed you two ways to produce a C loop: the while loop and the do-while loop. The next chapter extends your knowledge of loops by showing you how to create a determinate loop, called the for loop. The for loop is useful when you want a section of code to loop for a specified number of times instead of repeating based on a conditional test only.

11

The for Loop

The for loop enables you to repeat sections of your program for a specific number of times. Unlike the while and do-while loops, the for loop is a *determinate loop*. This means when you write your program you can usually determine how many times the loop takes place. The while and do-while loops continue only until a condition is met. The for loop does this and more: It continues looping until a count (or countdown) is reached. After the final for loop count is reached, execution continues with the next statement, in sequence.

This chapter teaches you the following topics:

- The for statement
- How for statements terminate
- Benefits of nested for loops

The for Statement

The for statement encloses one or more C statements that form the body of the loop. These statements in the loop continuously repeat for a certain number of times. You, as the programmer, control the number of loop repetitions.

The format of the for loop is

```
for (start expression; test expression; count expression)
   { Block of one or more C statements; }
```

C evaluates the *start expression* before the loop begins. Typically, the *start expression* is an assignment statement (such as ctr=1;), but it can be any legal expression you specify. C looks at and evaluates *start expression* only once, at the top of the loop.

CAUTION

Do not put a semicolon after the right parenthesis. If you do, the for loop "thinks" the body of the loop is zero statements long. It would continue looping—doing nothing each time—until the *test expression* becomes False.

Every time the body of the loop repeats, the *count expression* executes, usually incrementing or decrementing a variable. The *test expression* evaluates to True (nonzero) or False (zero), and then determines if the body of the loop repeats again.

TIP

If only one C statement resides in the for loop's body, braces are not required, but they are recommended. If you add more statements later, the braces are there already, so you cannot inadvertently leave them out.

The Concept of for Loops

You use the concept of for loops throughout your day-to-day life. Any time you need to repeat a certain procedure a specified number of times, that repetition becomes a good candidate for a computerized for loop.

To illustrate the concept of a for loop further, suppose you are putting up 10 new shutters on your house. You must do the following steps for each shutter:

1. Move the ladder to the location of the shutter.

2. Take a shutter, hammer, and nails up the ladder.

3. Hammer the shutter to the side of the house.

4. Climb down the ladder.

You must perform each of these four steps exactly 10 times because you have 10 shutters. After 10 times, you don't put another shutter up because the job is finished. You are looping through a procedure that has several steps (the block of the loop). These steps are the body of the loop. It is not an endless loop because there are a fixed number of shutters; you run out of shutters only after you have gone through all 10 of them.

For a less physical example that might be more easily computerized, suppose you need to fill out a tax return for each of your three teenage children. (If you have three teenage children, you probably need more than just a computer to help you get through the day.) For each child, you must perform the following steps:

1. Add up the total income.

2. Add up the total deductions.

3. Fill out a tax return.

4. Put it in an envelope.

5. Mail it.

You then must repeat this entire procedure two more times.

Notice how the sentence before these steps began: For each child. This signals an idea similar to the for loop construct.

NOTE

The for loop tests at the top of the loop. If the *test expression* is False when the for loop begins, the body of the loop never executes.

THE CHOICE OF LOOPS

Any loop construct can be written with a for loop, a while loop, or a do-while loop. Generally, you use the for loop when you want to count or loop a specific number of times, and reserve the while and do-while loops for looping until a False condition is met.

EXAMPLE

1. To give you a glimpse of the for loop's capabilities, this example shows you two programs: one that uses a for loop and one that does not. The first one is a counting program. Before studying its contents, look at the output. The results basically speak for themselves and illustrate the for loop very well.

The program with a for loop follows:

```
/* Filename: C11FOR1.C
   Introduces the for loop */
#include <stdio.h>
main()
```

```
    {
        int ctr;
        for (ctr=1; ctr<=10; ctr++)          /* Start ctr at 1,
                                                increment through loop */
            { printf("%d \n", ctr); }        /* Body of for loop */
        return 0;
    }
```

Here is the same program using a do-while loop:

```
/* Filename: C11WHI1.C
    Simulating a for loop with a do-while loop */
#include <stdio.h>
main()
{
    int ctr=1;
    do
        { printf("%d \n", ctr); /* Body of do-while loop */
            ctr++; }
    while (ctr <= 10);

    return 0;
}
```

Notice that the for loop is a cleaner way of controlling the looping process. The for loop does several things that require extra statements in a while loop. With for loops, you do not need to write extra code to initialize variables and increment or decrement them. You can see at a glance (in the expressions in the for statement) exactly how the loop executes, unlike the do-while, which forces you to look at the bottom of the loop to see how the loop stops.

Both of these equivalent programs produce this output:

OUTPUT

```
1
2
3
4
5
6
7
8
9
10
```

2. Both of the following sample programs add the numbers from 100 to 200. The first one uses a for loop, and the second one doesn't. The first example starts with a *start expression* other than 1, starting the loop with a bigger *count expression*.

This program has a for loop:

```
/* Filename: C11FOR2.C
   Demonstrates totaling using a for loop */
#include <stdio.h>
main()
{
    int total, ctr;

    total = 0;                    // Will hold total of 100 to 200

    for (ctr=100; ctr<=200; ctr++)        // ctr is 100, 101,
                                          // 102,...200
       { total += ctr; }  // Add value of ctr each iteration

    printf("The total is %d", total);
    return 0;
}
```

The same program without a for loop follows:

```
/* Filename: C11WHI2.C
   A totaling program using a do-while loop */
#include <stdio.h>
main()
{
    int total=0;        // Initialize total
    int num=100;          // Starting value

    do
       {  total += num;        // Add to total
          num++;              // Increment counter
       } while (num <= 200);
    printf("The total is %d", total);
    return 0;
}
```

Both programs produce this output:

```
The total is 15150
```

The body of the loop in both programs executes 100 times. The starting value is 100, not 1 as in the previous example. Notice that the for loop is less complex than the do-while because the initialization, testing, and incrementing are performed in the single for statement.

TIP

Notice how the body of the for loop is indented. This is a good habit to develop because it makes it easier to see the beginning and ending of the loop's body.

The following is the last example that compares the for loop to an equivalent program without a for loop.

3. The body of the for loop can have more than one statement. The following example requests five pairs of data values: children's first names and their ages. And, it prints the teacher assigned to each child, based on the child's age. This illustrates a for loop with printf() functions, a scanf() function, and an if statement in its body. Because exactly five children are checked, the for loop ensures that the program ends after the fifth child.

```c
/* Filename: C11FOR3.C
   Program that uses a loop to input and print
   the teacher assigned to each child */
#include <stdio.h>
main()
{
    char child[25];        /* Holds child's first name */
    int age;                        /* Holds child's age */
    int ctr;              /* The for loop counter variable */

    for (ctr=1; ctr<=5; ctr++)
      { printf("What is the next child's name? ");
        scanf(" %s", child);
        printf("What is the child's age? ");
        scanf(" %d", &age);
        if (age <= 5)
           { printf("\n%s has Mrs. Jones for a teacher\n",
                   child);}
        if (age == 6)
           { printf("\n%s has Miss Smith for a teacher\n",
                   child); }
        if (age >= 7)
           { printf("\n%s has Mr. Anderson for a teacher\n",
```

```
                               child); }
              }   /* Quits after 5 times */

         return 0;
     }
```

Here is the output from this program. You can improve this program further, after you learn the switch statement in the next chapter.

```
What is the next child's name? Jim
What is the child's age? 6

Jim has Miss Smith for a teacher

What is the next child's name? Linda
What is the child's age? 3

Linda has Mrs. Jones for a teacher

What is the next child's name? Elizabeth
What is the child's age? 7

Elizabeth has Mr. Anderson for a teacher

What is the next child's name? Bob
What is the child's age? 5

Bob has Mrs. Jones for a teacher

What is the next child's name? Walter
What is the child's age? 3

Walter has Mrs. Jones for a teacher
```

4. The previous examples used an increment as the *count expression*. You can make the for loop increment the loop variable by any value. It does not need to increment by 1.

   The following program prints the even numbers from 1 to 20. It then prints the odd numbers from 1 to 20. To do this, 2 is added to the counter variable (instead of 1 as shown in the previous examples) each time the loop executes:

```
/* Filename: C11EVOD.C
   Prints the even numbers from 1 to 20,
   then the odd numbers from 1 to 20 */
#include <stdio.h>
```

```
main()
{
    int num;                        // The for loop variable

    printf("Even numbers below 21\n");          // Title
    for (num=2; num<=20; num+=2)
      { printf("%d ", num); } // Prints every other number

    printf("\nOdd numbers below 20\n");    // A second title
    for (num=1; num<=20; num+=2)
      { printf("%d ", num); } // Prints every other number

    return 0;
}
```

There are two loops in this program. The body of each one consists of a single printf() function. In the first half of the program, the loop variable, num, is 2 and not 1. If it was 1, the number 1 would print first, as it does in the odd number section.

The two printf() functions that print the titles are not part of either loop. If they were, the program would print a title before each number. The following shows the result of running this program:

```
Even numbers below
2 4 6 8 10 12 14 16 18 20
Odd numbers below
1 3 5 7 9 11 13 15 17 19
```

5. You can decrement the loop variable as well. If you do, the value is subtracted from the loop variable each time through the loop.

The following example is a rewrite of the counting program. It produces the reverse effect by showing a countdown:

```
/* Filename: C11CNTD1.C
   Countdown to the lift-off */
#include <stdio.h>
main()
{
    int ctr;

    for (ctr=10; ctr!=0; ctr--)
      { printf("%d \n", ctr); }    // Print ctr as it
                                   // counts down
    printf("*** Blast off! ***");
    return 0;
}
```

When decrementing a loop variable, the initial value should be larger than the end value being tested. In this example, the loop variable, ctr, counts down from 10 to 1. Each time through the loop (each iteration), ctr is decremented by 1.

You can see how easy it is to control a loop by looking at this program's output, as follows:

OUTPUT

```
10
 9
 8
 7
 6
 5
 4
 3
 2
 1
*** Blast Off! ***
```

TIP

This program's for loop test illustrates a redundancy that you can eliminate thanks to C. The *test expression* ctr!=0; tells the for loop to continue looping until ctr is not equal to zero. However, if ctr becomes zero, that is a False value in itself; there is no reason to add the additional !=0 except for clarity. The for loop can be rewritten

```
for (ctr=10; ctr; ctr--)
```

without loss of meaning. This is more efficient, and it is such an integral part of C that you should become comfortable with it. There is little loss of clarity once you get used to it.

---

6. You can also make a for loop test for something other than a constant value. The following program combines much of what you have learned so far. It asks for student grades and computes an average. Because there might be a different number of students each semester, the program first asks the user for the number of students. Next, the program loops until the user enters that many scores. It then computes the average based on the total and the number of student grades entered.

```
/* Filename: C11FOR4.C
   Computes a grade average with a for loop */
#include <stdio.h>
main()
{
   float grade, avg;
   float total=0.0;
   int num;                        // Total number of grades
```

```
    int loopvar;                    // Used to control for loop

    printf("\n*** Grade Calculation ***\n\n");  // Title
    printf("How many students are there? ");
    scanf(" %d", &num);          // Get total number to enter

    for (loopvar=1; loopvar<=num; loopvar++)
        { printf("\nWhat is the next student's grade? ");
          scanf(" %f", &grade);
          total += grade;  }      // Keep a running total

    avg = total / num;
    printf("\n\nThe average of this class is: %.1f", avg);
    return 0;
}
```

Due to the for loop, the total and the average calculations do not need to be changed if the number of students changes.

7. Because characters and integers are so closely associated in C, you can increment character variables in a for loop. The following program prints the letters A through Z with a simple for loop:

```
/* Filename: C11FOR5.C
    Prints the alphabet with a simple for loop */
#include <stdio.h>
main()
{
    char letter;

    printf("Here is the alphabet:\n");
    for (letter='A'; letter<='Z'; letter++) // Loops A to Z
        { printf("%c ", letter); }

    return 0;
}
```

OUTPUT

This program produces the following output:

```
Here is the alphabet:
A B C D E F G H I J K L M N O P Q R S T U V W X Y Z
```

8. A for expression can be blank, or a *null expression*. In the following for loop, all the expressions are blank:

```
for (;;)
    { printf("Over and over..."); }
```

This loops forever. Although you should avoid infinite loops, your program might dictate that you make a for loop expression blank. If you already initialized the *start expression* earlier in the program, you would be wasting computer time to repeat it in the for loop—and C does not require it.

The following program omits the *start expression* and the *count expression*, leaving only the for loop's *test expression*. Most of the time, you need to omit only one of them. If you use a for loop without two of its expressions, consider replacing it with a while loop or a do-while loop.

```c
/* Filename: C11FOR6.C
   Uses only the test expression in
   the for loop to count by 5s */
#include <stdio.h>
main()
{
    int num=5;                              // Starting value

    printf("\nCounting by 5s: \n");         // Title
    for (; num<=100;)  // Contains only the test expression
      { printf("%d\n", num);
        num+=5;    // Increment expression outside the loop
      }                          // End of the loop's body

    return 0;
}
```

OUTPUT

The output from this program follows:

```
Counting by 5s:
5
10
15
20
25
30
35
40
45
50
55
60
```

```
65
70
75
80
85
90
95
100
```

Nested for Loops

Any C statement can go inside the body of a for loop—even another for loop. When you put a loop within a loop, you are creating a *nested loop*. The clock in a sporting event works like a nested loop. You might think this is stretching an analogy a little too far, but it truly works. A football game counts down from 15 minutes to 0. It does this four times. The first count-down loops from 15 to 0 (for each minute). That countdown is nested in another that loops from 1 to 4 (for each of the four quarters).

If your program needs to repeat a loop more than one time, it is a good can-didate for a nested loop. Figure 11.1 shows two outlines of nested loops. You can think of the inside loop as looping "faster" than the outside loop. In the first example, the inside for loop counts from 1 to 10 before the outside loop (the variable out) can finish its first iteration. When the outside loop finally does iterate a second time, the inside loop starts over.

```
                for (out=1; out<=100; out++}
                   {
Outside loop        for {in=1; in<=10; in++)
                      { /*Body of inside loop*/ }────── Inside loop
                   }
                for {out=1; out<=100; out++}
                   {
                    for (in1=1; in1<=5; in1++)
                      { /* Body of 1st inner loop*/ }───── Inside loop
Outside loop        for {in2=1; in2<=5; in2++}
                      {/* Body of 2nd inner loop*/ }───── Inside loop
                   }
```

Figure 11.1: Here are the outlines of two nested loops.

The second nested loop outline shows two loops within an outside loop. Both of these loops execute in their entirety before the outside loop finishes its first iteration. When the outside loop starts its second iteration, the two inside loops repeat again.

Notice the order of the braces in each example. The inside loop always finishes, and therefore its ending brace must come before the outside loop's ending brace. Indention makes this much clearer because you can "line up" braces of each loop.

Nested loops become important later when you use them for array and table processing.

EXAMPLE

1. The following program contains a loop within a loop—a nested loop. The inside loop counts and prints from 1 to 5. The outside loop counts from 1 to 3. Therefore, the inside loop repeats, in its entirety, 3 times. In other words, this program prints the values 1 to 5 and does so 3 times.

```c
/* Filename: C11NEST1.C
   Print the numbers 1 to 5 three times
   using a nested loop */
#include <stdio.h>
main()
{
    int times, num;   // Outer and inner for loop variables

    for (times=1; times<=3; times++)
    {
        for (num=1; num<=5; num++)
            { printf("%d", num); }     // Inner loop body
        printf("\n");
    }                                   // End of outer loop

    return 0;
}
```

OUTPUT

The indention follows the standard of for loops; every statement in each loop is indented a few spaces. Because the inside loop is already indented, its body is indented another few spaces. The program's output follows:

```
12345
12345
12345
```

2. The outside loop's counter variable changes each time through the loop. If one of the inside loop's control variables is the outside loop's counter variable, you see effects such as that shown in the following program:

```
/* Filename: C11NEST2.C
   An inside loop controlled by the outer loop's
   counter variable */
#include <stdio.h>
main()
{
    int outer, inner;

    for (outer=5; outer>=1; outer--)
      { for (inner=1; inner<=outer; inner++)
            { printf("%d", inner); }  // End of inner loop
      printf("\n");
      }
      return 0;
}
```

OUTPUT

The output from this program follows. The inside loop repeats five times (as outer counts down from 5 to 1) and prints from five numbers to one number:

```
12345
1234
123
12
1
```

The following table traces the two variables through this program. Sometimes you need to "play computer" when learning a new concept such as nested loops. By executing a line at a time, writing down each variable's contents, you produce the following list.

The outer variable	The inner variable
5	1
5	2
5	3
5	4
5	5
4	1
4	2
4	3
4	4
3	1

3	2
3	3
2	1
2	2
1	1

TIP FOR MATHEMATICIANS

The for statement is identical to the mathematical summation symbol. When you write programs to simulate the summation symbol, the for statement is an excellent candidate. A nested for statement is good for double summations.

For example, the following summation

$$\sum_{i=1}^{i=30} (i\ /\ 3\ *\ 2)$$

can be rewritten as

```
total = 0;
for (i=1; i<=30; i++)
    { total += (i / 3 * 2); }
```

---

4. A factorial is a mathematical number used in probability theory and statistics. A factorial of any number is the multiplied product of every number from 1 to that number.

   For instance, the factorial of 4 is 24 because 4 * 3 * 2 * 1 = 24. The factorial of 6 is 720 because 6 * 5 * 4 * 3 * 2 * 1 = 720. The factorial of 1 is 1 by definition.

   Nested loops are good candidates for writing a factorial number-generating program. The following program asks the user for a number, and then prints every factorial up to, and including, that number:

```
/* Filename: C11FACT.C
   Computes the factorial of numbers through
   the user's number */
#include <stdio.h>
main()
{
    int outer, num, fact, total;

    printf("What factorial do you want to see? ");
    scanf(" %d", &num);
```

```
for (outer=1; outer <= num; outer++)
  { total = 1;   // Initialize total for each factorial
    for (fact=1; fact<= outer; fact++)
      { total *= fact; }      // Compute each factorial
  }

printf("The factorial for %d is %d", num, total);

return 0;
}
```

OUTPUT

The following shows the first seven factorials. You can run this program, entering different values when asked, and see various factorials. Be careful: factorials multiply quickly. (A factorial of 11 won't fit in an integer variable.)

```
What factorial do you want to see? 7
The factorial for 7 is 5040
```

What's Next

You have now seen C's three loop constructs: the while loop, the do-while loop, and the for loop. They are similar, but behave differently in how they test and initialize variables. No loop is better than the others. The programming problem should dictate which loop you choose. The next chapter shows you additional C tools with which you can control loops. You will learn how to break out of loops early and force the continuation of a loop that would otherwise terminate.

Controlling Flow

Now that you have mastered the looping constructs, you should learn some loop-related statements. This chapter explains two additional looping commands, the break and continue statements, which control the way loops operate. These statements work with while loops and for loops. In addition to completing your study of C loops, you'll also learn two new control statements, the switch and the goto statements. They improve upon the if and else-if constructs by streamlining the multiple-choice decisions your programs make. switch does not replace the if statement, but you may prefer switch when your programs must perform one of many different actions. goto enables you to modify the order that your program's statements execute.

This chapter teaches you the following topics:

- Using break with for loops

- The continue statement

- How to control conditional flow with switch

- Working with goto

The break and for Statements

The for loop was designed to execute for a specified number of times. Sometimes, though rarely, the for loop should quit before the counting variable has reached its final value. As with while loops, you use the break statement to quit a for loop early.

The break statement goes in the body of the for loop. Programmers rarely put break on a line by itself, and it almost always comes after an if test. If the break were on a line by itself, the loop would always quit early, defeating the purpose of the for loop.

EXAMPLE

1. The following program shows what can happen when C encounters an *unconditional* break statement, that is, one not proceeded by an if statement:

```
/* Filename: C12BRAK1.C
   A for loop defeated by the break statement */
#include <stdio.h>
main()
{
    int num;

    printf("Here are the numbers from 1 to 20\n");
    for(num=1; num<=20; num++)
      { printf("%d \n", num);
         break;  }   // This exits the for loop immediately

    printf("That's all, folks!");
    return 0;
}
```

OUTPUT

The following shows you the result of running this program. Notice that the break immediately terminates the for loop. The for loop might as well not be in this program.

```
Here are the numbers from 1 to 20
1
That's all, folks!
```

2. The following program is an improved version of the preceding example. It asks users if they want to see another number. If so, the for loop continues its next iteration. If not, the break statement terminates the for loop.

```
/* Filename: C12BRAK2.C
   A for loop running at the user's request */
```

```
#include <stdio.h>
main()
{
    int num;     // Loop counter variable
    char ans;

    printf("Here are the numbers from 1 to 20\n");

    for (num=1; num<=20; num++)
      { printf("%d \n", num);
        printf("Do you want to see another (Y/N)? ");
        scanf(" %c", &ans);
        if ((ans == 'N') || (ans == 'n'))
           { break; }      // Will exit the for loop
                           // if user wants
      }

    printf("\nThat's all, folks!");
    return 0;
}
```

OUTPUT

The following display shows a sample run of this program:

```
Here are the numbers from 1 to 20
1
Do you want to see another (Y/N)? Y
2
Do you want to see another (Y/N)? Y
3
Do you want to see another (Y/N)? Y
4
Do you want to see another (Y/N)? Y
5
Do you want to see another (Y/N)? Y
6
Do you want to see another (Y/N)? Y
7
Do you want to see another (Y/N)? Y
8
Do you want to see another (Y/N)? Y
9
Do you want to see another (Y/N)? Y
10
Do you want to see another (Y/N)? N

That's all, folks!
```

The for loop prints 20 numbers, as long as the user does not answer **N** to the prompt. Otherwise, the break takes over and terminates the for loop early. The statement after the body of the loop always executes next if the break occurs. If you nest one loop inside another, the break terminates the "most active" loop, that is, the innermost loop in which the break statement resides.

3. Use the *conditional* break (an if statement followed by a break) when you are missing data. For example, when you process data files, or large amounts of user data-entry, you might expect 100 input numbers and get only 95. You could use a break to terminate the for loop before it cycles through the 96th iteration.

Suppose the teacher using the grade averaging program in the preceding chapter (C11FOR4.C) entered an incorrect total number of students. Maybe she typed 16, but there are only 14 students. The previous for loop looped 16 times, no matter how many students there are, because it relies on the teacher's count.

The following grade averaging program is more sophisticated than that. It asks the teacher for the total number of students, but if the teacher wants, she can enter –99 as a student's score. The –99 does not get averaged; it is used as a trigger value to break out of the for loop before its normal conclusion.

```
/* Filename: C12BRAK3.C
    Computes a grade average with a for loop,
    allowing an early exit with a break statement */
#include <stdio.h>
main()
{
    float grade, avg;
    float total=0.0;
    int num, count=0; // Total number of grades and counter
    int loopvar;                     // Used to control for loop

    printf("\n*** Grade Calculation ***\n\n");     // Title
    printf("How many students are there? ");
    scanf(" %d", &num);          // Get total number to enter

    for (loopvar=1; loopvar<=num; loopvar++)
        { printf("\nWhat is the next student's grade? (-99 to
➥quit) ");
            scanf(" %f", &grade);
            if (grade =< 0.0)               // A negative number
```

```
                                        //      triggers break
            { break; }                  // Leave the loop early
        count++;
        total += grade;   }             // Keep a running total

    avg = total / count;
    printf("\n\nThe average of this class is: %.1f", avg);
    return 0;
}
```

Notice that grade is tested for less than 0, not –99.0. You cannot reliably use floating-point values to compare for equality (due to their bit-level representations). Because no grade is negative, any negative number triggers the break statement.

OUTPUT

The following shows how this program works:

```
*** Grade Calculation ***

How many students are there? 10

What is the next student's grade? (-99 to quit) 87

What is the next student's grade? (-99 to quit) 97

What is the next student's grade? (-99 to quit) 67

What is the next student's grade? (-99 to quit) 89

What is the next student's grade? (-99 to quit) 94

What is the next student's grade? (-99 to quit) -99


The average of this class is: 86.8
```

The continue **Statement**

The break statement exits a loop early, but the continue statement forces the computer to perform another iteration of the loop. If you put a continue statement in the body of a for or a while loop, the computer ignores any statement in the loop that follows continue.

The format of continue is

```
continue;
```

You use the continue statement when data in the body of the loop is bad, out of bounds, or unexpected. Instead of acting on the bad data, you might want to go back to the top of the loop and get another data value. The following examples help illustrate this use of the continue statement.

TIP

The continue statement forces a new iteration of any of the three loop constructs: the for loop, the while loop, and the do-while loop.

Figure 12.1 shows the difference between the break and continue statements.

```
for (i=0;i<=10;i++)
    {                          —— break terminates loop immediately
     break: ◄
     printf("Loop now\n") // This NEVER prints!
    }◄
for (i=0; i<=10;i++)◄
    {                      —— continue causes loop to repeat once again
     continue;◄
     printf("Loop now\n"); // This NEVER prints!
    }
```

Figure 12.1: *This diagram illustrates the difference between* break *and* continue.

EXAMPLE

1. Although the following program appears to print the numbers 1 through 10, each followed by "C Programming," it does not. The continue in the body of the for loop causes an early finish to the loop. The first printf() in the for loop executes, but the second does not—due to the continue.

```c
/* Filename: C12CON1.C
   Demonstrates use of continue statement */
#include <stdio.h>
main()
{
    int ctr;

    for (ctr=1; ctr<=10; ctr++)        // Loop 10 times
       { printf("%d ", ctr);
           continue;              // Causes body to end early
           printf("C Programming\n");
       }
    return 0;
}
```

This program produces the following output:

```
1 2 3 4 5 6 7 8 9 10
```

On some compilers, you get a warning message when you compile this type of program. The compiler recognizes that the second printf() is *unreachable* code—it never executes due to the continue statement.

Because of this, most programs do not use a continue, except after an if statement. This makes it a conditional continue statement, which is more useful. The following two examples demonstrate the conditional use of continue.

2. This program asks users for five lowercase letters, one at a time, and prints their uppercase equivalents. It uses the ASCII table (see Appendix C, "ASCII Table") to ensure that users enter lowercase letters. (These are the letters whose ASCII numbers range from 97 to 122.) If users do not type a lowercase letter, the program ignores this with the continue statement.

```c
/* Filename: C12CON2.C
   Prints uppercase equivalents of 5 lowercase letters */
#include <stdio.h>
main()
{
    char letter;
    int ctr;

    for (ctr=1; ctr<=5; ctr++)
      { printf("Please enter a lowercase letter ");
        scanf(" %c", &letter);
        if ((letter < 97) || (letter > 122))   // See if
                                                // out-of-range
            { continue; }                       // Go get another
        letter -= 32;        // Subtract 32 from ASCII value
                             //             to get uppercase
        printf("The uppercase equivalent is: %c \n", letter);
      }
    return 0;
}
```

Because of the continue statement, only lowercase letters are converted to uppercase.

3. Suppose you want to average the salaries of employees in your company who make over $10,000 a year, but you have only their monthly gross pay figures. The following program might be useful. It prompts for each monthly employee salary, annualizes it (multiplying by 12),

and computes an average. The `continue` statement ensures that salaries less than or equal to $10,000 are ignored in the average calculation. It enables the other salaries to "fall through."

If you enter **-1** as a monthly salary, the program quits and prints the result of the average:

```
/* Filename: C12CON3.C
    Average salaries over $10,000 */
#include <stdio.h>
main()
{
    float month, year;          /* Monthly and yearly salaries */
    float avg=0.0, total=0.0;
    int count=0;

    do
       { printf("What is the next monthly salary (-1 to quit)?
");
            scanf(" %f", &month);
            if ((year=month*12.00) <= 10000.00)   /* Do not add */
                { continue; }                      /* low salaries */
            if (month < 0.0)
                { break; }                 /* Quit if user entered -1 */
            count++;                       /* Add 1 to valid counter */
            total += year;         /* Add yearly salary to total */
       } while (month > 0.0);

    avg = total / (float)count;            /* Compute average */
    printf("\n\nThe average of high salaries is $%.2f", avg);
    return 0;
}
```

Notice this program uses both a `continue` and a `break` statement. The program does one of three things, depending on each user's input. It adds to the total, or continues another iteration if the salary is too low, or exits the `while` loop (and the average calculation) if the user types a −1.

The following display is the output from this program:

OUTPUT

```
What is the next monthly salary (-1 to quit)? 500.00
What is the next monthly salary (-1 to quit)? 2000.00
```

```
What is the next monthly salary (-1 to quit)? 750.00
What is the next monthly salary (-1 to quit)? 4000.00
What is the next monthly salary (-1 to quit)? 5000.00
What is the next monthly salary (-1 to quit)? 1200.00
What is the next monthly salary (-1 to quit)? -1

The average of high salaries is $36600.00
```

The switch Statement

The switch statement is sometimes called the *multiple-choice statement*. The switch statement lets your program choose from several alternatives. The format of the switch statement is a little longer than the format of other statements you have seen. Here is the format of the switch statement:

```
switch (expression)
   { case (expression1): { one or more C statements; }
     case (expression2): { one or more C statements; }
     case (expression3): { one or more C statements; }
     ...
     ...
     ...
     default: { one or more C statements; }
   }
```

The *expression* can be an integer expression, a character, a constant, or a variable. The subexpressions (*expression1*, *expression2*, and so on) can be any other integer expression, character, constant, or variable. The number of case expressions following the switch line is determined by your application. The *one or more C statements* can be any block of C code. If the block is only one statement long, you do not need the braces, but they are recommended.

The default line is optional; most (but not all) switch statements include the default. The default line does not have to be the last line of the switch body. Programmers generally put the default line as the final line in switch but if the default will likely occur more often than the other switch statement options, moving default higher in the statement will make the code more efficient—the more likely default will be seen sooner by the compiler.

If *expression* matches *expression1*, the statements to the right of *expression1* execute. If *expression* matches *expression2*, the statements to the right of *expression2* execute. If none of the expressions match that of the switch *expression*, the default case block executes. The case expression does not need parentheses, but they sometimes make the value easier to find.

TIP

Use a break statement after each case block to keep execution from "falling through" to the remaining case statements.

Using the switch statement is easier than its format might lead you to believe. Anywhere an if-else-if combination of statements can go, you can usually put a clearer switch statement instead. The switch statement is much easier to follow than an if-within-an-if-within-an-if, as you have had to write previously.

However, the if and else-if combinations of statements are not bad to use or difficult to follow. When the relational test that determines the choice is complex and contains many && and ¦¦ operators, the if may be a better candidate. The switch statement is preferred whenever multiple-choice possibilities are based on a single constant, variable, or expression.

TIP

Arrange case statements in the most-often to least-often executed order to improve your program's speed.

The following examples clarify the switch statement. They compare the switch statement to if statements to help you see the difference.

EXAMPLE

1. Suppose you are writing a program to teach your child how to count. Your program should ask the child for a number. It then beeps (rings the computer's alarm bell by issuing the \a alarm escape sequence) as many times as necessary to match that number.

   The following program assumes the child presses a number key from 1 to 5. This program uses the if-else-if combination to accomplish this counting-and-beeping teaching method:

```
/* Filename: C12BEEP1.C
   Beeps a certain number of times */
#include <stdio.h>

/* Define a beep printf() to save repeating printf()s
   throughout the program */
#define BEEP printf("\a \n")
main()
```

```
{
    int num;

    // Get a number from the child (you may have to help)
    printf("Please enter a number ");
    scanf(" %d", &num);

    /* Use multiple if statements to beep */
    if (num == 1)
      { BEEP; }
    else if (num == 2)
          { BEEP; BEEP; }
        else if (num == 3)
                { BEEP; BEEP; BEEP; }
              else if (num == 4)
                    { BEEP; BEEP; BEEP; BEEP; }
                  else if (num == 5)
                        { BEEP; BEEP; BEEP; BEEP; BEEP; }
    return 0;
}
```

No beeps are sounded if the child enters something other than 1 through 5. This program takes advantage of the #define preprocessor directive to define a shortcut to an alarm print() function. In this case, the BEEP is a little clearer to read, as long as you remember that BEEP is not a command, but gets replaced with the printf() everywhere it appears.

One drawback to this type of if-within-an-if program is its readability. By the time you indent the body of each if and else, the program is shoved too far to the right. There is no room for more than five or six possibilities. More importantly, this type of logic is difficult to follow. Because it involves a multiple-choice selection, a switch statement is much better to use, as you can see with the following improved version:

```
/* Filename: C12BEEP2.C
   Beeps a certain number of times using a switch */
#include <stdio.h>

/* Define a beep printf() to save repeating printf()s
   throughout the program */
#define BEEP printf("\a \n")
main()
```

```
{
    int num;

    // Get a number from the child (you may have to help)
    printf("Please enter a number ");
    scanf(" %d", &num);

    switch (num)
    { case (1): { BEEP;
                    break; }
      case (2): { BEEP; BEEP;
                    break; }
      case (3): { BEEP; BEEP; BEEP;
                    break; }
      case (4): { BEEP; BEEP; BEEP; BEEP;
                    break; }
      case (5): { BEEP; BEEP; BEEP; BEEP; BEEP;
                    break; }
    }
    return 0;
}
```

This example is much clearer than the previous one. The value of num controls the execution—only the case that matches num executes. The indention helps separate each case.

If the child enters a number other than 1 through 5, no beeps are sounded because there is no case expression to match any other value and there is no default case.

Because the BEEP preprocessor directive is so short, you can put more than one on a single line. This is not a requirement, however. The block of statements following a case can also be more than one statement long.

If more than one case expression is the same, only the first expression executes.

2. If the child does not type a 1, 2, 3, 4, or 5, nothing happens in the last program. What follows is the same program modified to take advantage of the default option. The default block of statements executes if none of the previous cases match:

```
/* Filename: C12BEEP3.C
   Beeps a certain number of times using a switch */
#include <stdio.h>
```

```
/* Define a beep printf() to save repeating printf()s
    throughout the program */
#define BEEP printf("\a \n")
main()
{
    int num;

    // Get a number from the child (you may have to help)
    printf("Please enter a number ");
    scanf(" %d", &num);

    switch (num)
    { case (1): { BEEP;
                    break; }
      case (2): { BEEP; BEEP;
                    break; }
      case (3): { BEEP; BEEP; BEEP;
                    break; }
      case (4): { BEEP; BEEP; BEEP; BEEP;
                    break; }
      case (5): { BEEP; BEEP; BEEP; BEEP; BEEP;
                    break; }
      default:  { printf("You must enter a number from 1 to
➡5\n");

                    printf("Please run this program again\n");
                    break; }
    }
    return 0;
}
```

The break at the end of the default case might seem redundant. After all, no other case statements execute by "falling through" from the default case. It is a good habit to put a break after the default case anyway. If you move the default higher in the switch (it doesn't have to be the last switch option), you are more inclined to move the break with it (where it is then needed).

3. To show the importance of using break statements in each case expression, here is the same beeping program without any break statements.

```
/* Filename: C12BEEP4.C
    Incorrectly beeps using a switch */
#include <stdio.h>
```

```
/* Define a beep printf() to save repeating printf()s
   throughout the program */
#define BEEP printf("\a \n")
main()
{
    int num;

    // Get a number from the child (you may have to help)
    printf("Please enter a number ");
    scanf(" %d", &num);

    switch (num)                              /* Warning! */
    { case (1): { BEEP; }       /* Without a break, this code */
      case (2): { BEEP; BEEP; }        /* falls through to the */
      case (3): { BEEP; BEEP; BEEP; } /* rest of the beeps! */
      case (4): { BEEP; BEEP; BEEP; BEEP; }
      case (5): { BEEP; BEEP; BEEP; BEEP; BEEP; }
      default:  { printf("You must enter a number from 1 to
➥5\n");

                        printf("Please run this program again\n"); }
    }
    return 0;
}
```

If the user types a **1**, the program beeps 15 times! The break is not
there to stop the execution from falling through to the other cases.
Unlike other programming languages, such as Pascal, C's switch
statement requires that you insert break statements between each
case if you want only one case executed. This is not necessarily a
drawback. The trade-off of having to specify break statements gives
you more control in how you handle specific cases, as shown in the
next example.

4. This program controls the printing of end-of-day sales totals. It first
   asks for the day of the week. If the day is Monday through Thursday,
   a daily total is printed. If the day is a Friday, a weekly total and a
   daily total are printed. If the day happens to be the end of the month,
   a monthly sales total is printed as well.

   In a real application, these totals would come from the disk drive
   rather than be assigned at the top of the program. Also, instead of
   individual sales figures being printed, a full daily, weekly, and
   monthly report of many sales totals would probably be printed. You
   are on your way to learning more about expanding the power of your

C programs. But for now, concentrate on the switch statement and its possibilities.

The daily; daily and weekly; and daily, weekly, and monthly sales figures are handled through a hierarchy of case statements. Because the daily amount is the last case, it is the only report printed if the day of the week is Monday through Thursday. If the day of the week is Friday, the second case prints the weekly sales total and then falls through to the daily total (because Friday's daily total must be printed as well). If it is the end of the month, the first case executes, falling through to the weekly total, then to the daily sales total as well. In this example, the use of a break statement would be harmful. Other languages that do not offer this "fall through" flexibility are more limiting.

```c
/* Filename: C12SALE.C
   Prints daily, weekly, and monthly sales totals */
#include <stdio.h>
main()
{
    float daily=2343.34;    /* Later, these figures will */
    float weekly=13432.65;  /* come from a disk file      */
    float monthly=43468.97; /* instead of being assigned */
                            /* as they are here          */
    char ans;
    int day;        // Day value to trigger correct case

    /* Month is assigned 1 through 5 (for Monday through
       Friday) or 6 if it is the end of the month. Assume
       a monthly, weekly, and daily prints if it is the end of the
       month, no matter what the day is. */
    printf("Is this the end of the month? (Y/N) ");
    scanf(" %c", &ans);
    if ((ans=='Y') || (ans=='y'))
        { day=6; }                          // Month value
    else
        { printf("What day number, 1 through 5 (for Mon-Fri)is it?
");
          scanf(" %d", &day); }

    switch (day)
```

```
      { case (6): printf("The monthly total is: $%.2f \n",
➥monthly);
        case (5): printf("The weekly total is: $%.2f \n",
➥weekly);
        default:  printf("The daily total is: $%.2f \n",
➥daily);
      }
    return 0;
}
```

5. The order of the case statements is not fixed. You can rearrange them to make them more efficient. If only one or two cases are being selected most of the time, put those cases near the top of the switch statement.

   For example, in the last program most of the company's employees are engineers, but their option is third in the case statements. By rearranging the case statements so that Engineering is at the top, you can speed up this program because C will not have to scan through two case expressions that it rarely executes.

```
/* Filename: C12DEPT2.C
   Prints message depending on the department entered */
#include <stdio.h>
main()
{
   char choice;

   do    /* Display menu and ensure that user enters a
            correct option */
     { printf("\n Choose your department: \n");
       printf("S - Sales \n");
       printf("A - Accounting \n");
       printf("E - Engineering \n");
       printf("P - Payroll \n");
       printf("What is your choice? ");
       scanf(" %c", &choice);
       /* Convert choice to uppercase (if they
          entered lowercase) with the ASCII table */
       if ((choice>=97) && (choice<=122))
          { choice -= 32; }      /* Subtract enough to make
                                     uppercase */
     } while ((choice!='S')&&(choice!='A')&&
              (choice!='E')&&(choice!='P'));
```

```
     /* Put Engineering first because it occurs most often */
     switch (choice)
     { case ('E') : { printf("\n Your meeting is at 2:30");
                        break; }
        case ('S') : { printf("\n Your meeting is at 8:30");
                        break; }
        case ('A') : { printf("\n Your meeting is' at 10:00");
                        break; }
        case ('P') : { printf("\n Your meeting has been canceled");
                        break; }
     }
     return 0;
}
```

The goto Statement

Early programming languages did not offer the flexible constructs that C gives you, such as for loops, while loops, and switch statements. Their only means of looping and comparing was with the goto statement. C still includes a goto, but the other constructs are more powerful, flexible, and easier to follow in a program.

The goto statement causes your program to jump to a different location, rather than execute the next statement in sequence. The format of the goto statement is

goto *statement label*

A *statement label* is named just as variables are (refer to Chapter 3, "Variables and Constants"). A *statement label* cannot have the same name as a C command, a C function, or another variable in the program. If you use a goto statement, there must be a *statement label* elsewhere in the program that the goto branches to. Execution then continues at the statement with the *statement label*.

The *statement label* precedes a line of code. Follow all *statement labels* with a colon (:) so C knows they are labels and doesn't get them confused with variables. You have not seen statement labels in the C programs so far in this book because none of the programs needed them. A *statement label* is optional, unless you have a goto that branches to one.

The following four lines of code each have a different statement label. This is not a program, but individual lines that might be included in a program. Notice that the statement labels are to the left of the lines:

```
pay: printf("Place checks in the printer \n);
Again: scanf(" %s", name);
```

```
EndIt: printf("That is all the processing. \n");
CALC: amount = (total / .5) * 1.15;
```

The statement labels are not intended to replace comments, although their names should reflect the code that follows. Statement labels give goto statements a tag to go to. When your program gets to the goto, it branches to the statement labeled by the statement label. The program then continues to execute sequentially until the next goto changes the order again (or until the program ends).

TIP

Use identifying line labels. A repetitive calculation deserves a label such as CalcIt and not x15z. Even though both are allowed, the first one is a better indication of the code's purpose.

USE goto JUDICIOUSLY

The goto is not considered a good programming statement when overused. There is a tendency, especially for beginning programmers, to include too many goto statements in a program. When a program branches all over the place, it becomes difficult to follow. Some people call programs with lots of goto statements "spaghetti code."

To eliminate goto statements and write better structured programs, use the other looping and switch constructs seen in the last few chapters.

But the goto is not necessarily a bad statement—if used judiciously. Starting with the next chapter, you begin to break your programs into smaller modules called functions, and the goto becomes less and less important as you write more and more functions.

For now, become familiar with goto so you can understand programs that use it. Some day, you might be called on to correct the code of someone who used the goto.

EXAMPLE

1. The following program has a problem that is a direct result of the goto, but it is still one of the best illustrations of the goto statement. The program consists of an *endless loop* (or an infinite loop). The first three lines (after the opening brace) execute, then the goto in the fourth line causes execution to loop back to the beginning and repeat the first three lines. The goto continues to do this until you press Ctrl+Break or ask your system administrator to cancel the program.

```
/* Filename: C12GOTO1.C
   Program to show use of goto. This program ends
   only when the user presses Ctrl+Break. */
#include <stdio.h>
main()
{
    Again: printf("This message \n");
    printf("\t keeps repeating \n");
    printf("\t\t over and over \n");
```

```
        goto Again;    /* Repeat continuously */

        return 0;
}
```

Notice that the statement label has a colon to separate it from the rest of the line, but you never add the colon to the label at the goto statement.

The output from this program appears below:

```
This message
        keeps repeating
                over and over
This message
        keeps repeating
                over and over
This message
        keeps repeating
                over and over
This message
        keeps repeating
                over and over
This message
        keeps repeating
                over and over
This message
        keeps repeating
                over and over
This message
```

2. It is sometimes easier to read your program's code when you put the statement labels on lines by themselves. Remember that writing maintainable programs is the goal of every good programmer. Making your programs easier to read should be a prime consideration when you write them. The following program is the same repeating program shown in the previous example, except the statement label is placed on a line by itself:

```
/* Filename: C12GOTO2.C
   Program to show use of goto. This program ends
   only when the user presses Ctrl+Break. */
#include <stdio.h>
main()
{

Again:
    printf("This message \n");
```

```
    printf("\t keeps repeating \n");
    printf("\t\t over and over \n");

    goto Again;    /* Repeat continuously */

    return 0;
}
```

The line following the statement label is the one that executes next, after control is passed (by the goto) to the label.

Of course, these are silly examples. You really don't want to write programs with infinite loops. The goto is a statement best preceded with an if, so that the goto eventually stops branching without intervention from the user.

3. The following program is one of the worst-written programs ever. It is the epitome of spaghetti code. However, do your best to follow it and understand its output. By understanding the flow of this output, you can hone your understanding of the goto. You might also appreciate the fact that the rest of this book uses the goto only when needed to make the program clearer.

```
/* Filename: C12GOTO3.C
   This program demonstrates the overuse of goto */
#include <stdio.h>
main()
{
    goto Here;

    First:
    printf("A \n");
    goto Final;

    There:
    printf("B \n");
    goto First;

    Here:
    printf("C \n");
    goto There;

    Final:
    Return 0;
}
```

At first glance, this program appears to print the first three letters of the alphabet, but the goto statements make them print in the reverse order, C, B, A. Although the program is not a well-designed program, some indention of the lines without statement labels make it a little more readable. This enables you to quickly separate the statement labels from the rest of the code, as you can see from the following program:

```
/* Filename: C12GOTO4.C
   This program demonstrates the overuse of goto */
#include <stdio.h>
main()
{
    goto Here;

First:
    printf("A \n");
    goto Final;

There:
    printf("B \n");
    goto First;

Here:
    printf("C \n");
    goto There;

Final:
    Return 0;
}
```

This program's listing is slightly easier to follow than the previous one, even though both do the same thing. The remaining programs in this book that use statement labels also use such indention.

Obviously, this program's output would be better produced by the following three lines:

```
printf("C \n");
printf("B \n");
printf("A \n");
```

The goto warning is worth repeating: Use goto sparingly and only when its use would make your program more readable and maintainable. Usually, you can use much better commands.

What's Next

This ends the part of the book about program control. The next part, "Variable Scope and Structuring Code," introduces user-written functions. So far, you have been using C's built-in functions, such as `printf()` and `scanf()`. Now it's time to write your own.

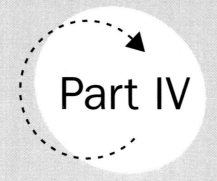

Part IV

Variable Scope and Structuring Code

13

Introduction to C Functions

You can take advantage of your computer's repetitive nature by looking at your programs in a new way—as a series of small routines that execute whenever you need them, however many times you require. This chapter approaches its subject a little differently from previous chapters. It concentrates on teaching the need for writing your own functions, which are *modules* of code that you execute and control from the main() function. So far, all programs in this book have consisted of a single long function called main(). As you learn here, the main() function's primary purpose is to control the execution of other functions that follow it.

This chapter stresses the use of *structured programming*, sometimes called *modular programming*. C was designed to make it easy to write your programs in several modules instead of as one long program. By breaking the program into several smaller routines (functions), you can isolate problems, write correct programs faster, and produce programs that are easier to maintain.

This chapter teaches you the following topics:

- The need for functions
- How to trace functions
- How to write functions
- How to call and return from functions

Function Basics

When you approach an application that needs to be programmed, it is best not to sit down at the keyboard and start typing. Rather, you should first think about the program and what it is supposed to do. One of the best ways to attack a program is to start with the overall goal, and then divide this goal into several smaller tasks. You should never lose sight of the overall goal, but you should think also of how individual pieces can fit together to accomplish such a goal.

When you finally do sit down to begin coding the problem, continue to think in terms of those pieces fitting together. Don't approach a program as if it were one giant problem; rather, continue to write those small pieces individually.

This does not mean that you must write separate programs to do everything. You can keep individual pieces of the overall program together—if you know how to write functions. This way, you can use the same functions in many different programs.

C programs are not like QBasic or FORTRAN programs. C was designed to force you to think in a modular, or subroutine-like, functional style. Good C programmers write programs that consist of many small functions, even if their programs execute one or more of these functions only once. But those functions work together to produce a program quicker and easier than if the program had to be written from scratch.

TIP

Rather than code one very long program, you should write several smaller routines, called functions. One of those functions must be called main(). The main() function is always the first to execute. It doesn't need to be first in a program, but it usually is.

Breaking Down Problems

If your program does very much, break it into several functions. Each function should do one primary task. For example, if you were writing a C program to get a list of characters from the keyboard, alphabetize them, and then print them to the screen, you could—but shouldn't—write all that into one big main() function, as the following C *skeleton* (program outline) shows:

```
main()
{
    /* :
        C code to get a list of characters
        :
```

```
      C code to alphabetize the characters

      :

      C code to print the alphabetized list on the screen

      :  */

   return 0;

}
```

This skeleton is not a good way to write this program. Even though you could type this program in only a few lines of code, it would be much better to get in the habit of breaking up every program into distinct tasks. You should not use main() to do everything—in fact, you should use main() to do little except call each of the functions that do the work.

A better way to organize this program is to write a separate function for each task the program is supposed to do. This doesn't mean that each function should be only one line long. Rather, it means you should make every function a building block that performs only one distinct task in the program.

The following program outline shows you a better way to write the program just described:

```
main()
{
    getletters();   /* Calls a function to get the numbers */
    alphabetize();  /* Calls a function to alphabetize
                         letters */
    printletters(); /* Calls a function to print letters
                         onscreen */
    return 0;            /* Return to the operating system */
}
getletters()
{
    /* :
       C code to get a list of characters
       :  */
    return 0;   /* Returns to main() */
}


alphabetize()
{
    /* :
```

```
        C code to alphabetize the characters
        :   /*
    return 0;    /* Returns to main() */
}


printletters()
{
    /* :
        C code to print the alphabetized list on the screen
        :  */
    return 0;    /* Returns to main() */
}
```

The program outline shows you a much better way of writing this program. It is longer to type, but much better organized. The only thing the main() function does is control the other functions by showing in one place the order in which they are called. Each separate function executes its instructions, and then returns to main(), whereupon main() calls the next function until no more functions remain. The main() function then returns control of the computer to the operating system.

TIP

A good rule of thumb is that a function should not be more than one screen in length. If it is longer, you are probably doing too much in that function and should therefore break it into two or more functions.

The first function called main() is what you previously used to hold the entire program. From this point, in all but the smallest of programs, main() simply controls other functions that do the work.

These listings are not examples of real C programs; instead, they are skeletons, or outlines, of programs. From these outlines, it is easier to develop the actual full program. But before going to the keyboard to write a program such as this, you should know that there will be four distinct sections: a primary function-calling main() function, a keyboard data-entry function, an alphabetizing function, and a printing function.

You should never lose sight of the original programming problem and, with the approach just described, you never do. Look again at the main() calling routine in the preceding program. Notice that you can glance at main() and get a feel for the overall program, without the remaining statements getting in the way. This is a good example of structured, modular programming. A large programming problem has been broken down into distinct, separate modules called functions, and each function performs one primary job in a few C statements.

Considering More Function Basics

Little has been said about naming and writing functions, but you probably understand much of the goals of the previous listing already. C functions generally adhere to the following rules:

1. Every function must have a name.

2. Function names are made up and assigned by the programmer (you!) following the same rules that apply to naming variables; they can contain up to 31 characters, they must begin with a letter, and they can consist of letters, numbers, and the underscore (_) character.

3. All function names have one set of parentheses immediately following them. This helps you (and C) differentiate them from variables. The parentheses might or might not contain something. So far, all such parentheses in this book have been empty.

4. The body of each function, starting immediately after the closing parenthesis of the function name, must be enclosed by braces. This means that a block containing one or more statements makes up the body of each function.

Although the outline shown in the previous listing is a good example of structured code, it can be further improved—and not only by putting the actual C statements inside the program to make it work. You can improve this program also by using the underscore character (_) in the function names. Do you see how get_letters() and print_letters() are much easier to read than are getletters() and printletters()? Then again, if you use uppercase letters, you may prefer to capitalize each word in the function name after the initial once, such as getLetters() and printLetters(). The selection of uppercase and lowercase or the underscore in function and variable names depends solely on the programmer's preference.

CAUTION

Be sure to use the underscore character (_) and not the hyphen (-) when naming functions and variables. If you use a hyphen, C becomes very confused and produces misleading error messages.

The following listing shows you an example of a C function. You can already tell quite a bit about this function. You know, for instance, that it isn't a complete program because it has no main() function. (All programs *must* have a main() function.) You know also that the function name is calcIt because parentheses follow this name. These parentheses happen to have something in them. You know also that the body of the function is enclosed in a block of braces. Inside that block is a smaller block, the body of a while loop. Finally, you recognize that the return statement is the last line of the function:

```
calcIt(int n)
{
    /* Function to print the square of a number */
    int square;

    while (square <= 250)
      { square = n * n;
        printf("The square of %d is %d \n", n, square);
        n++; }      /* A block within the function */

    return 0;
}
```

TIP

Not all functions require a `return` statement for their last line, but it is recommended that you always include one because it helps to show your intention to return to the calling function at that point. Later in the book, you learn when the `return` is required. For now, you should just get in the habit of including a `return` statement.

Calling and Returning Functions

You have been reading much about "function calling" and "returning control." Although you may already understand these phrases from their context, you can probably learn them better through an illustration of what is meant by a function call.

A function call in C is like a detour on a highway. Imagine you are traveling along the "road" of the primary function called `main()` and then run into a function-calling statement. You must temporarily leave the `main()` function and go execute the function that was called. After that function finishes (its `return` statement is reached), program control reverts to `main()`. In other words, when you finish a detour, you end up back on the "main" route and continue the trip. Control continues as `main()` calls other functions.

NOTE

Generally, the primary function that controls function calls and their order is referred to as a *calling function*. Functions controlled by the calling function are known as *called functions*.

EXAMPLE

A complete C program, with functions, should make this clear. The following program prints several messages to the screen. Each message printed is determined by the order of the functions. Before worrying too much about what this program does, take a little time to study its structure. You should be able to see three functions defined in the program: `main()`, `nextFun()`, and thirdFun(). A fourth function is used also, but it is the built-in C printf() function. The three defined functions appear sequentially, one after the other. The body of each is enclosed in braces, and each has a return statement at its end:

```
/* C13FUN1.C

   The following program illustrates function calls */
#include <stdio.h>

main()  /* main() is always the first C function executed */
{
    printf("First function called main() \n");
    nextFun();            /* Second function is called here */
    thirdFun();            /* This function is called here */
    printf("main() is completed \n");      /* All control
                                               returns here */
    return 0;                       /* Control is returned to
                                         the operating system   */
}                       /* This brace concludes main() */


nextFun()                                    /* Second function;
                                    parentheses always required */
{
    printf("Inside nextFun() \n");    /* No variables are
                                          defined in the program */
    return 0;              /* Control is now returned to main() */
}


thirdFun()                  /* Last function in the program */
{
    printf("Inside thirdFun() \n");
    return 0;                  /* Always return from all functions */
}
```

OUTPUT

The output of this program follows:

```
First function called main()

Inside nextFun()

Inside thirdFun()

main() is completed
```

Figure 13.1 shows a tracing of this program's execution. Notice that main()
controls which of the other functions is called, as well as the order of the
calling. Control always returns to the calling function after the called function finishes.

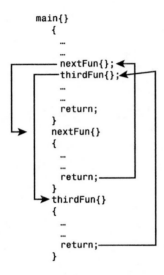

```
main{}
  {
    ...
    ...
    nextFun{};
    thirdFun{};
    ...
    ...
    return;
  }
  nextFun{}
  {
    ...
    ...
    return;
  }
  thirdFun{}
  {
    ...
    ...
    return;
  }
```

Figure 13.1: Use this figure to follow this function call trace.

To call a function, simply type its name—including the parentheses—and
follow it with a semicolon. Remember that semicolons follow all executable statements in C, and a function call (sometimes called a *function
invocation*) is an executable statement. The execution is the function's code
being called. Any function can call any other function. It just happens that
main() is the only function that calls other functions in this program.

Now, you can tell that the following statement is a function call:

```
printTotal();
```

Because printTotal is not a C command or built-in function name, it must
be a variable or a written function's name. Only function names end with
the parentheses, so it must be a function call or the start of a function's
code. Of the last two possibilities, it must be a call to a function because it
ends with a semicolon. If it didn't have a semicolon, it would have to be the
start of a function definition.

When you define a function (that is, when you type the function name and
its subsequent code inside braces), you never follow the name with a semicolon. Notice in the previous program that main(), nextFun(), and
thirdFun() have no semicolons when they appear in the body of the program. A semicolon follows their names only in main(), where these functions are called.

CAUTION
Never define a function within another function. All function code must be listed sequentially, one after the other, throughout the program. A function's closing brace must appear before another function's code can be listed.

EXAMPLE

1. Suppose you are writing a program that does the following. First, it asks users for their departments. Next, if they are in accounting, they should receive the accounting department's report. If they are in engineering, they should receive the engineering department's report. And if they are in marketing, they should receive the marketing department's report.

The skeleton of such a program follows. The code for main() is shown in its entirety, but only a skeleton of the other functions are shown. The switch statement is a perfect function-calling statement for such multiple-choice selections:

```
/* Skeleton of a departmental report program */
#include <stdio.h>
main()
{
    int choice;

    do
      { printf("Choose your department from the
                 following list\n");
        printf("\t1. Accounting \n");
        printf("\t2. Engineering \n");
        printf("\t3. Marketing \n");
        printf("What is your choice? ");
        scanf(" %d", &choice);
      } while ((choice<1) || (choice>3));   /* Ensure 1, 2,
                                                  or 3 */

    switch choice
    { case(1): { acctReport(); /* Call accounting function */
                 break; }         /* Don't fall through */
      case(2): { engReport(); /* Call engineering function */
                 break; }
      case(3): { mtgReport(); /* Call marketing function */
                 break; }
    }
    return 0;   /* Program returns to the operating system
                   when finished */
```

```
}

acctReport()
{
    /* :
        Accounting report code goes here */
        :   */
    return 0;
}

engReport()
{
    /* :
        Engineering report code goes here */
        :   */
    return 0;
}

mtgReport()
{
    /* :
        Marketing report code goes here */
        :   */
    return 0;
}
```

The bodies of switch statements normally contain function calls. You can tell that these case statements execute functions. For instance, acctReport(); (which is the first line of the first case) is not a variable name or a C command. It is the name of a function defined later in the program. If users enter 1 at the menu, the function called acctReport() executes. When it finishes, control returns to the first case body, whose break statement causes the switch statement to end. The main() function returns to DOS (or to your integrated C environment if you are using one) when its return statement executes.

2. In the previous example, the main() routine is not very modular. It displays the menu, but that should be done in a separate function. Remember that main() should do very little except control the other functions, which do all the work.

Here is a rewrite of this sample program, with a fourth function to print the menu to the screen. This is truly a modular example, with each function performing a single task. Again, the last three functions show only skeleton code because the goal here is simply to illustrate function calling and returning:

```c
/* Second skeleton of a departmental report program */
#include <stdio.h>
main()
{
    int choice;

    do
        {  menuPrint();   /* Call function to print the menu */
           scanf(" %d", &choice);
        } while ((choice<1) || (choice>3));   /* Ensure 1, 2,
                                                         or 3 */

    switch choice
    { case(1): { acctPeport(); /* Call accounting function */
                    break; }           /* Don't fall through */
      case(2): { engReport(); /* Call engineering function */
                    break; }
      case(3): { mtgReport(); /* Call marketing function */
                    break; }
    }
    return 0;   /* Program returns to the operating system
                    when finished */
}

menuPrint()
{
    printf("Choose your department from the following list\n");
    printf("\t1. Accounting \n");
    printf("\t2. Engineering \n");
    printf("\t3. Marketing \n");
    printf("What is your choice? ");
    return 0;   /* Return to main() */
}

acctReport()
{
    /* :
        Accounting report code goes here */
        :   */
    return 0;
}
```

```
engReport()
{
    /* :
        Engineering report code goes here */
        :   */
    return 0;
}

mtgReport()
{
    /* :
        Marketing report code goes here */
        :   */
    return 0;
}
```

The menu printing function doesn't have to follow main(). Because it's the first function called, however, it seems best to define it there.

3. Readability is the key, so programs broken into separate functions result in better written code. You can write and test each function, one at a time. After you write a general outline of the program, you can list a lot of function calls in main(), and define their skeletons after main().

The body of each function initially should consist of a single return statement, so that the program compiles in its skeleton format. As you complete each function, you can compile and test the program. This enables you to develop more accurate programs more quickly. The separate functions let others (who might later modify your program) "zero in" on whatever code they need to change, without affecting the rest of the program.

Another useful habit, popular with many C programmers, is to separate functions from each other with a comment consisting of a line of asterisks (*) or dashes (—). This makes it easy, especially in longer programs, to see where a function begins and ends. What follows is another listing of the previous program, but now with its four functions more clearly separated by this type of comment line:

```
/* Third skeleton of a departmental report program */
#include <stdio.h>
main()
{
    int choice;

    do
```

```
      {  menuPrint();  /* Call function to print the menu */
         scanf(" %d", &choice);
      } while ((choice<1) |¦ (choice>3));  /* Ensure 1, 2,
                                                    or 3 */

   switch choice
   { case(1): { acctReport(); /* Call accounting function */
                  break; }           /* Don't fall through */
     case(2): { engReport(); /* Call engineering function */
                  break; }
     case(3): { mtgReport();    /* Call marketing function */
                  break; }
   }
   return 0;   /* Program returns to the operating system
                  when finished */
}


/************************************************************/
menuPrint()
{
   printf("Choose your department from the following list\n");
   printf("\t1. Accounting \n");
   printf("\t2. Engineering \n");
   printf("\t3. Marketing \n");
   printf("What is your choice? ");
   return 0;   /* Return to main() */
}


/************************************************************/
acctReport()
{
   /* :
      Accounting report code goes here */
      :   */
   return 0;
}


/************************************************************/
engReport()
{
   /* :
```

```
          Engineering report code goes here */
          :   */
      return 0;
}


/**********************************************************/
mtgReport()
{
    /* :
        Marketing report code goes here */
        :   */
    return 0;
}
```

Due to space limitations, not all program listings in this book separate the functions in this manner. You might find, however, that your listings are easier to follow if you put these separating comments between your functions.

4. You can execute a function more than once simply by calling it from more than one place in a program. If you put a function call in the body of a loop, the function executes repeatedly until the loop finishes.

The following program prints the message C is fun! several times onscreen—forward and backward—using functions. Notice that main() does not make every function call. The second function, namePrint(), calls the function named reversePrint(). Trace the execution of this program's printf()s:

```
/* Filename: C13FUN2.C
    Prints C is fun! several times on the screen */
#include <stdio.h>
main()
{
    int ctr;   /* To control loops */

    for (ctr=1; ctr<=5; ctr++)
        { namePrint(); }              // Calls function 5 times

    onePerLine();                     // Calls last function once
    return 0;
}


/**********************************************************/
namePrint()
{
    // Prints C is fun! across a line, separated by tabs
```

```
        printf("C is fun!\tC is fun!\tC is fun!\tC is fun!\n");
        printf("C  i  s  f  u  n !\tC  i  s  f  u  n !\tC  i  s  f  u  n
➡ !\n");

        reversePrint();        // Call next function from here
        return 0;                              // Returns to main()
    }


/******************************************************/
reversePrint()
{
        // Prints several C is fun! messages,
        //     in reverse, separated by tabs
        printf("!nuf si C\t!nuf si C\t!nuf si C\t\n");

        return 0;                              // Returns to namePrint()
    }


/******************************************************/
onePerLine()
{
        // Prints C is fun! down the screen
        printf("C\n \ni\ns\n \nf\nu\nn\n!\n");
        return 0;    // Returns to main()
    }
```

OUTPUT

Here is the program's output that you can use to trace the order of function execution:

```
C is fun!        C is fun!        C is fun!        C is fun!
C  i  s  f  u  n !C  i  s  f  u  n !C  i  s  f  u  n !
!nuf si C        !nuf si C        !nuf si C
C is fun!        C is fun!        C is fun!
C is fun!        C is fun!        C is fun!        C is fun!
C  i  s  f  u  n !C  i  s  f  u  n !C  i  s  f  u  n !
!nuf si C        !nuf si C        !nuf si C
C is fun!        C is fun!        C is fun!
C is fun!        C is fun!        C is fun!        C is fun!
C  i  s  f  u  n !C  i  s  f  u  n !C  i  s  f  u  n !
!nuf si C        !nuf si C        !nuf si C
C is fun!        C is fun!        C is fun!
C is fun!        C is fun!        C is fun!        C is fun!
C  i  s  f  u  n !C  i  s  f  u  n !C  i  s  f  u  n !
!nuf si C        !nuf si C        !nuf si C
```

```
C is fun!      C is fun!      C is fun!
C is fun!      C is fun!      C is fun!      C is fun!
C  is  fun ! C  is  fun ! C  is  fun !
!nuf si C      !nuf si C      !nuf si C
C

i

s

f
u
n
!
```

What's Next

You have now been exposed to truly structured programs. Instead of typing a long program, you can break it up into separate functions. This isolates your routines from each other, so that surrounding code doesn't get in the way when you are concentrating on one section of your program. The next chapter builds on the fundamentals of functions you learned here by showing you how you transfer the values of variables between functions.

14

Variable Scope

Variable scope is most important when you write functions. Variable scope determines which functions recognize certain variables. If a function recognizes a variable, the variable is *visible* to that function. Variable scope protects variables in one function from other functions that might overwrite them. If a function doesn't need access to a variable, that function shouldn't be able to see or change the variable. In other words, the variable should not even be "visible" to that particular function.

This chapter teaches you the following topics:

- Global and local variables
- Passing arguments
- Automatic and static variables
- Passing parameters

Global Versus Local Variables

Global variables are variables that are recognized from any statement in the program. Global variables can be dangerous to use; parts of a program can inadvertently change a variable that shouldn't be changed. For example, suppose you are writing a program that keeps track of a grocery store's inventory. You might keep track of sale percentages, discounts, retail prices, wholesale prices, produce prices, dairy prices, delivered prices, price changes, sales tax percentages, holiday markups, post-holiday markdowns, and so on.

The huge number of prices in such a system is confusing. When writing a program to keep track of each of these prices, it would be easy to mistakenly call both the dairy prices dPrices and the delivered prices dPrices. Either C disallows it (does not let you define the same variable twice) or you overwrite a value used for something else. Whatever happens, keeping track of all of these different—but similarly named—prices makes this program confusing to write.

Global variables can be dangerous because code can inadvertently overwrite a variable initialized elsewhere in the program. It is better to make every variable *local* in your programs. Then, only functions that should be able to change the variables can do so.

Local variables can be seen (and changed) only from the function they are defined in. Therefore, if a function defines a variable as local, that variable's scope is protected. The variable cannot be used, changed, or erased by any other function—without special programming that you learn about shortly.

If you use only one function, main(), the concept of local and global is academic. But you know from the last chapter that single-function programs are not recommended. It is best to write modular, structured programs made up of many smaller functions. Therefore, you should know how to define variables as local to only those functions that need them.

Variable Scope

When you first learned about variables in Chapter 3, "Variables and Constants," you learned that you can define variables in two places:

- After the opening brace of a block of code (usually at the top of a function)
- Before a function name, such as main()

All examples in this book so far have declared variables using the first method. You have yet to see an example of the second method. Because most of these programs have consisted entirely of a single main() function, there has been no reason to differentiate the two methods. It is only after you start using several functions in one program that these two variable definition methods become critical.

The following rules, specific to local and global variables, are very important:

- A variable is local if and only if you define it after the opening brace of a block, usually at the top of a function.

- A variable is global if and only if you define it outside of a function.

All variables you have seen so far have been local. They have all been defined immediately after the opening braces of main(). Therefore, they have been local to main(), and only main() can use them. Other functions have no idea these variables even exist because they belong to main() only. When the function (or block) ends, all its local variables are destroyed.

TIP

All local variables disappear (lose their definition) when their block ends.

Global variables are visible ("known") from their point of definition downward in the source code. That is, if you define a global variable, any line throughout the rest of the program—no matter how many functions and code lines follow it—is able to use that global variable.

EXAMPLE

1. The following section of code defines two local variables, i and j:

```
main()
{
    int i, j;                      /* Local because they're
                                      defined after the brace */
    // Rest of main() goes here
}
```

These variables are visible to main() and not to any other function that might follow or be called by main().

2. The following section of code defines two global variables, g and h:

```
#include <stdio.h>
int g, h;                      /* Global because they're
                                  defined before a function */
main()
{
    /* main()'s code goes here */
}
```

It really doesn't matter whether your #include lines go before or after global variable declarations.

3. Global variables can appear before any function. In the following program, main() uses no variables. However, both of the two functions after main() can use sales and profit because these variables are global:

```c
/* Filename: C14GLO.C
   Program that contains two global variables */
#include <stdio.h>
main()
{
    printf("No variables defined in main() \n\n");
    doFun();                    // Call the first function
    return 0;
}

float sales, profit;            // Two global variables
doFun()
{
    sales = 20000.00;        // This variable is visible
                             // from this point down.
    profit = 5000.00;        // So is this one. They are
                             // both global.

    printf("The sales in the second function are: %.2f \n",
            sales);
    printf("The profit in the second function is: %.2f \n\n",
            profit);

    thirdFun();             // Call the third function to
                            // show that globals are visible
    return 0;
}

thirdFun()
{
    printf("In the third function: \n");
    printf("The sales in the third function are: %.2f \n",
            sales);
    printf("The profit in the third function is: %.2f \n",
            profit);
    /* If sales and profit were local, they would not be
       visible by more than one function */
```

```
                    return 0;
              }
```

Note that the main() function can never use sales and profit because they are not visible to main()—even though they are global. Remember, global variables are visible only from their point of definition downward in the program. Statements that appear before global variable definitions cannot use those variables.

Here is the result of running this program:

OUTPUT

```
No variables defined in main()

The sales in the 2nd function are: 20000.00
The profit in the 2nd function is: 5000.00

In the third function:
The sales in the 3rd function are: 20000.00
The profit in the 3rd function is: 5000.00
```

TIP

Declare all global variables at the top of your programs. Even though you can define them later (between any two functions), you can spot them faster if you declare them at the top.

4. The following program uses both local and global variables. It should now be obvious to you that j and p are local and i and z are global.

```
/* Filename: C14GLLO.C
   Program with both local and global variables
   Local Variables          Global Variables
          j, p                    i, z                    */
#include <stdio.h>
int i = 0;                       // Global variable because it's
                                 // defined outside main()

main()
{
    float p ;                              // Local to main() only
    p = 9.0;                    // Put value in global variable
    printf("%d  %f\n", i, p);              // Prints global i
                                           //       and local p
    prAgain();                    // Calls next function
    return 0;                             // Returns to DOS

}

float z = 9.0;                   // Global variable because it's
```

```
                                    // defined before a function
prAgain()
{
    int j = 5;                      // Local to only prAgain()
    printf("%d %f %d", j, z, i);    // This couldn't print p!
    return 0;                       // Return to main()
}
```

Even though j is defined in a function that main() calls, main() cannot use j because j is local to prAgain(). When prAgain() finishes, j is no longer defined. The variable z is global from its point of definition down. This is why main() cannot print z. Also, the function prAgain() cannot print p because p is local to main() only.

Make sure you can recognize local and global variables before you continue. A little study here makes the rest of this chapter very easy to understand.

5. Two variables can have the same name, as long as they are local to two different functions. They are distinct variables, even though they are named identically.

The following short program uses two variables, both named age. They have two different values, and they are considered to be two different variables. The first age is local to main(), and the second age is local to getAge():

```
/* Filename: C14LOC2.C
   Two different local variables with the same name */
#include <stdio.h>
main()
{
    int age;
    printf("What is your age? ");
    scanf(" %d", &age);

    getAge();                       // Call the second function
    printf("main()'s age is still: %d", age);

    return 0;
}

getAge()
{
    int age;                        // A different age. This one
                                    // is local to getAge()
    printf("What is your age again? ");
```

```
    scanf(" %d", &age);
    return 0;
}
```

The output of this program follows. Study this output carefully. Notice that main()'s last printf() does not print the newly changed age. Rather, it prints only the age known to main()—the age that is local to main(). Even though they are named the same, main()'s age has nothing to do with getAge()'s age. They might as well have two different variable names.

```
What is your age? 28
What is your age again? 56
main()'s age is still 28
```

You should be careful when naming variables. Having two variables with the same name is misleading. It would be easy to become confused while changing this program later. If these variables truly need to be separate, name them differently, such as oldAge and newAge, or age1 and age2. This helps you remember that they are different.

6. There are a few times when overlapping local variable names does not add confusion, but be careful about overdoing it. Programmers often use the same variable name as the counter variable in a for loop. For example, the two local variables in the following program have the same name:

```
/* Filename: C14LOC3.C
   Using two local variables with the same name
   as counting variables */
#include <stdio.h>
main()
{
    int ctr;                            // Loop counter
    for (ctr=0; ctr<=10; ctr++)
       { printf("main()'s ctr is: %d \n", ctr); }
    doFun();                            // Call second function

    return 0;
}

doFun()
{
    int ctr;
    for (ctr=10; ctr>=0; ctr--)
       { printf("doFun()'s ctr is: %d \n", ctr); }
```

```
        return 0;                          // Return to main()
    }
```

Although this is a nonsense program that simply prints 0 through 10 and then prints 10 through 0, it shows that the use of ctr in both functions is not a problem. These variables do not hold important data that must be processed; rather, they are for loop counting variables. Calling them both ctr leads to little confusion because their use is limited to controlling for loops. Because a for loop initializes and increments variables, the functions never rely on the other one's ctr to do anything.

7. Be careful about creating local variables with the same name in the same function. If you define a local variable early in a function and then define another local variable with the same name inside a new block, C uses only the innermost variable, until its block ends.

The following example helps clarify this confusing problem. The program contains one function with three local variables. See if you can find these three variables:

```
/* Filename: C14MULI.C
   Program with multiple local variables called i */
#include <stdio.h>
main()
{
   int i;                                 /* Outer i */
   i = 10;

   { int i;                              /* New block's i */
     i = 20;                   /* Outer i still holds a 10 */
     printf("%d %d \n", i, i);           /* Prints 20 20 */

     { int i;  /* Another new block and local variable */
       i = 30;                          /* Innermost i only */
       printf("%d %d %d \n", i, i, i); /* Prints 30 30 30 */
     }               /* Innermost i is now gone forever */

   }       * Second i is gone forever (its block ended) */

   printf("%d %d %d", i, i, i);       /* Prints 10 10 10 */
   return 0;
}               /* main() ends and so does its variables */
```

All local variables are local to the block in which they are defined. This program has three blocks, each one nested within another.

Because you can define local variables immediately after an opening brace of a block, there are three distinct i variables in this program.

The local i disappears completely when its block ends (that is, when the closing brace is reached). C always prints the variable that it sees as the most local—the one that resides within the innermost block.

Use Global Variables Sparingly

You may be asking yourself, "Why do I need to know about global and local variables?" At this point, that is an understandable question, especially if you have been programming mostly in QBasic without taking advantage of the structured routines QBasic allows. Here is the bottom line: Global variables can be dangerous. Code can inadvertently overwrite a variable that was initialized in another place in the program. It is better to have every variable in your program be local to the function that needs to access it.

Read that last sentence again. Even though you now know how to make variables global, you should avoid doing so. Try to never use another global variable. It may seem easier to use global variables when you write programs having more than one function: If you make every variable used by every function global, you never have to worry if one is visible or not to any given function. On the other hand, a function can accidentally change a global variable when it has no right to change it. If you keep variables local only to functions that need them, you protect their values, and you also keep your programs, both the code and all your data, fully modular.

The Need for Passing Variables

You just learned the difference between local and global variables. You saw that by making your variables local, you protect their values because the function that sees the variable is the only one that can modify it.

What do you do, however, if you have a local variable you want to use in *two or more* functions? In other words, you may need a variable to be both inputted from the keyboard in one function and printed in another function. If the variable is local only to the first function, how can the second one access it?

You have two solutions if more than one function needs to share a variable. One, you can declare the variable globally. This is bad because you want only those two functions to "see" the variable, but all other functions can "see" it if it is global. The other alternative—and the better one by far—is to pass the local variable from one function to another. This has a big advantage: The variable is only known to those two functions. The rest of the program still has no access to it.

CAUTION

Never pass a global variable because C will get confused. There is no reason to pass global variables anyway because they are already visible to all functions.

When you pass a local variable from one function to another, you pass an argument from the first function to the next. You can pass more than one argument (variable) at a time, if you want several local variables sent from one function to another. The receiving function receives a parameter (variable) from the function that sends it. You shouldn't worry too much about what you call them—either arguments or parameters. The important thing to remember is that you are sending local variables from one function to another.

NOTE

You have already passed arguments to parameters when you passed data to the `printf()` function. The constants, variables, and expressions in the `printf()` parentheses are arguments. The built-in `printf()` function receives these values (called parameters on the receiving end) and displays them.

A little more terminology is needed before you see some examples. When a function passes an argument, it is called the *passing function*. The function that receives the argument (called a parameter when it is received) is called the *receiving function*. Figure 14.1 explains these terms.

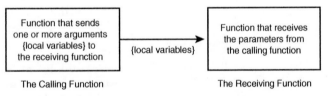

Figure 14.1: *The calling and receiving functions.*

To pass a local variable from one function to another, you must place the local variable in parentheses in both the calling function and the receiving function. For example, the local and global examples presented earlier did not pass local variables from `main()` to `doFun()`. If a function name has empty parentheses, nothing is being passed to it. Given this, the following line passes two variables, `total` and `discount`, to a function called `doFun()`:

```
doFun(total, discount);
```

It is sometimes said that a variable or function is *defined*. This has nothing to do with the `#define` preprocessor directive, which defines constants. You define variables with statements such as the following:

```
int i, j;
int m=9;
```

```
float x;
char ara[] = "Tulsa";
```

These statements tell the program that you need these variables and want them reserved. A function is defined when the C compiler reads the first statement in the function that describes the name and also reads any variables that may have been passed to that function. Never follow a function definition with a semicolon, but always follow the statement that calls a function with a semicolon.

NOTE

To some C purists, a variable is only declared when you write int i; and only truly defined when you assign it a value, such as i=7;. They say that the variable is both declared and defined when you declare the variable and assign it a value at the same time, such as int i=7;.

The following program contains two function definitions, main() and prIt():

```
main()                      /* The main() function definition */
{
  int i=5;                      /* Define an integer variable */
  prIt(i);                          /* Calls the prIt()
                                function and passes it i */
  return 0;                   /* Return to the operating system */
}


prIt(int i)             /* The prIt() function definition */
{
    printf("%d \n", i);     /* Calls the printf() function */
    return 0;                          /* Returns to main() */
}
```

Because a passed parameter is treated like a local variable in the receiving function, the printf() in prIt() prints a 5, even though the main() function initialized this variable.

When you pass arguments to a function, the receiving function has no idea about the data types of the incoming variables. Therefore, you must include each parameter's data type in front of the parameter's name. In the previous example, the definition of prIt() (the first line of the function) contains the type, int, of the incoming variable i. Notice that the main() calling function does not need to indicate the variable type. In this example, main() already knows the type of variable i (an integer); only prIt() needs to know that i is an integer.

TIP

Always declare the parameter types in the receiving function. Precede each parameter in the function's parentheses with int, float, or whatever each passed variable's data type happens to be.

EXAMPLE

1. Here is a main() function that contains three local variables. main() passes one of these variables to the first function and two of them to the second function:

```
/* Filename: C14LOC4.C
    Pass three local variables to functions */
#include <stdio.h>
main()
{
    char initial;              // 3 variables local to main()
    int age;
    float salary;

    /* Fill these variables in main() */
    printf("What is your initial? ");
    scanf(" %c", &initial);
    printf("What is your age? ");
    scanf(" %d", &age);
    printf("What is your salary? ");
    scanf(" %f", &salary);

    prInit(initial);                    // Call prInit() and
                                        //    pass it initial
    prOther(age, salary);        // Call prOther() and
                                 // pass it age and salary

    return 0;
}

prInit(char initial)            // Never put a semicolon in
                                // the function definition
{
    printf("Your initial is really %c? \n", initial);
    return 0;                           // Return to main()
}

prOther(int age, float salary)          // Must type both
                                        //     parameters
{
    printf("You look young for %d \n", age);
    printf("And $%.2f is a LOT of money!", salary);
```

```
    return 0;                            // Return to main()
}
```

2. A receiving function can contain its own local variables. As long as the
names are not the same, these local variables do not conflict with the
passed ones. In the following program, the second function receives a
passed variable from main() and also defines its own local variable
called pricePer:

```
/* Filename: C14LOC5.C
    Second function has its own local variable */
#include <stdio.h>
main()
{
    int gallons;

    printf("Richard's Paint Service \n");
    printf("How many gallons of paint did you buy? ");
    scanf(" %d", &gallons);          // Get gallons in main()

    computeSale(gallons);     // Compute total in function
    return 0;
}

computeSale(int gallons)
{
    float pricePer = 12.45;     // Local to computeSale()

    printf("The total is: $%.2f \n",
            (pricePer*(float)gallons) );
        // Had to type cast gallons because it was integer
    return 0;                             // Return to main()
}
```

3. The following sample code lines test your skill at recognizing calling
functions and receiving functions. Being able to recognize the difference is half the battle of understanding them:

```
doIt()
```

This must be the first line of a new function because it does not end
with a semicolon:

```
doIt2(sales);
```

This calls a function named doIt2(). The calling function passes the
variable called sales to doIt2():

```
prIt(float total)
```

This is the first line of a function that receives a floating-point variable from another function that called it. All receiving functions must specify the type of each variable being passed.

```
prThem(float total, int number)
```

This is the first line of a function that receives two variables—one is a floating-point variable and the other is an integer. This line cannot be calling the function prThem because there is no semicolon at the end of the line.

Automatic Versus Static Variables

The terms *automatic* and *static* describe what happens to local variables when a function returns to the calling procedure. By default, all local variables are automatic, meaning that they are erased when their function ends. To declare a variable as an automatic variable, prefix its definition with the term auto. The auto keyword is optional with local variables because they are automatic by default.

The two statements after main()'s opening brace declare automatic local variables:

```
main()
{
    int i;
    auto float x;
    /* Rest of main() goes here */
```

Because auto is the default, we did not need to include the term auto with x.

NOTE

C programmers rarely use the auto keyword with local variables because they are automatic by default.

The opposite of an automatic variable is a static variable. All global variables are static and, as mentioned, all static variables retain their values. Therefore, if a local variable is static, it too retains its value when its function ends—in case the function is called a second time. To declare a variable as static, place the static keyword in front of the variable when you define it. The following code section defines three variables, i, j, and k. The variable i is automatic, but j and k are static:

```
myFun()           /* Start of new function definition */
{
    int i;
```

```
static j=25;    /* Both j and k are static variables */
static k=30;
```

If local variables are static, their values remain in case the function is called again.

Always assign an initial value to a static variable when you declare it, as shown here in the last two lines. This initial value is placed in the static variable only the first time myFun() executes. If you don't assign a static variable an initial value, C initializes it to zero.

TIP

Static variables are good to use when you write functions that keep track of a count or add to a total when called. If the counting or total variables were local and automatic, their values would disappear when the function finished—destroying the totals.

AUTOMATIC AND STATIC RULES FOR LOCAL VARIABLES

Local automatic variables disappear when their block ends. All local variables are automatic by default. You can prefix a variable (when you define it) with the auto keyword, or you can omit it; the variable is still automatic and its value is destroyed when the block it is local to ends.

Local static variables do not lose their values when their function ends. They remain local to that function. When the function is called after the first time, the static variable's value is still in place. You declare a static variable by placing the static keyword before the variable's definition.

EXAMPLE

1. Consider this program:

```
/* Filename: C14STA1.C
   Tries to use a static variable
   without a static declaration */
#include <stdio.h>
main()
{
    int ctr;                        // Used in the for loop to
                                    // call a function 25 times
    for (ctr=1; ctr<=25; ctr++)
      { tripleIt(ctr); }            // Pass ctr to a function
                                    //       called tripleIt()
    return 0;
}


tripleIt(int ctr)
{
    int total, ans;        // Local automatic variables
    // Triples whatever value is passed to it
```

```
        // and adds the total

        ans = ctr * 3;                    // Triple number passed
        total += ans;  // Add triple numbers as this is called

        printf("The number %d, multiplied by 3 is: %d \n",
                ctr, ans);

        if (total > 300)
            { printf("The total of the triple numbers is over 300
➥\n"); }
        return 0;
}
```

This is a nonsense program that doesn't do much, yet you may sense something is wrong. The program passes numbers from 1 to 25 to the function called tripleIt. The function triples the number and prints it.

The variable called total is initially set to 0. The idea here is to add each tripled number and print a message when the total is larger than 300. However, the printf() never executes. For each of the 25 times that this subroutine is called, total is reset to 0. The total variable is an automatic variable whose value is erased and initialized every time its procedure is called. The next example corrects this.

2. If you want total to retain its value after the procedure ends, you must make it static. Because local variables are automatic by default, you need to include the static keyword to override this default. Then the value of the total variable is retained each time the subroutine is called.

The following corrects the mistake in the previous program:

```
/* Filename: C14STA2.C
   Uses a static variable with the static declaration */
#include <stdio.h>
main()
{
    int ctr;                        // Used in the for loop to
                                    // call a function 25 times
    for (ctr=1; ctr<=25; ctr++)
        { tripleIt(ctr); }          // Pass ctr to a function
                                    //       called tripleIt()

    return 0;
}
```

```
tripleIt(int ctr)
{
    static int total=0;                    // Local and static
    int ans;                               // Local and automatic
    // total will be set to 0 only the first time this
    // function is called.

    // Triples whatever value is passed to it and add
    // the total

    ans = ctr * 3;                         // Triple number passed
    total += ans;   // Add triple numbers as this is called

    printf("The number %d, multiplied by 3 is %d \n",
            ctr, ans);

    if (total > 300)
        { printf("The total of the triple numbers is over 300
➥\n"); }
    return 0;
}
```

OUTPUT

The program's output appears next. Notice that the function's printf() is triggered, even though total is a local variable. Because total is static, its value is not erased when the function finishes. When the function is called a second time by main(), total's previous value (when you left the routine) is still there.

```
The number 1, multiplied by 3 is 3
The number 2, multiplied by 3 is 6
The number 3, multiplied by 3 is 9
The number 4, multiplied by 3 is 12
The number 5, multiplied by 3 is 15
The number 6, multiplied by 3 is 18
The number 7, multiplied by 3 is 21
The number 8, multiplied by 3 is 24
The number 9, multiplied by 3 is 27
The number 10, multiplied by 3 is 30
The number 11, multiplied by 3 is 33
The number 12, multiplied by 3 is 36
The number 13, multiplied by 3 is 39
The number 14, multiplied by 3 is 42
The number 15, multiplied by 3 is 45
The number 16, multiplied by 3 is 48
The number 17, multiplied by 3 is 51
The number 18, multiplied by 3 is 54
```

```
The number 19, multiplied by 3 is 57
The number 20, multiplied by 3 is 60
The number 21, multiplied by 3 is 63
The number 22, multiplied by 3 is 66
The number 23, multiplied by 3 is 69
The number 24, multiplied by 3 is 72
The number 25, multiplied by 3 is 75
```

This does not mean that local static variables become global. The main program cannot refer, use, print, or change total because it is local to the second function. Static simply means that the local variable's value is still there if the program calls the function again.

Three Issues of Parameter Passing

To have a complete understanding of programs with several functions, you need to learn three additional concepts:

- Passing arguments (variables) by value (also called "by copy")

- Passing arguments (variables) by address (also called "by reference")

- Returning values from functions

The first two concepts deal with the way local variables are passed and received. The third concept describes how receiving functions send values back to the calling functions. The next chapter concludes this discussion by explaining these three methods for passing parameters and returning values.

What's Next

Parameter passing is necessary because local variables are better than global. Local variables are protected in their own routines, but sometimes they must be shared with other routines. If local data is to remain in those variables (in case the function is called again in the same program), the variables should be static because otherwise their automatic values would disappear.

Most of the information in this chapter should become more obvious as you use functions in your own programs. The next chapter goes into more detail on the actual passing of parameters and shows you two different ways to do it.

15

Passing Values Between Functions

C passes variables between functions using two different methods. The one you use depends on how you want the passed variables to be changed. This chapter explores these two methods. The concepts discussed here are not new to the C language. Other programming languages, such as Pascal, FORTRAN, and QBasic, pass parameters using similar techniques. A computer language must have the capability to pass information between functions, before it can be called truly structured.

This chapter teaches you the following topics:

- Passing variables by value
- Passing arrays by address
- Passing nonarrays by address

Passing by Value (by Copy)

The two wordings "passing by value" and "passing by copy" mean the same thing in computer terms. Some textbooks and C programmers say that arguments are passed by value, and some say they are passed by copy. Both of these phrases describe one of the two methods by which arguments are passed to receiving functions. (The other method is called "by address," and it is covered later in the chapter.)

When an argument (local variable) is passed by value, a copy of the variable's value is sent to—and is assigned to—the receiving function's parameter. If more than one variable is passed by value, a copy of each of their values is sent to—and is assigned to—the receiving function's parameters.

Figure 15.1 shows the passing by copy in action. The value of i—not the variable itself—is passed to the called function, which receives it as a variable i. There are two variables called i, not one. The first is local to main(), and the second is local to prIt(). They both have the same names, but because they are local to their respective functions, there is no conflict. The variable does not have to be called i in both functions, and because the value of i is sent to the receiving function, it does not matter what the receiving function calls the variable that receives this value.

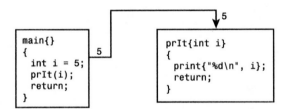

Figure 15.1: *Passing the variable i by value sends only the value.*

In this case, when passing and receiving variables between functions, it is wisest to retain the same names. Even though they are not the same variables, they hold the same value. In this example, the value 5 is passed from main()'s i to prIt()'s i.

Because a copy of i's value (and not the variable itself) is passed to the receiving function, if prIt() changed i, it would be changing only its copy of i and not main()'s i. This makes for true separation of functions and variables. You now have the technique for passing a copy of a variable to a receiving function, with the receiving function being unable to modify the calling function's variable.

All of C's nonarray variables that you have seen so far are passed by value. You do not have to do anything special to pass variables by value, except to pass them in the calling function's argument list and receive them in the receiving function's parameter list.

NOTE

The default method for passing parameters is by value, as just described, unless you pass arrays. Arrays are always passed by the other method, by address, as described later in this chapter.

EXAMPLE

1. The following program asks users for their weight. It then passes that weight to a function that calculates the equivalent weight on the moon. Notice that the second function uses the passed value, and calculates with it. After the weight is passed to the second function, that function can treat it as though it were a local variable:

```c
/* Filename: C15PASS1.C
   Calculate the user's weight in a second function */
#include <stdio.h>
main()
{
    int weight;                     // main()'s local weight
    printf("How many pounds do you weigh? ");
    scanf(" %d", &weight);

    moon(weight);                   // Call the moon() function and
                                    // pass it the weight
    return 0;                       // Return to the operating system
}

moon(int weight)                    // Declare the passed parameter
{
    /* Moon weights are 1/6th earth's weights */
    weight /= 6;                    // Divide the weight by 6

    printf("You weigh only %d pounds on the moon!", weight);
    return 0;                               // Return to main()
}
```

OUTPUT

The output of this program follows:

```
How many pounds do you weigh? 120
You weigh only 20 pounds on the moon!
```

2. You can rename passed variables in the receiving function. They are distinct from the passing function's variable. The following is the same program as in Example 1, except the receiving function calls the passed variable earthWeight. A new variable, called moonWeight, is

local to the called function and is used for the moon's equivalent weight:

```
/* Filename: C15PASS2.C
   Calculate the user's weight in a second function */
#include <stdio.h>
main()
{
    int weight;                         // main()'s local weight
    printf("How many pounds do you weigh? ");
    scanf(" %d", &weight);

    moon(weight);              // Call the moon() function and
                               //   pass it the weight
    return 0;                  // Return to the operating system
}

moon(int earthWeight)      // Declare the passed parameter
{
    int moonWeight;               // Local to this function

    /* Moon weights are 1/6th earth's weights */
    moonWeight = earthWeight / 6;   // Divide weight by 6

    printf("You only weigh %d pounds on the moon!", moonWeight);
    return 0;                              // Return to main()
}
```

The resulting output is identical to that of the previous program. Renaming the passed variable changes nothing.

3. The next example passes three variables—of three different types—to the called function. In the receiving function's parameter list, each of these variable types must be declared.

This program prompts users for three values in the main() function. The main() function then passes these variables to the receiving function, which calculates and prints values related to those passed variables. When the called function modifies a variable passed to the function, notice again that this does not affect the calling function's variable. When variables are passed by value, the value—not the variable itself—is passed:

```
/* Filename: C15PASS3.C
   Get grade information for a student */
#include <stdio.h>
main()
{
   char lgrade;                                    // Letter grade
   int  tests;                   // Number of tests not yet taken
   float average; // Student's average based on 4.0 scale

   printf("What letter grade do you want? ");
   scanf(" %c", &lgrade);
   printf("What is your current test average? ");
   scanf(" %f", &average);
   printf("How many tests do you have left? ");
   scanf(" %d", &tests);

   checkGrade(lgrade, average, tests);   // Call function
                       // and pass three variables by value
   return 0;
}


checkGrade(char lgrade, float average, int tests)
{
   switch (tests)
   {
     case (0): { printf("You will get your current grade \
                          of %c", lgrade);
                 break; }
     case (1): { printf("You still have time to bring your \
                          average ");
                 printf("of %.1f up. Study hard!", average);
                 break; }
     default:  { printf("Relax. You still have plenty of \
                          time.");
                 break; }
   }
   return 0;
}
```

Passing by Address

The previous section described passing arguments by value (or by copy).
This section describes how to pass arguments by address.

When you pass an argument (local variable) by address, the variable's address is sent to—and is assigned to—the receiving function's parameter. (If you pass more than one variable by address, each of their addresses is sent to—and is assigned to—the receiving function's parameters.)

Variable Addresses

All variables in memory (RAM) are stored at memory addresses (see Figure 15.2). If you want more information on the internal representation of memory, you should see Appendix A, "Memory Addressing, Binary, and Hexadecimal."

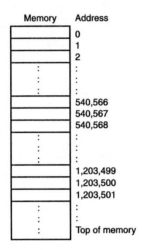

Memory	Address
	0
	1
	2
:	:
:	:
:	:
	540,566
	540,567
	540,568
:	:
:	:
:	:
	1,203,499
	1,203,500
	1,203,501
:	:
:	:
:	Top of memory

Figure 15.2: *Each memory content resides at a different address.*

When you tell C to define a variable (such as int i;), you are requesting C to find an unused place in memory and assign that place (or memory address) to i. When your program uses the variable called i, C knows to go to i's address and use whatever is there.

If you define five variables as follows

```
int i;
float x=9.8;
char ara[2] = {'A', 'B'};
int j=8, k=3;
```

C might arbitrarily place them in memory at the addresses shown in Figure 15.3.

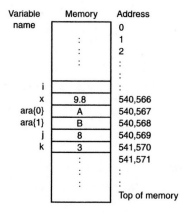

Figure 15.3: C might store the variables in these memory locations.

You don't know what is contained in the variable called i because you haven't put anything in it yet. Before you use i, you should initialize it with a value. (All variables—except character variables—usually take up more than one byte of memory.)

Analyzing a Sample Program

The address of the variable, not its value, is copied to the receiving function when you pass a variable by address. In C, all arrays are passed by address. (Actually, a copy of their address is passed, but you will understand this better when you learn more about arrays and pointers.) The following important rule holds true for programs that pass by address:

- Every time you pass a variable by address, if the receiving function changes the variable, it is changed also in the calling function.

Therefore, if you pass an array to a function and the function changes the array, those changes are still with the array when it returns to the calling function. Unlike passing by value, passing by address gives you the ability to change a variable in the called function and keep those changes in effect in the calling function. The following sample program should help to illustrate this concept:

```
/* Filename: C15ADD1.C

   Passing by address example */
#include <stdio.h>
main()
{
    char name[4]="ABC";
```

```
        changeIt(name);              // Passes by address because
                                     //        it is an array
        printf("%s \n", name);       // Called function can
                                     //           change array

        return 0;
    }


    changeIt(char c[4])              // You must tell the function
                                     // that c is an array
    {
        printf("%s \n", c);          // Print as it is passed
        strcpy(c, "USA");            // Change the array, both
                                     //        here and in main()

        return 0;
    }
```

Here is the output from this program:

```
ABC
USA
```

At this point, you should have no trouble understanding that the array is passed from main() to the function called changeIt(). Even though changeIt() calls the array c, it refers to the same array passed by the main() function (name).

Figure 15.4 shows how the array is passed. Although the address of the array—and not its value—is passed from name to c, both arrays are the same.

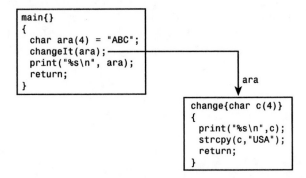

Figure 15.4: *Passing an array by address does not send the data value.*

Before going any further, a few additional comments are in order. Because the address of name is passed to the function—even though the array is called c in the receiving function—it is still the same array as name. Figure 15.5 shows how C accomplishes this at the memory-address level.

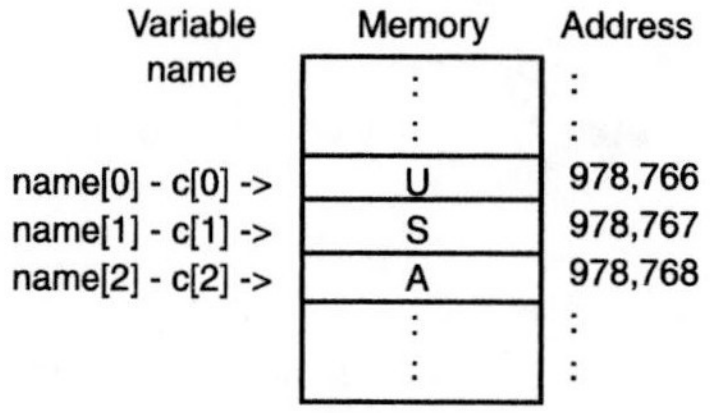

Variable name	Memory	Address
	:	:
	:	:
name[0] - c[0] ->	U	978,766
name[1] - c[1] ->	S	978,767
name[2] - c[2] ->	A	978,768
	:	:
	:	:

Figure 15.5: *The array being passed is the same array in both functions.*

The variable array is referred to as name in main() and as c in changeIt(). Because the address of name is copied to the receiving function, the variable gets changed no matter what it is called in either function. Because changeIt() changes the array, the array is changed also in main().

EXAMPLE

1. You can now use a function to fill an array with user input. The following function asks users for their first name in the function called getName(). As users type the name in the array, it is also entered in main()'s array. The main() function then passes the array to prName(), where it is printed. (If arrays were passed by value, this program would not work. Only the array value would be passed to the called functions.)

```
/* Filename: C15ADD2.C
   Get a name in an array, then print it using
   separate functions */
#include <stdio.h>
main()
{
    char name[25];
    getName(name);                      // Get the user's name
    printName(name);                    // Print the user's name
    return 0;
}

getName(char name[25])       // Pass the array by address
{
    printf("What is your first name? ");
    scanf(" %s", name);
    return 0;
}
```

```
printName(char name[25])
{
    printf("\n\n Here it is: %s", name);
    return 0;
}
```

When you pass an array, be sure to specify the array's type in the receiving function's parameter list. If the previous program declared the passed array with

```
getName(char name)
```

the function getName() would think it is being passed a single character variable, not a character array. You never need to put the array size in brackets. The following statement would also work as the first line of getName():

```
getName(char name[])
```

Most C programmers put the array size in the brackets even though the size is not needed.

2. Many programmers pass character arrays to functions in order to erase them. Here is a function called clearIt(). It expects two parameters: a character array and the total number of elements declared for that array. The array is passed by address (as are all arrays) and the number of elements, numEls, is passed by value (as are all nonarrays). When the function finishes, the array is cleared (that is, all its elements are reset to null zero). Subsequent functions that use it can then have an empty array:

```
clearIt(char ara[10], int numEls)
{
    int ctr;
    for (ctr=0; ctr<numEls; ctr++)
      { ara[ctr] = '\0'; }
    return 0;
}
```

The brackets after ara do not need to contain a number, as described in the previous example. The 10 in this example is simply a placeholder for the brackets. Any value (or no value) would work as well.

Passing Nonarrays by Address

You now should see the difference between passing variables by address and by value. Arrays can be passed by address, and nonarrays can be passed by value. You can override the by value default for nonarrays. This is helpful sometimes, but it is not always recommended because the called function can damage values in the calling function.

If you want a nonarray variable changed in a receiving function and also want the changes kept in the calling function, you must override the default and pass the variable by address. (You should understand this section better after you learn how arrays and pointers relate.) To pass a nonarray by address, you must do the following:

1. Precede the variable in the calling function with an ampersand (&).

2. Precede the variable in the receiving function with an asterisk (*), everywhere the variable appears.

This might sound strange to you (and it is, at this point). Few C programmers override the default of passing by address. When you learn about pointers later, you should have little need for this. Most C programmers don't like to clutter their code with these extra ampersands and asterisks, but they know they can do this if necessary.

The following examples demonstrate how to pass nonarray variables by address:

EXAMPLE

1. The following program passes a variable by address from main() to a function. The function changes it and returns to main(). Because the variable is passed by address, main() recognizes the new value:

```
/* Filename: C15ADD3.C
   Demonstrate passing nonarrays by address */ ·
#include <stdio.h>
main()
{
    int amt;

    amt = 100;                     // Assign a value in main()
    printf("In main(), amt is %d \n", amt);

    doFun(&amt);          // The & means pass it by address
    printf("After return, amt is %d in main() \n", amt);
    return 0;
}

doFun(int *amt)                         // Inform function of
                                        //  passing by address
{
    *amt = 85;                     // Assign new value to amt
    printf("In doFun(), amt is %d \n", *amt);
    return 0;
}
```

OUTPUT

The output from this program follows:

```
In main(), amt is 100
In doFun(), amt is 85
After return, amt is 85 in main()
```

Notice that amt changed in the called function. Because it was passed by address, it gets changed also in the calling function.

HOW scanf() PASSES VALUES

You can now understand some of the strangeness of the built-in scanf() function. The scanf() function passes arguments to its internal code. The arguments are control strings and variables that fill up with keyboard input.

Recall that you must put an ampersand (&) before each nonarray variable in the scanf() list. For example, to input three integers from the keyboard, you have to code scanf() as follows:

```
scanf("%d %d %d", &i1, &i2, &i3);
```

Think about what is happening. If you did not force these variables to be passed by address, the calling function would not be able to access the values typed from the keyboard. When a user types in values, the scanf() function fills its parameters with those typed values because you pass the variables by address. The calling program also recognizes those values because they get changed in both places.

No ampersand is needed in front of scanf() array variables. To get a name from the keyboard, you would type the following scanf() statement:

```
scanf(name);
```

The ampersand is not needed because all arrays are automatically passed by address. When scanf() gets the keyboard values into the array, the calling program (your program) recognizes them because the array is changed in both places.

2. You can use a function to get the user's keyboard values. The main() function recognizes those values as long as you pass them by address. The following program calculates the cubic feet in a swimming pool. In one function, it requests the width, length, and depth. In another function, it calculates the cubic feet of water. Finally, in a third function, it prints the answer. The main() function is clearly a controlling function, passing variables between these functions by address:

```
/* Filename: C15POOL.C
   Calculate the cubic feet in a swimming pool */
#include <stdio.h>
main()
{
    int length, width, depth, cubic;

    getValues(&length, &width, &depth);
    calcCubic(&length, &width, &depth, &cubic);
    printCubic(&cubic);
```

```
    return 0;
}

getValues(int *length, int *width, int *depth)
{
    printf("What is the pool's length? ");
    scanf(" %d", &*length);
    printf("What is the pool's width? ");
    scanf(" %d", &*width);
    printf("What is the pool's average depth? ");
    scanf(" %d", &*depth);
    return 0;
}

calcCubic(int *length, int *width, int *depth, int *cubic)
{
    /* This may look confusing, but you must
       precede each variable with an asterisk */
    *cubic = (*length) * (*width) * (*depth);
    return 0;
}

printCubic(int *cubic)
{
    printf("\nThe pool has %d cubic feet\n", *cubic);
    return 0;
}
```

The output follows:

```
What is the pool's length? 16
What is the pool's width? 32
What is the pool's average depth? 6
The pool has 3072 cubic feet
```

Notice the strange scanf() parameters. All variables in a function must be preceded with an asterisk if they are to be passed by address. Because scanf() requires an ampersand before its nonarray variables, this technique adds confusion to the scanf() statement. As you learn in a later chapter, & and * cancel each other. If you find yourself using scanf() in functions (on nonarray variables passed by address), you can omit &*. For example, the first scanf() could be rewritten as follows without any change in the program's output:

```
scanf(" %d", length);
```

What's Next

Whenever you pass values, you must ensure that they match in number and type. If you don't match them, you could have problems. For example, suppose you pass an array and a floating-point variable, but in the receiving function, you receive a floating-point variable followed by an array. The data is not getting to the receiving function properly because the parameter data types do not match the variables being passed. The next chapter shows you how to protect against such disasters by prototyping all your functions.

16

Returning Function Values

You know how to pass variables to functions in only one direction—a calling function passed data to a receiving function. You have yet to see how data is passed back from the receiving function to the calling function. When you pass variables by address, the data gets changed in both functions—but this is different from passing data back. This chapter focuses on writing function return values that improve your programming power.

After you learn to pass and return values, you need to *prototype* the functions you write—as well as C's built-in functions, such as printf() and scanf(). By prototyping your functions, you ensure the accuracy of passed and returned values.

This chapter teaches you the following topics:

- Returning values from functions
- Prototyping functions
- Header files

Function Return Values

Until now, all functions in this book have been *subroutines* or *subfunctions*. A C subroutine is a function that is called from another function, but it does not return any values. The difference between subroutines and functions is not as critical in C as it is in other languages. All functions, whether they are subroutines or functions that return values, are defined in the same way. You can pass variables to each of them, as you have seen throughout Part IV, "Variable Scope and Structuring Code."

Functions that return values offer you a new approach to programming. In addition to passing data one way, from calling to receiving function, you can pass data back from a receiving function to its calling function. When you want to return a value from a function to its calling function, put the return value after the `return` statement. To make the return value clearer, many programmers put parentheses around the return value, as shown in the following syntax:

```
return (return value);
```

CAUTION

Do not return global variables. There is no need to do it because their values are already known throughout the code.

EXAMPLE

The calling function must have a use for the return value. For example, suppose you wrote a function that calculated the average of any three integer variables passed to it. If you return the average, the calling function has to receive that return value. The following sample program helps to illustrate this principle:

```
/* Filename: C16AVG.C
   Calculates the average of three input values */
#include <stdio.h>
main()
{
    int num1, num2, num3;
    int avg;                    // Will hold the return value

    printf("Please type three numbers (such as 23, 54, 85) ");
    scanf(" %d, %d, %d", &num1, &num2, &num3);

    // Call the function, passing the numbers,
    // and accept the return value
    avg = calcAv(num1, num2, num3);
```

```
        printf("\n\nThe average is %d", avg);   // Print the
                                                 // return value

        return 0;
}


int calcAv(int num1, int num2, int num3)
{
        int localAvg;   // Holds the average for these numbers
        localAvg = (num1+num2+num3) / 3;

        return (localAvg);
}
```

OUTPUT

Here is a sample output from the program:

```
Please type three numbers (such as 23, 54, 85) 30, 40, 50
The average is 40
```

Study this program carefully. It is similar to many you have seen, but a few additional points should be considered now that the function returns a value. It may help to walk through this program a few lines at a time.

The first part of main() is similar to many programs you have seen. It declares its local variables: three for user input and one for the calculated average. The printf() and scanf() are familiar to you. The function call to calcAv() is also familiar; it passes three variables (num1, num2, and num3) by value to calcAv(). (If it passed them by address, an ampersand (&) would have to precede each argument, as discussed in the previous chapter.)

The receiving function, calcAv(), seems similar to others you have seen, except the first line, the function's definition line, has one addition—the int before its name. This is the type of the return value. You must always precede a function name with its return data type. If you do not specify a type, C assumes a type of int. Therefore, if this example had no return type, it would work just as well because C always assumes an int return type. Even main() assumes an int return data type, hence, the return 0; instead of just a return; statement without an integer return value.

You can also see that the return statement of calcAv() includes the return value, localAvg. This is the variable being sent back to the calling function, main(). You can return only a single variable to a calling function.

This introduces a rule for returning variables. Even though a function can receive more than one parameter, it can return only a single value to the calling function. If a receiving function will be modifying more than one value from the calling function, you must pass the parameters by address; you cannot return multiple values using a return statement.

After the receiving function, calcAv(), returns the value, main() must do something with that returned value. So far, you have seen function calls on lines by themselves. Notice in main() that the function call appears on the right side of the following assignment statement:

```
avg = calcAv(num1, num2, num3);
```

When the calcAv() function returns its value—the average of the three numbers—that value replaces the function call. If the average computed in calcAv() is 40, the C compiler "sees" the following statement in place of the function call:

```
avg = 40;
```

You typed a function call to the right of the equal sign, but the program replaces a function call with its return value when the return takes place. In other words, a function that returns a value becomes that value. You must put such a function anywhere you would put any variable or constant, usually to the right of an equal sign, or in an expression, or in printf(). The following is an incorrect way of calling calcAv():

```
calcAv(num1, num2, num3);
```

If you did this, C would have nowhere to put the return value of 40 (or whatever it happens to be).

CAUTION

Function calls that return values usually never appear on lines by themselves. Because the function call is replaced by the return value, you should do something with that return value (such as assign it to a variable or use it in an expression). Return values can be ignored, but doing so usually defeats the purpose of using them.

EXAMPLE

1. The following program passes a number to a function called doub(). The function doubles the number and returns the result:

```
/* Filename: C16DOUB.C
   Doubles the user's number */
#include <stdio.h>
main()
{
    int number;                      // Holds user's input
    int dNumber;        // Will hold double the user's input
    printf("What number do you want doubled? ");
    scanf(" %d", &number);

    dNumber = doub(number);          // Assign return value
    printf("%d doubled is %d", number, dNumber);
```

```
    return 0;
}

int doub(int num)
{
    int dNum;
    dNum = num * 2;                 // Double the number
    return (dNum);                  // Return the result
}
```

OUTPUT

The program produces output such as this:

```
What number do you want doubled? 5
5 doubled is 10
```

2. Function return values can be used anywhere constants, variables, and expressions can be used. The following program is similar to the last. The difference is in main().

   The function call is performed not on a line by itself, but from a printf(). This is a nested function call. You call the built-in function printf() using the return value from one of the program's functions named doub(). Because the call to doub() is replaced by its return value, the printf() has enough information to proceed as soon as doub() returns. This gives main() less overhead because it no longer needs a variable called dNumber, although you must use your own judgment as to whether this program is easier to maintain. Sometimes it is wise to include function calls within other expressions; other times it is clearer to call the function and assign its return value to a variable before using it:

```
/* Filename: C16DOUB2.C
   Doubles the user's number */
#include <stdio.h>
main()
{
    int number;                       // Holds user's input
    printf("What number do you want doubled? ");
    scanf(" %d", &number);

    // The third printf() parameter is
    // replaced with a return value
    printf("%d doubled is %d", number, doub(number));

    return 0;
}
```

```
int doub(int num)
{
    int dNum;
    dNum = num * 2;                     // Double the number
    return (dNum);                      // Return the result
}
```

3. The following program asks the user for a number. That number is
   then passed to a function called sum(), which adds the numbers from 1
   to that number. In other words, if the user types a 6, the function
   returns the result of the following calculation:

```
1 + 2 + 3 + 4 + 5 + 6
```

This is known as the sum of the digits calculation, and it is sometimes
used for depreciation in accounting.

```
/* Filename: C16SUMD.C
   Compute the sum of the digits */
#include <stdio.h>
main()
{
    int num, sumd;

    printf("Please type a number: ");
    scanf(" %d", &num);

    sumd = sum(num);
    printf("The sum of the digits is %d", sumd);
    return 0;
}

int sum(int num)
{
    int ctr;                           // Local loop counter
    int sumd=0;                        // Local to this function
    if (num <= 0)   // Check whether parameter is too small
        { sumd = num; }      // Returns parameter if too small
    else
        { for (ctr=1; ctr<=num; ctr++)
            { sumd += ctr; }
        }
    return(sumd);
}
```

Following is a sample output from this program:

```
Please type a number: 6
The sum of the digits is 21
```

4. The following program contains two functions that return values. The first function, maximum(), returns the larger of two numbers entered by the user. The second one, minimum(), returns the smaller:

```c
/* Filename: C16MINMX.C
   Finds minimum and maximum values in functions */
#include <stdio.h>
main()
{
    int num1, num2;                     // User's two numbers
    int min, max;

    printf("Please type two numbers (such as 46, 75) ");
    scanf(" %d, %d", &num1, &num2);

    max = maximum(num1, num2);     // Assign the return
    min = minimum(num1, num2);     // value of each
                                   // function to variables

    printf("The minimum number is %d \n", min);
    printf("The maximum number is %d \n", max);
    return 0;
}

int maximum(int num1, int num2)
{
    int max;                 // Local to this function only
    max = (num1 > num2) ? (num1) : (num2);
    return (max);
}

int minimum(int num1, int num2)
{
    int min;                 // Local to this function only
    min = (num1 < num2) ? (num1) : (num2);
    return (min);
}
```

Here is a sample output from this program:

```
Please type two numbers (such as 46, 75) 72, 55
The minimum number is 55
The maximum number is 72
```

If the user types the same number, `minimum` and `maximum` are the same.

These two functions can be passed to any two integer values. In such a simple example as this one, the user certainly already knows which number is lower or higher. The point of such an example is to show how to code return values. You might want to use similar functions in a more useful application, such as finding the highest paid employee from a payroll disk file.

Function Prototypes

The word *prototype* is sometimes defined as a model. In C, a function prototype models the actual function. Before completing your study of functions, parameters, and return values, you must understand how to prototype each function in your program.

You should prototype each function in your program. By prototyping, you inform C of the function's parameter types and its return value, if any. You do not always need to prototype functions, but it is always recommended. Sometimes, a prototype is mandatory before your functions can work properly.

A simple example should help to clarify the need for prototyping. The following simple program asks the user for a temperature in Celsius, and then converts it to Fahrenheit. The parameter and the return type are both floating-point. You know the return type is floating-point due to the word `float` before the `convert()` function's definition. See if you can follow this program. Other than the Celsius calculation, it is similar to others you have seen:

```c
/* Filename: C16TEMP.C
   Converts Celsius temperature to Fahrenheit */
#include <stdio.h>
main()
{
    float cTemp;                 // Holds Celsius temperature
                                        // from the user
    float fTemp;             // Holds converted temperature
    printf("What is the Celsius temperature to convert? ");
    scanf(" %f", &cTemp);
```

```
    fTemp = convert(cTemp);        // Convert the temperature


    printf("The Fahrenheit equivalent is %.1f", fTemp);
    return 0;
}


float convert(float cTemp)          // The return var and
                                    //   parameter are both
                                    // floating-point values
{
    float fTemp;                    // Local variable
    fTemp = cTemp * (9.0 / 5.0) + 32.0;
    return (fTemp);
}
```

If you run this program, your C compiler will refuse to compile it or you will get incorrect results, at best. Yet this program seems similar to many you have seen previously. The primary difference is the return type; when you return a data type that is not int, you must prototype the function to ensure that it works.

Although prototyping is not required for functions that return integers, you should prototype them as well. Taking this one step further, you should prototype all functions, whether they return a value or not.

To prototype a function, copy the function's definition line to the top of your program (immediately before or after the #include <stdio.h> line is fine). Place a semicolon at the end of it, and you have the prototype. The definition line (the function's first line) contains the return type, the function name, and the type of each argument, so the function prototype serves as a model of the function that will follow.

If a function does not return a value, or if that function has no arguments passed to it, you should still prototype it. Place the keyword void in place of the return type or the parameters. Even main() can be prototyped. The following listing shows the corrected version of the previous program—now with the prototype lines. Because there are two functions, main() and convert(), there are two prototypes:

```
/* Filename: C16TEMP2.C
    Converts Celsius to Fahrenheit */
#include <stdio.h>
void main(void);                // main()'s prototype
float convert(float cType);     // convert()'s prototype
```

```
     void main(void)                    // The function must match
                                        // its prototype
{
   float cTemp;              // Holds Celsius temperature
                                        // from the user
   float fTemp;              // Holds converted temperature
   printf("What is the Celsius temperature to convert? ");
   scanf(" %f", &cTemp);

   fTemp = convert(cTemp);   // Convert the temperature

   printf("The Fahrenheit equivalent is %.1f", fTemp);
   return 0;
}

float convert(float cTemp)       // The return var and
                                 //    parameter are both
                                 //    floating-point values

{
   float fTemp;                          // Local variable
   fTemp = cTemp * (9.0 / 5.0) + 32.0;
   return (fTemp);
}
```

All functions must match their prototypes. Because main()'s prototype
includes the two void keywords, which means there are no return types
and no arguments to main(), the first line of main() must also have voids.
But you have to list only the data types of each parameter—not the individual parameter names—in the parentheses of the function's prototype.

You can look at a statement and tell whether it is a prototype or a function
definition (the function's first line) by the semicolon at the end. If the semicolon does not appear, C assumes the statement is the first line in a new
function, and compiler errors will likely occur until the programmer adds
the semicolon.

Prototype for Safety

Prototyping protects you from programming mistakes. Suppose you write a
function that expects two arguments: an integer followed by a floating-point
value. Here is the definition line of such a function:

```
myFun(int num, float amount)
```

What if you passed incorrect data types to `myFun()`? If you were to call this function by passing it two constants, a floating-point followed by an integer, as in

```
myFun(23.43, 5);          /* Call the myFun() function */
```

the function would not receive correct parameters. It is expecting an integer followed by a floating-point, but you did the opposite and sent it a floating-point followed by an integer.

Despite the power of your C compiler, you do not get an error message if you do this. C enables you to pass such incorrect values if you don't prototype first. By prototyping such a function at the top of the program, such as

```
void myFun(int num, float amount);       // Prototype
```

you tell the compiler to check this function for accuracy. You inform the compiler to expect nothing after the `return` statement (due to the `void` keyword) and to expect an integer followed by a floating-point in the parentheses.

If you break any of the prototype's rules, the compiler informs you of the problem and you can correct it. Without the prototype, the program would compile but the results would be wrong. Such a program would be difficult to debug, at best.

Prototype All Functions

You should prototype every function in your program, even `main()` as the previous example shows. As just described, the prototype defines (for the rest of the program) which functions follow, their return types, and their parameter types. You should also prototype C's built-in functions, such as `printf()` and `scanf()`.

Think about how you would prototype `printf()`. You don't always pass it the same types of parameters because you print different data with each `printf()`. Prototyping functions that you write is easy: The prototype is basically the first line in the function. Prototyping functions that you do not write may seem difficult, but it isn't—you have already done it with every program in this book.

The designers of C realized that all functions should be prototyped. They realized also that you cannot prototype built-in functions, so they did it for you and placed the prototypes in header files on your disk. You have been including the `printf()` and `scanf()` prototypes in each program with the following statement:

```
#include <stdio.h>
```

Inside the `stdio.h` file is a prototype of many of C's input and output functions. By having prototypes of these functions, you ensure that they cannot be passed bad values. If someone attempts to pass incorrect values, C catches the problem.

Prototyping is the primary reason why you should always include the matching header file when you use C's built-in functions. The `strcpy()` function you saw in previous chapters requires the following line:

```
#include <string.h>
```

This is the header file for the `strcpy()` function. Without it, the program might or might not work, depending on how careful you are with the data you pass to `strcpy()`. It is best to be safe and prototype. If you want values other than `int` to be returned from a function, a prototype is required.

EXAMPLE

1. You should prototype all programs, even those with only a single `main()` function. The following program includes two prototypes: one for `main()` and an included header file for `printf()` and `scanf()`:

```
/* Filename: C16PRO1.C
   Calculates sales tax on a sale */
#include <stdio.h>            // Prototype built-in functions
void main(void);                         // Prototype main()
void main(void)
{

    float totalSale;
    float taxRate = .07;                 // Assume 7% tax rate

    printf("What is the total sale? ");
    scanf(" %f", &totalSale);

    totalSale += (taxRate * totalSale);
    printf("The total sale is %.2f", totalSale);
    return 0;
}
```

2. The following program asks the user for a number in `main()`, and passes that number to `ascii()`. The `ascii()` function returns the ASCII character that matches the user's number. This illustrates a character return type. Functions can return any data type:

```
/* Filename: C16ASC.C
   Prints the ASCII character of the user's number */
/* Prototypes follow */
#include <stdio.h>
char ascii(int num);

main()
```

```
{
    int num;
    char ascChar;

    printf("Enter an ASCII number? ");
    scanf(" %d", &num);

    ascChar = ascii(num);
    printf("The ASCII character for %d is %c", num, ascChar);
    return 0;
}

char ascii(int num)
{
    char ascChar;
    ascChar = (char)num;
    return (ascChar);
}
```

The output from this program follows:

```
Enter an ASCII number? 67
The ASCII character for 67 is C
```

3. Suppose you need to calculate net pay for a company. You find yourself multiplying the hours worked by the hourly pay, then deducting taxes to compute the net pay. The following program includes a function that does this for you. It requires three arguments: the hours worked, the hourly pay, and the tax rate (as a floating-point decimal, such as .30 for 30%). The function returns the net pay. The main() calling program tests the function by sending three different payroll values to the function and printing the three return values:

```
/* Filename: C16NPAY.C
   Defines a function that computes net pay */
#include <stdio.h>
void main(void);
float netpayfun(float hours, float rate, float taxrate);

void main(void)
{
    float netPay;

    netPay = netpayfun(40.0, 3.50, .20);
    printf("The pay for 40 hours at $3.50/hr., and a \
```

```
                    20% tax rate is:");
        printf("$%.2f", netPay);

        netPay = netpayfun(50.0, 10.00, .30);
        printf("The pay for 50 hours at $10.00/hr., and a \
                30% tax rate is:");
        printf("$%.2f", netPay);

        netPay = netpayfun(10.0, 5.00, .10);
        printf("The pay for 10 hours at $5.00/hr., and a \
                10% tax rate is:");
        printf("$%.2f", netPay);

        return 0;
}

float netpayfun(float hours, float rate, float taxrate)
{
    float grossPay, taxes, netPay;
    grossPay = (hours * rate);
    taxes = (taxrate * grossPay);
    netPay = (grossPay - taxes);
    return (netPay);
}
```

What's Next

You learned how to build your own collection of functions. When you write a function, you might want to use it in more than one program—there is no need to reinvent the wheel. Many programmers write useful functions and use them in more than one program. The rest of this book incorporates concepts presented in this part to take advantage of separate, modular functions and local data. You are ready to learn more about how C performs input and output. The next chapter teaches you the theory behind I/O in C, and introduces more built-in functions.

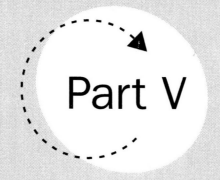

Part V

Standard Input, Output, and Intrinsic Functions

Device and Character I/O

String and Numeric Functions

17

Device and Character I/O

Unlike many programming languages, C contains no input or output commands. C is an extremely *portable* language, meaning that a C program compiled and run on one computer can compile and run also on another computer. Most incompatibilities between computers reside in their input/output (I/O) mechanics. Each different device requires a different method of performing I/O. By putting all I/O capabilities in common functions supplied with each computer's compiler—and not in C statements—the designers of C ensured that programs were not tied to specific hardware for input and output. Your Windows programming language, such as Visual C++'s C compiler, offers specific functions that mimic and build upon many of the fundamental I/O functions that you learn here. Keep in mind as you learn this chapter's character-based I/O functions that they form the basis for all I/O you will subsequently write, no matter which environment you write for. I/O should be simple once you know the basics.

This chapter teaches you the following topics:

- Stream and character I/O
- Buffered and non-buffered I/O
- Standard I/O
- Redirecting I/O
- Printing formatting output

Character Stream I/O

C views all input and output as streams of characters. Whether your program gets input from the keyboard, a disk file, a modem, or a mouse, C sees only a stream of characters. C does not "know" or "care" what type of device is supplying the input. C lets the operating system take care of the device specifics. The designers of C want your programs to operate on characters of data without regard to whatever physical method is taking place.

This stream I/O means that the functions you use to get input from the keyboard can be used to get input also from the modem or any other input device. You can use the same functions to write to a disk file, a printer, or the screen. You must have some way of routing that stream input or output to the proper device, but each program's I/O functions work in a similar manner.

THE NEWLINE CHARACTER: \n

Portability is the key to C's success. Few companies have the resources to rewrite every program they use when they change computer equipment. They need a programming language that works on many platforms (hardware combinations). C achieves true portability better than almost all other programming languages.

It is because of portability that C uses the generic newline character, \n, instead of the specific carriage return and line feed sequences that other languages use. This is also why C uses \t for tab and all the other control characters utilized in I/O functions.

If C relied on a specific ASCII code to represent these special characters, your programs would not be portable. Suppose you wrote a C program on one computer, and used a carriage return value such as 12—but 12 may not be the carriage return value on another type of computer.

By using the newline character and the other control characters available in C, you ensure that your program works on any computer on which it is compiled. The specific compilers substitute their computer's actual codes for the control codes in your programs.

Standard Devices

Table 17.1 shows a listing of standard I/O devices. C always assumes that input comes from stdin, or the *standard input device*. This is usually the keyboard, although you can reroute this default. C assumes that all output goes to stdout, or the *standard output device*. There is nothing magic in the words "stdin" and "stdout," but many people see these words for the first time only in the C language.

Table 17.1: Standard I/O devices in C.

I/O Device	C Name
Screen	stdout
Keyboard	stdin
Printer	stdprn
Serial port	stdaux
Error messages	stderr
Disk files	none

✔ If you want to route I/O to a second printer or serial port, read Chapter 24, "Simple C File Processing," page 418.

If you program on a mainframe, you must use JCL (Job Control Language) to route C's standard devices, such as stdin and stdout, to your preferred local or remote I/O devices. If you are new to programming, you may have to contact your system administrator to help you with setting up a JCL file that connects C programs to the appropriate I/O devices.

If you write for Windows, you'll use built-in Windows functions, ones that are generally specific to the compiler you use, for producing output in the windowed environment. In spite of the non-standard windowing functions available for I/O, all of the functions attempt to maintain C's goal of the device independence that this chapter stresses so much. In addition, you'll understand how to control the Windows functions better if you understand the low-level functions explained here.

Printing Formatted Output

It is easy to send program output to the printer using the fprintf() function. The format of fprintf() follows:

```
fprintf(device, controlString [, one or more values]);
```

You might notice that the format of fprintf() is similar to that of printf(). The only difference between fprintf() and printf() (besides the names) is that fprintf() requires a *device* as its first argument. Usually, this device is the standard printer, stdprn. In Chapter 24, "Simple C File Processing," you learn how to write formatted data to a disk file by using fprintf().

CAUTION

Some compilers, despite following the ANSI C standard, do not allow fprintf() to print to a printer using the stdprn device. If yours does not, you need to learn more about file I/O. See Part VII, "Advanced C," to learn how to route output to the printer using a file pointer.

The following program asks users for their first and last names. It then prints the full name—last name first—to the printer:

```
/* Filename: C17FPR1.C
   Prints a name on the printer */
#include <stdio.h>
main()
{
    char first[20];
    char last[20];

    printf("What is your first name? ");
    scanf(" %s", first);

    printf("What is your last name? ");
    scanf(" %s", last);

    /* Send names to the printer */
    fprintf(stdprn, "In a phone book, your name");
    fprint(stdprn, " looks like this: \n");
    fprintf(stdprn, " %s, %s", last, first);
    return 0;
}
```

Character I/O Functions

Because all I/O is actually character I/O, C provides many functions that perform character input and output. The printf() and scanf() functions, however, are not character I/O functions. The printf() and scanf() functions are called *formatted I/O functions* because they give you formatting control (using conversion characters) over your input and output.

There is nothing wrong with using printf() for formatted output, but scanf() has many problems, some of which you have seen. In this section, you learn how to write your own character input routines that replace scanf(). To prepare you for the upcoming chapters on disk files, you also learn how to use character output functions. These functions are generally easier to use than scanf() and printf() because they don't require formatting codes.

The `getc()` and `putc()` Functions

The most fundamental character I/O functions are getc() and putc(). The putc() function writes a single character to the standard output device, which is the screen, unless you redirect it from your operating system. The getc() function inputs a single character from the standard input device, which is the keyboard, unless you redirect it.

The format for getc() follows:

```
intVar = getc(device);
```

Don't let the integer *intVar* confuse you. Even though getc() is a character function, you use an integer variable to store the getc() input value. getc() returns a –1 when an end-of-file condition occurs. If you are using getc() to read information from a disk file, the –1 is read when the end of the file is reached. If you used a character variable, the –1 would be interpreted as 255. You learn more about end-of-file conditions in Chapter 24. As with all integer variables, you can use the integer input value as though it were a character.

The getc() *device* can be any C standard input device. If you are getting character input from the keyboard, use stdin as the *device*. If you initialize your modem and want to receive characters from it, use stdaux for the *device*.

The format of putc() follows:

```
putc(intVal, device);
```

The *intVal* can be an integer variable, expression, or constant. You output character data with putc(). The *device* can be any standard output C device. To write a character to your printer, use stdprn for the *device*.

NOTE

Most of the character I/O functions, including getc() and putc(), are actually called *macros*. These are not true functions, but rather a form of preprocessor directives. Most C programmers program for years and never notice the difference, and you probably won't either. As a precaution, however, be sure you do not include an expression in putc(), such as putc(mychar++);. A macro might not evaluate this properly.

EXAMPLE

1. The following program asks users for their initials, one character at a time. Notice that the program uses both printf() and putc(). The printf() is still useful for formatted output, such as messages to the user. Writing individual characters is best achieved with putc().

   The program must call two getc() functions for each character typed. When you answer a getc() prompt, by typing a character followed by an Enter keypress, C sees that input as a stream of two characters. The getc() first gets the letter you typed, and then it gets the \n (newline, supplied to C when you press Enter). The following examples correct this double-getc() problem:

```
/* Filename: C17CH1.C
   Introduces getc() and putc() */
#include <stdio.h>
main()
{
    int inChar;                      // Holds incoming initial
    char first, last;                // Holds converted first
                                     //   and last initial

    printf("What is your first name initial? ");
    inChar = getc(stdin);            // Wait for first initial
    first = inChar;
    inChar = getc(stdin);                     // Ignore newline

    printf("What is your last name initial? ");

    inChar = getc(stdin);            // Wait for last initial
    last = inChar;
    inChar = getc(stdin);                     // Ignore newline

    printf("\nHere they are: \n");
    putc(first, stdout);
    putc(last, stdout);
    return 0;
}
```

Here is the output from this program:

```
What is your first name initial? G
What is your last name initial? P

Here they are:
GP
```

2. You can add carriage returns to better space the output. To print the two initials on two separate lines, use putc() to send a newline character to stdout. The following program does this:

```
/* Filename: C17CH2.C
   Introduces getc() and putc() and uses
   putc() to output newline */
#include <stdio.h>
main()
{
```

```
        int inChar;                    // Holds incoming initial
        char first, last;                 // Holds converted first
                                          //   and last initial

        printf("What is your first name initial? ");
        inChar = getc(stdin);          // Wait for first initial
        first = inChar;
        inChar = getc(stdin);                 // Ignore newline

        printf("What is your last name initial? ");

        inChar = getc(stdin);          // Wait for last initial
        last = inChar;
        inChar = getc(stdin);                 // Ignore newline

        printf("\nHere they are: \n");
        putc(first, stdout);
        putc('\n', stdout);            // A newline is output
        putc(last, stdout);
        return 0;
    }
```

3. It may be clearer to define the newline character as a constant. At the top of the program, you could have

```
#define NEWLINE '\n'
```

The putc() could then read

```
putc(NEWLINE, stdout);
```

Some programmers prefer to define their character formatting constants and refer to them by name. You can decide whether you think this is clearer or whether you want to continue using the \n character constant in putc().

The getchar() and putchar() Functions

When you perform character I/O, the getchar() and putchar() functions are easier to use than getc() and putc() are. The getchar() and putchar() functions are identical to getc() and putc(), except you do not specify a device because they assume that the standard input and output devices are stdin and stdout (typically, the screen and the keyboard). In the following,

```
inChar=getc(stdin);
```

is identical to

```
c1
```

```
inChar=getchar();
```

and

```
putc(var, stdout);
```

is identical to

```
putchar(var);
```

The `getchar()` and `putchar()` functions are two of the most frequently used character I/O functions in C. Most I/O is performed on the keyboard and screen, and these two devices are generally routed to `stdin` and `stdout` by the operating system, unless you redirect them.

The `getchar()` and the `getc()` functions are both *buffered* input functions. That is, as you type characters, the data goes to a buffer rather than immediately to your program. The buffer is a section of memory managed by C (and has nothing to do with some computers' *typeahead buffers*).

Figure 17.1 shows you how this works. When your program gets to a `getc()` or a `getchar()`, the program temporarily waits as you type the input. The program does not see the characters because they are going to the buffer in memory. There is no limit to the size of the buffer; it keeps filling up with input until you press Enter. Pressing the Enter key signals the computer to release the buffer to your program.

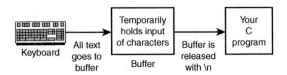

Figure 17.1: *The* `getc()` *and* `getchar()` *input goes to a buffer, where it is held until you press Enter.*

Most multiuser computers and windowed environments will buffer all input. Most PCs allow either buffered or nonbuffered input. The `getch()` function (shown later in this chapter) is nonbuffered. With `getc()` and `getchar()`, all input is buffered, and this affects the timing of your program's input. Your program receives no characters from a `getchar()` or `getc()` until you press Enter. Suppose that you ask a question such as

```
Do you want to see the report again (Y/N)?
```

and use `getchar()` for input. If the user presses a Y, the program does not know this until the user presses Enter, too. The Y and Enter key-presses are sent, one character at a time, to the program, where the input is processed. If you want immediate response to a user's typing (such as `Inkey$` does, if you are familiar with QBasic), you must use `getch()`.

TIP

By using buffered input, the user can type a string of characters in response to repeated getc() requests, and correct the input with the Backspace key before pressing Enter. If the input is non-buffered, the Backspace becomes just one more character of data.

EXAMPLE

1. The following sample program illustrates getchar() and putchar(). The first getchar() gets a character from the keyboard; a second one gets the newline character produced when the user presses Enter. The putchar() echoes the typed character back to the screen. You might be able to see from this program why getchar() and putchar() are called *mirror-image functions*:

```
/* Filename: C17GPC.C
   Illustrates simple getchar() and putchar() */
#include <stdio.h>
main()
{
    int myChar;                        // Must be integer

    printf("Please type a character... ");
    myChar = getchar();                // Get the character
    getchar();                         // Discard the newline

    printf("You typed this: ");
    putchar(myChar);
    return 0;
}
```

This program must discard the newline character. It could have done so by assigning the input character—from getchar()—to an extra variable, as previous examples have done. Because we know that the user must press Enter after typing a character, we can ignore the second return value by not assigning getchar() to anything. You know the user must press Enter (to end the input), so it is all right to discard it with an unused getchar() function call.

2. The scanf() function has limited use when inputting strings such as names and sentences. The scanf() function allows only one word to be entered at a time. If you ask users for their full names with these lines,

```
printf("What are your first and last names? ");
scanf(" %s", names);           /* Get the name into the
                                  names character array */
```

the array called names would receive only the first name; scanf()
ignores all data to the right of the first space.

Using getchar(), you can build an input function that does not have a
single-word limitation. When you want to get a string of characters
from users, such as their first and last names, you can call the
getInStr() function shown in the next program:

```c
/* Filename: C17IN.C
   Program that builds an input string array
   using getchar() */
#include <stdio.h>
#define MAX 25                      // Size of character
                                    // array to be typed in
void main(void);
void getInStr(char str[], int len);


void main(void)
{
    char inputStr[MAX];   // Keyboard input will fill this
    printf("What is your full name? ");
    getInStr(inputStr, MAX);     // String from keyboard
    printf("After return, your name is %s", inputStr);
    return 0;
}

/***********************************************************
The following function requires that a string and the
maximum length of the string be passed to it. It accepts
input from the keyboard, and sends keyboard input into
the string. Upon return, the calling routine has access
to the string.
***********************************************************/
void getInStr(char str[], int len)
{
    int i=0, inputChar;        // Index and character typed
    inputChar = getchar(); // Get next character in string
    while (i<(len-1) && (inputChar!='\n'))
        {
            str[i] = inputChar;        // Build the string, one
                                       //    character at a time
            i++;
            inputChar = getchar();            // Get the next
                                       //    character in the string
        }
```

```
    str[i]='\0';         // Make the char array into a string
    return 0;
}
```

The `main()` function defines an array and prompts the user for a name. After the prompt, the program calls the `getInStr()` function and uses `getchar()` to build the input array, one character at a time. The function keeps looping, using the `while` loop, until the user presses Enter (signaled by the newline character, `\n`) or the maximum number of characters are typed.

You might want to use this function in your own programs. Be sure to pass it a character array and an integer that holds the maximum array size (you don't want the input string to be longer than the character array that holds the string). When control returns to `main()`—or to whichever function called `getInStr()`—the array has the user's full input, spaces and all.

NOTE

The loop checks for `len-1` to save room for the null terminating zero at the end of the input string.

---

3. Because the `getchar()` function is used frequently for building strings (as the last example showed), many programmers have chosen to insert it directly inside the `while` test.

   Here is a rewritten version of the `getInStr()` function shown in the last example. Notice that by putting the `getchar()` directly inside the `while` conditional test, you streamline the function. The `while` conditional test takes a little more room, but the improved efficiency is worth it. This is a common input procedure, and you should become familiar with seeing `getchar()` inside tests such as this. At first it may seem awkward and cumbersome, but many C programmers choose to use it because it gives them greater control over user input.

```
void getInStr(char str[], int len)
{
    int i=0, inputChar;         // Index and character typed
    // Get next character in string
    while (i<(len-1) && ((inputChar=getchar()) != '\n') )
      {
          str[i] = inputChar;         // Build the string, one
                                      // character at a time
          i++;
      }
    str[i]='\0';         // Make the char array into a string
```

```
        return 0;
}
```

The getch() and putch() Functions

The getch() and putch() functions are slightly different than the previous character I/O functions. Their formats are similar to getchar() and putchar(); they both assume that stdin and stdout are the standard input and output devices, and you cannot specify other devices (unless you redirect them with your operating system). The format of getch() and putch() follows:

intVar = getch();

and

putch(*intVar*);

The getch() and putch() functions are not ANSI C standard functions, but they are available on a large number of compilers and well worth mentioning. getch() and putch() are non-buffered functions. However, many multi-user computer systems buffer getch(), even though the function was not designed for buffered input. The putch() character output function is a mirror-image of getch(); it is a nonbuffered output function. Because almost every output device (except screens and modems) are inherently buffered, putch() effectively does the same thing as putc().

Another difference between getch() and the other character input functions is that getch() does not echo the input characters onscreen as it receives them. When you type characters in response to getchar(), you see the characters as you type them (as they are sent to the buffer). If you want to display onscreen the characters received by getch(), you must follow getch() with putch(). It is handy to echo the characters onscreen so that users can verify what they typed.

Both getch() and putch() assume that stdin and stdout are the standard input and output devices. When you want your program to respond immediately to keyboard input, use getch(). Some programmers want to make users press Enter after answering a prompt or selecting from a menu. They feel that buffered input gives users more time to decide if they really want to give that answer; users can press Backspace and correct the input before pressing Enter.

Other programmers like to "grab" the user's single-character answer (such as a menu response) and act on it immediately. They feel that pressing Enter is an added and unneeded burden for the user. The choice is yours. You should understand both buffered and non-buffered input, so you can use either one.

TIP

Although getche() is not an ANSI C standard function, you can use it on most computer systems. The getche() function is a non-buffered input function identical to getch(), except the input characters are echoed (displayed) to the screen as the user types them. Using getche() instead of getch() sometimes keeps you from having to echo the user's input to the screen.

EXAMPLE

1. The following program uses the getch() and putch() functions. The user is asked to enter five letters. These five letters are added to the character array named letters using a for loop. As you run this program, notice that the characters are not echoed to the screen as you type them. As you type the characters, the program receives each character, adds it to the array, and loops again, because getch() is non-buffered. (If this were buffered input, the program would not loop through the five iterations until you pressed Enter.)

A second loop uses putch() to print the five letters. A third loop uses putc() to print the five letters to the printer:

```c
/* Filename: C17GCH1.C
   Uses getch() and putch() for input and output */
#include <stdio.h>
#include <conio.h>
main()
{
   int ctr;                         // The for loop counter
   char letters[5];    /* Holds five input characters. No
                           room is needed for the null zero
                           because this array will never be
                           treated like a string.         */
   printf("Please type five letters... \n");
   for (ctr=0; ctr<5; ctr++)
     {
        letters[ctr] = getch();      // Add input to array
     }
   for (ctr=0; ctr<5; ctr++)  // Print them to the screen
     {
        putch(letters[ctr]);
     }
   for (ctr=0; ctr<5; ctr++) // Print them to the printer
     {
        putc(letters[ctr], stdprn);
     }
   return 0;
}
```

When you run this program, don't press Enter after typing the five letters. The loop ends automatically after the fifth letter (due to the for loop). This is possible only because of the non-buffered input allowed with getch().

What's Next

Although the methods of character I/O are primitive, their flexibility enables you to build on them and create your own input functions. One of the most often used C functions, a string-building character I/O function, was demonstrated in this chapter (the C17IN.C program). The next chapter introduces new character and string functions, including string I/O functions. The string I/O functions build on the principles presented here. You might be surprised at the extensive character and string manipulation functions available in the C language.

18

String and Numeric Functions

C provides many built-in functions in addition to the printf(), scanf(), and strcpy() functions you have seen so far throughout the book. These built-in functions increase your productivity and save you programming time. You don't need to write as much code because the built-in functions perform many useful tasks for you.

This chapter teaches you the following topics:

- Character conversion functions
- Character and string testing functions
- String manipulation functions
- String I/O functions
- Mathematic, trigonometric, and logarithmic functions

Character Functions

This section explores many of the character functions available in ANSI C. Generally, you pass character arguments to the functions, and the functions return values that you can store or print. By using these functions, you off-load much of your work to C and let it perform the more tedious manipulations of character and string data.

Character Testing Functions

Several functions test for certain characteristics of your character data. You can test to see if your character data is alphabetic, digital, uppercase, lowercase, and much more. You must pass a character variable or constant argument to the function (by placing the argument in the function parentheses) when you call it. These functions all return a True or False result, so you can test their return values inside an `if` statement or a `while` loop.

NOTE

All character functions presented in this section are prototyped in the `ctype.h` header file. Be sure to include `ctype.h` at the top of any program that uses them.

Alphabetic and Digital Testing

The following functions test for alphabetic conditions:

- `isalpha(c)`: Returns True (nonzero) if c is an uppercase or lowercase letter. Returns False (zero) if c is not a letter.

- `islower(c)`: Returns True (nonzero) if c is a lowercase letter. Returns False (zero) if c is not a lowercase letter.

- `isupper(c)`: Returns True (nonzero) if c is an uppercase letter. Returns False (zero) if c is not an uppercase letter.

Remember that any nonzero value is True in C, and zero is always False. If you use the return values of these functions in a relational test, the True return value is not always 1 (it can be any nonzero value), but it is always considered True for the test.

The following functions test for digits:

- `isdigit(c)`: Returns True (nonzero) if c is a digit 0 through 9. Returns False (zero) if c is not a digit.

NOTE

Although some character functions test for digits, the arguments are still character data and cannot be used in mathematical calculations, unless you calculate using the ASCII values of characters.

- isxdigit(c): Returns True (nonzero) if c is any of the hexadecimal digits 0 through 9 or A, B, C, D, E, F, a, b, c, d, e, or f. Returns False (zero) if c is anything else. (See Appendix A, "Memory Addressing, Binary, and Hexadecimal," for more information on the hexadecimal numbering system.)

The following function tests for numeric or alphabetical arguments:

- isalnum(c): Returns True (nonzero) if c is a digit 0 through 9 or an alphabetic character (either uppercase or lowercase). Returns False (zero) if c is not a digit or a letter.

CAUTION

You can pass to these functions only a character value or an integer value holding the ASCII value of a character. You cannot pass an entire character array to character functions. If you want to test the elements of a character array, you must pass the array one element at a time.

EXAMPLE

1. The following program asks users for their initials. If a user types anything but alphabetic characters, the program displays an error and asks again:

```
/* Filename: C18INI.C
   Asks for first initial and tests
   to ensure that it is correct */
#include <stdio.h>
#include <ctype.h>
main()
{
    char initial;
    printf("What is your first initial? ");
    scanf(" %c", &initial);

    while (! isalpha(initial))
      {
        printf("\nThat was not a valid initial! \n");
        printf("\nWhat is your first initial? ");
        scanf(" %c", &initial);
      }

    printf("\nThanks!");
    return 0;
}
```

This use of the not operator (!) is quite clear. The program continues to loop while the entered character is not alphabetic.

Special Character Testing Functions

A few character functions become useful when you need to read from a disk file, a modem, or another operating system device that you route input from. These functions are not used as much as the character functions you saw in the last section, but they can be useful for testing specific characters for readability.

The remaining character testing functions follow:

- `iscntrl(c)`: Returns True (nonzero) if c is a *control character* (any character from the ASCII table numbered 0 through 31). Returns False (zero) if c is not a control character.

- `isgraph(c)`: Returns True (nonzero) if c is any printable character (a non-control character) except a space. Returns False (zero) if c is a space or anything other than a printable character.

- `isprint(c)`: Returns True (nonzero) if c is a printable character (a non-control character) from ASCII 32 to ASCII 127, including a space. Returns False (zero) if c is not a printable character.

- `ispunct(c)`: Returns True (nonzero) if c is any punctuation character (any printable character other than a space, a letter, or a digit). Returns False (zero) if c is not a punctuation character.

- `isspace(c)`: Returns True (nonzero) if c is a space, newline (\n), carriage return (\r), tab (\t), or vertical tab (\v) character. Returns False (zero) if c is anything else.

Character Conversion Functions

Two remaining character functions can be very handy. Rather than test characters, these functions change characters to their lowercase or uppercase equivalents:

- `tolower(c)`: Converts c to lowercase. Nothing is changed if you pass `tolower()` a lowercase letter or a non-alphabetic character.

- `toupper(c)`: Converts c to uppercase. Nothing is changed if you pass `toupper()` an uppercase letter or a non-alphabetic character.

These functions return their changed character values. They are very useful for user input. Suppose you are asking users a yes-or-no question, such as the following:

```
Do you want to print the checks (Y/N)?
```

Before knowing `toupper()` and `tolower()`, you would need to check for both a *Y* and a *y* before printing the checks. Instead of testing for both conditions, you can convert the character to uppercase, and test for a *Y*.

EXAMPLE

1. Here is a program that prints an appropriate message if the user is a girl or a boy. The program tests for *G* and *B* after converting the user's input to uppercase. No check for lowercase needs to be done.

```c
/* Filename: C18GB.C
   Tests whether the user typed a G or a B */
#include <stdio.h>
#include <ctype.h>
main()
{
    char ans;                          // Holds user's response
    printf("Are you a girl or a boy (G/B)? ");
    ans=getchar();                              // Get answer
    getchar();                              // Discard newline

    ans = toupper(ans);      // Convert answer to uppercase
    switch (ans)
    {   case ('G'): { printf("You look pretty today!\n");
                      break; }
        case ('B'): { printf("You look handsome today!\n");
                      break; }
        default :   { printf("Your answer makes no sense!\n");
                      break; }
    }
    return 0;
}
```

OUTPUT

Here is the output from the program:

```
Are you a girl or a boy (G/B)? B
You look handsome today!
```

String Functions

Some of the most powerful built-in C functions are the string functions. They perform much of the tedious work for which you have been writing code so far, such as inputting strings from the keyboard and comparing strings.

As with the character functions, there is no need to "reinvent the wheel" by writing code when built-in functions do the same task. Use these functions as much as possible.

Now that you have a good grasp of the foundations of C, you can master the string functions. They enable you to concentrate on your program's primary purpose, rather than spend time coding your own string functions.

Useful String Functions

You can use a handful of useful string functions for string testing and conversion. You have already seen (in earlier chapters) the strcpy() string function, which copies a string of characters into a character array.

NOTE

All string functions in this section are prototyped in the string.h header file. Be sure to include string.h at the top of any program that uses the string functions.

Some string functions that test or manipulate strings follow:

- strcat(*s1*, *s2*): Concatenates (merges) the *s2* string to the end of the *s1* character array. The *s1* array must have enough reserved elements to hold both strings.

- strcmp(*s1*, *s2*): Compares the *s1* string with the *s2* string on an alphabetical, element-by-element basis. If *s1* alphabetizes before *s2*, strcmp() returns a negative value. If *s1* and *s2* are the same strings, strcmp() returns 0. If *s1* alphabetizes after *s2*, strcmp() returns a positive value.

- strlen(*s1*): Returns the length of *s1*. Remember, the length of a string is the number of characters up to—but not including—the null zero. The number of characters defined for the character array has nothing to do with the length of the string.

TIP

Before using strcat() to concatenate strings, use strlen() to ensure that the target string (the string being concatenate to) is large enough to hold both strings.

String I/O Functions

In the previous few chapters, you have used a character input function, getchar(), to build input strings. Now you can begin to use the string input and output functions. Although the goal of the string-building functions has been to teach you the specifics of the language, these string I/O functions are much easier to use than writing a character input function is.

The string input and output functions are listed as follows:

- gets(*s*): Stores input from stdin (usually directed to the keyboard) into the string named *s*.

- puts(*s*): Outputs the *s* string to stdout (usually directed to the screen by the operating system).

- fgets(s, *len*, *dev*): Stores input from the standard device specified by *dev* (such as stdin or stdaux) in the s string. If more than *len* characters are input, fgets() discards them.

- fputs(s, *dev*): Outputs the s string to the standard device specified by *dev*.

These four functions make the input and output of strings easy. They work in pairs. That is, strings input with gets() are usually output with puts(). Strings input with fgets() are usually output with fputs().

TIP

gets() replaces the string-building input function you saw developed in earlier chapters.

Terminate gets() or fgets() input by pressing Enter. Each of these functions handles string-terminating characters in a slightly different manner, as follows:

gets()   A newline input becomes a null zero (\0).

puts()   A null at the end of the string becomes a newline character (\n).

fgets() A newline input stays, and a null zero is added after it.

fputs() The null zero is dropped, and a newline character is not added.

Therefore, when you enter strings with gets(), C places a string-terminating character in the string at the point where you press Enter. This creates the input string. (Without the null zero, the input would not be a string.) When you output a string, the null zero at the end of the string becomes a newline character. This is good because you typically prefer a newline at the end of a line of output (to put the cursor on the next line).

Because fgets() and fputs() can input and output strings from devices such as disk files and modems, it may be critical that the incoming newline characters are retained for the data's integrity. When outputting strings to these devices, you do not want C inserting extra newline characters.

CAUTION

Neither gets() nor fgets() ensures that its input strings are large enough to hold the incoming data. It is up to you to make sure enough space is reserved in the character array to hold the complete input.

One final function is worth noting, although it is not a string function. It is the fflush() function, which flushes (empties) whatever standard device is listed in its parentheses. To flush the keyboard of all its input, you would code as follows:

```
fflush(stdin);
```

When doing string input and output, sometimes an extra newline character gets into the keyboard buffer. A previous answer to gets() or getc() might have an extra newline you forgot to discard. When a program seems to ignore gets(), you might have to insert fflush(stdin) before gets().

Flushing the standard input device causes no harm, and using it can clear the input stream so that your next gets() works properly. You can also flush standard output devices with fflush() to clear the output stream of any characters you may have sent into it.

NOTE

The header file for fflush() is in stdio.h.

EXAMPLE

1. The following program shows you how easy it is to use gets() and puts(). The program requests the name of a book from the user using a single gets() function call, then prints the book title with puts():

```
/* Filename: C18GPS1.C
   Gets and puts strings */
#include <stdio.h>
#include <string.h>
main()
{
    char book[30];

    printf("What is the book title? ");
    gets(book);                     /* Get an input string */
    puts(book);                     /* Display the string */
    printf("Thanks for the book!\n");
    return 0;
}
```

OUTPUT

The output of the program follows:

```
What is the book title? Mary and Her Lambs
Mary and Her Lambs
Thanks for the book!
```

Converting Strings to Numbers

Sometimes you need to convert numbers stored in character strings to a numeric data type. ANSI C provides three functions that let you do this:

- atoi(s): Converts s to an integer. The name stands for *a*lphabetic *to i*nteger.

- atol(s): Converts s to a long integer. The name stands for *a*lphabetic *to l*ong integer.

- atof(s): Converts s to a floating-point number. The name stands for *a*lphabetic *to f*loating-point.

NOTE

These three ato() functions are prototyped in the stdlib.h header file. Be sure to include stdlib.h at the top of any program that uses the ato() functions.

The string must contain a valid number. Here is a string that can be converted to an integer:

```
"1232"
```

The string must hold a string of digits short enough to fit in the target numeric data type. The following string could not be converted to an integer with the atoi() function:

```
"-1232495.654"
```

However, it could be converted to a floating-point number with the atof() function.

C cannot perform any mathematical calculation with such strings, even if the strings contain digits that represent numbers. Therefore, you must convert any string into its numeric equivalent before performing any arithmetic with it.

NOTE

If you pass a string to an ato() function and the string does not contain a valid representation of a number, the ato() function returns 0.

These functions become more useful to you later, after you learn about disk files, pointers, and command-line arguments.

Numeric Functions

This section presents many of the built-in C numeric functions. As with the string functions, these functions save you time by converting and calculating numbers instead of you having to write functions that do the same thing. Many of these are trigonometric and advanced math functions. You might use some of these numeric functions only rarely, but they are there if you need them.

This section concludes the discussion of C's standard built-in functions. After mastering the concepts in this chapter, you are ready to learn more about arrays and pointers. As you develop more skills in C, you might find yourself relying on these numeric, string, and character functions when you write more powerful programs.

Useful Mathematical Functions

Several built-in numeric functions return results based on numeric variables and constants passed to them. Even if you write only a few science and engineering programs, some of these functions may be useful.

NOTE

All mathematical and trigonometric functions are prototyped in the math.h header file. Be sure to include math.h at the top of any program that uses the numeric functions.

Here are the functions listed with their descriptions:

- ceil(*x*): The ceil(), or *ceiling*, function rounds numbers up to the nearest integer.

- fabs(*x*): Returns the absolute value of *x*. The absolute value of a number is its positive equivalent.

TIP

Absolute value is used for distances (which are always positive), accuracy measurements, age differences, and other calculations that require a positive result.

- floor(*x*): The floor() function rounds numbers down to the nearest integer.

- fmod(*x*, *y*): Returns the floating-point remainder of (*x*/*y*), with the same sign as *x*; *y* cannot be zero. Because the modulus operator (%) works only with integers, this function is supplied to find the remainder of floating-point number divisions.

- pow(*x*, *y*): Returns *x* raised to the *y* power, often written as x^y. If *x* is less than or equal to zero, *y* must be an integer. If *x* equals zero, *y* cannot be negative.

- sqrt(*x*): Returns the square root of *x*; *x* must be greater than or equal to zero.

THE NTH ROOT

No function returns the nth root of a number, only the square root does. In other words, you cannot call a function that gives you the 4th root of 65,536. (By the way, 16 is the 4th root of 65,536, because 16 times 16 times 16 times 16 = 65,536.)

You can use a mathematical trick to simulate the nth root, however. Because C lets you raise a number to a fractional power—with the pow() function—you can raise a number to the nth root by raising it to the (1/n) power. For example, to find the 4th root of 65,536, you could type this:

```
root = pow(65536.0, (1.0/4.0));
```

Note that the decimal point keeps the numbers in floating-point format. If you leave them as integers, such as

```
root = pow(65536, (1,4));
```

C produces incorrect results. The pow() function and most other mathematical functions require floating-point values as arguments.

To store the 7th root of 78,125 in a variable called root, for example, you would type

```
root = pow(78125.0, (1.0/7.0));
```

This stores 5.0 in root because 5^7 equals 78,125.

Knowing how to compute the nth root comes in handy in scientific programs and also in financial applications, such as time value of money problems.

1. The following program uses the fabs() function to compute the difference between two ages:

```c
/* Filename: C18ABS.C
   Prints the difference between two ages */
#include <stdio.h>
#include <math.h>
main()
{
   float age1, age2, diff;
   printf("\nWhat is the first child's age? ");
   scanf(" %f", &age1);
   printf("What is the second child's age? ");
   scanf(" %f", &age2);

   /* Calculate the positive difference */
   diff = age1 - age2;
   diff = fabs(diff);      // Determine the absolute value

   printf("\nThey are %.0f years apart.", diff);
   return 0;
}
```

The output from this program follows. Because of `fabs()`, the order of the ages doesn't matter. Without absolute value, this program would produce a negative age difference if the first age was less than the second. Because the ages are relatively small, floating-point variables are used in this example. C automatically converts floating-point arguments to double precision when passing them to `fabs()`:

```
What is the first child's age? 10
What is the second child's age? 12

They are 2 years apart.
```

Trigonometric Functions

The following functions are available for trigonometric applications:

- `cos(x)`: Returns the cosine of the angle *x*, expressed in radians.

- `sin(x)`: Returns the sine of the angle *x*, expressed in radians.

- `tan(x)`: Returns the tangent of the angle *x*, expressed in radians.

These are probably the least-used functions. This is not to belittle the work of scientific and mathematical programmers who need them, however. Certainly they are grateful that C supplies these functions. Otherwise, programmers would have to write their own functions to perform these three basic trigonometric calculations.

Most C compilers supply additional trigonometric functions, including hyperbolic equivalents of these three functions.

TIP

If you need to pass an angle that is expressed in degrees to these functions, convert the angle's degrees to radians by multiplying the degrees by π/180.0 (π equals approximately 3.14159).

Logarithmic Functions

Three highly mathematical functions are sometimes used in business and mathematics. They are listed as follows:

- `exp(x)`: Returns the base of natural logarithm (*e*) raised to a power specified by *x* (e^x); *e* is the mathematical expression for the approximate value of 2.718282.

- `log(x)`: Returns the natural logarithm of the argument *x*, mathematically written as `ln(x)`. *x* must be positive.

- `log10(x)`: Returns the base-10 logarithm of argument *x*, mathematically written as `log10(x)`. *x* must be positive.

What's Next

Functions save you programming time because they take over some of your computing tasks, leaving you free to concentrate on your programs. C's numeric functions round and manipulate numbers, produce trigonometric and logarithmic results, and produce random numbers. Now that you have learned most of C's built-in functions, you are ready to improve your ability to work with arrays. The following chapter extends your knowledge of character arrays and shows you how to produce arrays of any data type.

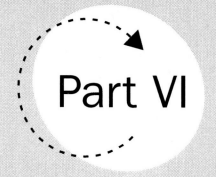

Part VI

Building Blocks

Working with Arrays

Pointer Storage

Using Pointers

19

Working with Arrays

This chapter discusses arrays and how C stores array contents in memory. You are already familiar with character arrays, which are the only method for storing character strings in the C language. A character array isn't the only kind of array you can use, however. There is an array for every data type in C. By learning how to process arrays, you greatly improve the power and efficiency of your programs. C provides many ways to access arrays. If you have programmed in other computer languages, you will find that some of C's array indexing techniques are different. Arrays in the C language are closely linked with *pointers*. Chapter 20, "Pointer Storage," describes the many ways pointers and arrays interact. Because pointers are so powerful, and because learning arrays well provides a good foundation for learning about pointers, this chapter describes, in detail, how C manages arrays inside your computer's memory.

This chapter teaches you the following topics:

- Array names, data types, and subscripts
- Initializing arrays
- How to search arrays
- Ordering arrays
- Advanced subscripting with arrays

Array Basics

Although you have seen a special use of arrays as character strings, you still need a review of arrays in general. An *array* is a list of more than one variable having the same name. Not all lists of variables are arrays. The following list of four variables, for example, does not qualify as an array:

```
sales      bonus_92     firstInitial      ctr
```

This is a list of variables (four of them), but they don't combine into an array because they each have different names. You might wonder how more than one variable can have the same name; this seems to violate the rules for variables. If two variables have the same name, how can C know which one you mean whenever you use that name?

Array variables, or array elements, are differentiated by a *subscript*, which is a number inside brackets. Suppose you want to store a person's name in a character array called name. You know you can do this with

```
char name[] = "Ray Krebbs";
```

or

```
char name[11] = "Ray Krebbs";
```

Because C knows to reserve an extra element for the null zero at the end of every string, you don't need to specify the 11 as long as you initialize the array with a value. The variable name is an array because brackets follow its name. The array has a single name called name, and it contains 11 elements.

NOTE

All array subscripts begin with 0.

You can manipulate individual elements in the array by their subscripts. For instance the following printf() function prints Ray's first and last initials:

```
printf("%c. %c", name[0], name[4]);
```

You can define an array as any data type in C. You can have integer arrays, long integer arrays, double floating-point arrays, short integer arrays, and so on. C recognizes that you are defining an array, and not a single nonarray variable, when you put brackets ([]) after the array name.

The following line defines an array called ages, consisting of 5 integers:

```
int ages[5];
```

The first element in the ages array is ages[0]. The second element is ages[1], and the last one is ages[4]. This declaration of ages does not assign values to the elements, so you don't know what is in ages and your program cannot assume that it contains zeros or anything else.

Here are some more array definitions:

```
int weights[25], sizes[100]; // Declare two integer arrays
float salaries[8];           // Declare a floating-point array
double temps[50];            // Declare a double floating-point
                             // array
char letters[15];            // Declare an array of letters
```

When you declare an array, you instruct C to reserve a specific number of memory locations for that array. C protects those elements. In the previous lines of code, if you assign a value to letters[2] you don't overwrite any data in weights, sizes, salaries, or temps. Also, if you assign a value to sizes[94], you don't overwrite data stored in weights, salaries, temps, or letters.

Each element in an array occupies the same amount of storage as a nonarray variable of the same data type. In other words, each element in a character array occupies one byte. Each element in an integer array occupies two or more bytes of memory—depending on the computer's internal architecture. The same is true for every other data type.

Your program might reference elements by using formulas for subscripts. As long as the subscript can evaluate to an integer, you can use a constant, a variable, or an expression for the subscript. All of the following are references to individual array elements:

```
ara[4]
sales[ctr+1]
bonus[month]
salary[month[i]*2]
```

All array elements are stored in a contiguous, back-to-back fashion. This is important to remember, especially as you write more advanced programs. You can always count on an array's first element preceding the second. The second element is always placed immediately before the third, and so on. Memory is not "padded"; that is, C ensures and guarantees there is no extra space between array elements. This is true for character arrays, integer arrays, floating-point arrays, and every other type of array. If a floating-point value occupies four bytes of memory on your computer, the next element in a floating-point array always begins exactly four bytes after that previous element. It might help to think of array memory as a pile of bricks; each brick consumes a specific amount of space and the next brick much be placed directly on top of the pile.

THE SIZE OF ARRAYS

The `sizeof()` function returns the number of bytes needed to hold its argument. If you request the size of an array name, `sizeof()` returns the number of bytes reserved for the entire array. For example, suppose you declare an integer array of 100 elements called scores. If you were to find the size of the array, as in

```
n = sizeof(scores);
```

n holds either 200 or 400, depending on the integer size of your computer. The `sizeof()` function always returns the reserved amount of storage, no matter what data is in the array.

If you request the size of an individual array element, however, as in

```
n = sizeof(scores[6]);
```

n holds either 2 or 4, depending on the integer size of your computer.

You must never go out-of-bounds of any array. For example, suppose you want to keep track of the exemptions and salary codes of five employees. You could reserve two arrays to hold such data like this:

```
int  exemptions[5];   // Holds up to 5 employee exemptions
char salCodes[5];        // Holds up to 5 employee codes
```

C stores these arrays back-to-back in memory. C knows to reserve five elements for exemptions from the array declaration. C starts reserving memory for salCodes after it reserves all five elements for exemptions. If you declare several more variables—either locally or globally—after these two lines, C always protects these reserved five elements for exemptions and salCodes.

Because C does its part to protect the data in the array, so must you. If you reserve five elements for exemptions, you have five integer array elements referred to as exemptions[0], exemptions[1], exemptions[2], exemptions[3], and exemptions[4]. C does not protect more than five elements for exemptions. Suppose that you put a value into an exemptions element that you did not reserve:

```
exemptions[6] = 4;               // Assign a value to an
                                 // out-of-range element
```

C lets you do this—but the results are damaging. C overwrites *other* data (in this case, salCodes[2] and salCodes[3] because they are reserved where the sixth element of exemptions has to be placed). No exemptions[6] exists; C doesn't tell you this, however. Instead, C counts forward seven integer spaces in memory, from C[0]'s starting point, and places the 4 there. The 4's location happens to be the same place where the salCodes array begins. Each salCodes item consumes a single byte of memory due to the array being defined as a character array.

CAUTION

Unlike most programming languages, ANSI C lets you assign values to out-of-range (nonreserved) subscripts. You must be very careful not to do this; otherwise, you start overwriting your other data or code. Most C compilers do offer an option you can select that will check for array boundary overflow.

Although you can define an array of any data type, you cannot declare an array of strings. A *string* is not a C variable data type. You learn how to hold multiple strings in an array-like structure in Chapter 21, "Using Pointers."

Initializing Arrays

You must assign values to array elements before using them. Here are the two ways to initialize elements in an array:

- Initialize the elements at declaration time
- Initialize the elements in the program

NOTE

C automatically initializes global arrays to null zeros. Therefore, global character array elements are all null, and numeric array elements all contain zero. You should limit your use of global arrays. If you use global arrays, explicitly initialize them to zero, even though C does this for you, to clarify your intentions.

Initializing Elements at Declaration Time

You already know how to initialize character arrays that hold strings when you define the arrays: You simply assign them a string. For example, the following declaration reserves six elements in a character array called `city`:

```
char city[6];                /* Reserve space for city */
```

If you also want to initialize `city` with a value, you could do it like this:

```
char city[6] = "Tulsa";      // Reserve space and
                             //   initialize city
```

The 6 is optional because C counts the elements needed to hold `Tulsa`, plus an extra element for the null zero at the end of the quoted string.

You can also reserve a character array and initialize it—a single character at a time—by using braces around the character data. The following line of code declares an array called `initials` and initializes it with eight characters:

```
char initials[8] = {'Q', 'K', 'P', 'G', 'V', 'M', 'U', 'S'};
```

The array initials is not a string! Its data does not end in a null zero. There is nothing wrong with defining an array of characters such as this one, but you must remember that you cannot treat the array as if it were a string. Do not use string functions with it, or attempt to print the array with the %s printf() format code.

By using braces, you can initialize any type of array. For example, if you want to initialize an integer array that holds your five children's ages, you could do it with the following declaration:

```
int childAges[5] = {2, 5, 6, 8, 12};   // Declare and
                                        // initialize array
```

In another example, if you want to keep track of the last three years' total sales, you could declare an array and initialize it at the same time with the following:

```
double sales[] = {454323.43, 122355.32, 343324.96};
```

As with character arrays, you do not need to state explicitly the array size when you declare and initialize an array of any type. C would know, in this case, to reserve three double floating-point array elements for sales.

NOTE

You cannot initialize an array, using the assignment operator and braces, after you declare it. You can initialize arrays in this manner only when you declare them. If you want to fill an array with data after you declare the array, you must do so element-by-element or by using functions as described in the next section.

Although C does not automatically zero-out (or initialize to any value) array elements, if you initialize some but not all of the elements when you declare the array, C finishes the job for you by assigning the remainder to zero.

TIP

To initialize every element of a large array to zero at the same time, declare the entire array and initialize its first value to zero. C finishes filling in the rest of the array to zero.

For instance, suppose you need to reserve array storage for profit figures of the three previous months as well as the three months to follow. You need to reserve six elements of storage, but you know values for only the first three of them. You can initialize the array as follows

```
double profit[6] = {67654.43, 46472.34, 63451.93};
```

Because you explicitly initialized three of the elements, C initializes the rest to zero. If you use an appropriate printf() to print the entire array, one element per line, you would get

```
67654.43
46472.34
```

```
63451.93
00000.00
00000.00
00000.00
```

CAUTION

Always declare an array with the maximum number of subscripts, unless you initialize the array at the same time. The following array declaration is illegal:

```
int count[];              // Bad array declaration!
```

C does not know how many elements to reserve for count, so it reserves none. If you then assign values to count's nonreserved elements, you might (and probably would) overwrite other data. The only time you can leave the brackets empty is if you also assign values to the array, such as the following:

```
int count[] = {15, 9, 22, -8, 12}; /* Good definition */
```

C can tell, from the list of values, how many elements to reserve. In this case, C reserves five elements for count.

EXAMPLE

1. Suppose you want to track the stock market averages for the last 90 days. Instead of storing them in 90 different variables, it is much easier to store them in an array. You could declare the array like this:

   ```
   float stock[90];
   ```

   The rest of the program could assign values to the averages.

2. Suppose that you just finished taking classes at a local university and want to average your six class scores. The following program initializes one array for the school name and another for the six classes. The body of the program averages each of the six scores.

   ```
   /* Filename: C19ARA1.C
      Averages six test scores */
   #include <stdio.h>
   main()
   {
       char sName[] = "Tri Star University";
       float scores[6] = {88.7, 90.4, 76.0, 97.0, 100.0, 86.7};
       float average=0.0;
       int ctr;

       /* Compute total of scores */
       for (ctr=0; ctr<6; ctr++)
           { average += scores[ctr]; }

       /* Compute the average */
       average /= (float)6;
   ```

```
    printf("At %s, your class average is %.1f.",
            sName, average);
    return 0;
}
```

The output follows:

```
At Tri Star University, your class average is 89.8.
```

Notice that using arrays makes processing lists of information much easier. Instead of averaging six differently named variables, you can use a for loop to step through each array element. If you had to average 1,000 numbers, you could still do so with a simple for loop, as in this example. If the 1,000 variables were not in an array, but were individually named, you would need to write a considerable amount of code just to add them.

3. The following program is an expanded version of the previous one. It prints the six scores before computing the average. Notice that you must print array elements individually; you cannot print an entire array in a single printf(). (You can print an entire character array with %s, but only if it holds a null-terminated string of characters.)

```
/* Filename: C19ARA2.C
    Prints and averages six test scores */
#include <stdio.h>
void main(void);
void prScores(float scores[]);

void main(void)
{
    char sName[] = "Tri Star University";
    float scores[6] = {88.7, 90.4, 76.0, 97.0, 100.0, 86.7};
    float average=0.0;
    int ctr;

    /* Call function to print scores */
    prScores(scores);

    /* Compute total of scores */
    for (ctr=0; ctr<6; ctr++)
        { average += scores[ctr]; }

    /* Compute the average */
    average /= (float)6;
```

```
      printf("At %s, your class average is %.1f.",
               sName, average);
      return 0;
}

void prScores(float scores[6])
{
   /* Prints the six scores */
   int ctr;

   printf("Here are your scores:\n");          // Title
   for (ctr=0; ctr<6; ctr++)
     printf("%.1f\n", scores[ctr]);
   return 0;
}
```

To pass an array to a function, you need to specify only its name. In the receiving function's parameter list, you must state the array type and include its brackets, which tell the function that it is an array. (You do not explicitly need to state the array size in the receiving parameter list as shown in the prototype.)

4. To improve the maintainability of your programs, define all array sizes with the #define preprocessor directive. What if you took four classes next semester but still wanted to use the same program? You could modify it by changing all the 6s to 4s, but if you had defined the array size with a defined constant, you would have to change only one line in order to change the program's subscript limits. Notice how the following program uses a defined constant for the number of classes:

```
/* Filename: C19ARA3.C
   Prints and averages six test scores */
#include <stdio.h>
void main(void);
void prScores(float scores[]);
#define CLASS_NUM 6

void main(void)
{
   char sName[] = "Tri Star University";
   float scores[CLASS_NUM] = {88.7, 90.4, 76.0, 97.0,
                                  100.0, 86.7};
   float average=0.0;
   int ctr;
```

```
                /* Call function to print scores */
                prScores(scores);

                /* Compute total of scores */
                for (ctr=0; ctr<CLASS_NUM; ctr++)
                    { average += scores[ctr]; }

                /* Compute the average */
                average /= (float)CLASS_NUM;

                printf("At %s, your class average is %.1f.",
                        sName, average);
                return 0;
            }

            void prScores(float scores[CLASS_NUM])
            {
                /* Prints the six scores */
                int ctr;

                printf("Here are your scores:\n");              // Title
                for (ctr=0; ctr<CLASS_NUM; ctr++)
                    printf("%.1f\n", scores[ctr]);
                return 0;
            }
```

For such a simple example, using a defined constant for the maximum subscript may not seem like a big advantage. If you were writing a larger program that processed several arrays, however, changing the defined constant at the top of the program is much easier than searching the program for each occurrence of that array reference.

Using defined constants for array sizes has the added advantage of protecting you from going out of the subscript bounds. You do not have to remember the subscript when looping through arrays; you can use the defined constant instead.

Initializing Elements in the Program

Rarely do you know the contents of arrays when you declare them. Usually, you fill an array with user input or a disk file's data. The for loop is a perfect tool for looping through arrays when you fill them with values.

CAUTION

An array name cannot appear on the left side of an assignment statement.

You cannot assign one array to another. Suppose you want to copy an array called totalSales to a second array called savedSales. You cannot do so with the following assignment statement:

```
savedSales = totalSales;                /* Invalid! */
```

Rather, you have to copy the arrays one element at a time, using a loop, such as the following section of code does:

```
for (ctr=0; ctr<ARRAY_SIZE; ctr++)
   { savedSales[ctr] = totalSales[ctr]; }
```

1. The following program uses the assignment operator to assign ten temperatures to an array:

```
/* Filename: C19ARA4.C
    Fill an array with ten temperature values */
#include <stdio.h>
#define NUM_TEMPS 10
main()
{
    float temps[NUM_TEMPS];
    int ctr;

    temps[0] = 78.6;      /* Subscripts always begin at 0 */
    temps[1] = 82.1;
    temps[2] = 79.5;
    temps[3] = 75.0;
    temps[4] = 75.4;
    temps[5] = 71.8;
    temps[6] = 73.3;
    temps[7] = 69.5;
    temps[8] = 74.1;
    temps[9] = 75.7;

    /* Print the temps */
    printf("Daily temperatures for the last %d days:\n",
            NUM_TEMPS);
    for (ctr=0; ctr<NUM_TEMPS; ctr++)
       { printf("%.1f \n", temps[ctr]); }

    return 0;
}
```

2. The following program uses a for loop and scanf() to assign eight integers entered individually by the user. The program then prints a total of all the numbers:

```
/* Filename: C19TOT.C
   Totals eight input values from the user */
#include <stdio.h>
#define NUM 8
main()
{
   int nums[NUM];
   int total = 0;        /* Holds total of user's 8 numbers */

   for (ctr=0; ctr<NUM; ctr++)
     { printf("Please enter the next number...");
       scanf("%d", &nums[ctr]);
       total += nums[ctr]; }

   printf("The total of the numbers is %d", total);
   return 0;
}
```

Searching Arrays

Arrays are one of the primary means by which data is stored in C programs. Many types of programs lend themselves to processing lists (arrays) of data, such as an employee payroll program, a scientific research of several chemicals, or customer account processing. Array data usually is read from the keyboard or, in quantity, from disk files. Later chapters describe disk file processing. For now, you should understand how to manipulate arrays so that you see the data exactly the way you want to see it.

The random access of C arrays can be powerful. Suppose that a high school used C programs for its grade reports. Suppose also that the school wanted to see a list of the top 10 grade-point averages. You could not print the first 10 grade-point averages in the list of student averages because the top 10 GPAs might not (and probably will not) appear as the first 10 array elements. Because the GPAs would not be in any sequence, the program would have to sort the array into numeric order, from high GPAs to low, or else search the array for the 10 highest GPAs.

You need a method for putting arrays in a specific order. This is called *sorting* an array. When you sort an array, you put that array in a specific order, such as in alphabetical or numerical order. A dictionary is in sorted order, and so is a phone book.

When you reverse the order of a sort, it is called a *descending sort*. For instance, if you wanted to look at a list of all employees in descending salary order, the highest-paid employees would be printed first.

Before you learn to sort, it would be helpful to learn how to search an array for a value. This is a preliminary step in learning to sort. What if one of those students received a grade change? The computer must be able to access that specific student's grade to change it (without affecting the others). As the next section shows, programs can search for specific array elements.

Searching for Values

You do not need to know any new commands to search an array for a value. Basically, the if and for loop statements are all you need. To search an array for a specific value, look at each element in that array, comparing with the if statement to see whether they match. If they do not, you keep searching down the array. If you run out of array elements before finding the value, it is not in the array.

You can perform several different kinds of searches. You might need to find the highest or the lowest value in a list of numbers. This is informative when you have much data and want to know the extremes of the data (such as the highest and lowest sales region in your division). You also can search an array to see whether it contains a matching value. For example, you can see whether an item is already in an inventory by searching a part number array for a match.

The following programs illustrate some of these array-searching techniques.

EXAMPLE

1. To find the highest number in an array, compare each element with the first one. If you find a higher value, it becomes the basis for the rest of the array. Continue until you reach the end of the array and you will have the highest value, as the following program shows:

```c
/* Filename: C19HIGH.C
   Finds the highest value in the array */
#include <stdio.h>
#define SIZE 15
main()
{
   /* Puts some numbers in the array */
   int ara[SIZE]={5,2,7,8,36,4,2,86,11,43,22,12,45,6,85};
   int highVal, ctr;

   highVal = ara[0];              /* Initializes with first
                                        array element */
   for (ctr=1; ctr<SIZE; ctr++)
     {                           /* Stores current value if it is
                                   higher than the highest so far */
       if (ara[ctr] > highVal)
```

```
                              { highVal = ara[ctr]; }
              }

          printf("The highest number in the list is %d.", highVal);
          return 0;
      }
```

The output of the program is the following:

```
The highest number in the list is 86.
```

You have to save the element if and only if it is higher than the one you are comparing. Finding the smallest number in an array is just as easy, except that you compare to see whether each succeeding array element is less than the lowest value found so far.

2. The next program fills an array with part numbers from an inventory. You must use your imagination, because the inventory array normally would fill more of the array, would be initialized from a disk file, and would be part of a larger set of arrays that holds descriptions, quantities, costs, selling prices, and so on. For this example, assignment statements initialize the array. The important idea from this program is not the array initialization, but the method for searching the array.

NOTE

If the newly entered part number is already on file, the program tells the user. Otherwise, the part number is added to the end of the array.

To see how the part numbers fill the array, study this program:

```
/* Filename: C19SERCH.C
   Searches a part number array for the input value. If
   the entered part number is not in the array, it is
   added. If the part number is in the array, a message
   is printed. */
#include <stdio.h>
#define MAX 100
void main(void);
void fillParts(long int parts[MAX]);

void main(void)
{
    long int searchPart;               /* Holds user request */
    long int parts[MAX];
    int ctr;
    int numParts=5;            /* Beginning inventory count */
```

```
      fillParts(parts);      /* Fills the first five elements */
      do
      {
        printf("\n\nPlease type a part number...")
        printf("(-9999 ends program) ");
        scanf("%ld", &searchPart);
        if (searchPart == -9999)
          { break; }           /* Exits loop if user wants */
        /* Scan array to see whether part is in inventory */
        for (ctr=0; ctr<numParts; ctr++) /* Checks each item */
        { if (searchPart == parts[ctr])        /* If it is in
                                                  inventory...*/
              { printf("\nPart %ld is already in inventory",
                        searchPart);
                break;
              }
          else
            { if (ctr == (numParts-1) )        /* If not there,
                                                  adds it */
                { parts[numParts] = searchPart;     /* Adds to
                                                  end of array */
                  numParts++;
                  printf("\n%ld was added to inventory\n",
                          searchPart);
                  break;
                 }
            }
        }
      } while (searchPart != -9999);      /* Loops until user
                                            signals end */
      return 0;
}

void fillParts(long int parts[MAX])
{
    /* Assigns five part numbers to array for testing */
    parts[0] = 12345;
    parts[1] = 24724;
    parts[2] = 54154;
    parts[3] = 73496;
    parts[4] = 83925;
    return 0;
}
```

Here is the output from this program:

```
Please type a part number...(-9999 ends program) 25432

25432 was added to inventory


Please type a part number...(-9999 ends program) 12345

Part 12345 is already in inventory

Please type a part number...(-9999 ends program) 65468

65468 was added to inventory


Please type a part number...(-9999 ends program) 25432

Part 25432 is already in inventory

Please type a part number...(-9999 ends program) -9999
```

Sorting Arrays

There are many times when you need to sort one or more arrays. Suppose that you were to take a list of numbers, write each number on a separate piece of paper, and throw all the pieces of paper into the air. The steps you would take—shuffling and changing the order of the pieces of paper, trying to put them in order—would be similar to what your computer goes through to sort numbers or character data into a sorted order.

Because sorting arrays requires exchanging values of elements back and forth, it helps if you first learn the technique for swapping variables. Suppose that you had two variables named score1 and score2. What if you wanted to reverse their values (putting score2 into the score1 variable, and vice versa)? You could not do this:

```
score1 = score2;    /* Does not swap the two values */
score2 = score1;
```

Why doesn't this work? In the first line, the value of score1 gets replaced with score2's value. When the first line finishes, both score1 and score2 contain the same value. Therefore, the second line cannot work as desired.

To swap two variables, you need to use a third variable to hold the intermediate result. (This is the only function of this third variable.) For instance, to swap `score1` and `score2`, use a third variable (called `holdScore` in this code), as in

```
holdScore = score1;    /* These three lines properly */
score1 = score2;       /* swap score1 and score2     */
score2 = holdScore;
```

This exchanges the two values in the two variables.

There are several different ways to sort arrays. These methods include the *bubble sort,* the *quicksort,* and the *shell sort.* The basic goal of each method is to compare each array element to another array element and swap them if the higher one is less than the other.

The theory behind these sorts is beyond the scope of this book; however, the bubble sort is one of the easiest to understand. Values in the array are compared to each other, a pair at a time, and swapped if they are not in back-to-back order. The lowest value eventually "floats" to the top of the array, like a bubble in a glass of soda.

The bubble sort steps through the array, comparing pairs of numbers, to see whether they need to be swapped. Several passes might have to be made through the array before it is finally sorted (no more passes are needed). Other types of sorts improve on the bubble sort. The bubble sort procedure is easy to program, but it is slower compared to many of the other methods.

EXAMPLE

1. The following program assigns 10 random numbers between 0 and 99 to an array, and then sorts the array. C's rand() function produces a different and random integer when you call it, and this program uses the integer division operator (%) to put the random number between 0 and 99. A nested for loop is perfect for sorting numbers in the array (as shown in the sortArray() function). Nested for loops provide a nice mechanism for working on pairs of values, swapping them if needed. As the outside loop counts down the list, referencing each element, the inside loop compares each of the remaining values to those array elements:

```
/* Filename: C19SORT1.C
   Sorts and prints a list of numbers */
#define MAX 10
#include <stdio.h>
#include <stdlib.h>
void fillArray(int ara[MAX]);
void printArray(int ara[MAX]);
void main(void);
void sortArray(int ara[MAX]);
```

```
void main(void)
{
    int ara[MAX];

    fillArray(ara);   /* Puts random numbers in the array */

    printf("Here are the unsorted numbers:\n");
    printArray(ara);        /* Prints the unsorted array */

    sortArray(ara);                  /* Sorts the array */

    printf("\n\nHere are the sorted numbers:\n");
    printArray(ara);     /* Prints the newly sorted array */
    return 0;
}

void fillArray(int ara[MAX])
{
    /* Puts random numbers in the array */
    int ctr;
    for (ctr=0; ctr<MAX; ctr++)
        { ara[ctr] = (rand() % 100); }   /* Forces number to
                                              0-99 range */

    return 0;
}

void printArray(int ara[MAX])
{
    /* Prints the array */
    int ctr;
    for (ctr=0; ctr<MAX; ctr++)
        { printf("%d\n", ara[ctr]); }
    return 0;
}

void sortArray(int ara[MAX])
{
    /* Sorts the array */
    int temp;          /* Temporary variable to swap with */
    int ctr1, ctr2;         /* Need two loop counters to */
                            /*   swap pairs of numbers    */
    for (ctr1=0; ctr1<(MAX-1); ctr1++)
        { for (ctr2=(ctr1+1); ctr2<MAX; ctr2++) /* Test pairs */
            { if (ara[ctr1] > ara[ctr2])    /* Swap if this */
```

```
                          { temp = ara[ctr1]; /* pair is not in order */
                            ara[ctr1] = ara[ctr2];
                            ara[ctr2] = temp;   /* "float" the lowest
                                                   to the highest */
                          }
                     }
               }
         return 0;
   }
```

OUTPUT

Here is the output from this program. If any two randomly generated numbers were the same, the bubble sort would work properly, placing them next to each other in the list:

```
Here are the unsorted numbers:
46
38
81
90
56
17
95
15
40
26

Here are the sorted numbers:
15
17
26
38
46
48
56
82
90
95
```

TIP

To produce a descending sort, use the less-than (<) logical operator when swapping array elements.

Advanced Referencing of Arrays

The array notation you have seen so far is common in computer programming languages. Most languages use subscripts inside brackets (or parentheses) to refer to individual array elements. For instance, you know that the following array references describe the first and fifth element of the array called sales (remember that the starting subscript is always 0):

```
sales[0]

sales[4]
```

C provides another approach to referencing arrays. Even though the title of this section includes the word "advanced," this array-referencing method is not difficult. It is very different, however, especially if you are familiar with another programming language's approach.

There is nothing wrong with referring to array elements in the manner you have seen so far. However, the second approach, unique to C, will be helpful when you learn about pointers in upcoming chapters. Actually, C programmers who have programmed for several years rarely use the subscript notation you have seen.

In C, an array's name is not just a label for you to use in programs. To C, the array name is the actual address where the first element begins in memory. Suppose that you define an array called amounts with the following statement:

```
int amounts[6] = {4, 1, 3, 7, 9, 2};
```

Figure 19.1 shows how this array is stored in memory. The figure shows the array beginning at address 405,332. (The actual addresses of variables are determined by the computer when you load and run your compiled program.) Notice that the name of the array, amounts, is located somewhere in memory and contains the address of amounts[0], or 405,332. The values are integers so two memory locations are used for each value although some compilers might store integers using more than two bytes.

You can refer to an array by its regular subscript notation, or by modifying the address of the array. Both of the following refer to the third element of amounts:

```
amounts[3]    (amounts + 3)[0]
```

Because C considers the array name to be an address in memory that contains the location of the first array element, nothing keeps you from using a different address as the starting address and referencing from there. Taking this one step further, each of the following also refers to the third element of amounts:

(amounts+0)[3]　　(amounts+2)[1]　　(amounts-2)[5]

(1+amounts)[2]　　(3+amounts)[0]　　(amounts+1)[2]

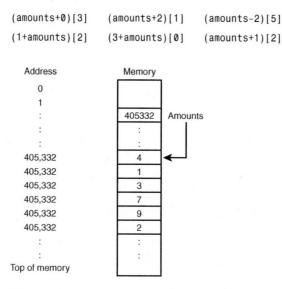

Figure 19.1: *The array name* amounts *holds the address of* amounts[0].

You can print any of these array elements with a printf() function using the standard integer %d control code.

CAUTION

The hierarchy table in Appendix B, "C's Precedence Table," shows that array subscripts have precedence over addition and subtraction. Therefore, you must enclose array names in parentheses if you want to modify the name as shown in these examples. The following are not equivalent:

(2+amounts)[1]　and　2+amounts[1]

The second example takes the value of amounts[1] (which is 1 in this example array) and adds 2 to it (resulting in a value of 3).

This second method of array referencing might seem like more trouble than it is worth, but learning to reference arrays in this fashion will make your transition to pointers much easier. An array name is actually a pointer itself, because the array contains the address of the first array element (it "points" to the start of the array).

When you print strings inside character arrays, referencing the arrays by their modified addresses is more useful than with integers. Suppose that you stored three strings in a single character array. You could initialize this array with the following statement:

```
char names[]={'T','e','d','\0','E','v','a','\0','S',
              'a','m','\0'};
```

Figure 19.2 shows how this array might look in memory. The array name, names, contains the address of the first element, names[0] (the letter T).

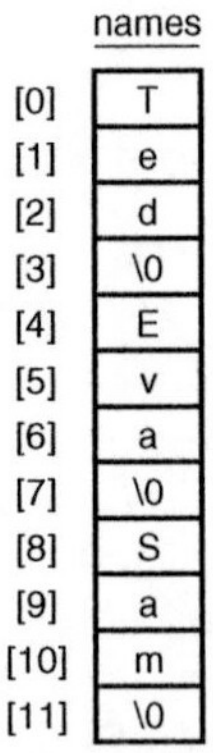

names

[0]	T
[1]	e
[2]	d
[3]	\0
[4]	E
[5]	v
[6]	a
[7]	\0
[8]	S
[9]	a
[10]	m
[11]	\0

Figure 19.2: *Storing more than one string in a single character array is possible.*

You have yet to see a character array that holds more than one string, but C allows it. The problem with such an array is how you reference, especially how you print, the second and third strings. If you were to print this array using the %s string control code (as you have been doing) with the following printf(),

```
printf("%s", names);
```

C would print the following:

```
Ted
```

As mentioned in Chapter 6, "Input and Output," (where this book introduces control codes), the %s control code prints the string starting at the address of the specified array. Without a different way to reference the array, you would have no way to print the three strings inside the single array (without resorting to printing them one element at a time).

Because the %s control code requires a starting address, you can print the three strings with the following printf() function calls:

```
printf("%s", names);        /* Prints Ted */
printf("%s", (names+4));    /* Prints Eva */
printf("%s", (names+8));    /* Prints Sam */
```

To test your understanding, what will the following printf() function calls print?

```
printf("%s", (names+1));
printf("%s", (names+6));
```

The first printf() prints ed. The %s prints the string starting at the address specified. The characters ed begin at (names+1) and the %s stops printing when it gets to the null zero. The second printf() prints a. Adding 6 to the address at names produces the address where the a is located. The "string" is only one character long because the null zero appears in the array immediately after the a.

To sum up character arrays, the following refer to individual array elements (single characters):

names[2] and (names+1)[1]

With such, you can print them with the %c control code, but not with %s. The following refer to addresses only, and as such, you can print them with the %s control code

names and (names+4)

but not with %c.

CAUTION

Never use %c to print an address reference, even if that address contains a character. Print strings by specifying an address with %s, and single characters by specifying the character element with %c.

The following examples are a little different from most you have seen. They do not perform "real-world" work; but they are study examples for you to familiarize yourself with this new method of array referencing. The next few chapters expand on these methods.

EXAMPLE

1. The following program stores the numbers from 100 to 600 in an array, then prints elements using the new method of array subscripting:

```
/* Filename: C19REF1.C
   Print elements of an integer array in different ways */
#include <stdio.h>
main()
{
    int num[6] = {100, 200, 300, 400, 500, 600};

    printf("num[0] is \t%d \n", num[0]);
    printf("(num+0)[0] is \t%d \n", (num+0)[0]);
    printf("(num-2)[2] is \t%d \n\n", (num-2)[2]);

    printf("num[1] is \t%d \n", num[1]);
    printf("(num+1)[0] is \t%d \n", (num+1)[0]);
    printf("(num-5)[4] is \t%d \n\n", (num-5)[4]);

    printf("num[5] is \t%d \n", num[5]);
    printf("(num+5)[0] is \t%d \n", (num+5)[0]);
    printf("(num+2)[3] is \t%d \n\n", (num+2)[3]);
```

```
        printf("(3+num)[1] is \t%d \n", (3+num)[1]);
        printf("3+num[1] is \t%d \n", 3+num[1]);
        return 0;
}
```

Here is the output of this program:

```
num[0] is          100
(num+0)[0] is      100
(num-2)[2] is      100

num[1] is          200
(num+1)[0] is      200
(num-5)[4] is      200

num[5] is          600
(num+5)[0] is      600
(num+2)[3] is      600

(3+num)[1] is      500
3+num[1] is        203
```

2. The following program prints strings and characters from a character array. The printf()s use %s and %c properly; you could not interchange any %s for %c (or %c for %s) and get correct output:

```
/* Filename: C19REF2.C
   Prints elements and strings from an array */
#include <stdio.h>
main()
{
    char names[]={'T','e','d','\0','E','v','a','\0','S',
                    'a','m','\0'};

    /* Must use extra percent (%) to print %s and %c */
    printf("names with \%s: %s\n", names);
    printf("names+0 with \%s: %s\n", names+0);
    printf("names+1 with \%s: %s\n", names+1);
    printf("names+2 with \%s: %s\n", names+2);
    printf("names+3 with \%s: %s\n", names+3);
    printf("names+5 with \%s: %s\n", names+5);
    printf("names+8 with \%s: %s\n\n", names+8);

    printf("(names+0)[0] with \%c: %c\n", (names+0)[0]);
    printf("(names+0)[1] with \%c: %c\n", (names+0)[1]);
    printf("(names+0)[2] with \%c: %c\n", (names+0)[2]);
    printf("(names+0)[3] with \%c: %c\n", (names+0)[3]);
    printf("(names+0)[4] with \%c: %c\n", (names+0)[4]);
    printf("(names+0)[5] with \%c: %c\n\n", (names+0)[5]);
```

```
        printf("(names+2)[0] with \%c: %c\n", (names+2)[0]);
        printf("(names+2)[1] with \%c: %c\n", (names+2)[1]);
        printf("(names+1)[4] with \%c: %c\n\n", (names+1)[4]);

        printf("(names-4)[6] with \%c: %c\n", (names-4)[6]);
        printf("(names-6)[11] with \%c: %c\n", (names-6)[11]);
        return 0;
}
```

OUTPUT

Study the output that follows by comparing the output to the program's code. You will learn more about strings, characters, and character array referencing from studying this one example than from 20 pages of textual description:

```
names with %s: Ted
names+0 with %s: Ted
names+1 with %s: ed
names+2 with %s: d
names+3 with %s:
names+5 with %s: variable
names+8 with %s: Sam

(names+0)[0] with %c: T
(names+0)[1] with %c: e
(names+0)[2] with %c: d
(names+0)[3] with %c:
(names+0)[4] with %c: E
(names+0)[6] with %c: v

(names+2)[0] with %c: d
(names+2)[1] with %c:
(names+1)[4] with %c: v

(names-4)[6] with %c: d
(names-6)[11] with %c: v
```

What's Next

You now know how to declare and initialize arrays consisting of various data types. You can initialize an array when you declare it or when it is in the body of your program. Array elements are much easier to process than many variables, each of which have a different name. You will use the concepts learned here for sorting and searching lists of character string data as well, as soon as you learn a little more about the way C manipulates strings and pointers. The next chapter introduces C pointers which are little more than arrays in disguise.

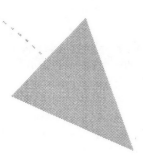

20

Pointer Storage

C reveals its true power through *pointer variables*. Pointer variables (or
pointers, as they generally are called) are variables that contain addresses
of other variables. All variables you have seen so far have held data values.
You understand that variables hold various data types: character, integer,
floating-point, and so on. Pointer variables contain the location of regular
data variables; they in effect point to the data because they hold the
address of the data. After you work with pointers for a while, you will find
that they are easier to use than arrays (and much more flexible).

This chapter teaches you the following topics:

- Pointer declarations
- The "address of" (&) operator
- The dereferencing (*) operator
- Arrays of pointers

Introduction to Pointer Variables

Pointers are variables. They follow all the normal naming rules of regular, nonpointer variables. As with regular variables, you must declare pointer variables before using them. There is a type of pointer for every data type in C; there are integer pointers, character pointers, floating-point pointers, and so on. You can declare global pointers or local pointers, depending on where you declare them.

About the only difference between pointer variables and regular variables is the data they hold. Pointers do not contain data in the usual sense of the word. Pointers contain addresses of data. If you need a quick review of addresses and memory, see Appendix A, "Memory Addressing, Binary, and Hexadecimal."

There are two pointer operators in C:

& The "address of" operator

* The dereferencing operator

Don't let the second operator throw you; you have seen the * before. The * means, of course, multiplication. The asterisk is called an *overloaded* operator. Overloaded operators perform more than one kind of operation depending on how you use them in your programs. C does not confuse * for multiplication when you use it as a dereferencing operator with pointers.

Any time you see the & used with pointers, think of the words "address of." The & operator always produces the memory address of whatever it precedes. The * operator, when used with pointers, either declares a pointer or dereferences the pointer's value. The next section explains each of these operators.

Declaring Pointers

Because you must declare all pointers before using them, the best way to begin learning about pointers is to understand how to declare and define them. Actually, declaring pointers is almost as easy as declaring regular variables. After all, pointers are variables.

If you need to declare a variable that will hold your age, you could do so with the following variable declaration:

```
int age=30;      // Declare a variable to hold my age
```

Declaring age like this does several things. C now knows that you will need a variable called age, so C reserves storage for that variable. C also knows that you will store only integers in age, not floating-point or double floating-point data. The declaration also requests that C store the value of 30 in age after it reserves storage for age.

Where did C store age in memory? As the programmer, you do not really care where C decided to store age. You do not need to know the variable's address because you will never refer to age by its address. If you want to calculate or print with age, you will call it by its name, age.

TIP

Make your pointer variable names meaningful. The name `filePtr` makes more sense than x13 for a file-pointing variable, although either name is allowed.

Suppose that you want to declare a pointer variable. This pointer variable will not hold your age, but it will point to age, the variable that holds your age. (Why you would want to do this is explained in this and the next few chapters.) pAge might be a good name for the pointer variable. Figure 20.1 illustrates what you want to do. The figure assumes that C stored age at the address 350,606; however, your C compiler arbitrarily determines the address of age, so it could be anything.

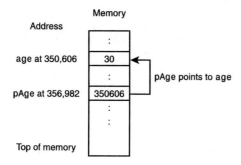

Figure 20.1: *pAge contains the address of* age; *pAge points to the* age *variable.*

The name pAge by itself has nothing to do with pointers, except that is the name you made up for the pointer to age. pAge could just as easily have been named house, x43344, space_trek, or whatever else you wanted to call it, just as you can name variables anything (as long as the name follows the legal naming rules of variables). This reinforces the idea that a pointer is just a variable that you must reserve in your program. Make up meaningful variable names, even for pointer variables. pAge is a good name for a variable that points to age (as would be ptrAge and ptrToAge).

To declare the pAge pointer variable, you must do the following:

```
int * pAge;              // Declare an integer pointer
```

Similar to the declaration for age, this declaration reserves a variable called pAge. pAge is not a normal integer variable, however. Because of the dereferencing operator (*), C knows that this is to be a pointer variable. Some C programmers prefer to declare such a variable without a space after the *, as follows:

```
int *pAge;                 // Declare an integer pointer
```

Either method is okay, but you must remember that the * is not part of the name. When you later use pAge, you will not always prefix the name with the *, unless you are dereferencing it at the time (as later examples show).

TIP
Whenever the dereferencing operator (*) appears in a variable definition, the variable being declared is always a pointer variable.

Consider the declaration for pAge if the asterisk were not there: C would think you were declaring a regular integer variable. The * is important, because it tells C to interpret pAge as a pointer variable, not as a normal, data variable.

Assigning Values to Pointers

pAge is an integer pointer. This is very important. pAge can point only to integer values, never to floating-point, double floating-point, or even character variables. If you needed to point to a floating-point variable, you might do so with a pointer declared as

```
float *point;     // Declares a floating-point pointer
```

As with any automatic variable, C does not initialize pointers when you declare them. If you declared pAge as previously described, and you wanted pAge to point to age, you would have to explicitly assign pAge to the address of age. The following statement does this:

```
pAge = &age;     // Assign the address of age to pAge
```

What value is now in pAge? You do not know exactly, but you know it is the address of age, wherever that is. Instead of assigning the address of age to pAge with an assignment operator, you can declare and initialize pointers at the same time. These lines declare and initialize both age and pAge:

```
int age=30;        /* Declares a regular integer
                      variable, putting 30 in it         */
int *pAge=&age;    /* Declares an integer pointer,
                      initializing it with the address
                      of pAge                            */
```

These two lines produce the variables described in Figure 20.1.

If you wanted to print the value of age, you could do so with the following printf():

```
printf("%d", age);              // Prints the value of age
```

You also can print the value of age like this:

```
printf("%d", *pAge);            // Dereferences pAge
```

The dereference operator produces a value that tells the pointer where to point. Without the *, the last `printf()` would print an address (the address of age). With the *, the `printf()` prints the value at that address.

You can assign a different value to age with the following statement:

```
age=41;                 /* Assign a new value to age */
```

You also can assign a value to age like this:

```
*pAge=41;
```

This declaration assigns 41 to the value to which pAge points.

TIP

The * appears before a pointer variable in only two places—when you declare a pointer variable, and when you dereference a pointer variable (to find the data it points to).

Pointers and Parameters

Now that you understand the pointer's * and & operators, you can finally see why `scanf()`'s requirements were not really as strict as they first appeared. While passing a regular variable to `scanf()`, you had to prefix the variable with the & operator. For instance, the following `scanf()` gets three integer values from the user:

```
scanf(" %d %d %d", &num1, &num2, &num3);
```

This `scanf()` does not pass the three variables, but passes the addresses of the three variables. Because `scanf()` knows the exact locations of these parameters in memory (because their addresses were passed), it goes to those addresses and puts the keyboard input values into those addresses.

This is the only way `scanf()` could work. If you passed these variables by copy, without putting the "address of" operator (&) before them, `scanf()` would get the keyboard input and fill a copy of the variables, but not the actual variables num1, num2, and num3. When `scanf()` then returned control to your program, you would not have the input values.

You might recall from Chapter 15, "Passing Values Between Functions," that you can override C's normal default of passing by value. To pass by address, pass a variable preceded by an & and put an asterisk before the parameter everywhere it appears in the receiving function. The following function call passes tries by address to the receiving function called prIt():

```
prIt(&tries);   /* Pass integer tries to prIt() by
                   address (tries would normally pass
                   by copy)                           */
```

The following function, prIt(), receives the address of tries, in effect receiving tries by address:

```
prIt(int *tries)            /* Receive tries by address
                               (dereference its value)   */

{
*tries++;                   /* This changes tries in calling
                               and receiving functions      */

        return 0;

}
```

Now that you understand the & and * operators, you can completely understand the passing of nonarray parameters by address to functions. (Arrays default to passing by address without requiring that you use & and *.)

EXAMPLE

1. The following section of a program declares three regular variables of three different data types, and pointers that point to those variables:

```
char initial= 'Q';    /* Declares three regular variables */
int num=40;           /* of three different types            */
float sales=2321.59;

char *pInitial=&initial;  /* Declares three pointers.    */
int * ptrNum=&num;        /* Pointer names and spacing   */
      float * salesAdd = &sales; /* after * are not critical. */
```

2. You can initialize pointers, just as with regular variables, with assignment statements. You do not have to initialize them when you declare them. The next few lines of code are equivalent to the code in the first example:

```
char initial;        /* Declares three regular variables */
int num;             /* of three different types           */
float sales;

char *pInitial;      /* Declares three pointers but does */
int * ptrNum;        /* not initialize them yet           */
float * salesAdd;

initial='Q';         /* Initializes the regular variables */
num=40;              /* with values                        */
sales=2321.59;

pInitial=&initial;   /* Initializes the pointers with */
ptrNum=&num;         /* the addresses of their          */
salesAdd=&sales;     /* corresponding variables         */
```

Notice that you do not put the * operator before the pointer variable names when assigning them values. You would prefix a pointer variable with the * only if you were dereferencing it.

NOTE

In this example, the pointer variables could have been assigned the addresses of the regular variables before the regular variables were assigned values. There would be no difference in the operation. The pointers are assigned the addresses of the regular variables no matter what the data in the regular variables is.

Keep the data type of each pointer consistent. Do not assign a floating-point variable to an integer's address. For instance, you cannot make the assignment statement

```
pInitial = &sales;      /* Invalid pointer assignment */
```

because pInitial can point only to character data, not to floating-point data.

3. The following program is an example you should study closely. It shows more about pointers and the pointer operators, & and *, than several pages of text can do.

```
/* Filename: C20POINT.C
   Demonstrates the use of pointer declarations
   and operators */
#include <stdio.h>
main()
{
    int num=123;                // A regular integer variable
    int *pNum;                  // Declares an integer pointer

    printf("num is %d\n", num);      // Prints value of num
    printf("The address of num is %ld \n", &num); // Prints
                                //        num's location
    pNum = &num;               // Puts address of num in pNum,
                                //  in effect making pNum point
                                //  to num
                                // No * in front of pNum
    printf("*pNum is %d \n", *pNum); // Prints value of num
    printf("pNum is %ld \n", pNum);   // Prints location of num

    return 0;
}
```

Here is the output from this program:

```
num is 123
The address of num is 65522
*pNum is 123
pNum is 65522
```

If you run this program, you probably will get different results for the value of pNum because your compiler will place num at a different location, depending on your memory setup. The actual address is moot, however. Because the pointer pNum always contains the address of num, and because you can dereference pNum to get num's value, the actual address is not critical.

4. The following program includes a function that swaps the values of any two integers passed to it. You might recall that a function can return only a single value. Therefore, before now, you could not write a function that changed two different values and returned both values to the calling function.

To swap two variables (reversing their values for sorting, as you saw in Chapter 19, "Working with Arrays"), you need the ability to pass both variables by address. Then, when the function reverses the variables, the calling function's variables also are swapped.

Notice the function's use of dereferencing operators before each occurrence of num1 and num2. You do not care at which addresses num1 and num2 are stored, but you must make sure that you dereference whatever addresses were passed to the function.

Be sure to pass arguments with the prefix & to functions that receive by address, as done here in main():

```c
/* Filename: C20SWAP.C
      Program that includes a function that swaps
      any two integers passed to it */
#include <stdio.h>
void swapThem(int *num1, int *num2);
void main(void);

void main(void)
{
     int i=10, j=20;
     printf("\n\nBefore swap, i is %d and j is %d\n\n",
             i, j);
     swapThem(&i, &j);
     printf("\n\nAfter swap, i is %d and j is %d\n\n",
             i, j);
```

```
        return 0;
}
void swapThem(int *num1, int *num2)
{
int temp;                       /* Variable that holds
                                     in-between swapped value. */
temp = *num1;                   // The asterisks ensure that the
*num1 = *num2;                  // calling function's variables
*num2 = temp;                   // (and not copies of them) are
                                // worked on in this function.
        return 0;
}
```

Arrays of Pointers

If you need to reserve many pointers for many different values, you might want to declare an array of pointers. You know that you can reserve an array of characters, integers, long integers, and floating-point values, as well as an array of every other data type available. You also can reserve an array of pointers, with each pointer being a pointer to a specific data type.

The following reserves an array of 10 integer pointer variables:

```
int *iptr[10]; // Reserves an array of 10 integer pointers
```

Figure 20.2 shows how C views this array. Each element holds an address (after being assigned values) that points to other values in memory. Each value pointed to must be an integer. You can assign an element from iptr an address just as you would for nonarray pointer variables. You can make iptr[4] point to the address of an integer variable named age by assigning it like this:

```
iptr[4] = &age;     /* Make iptr[4] point to address of age */
```

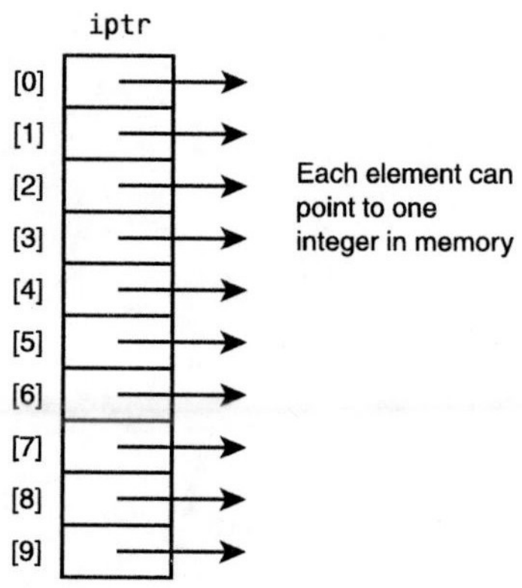

Figure 20.2: *An array of 10 integer pointers works like other arrays.*

The following reserves an array of 20 character pointer variables:

```
char *cpoint[20];          // Array of 20 character pointers
```

Again, the asterisk is not part of the array name. The asterisk lets C know that this is an array of integer pointers and not just an array of integers.

Some beginning C students get confused when they see such a declaration. Pointers are one thing, but reserving storage for arrays of pointers tends to bog down novices. However, reserving storage for arrays of pointers is easy to understand. Remove the asterisk from the last declaration

```
char cpoint[20];
```

and what do you have? You have just reserved a simple array of 20 characters. Adding the asterisk tells C to go one step further—rather than an array of character variables, you want an array of character-pointing variables. Instead of having each element be a character variable, you have each element hold an address that points to characters.

Reserving arrays of pointers will be much more meaningful after you learn about structures in the next few chapters. As with regular, nonpointing variables, an array makes processing several variables much easier. You can use a subscript to reference each variable (element) without having to use a different variable name for each value.

What's Next

Declaring and using pointers might seem like a lot of trouble at this point. Why assign *pNum a value when it is easier (and clearer) to assign a value directly to num? If you are asking yourself that question, you probably understand everything you should from this chapter and are ready to begin seeing the true power of pointers—combining pointers and array processing, which is described in the next chapter.

21

Using Pointers

Arrays and pointers are closely related in the C programming language. You can address arrays as if they were pointers and address pointers as if they were arrays. Being able to store and access pointers and arrays gives you the ability to store strings of data in array elements. Without pointers, you could not store strings of data in arrays because there is no fundamental string data type in C (no string variables, only string constants).

This chapter teaches you the following topics:

- Array names and pointers
- Character pointers
- Pointer arithmetic
- Ragged-edge arrays of string data

Array Names as Pointers

An array name is just a pointer, nothing more. To prove this, suppose that you have the following array declaration:

```
int ara[5] = {10, 20, 30, 40, 50};
```

If you printed ara[0], you would see 10. Because you now fully understand arrays, this is the value you would expect.

But what if you were to print *ara? Would *ara print anything? If so, what? If you thought an error message would print because ara is not a pointer but an array, you would be wrong. An array name is a pointer. If you print *ara, you also would see 10.

Recall how arrays are stored in memory. Figure 21.1 shows how ara would be mapped in memory. The array name, ara, is nothing more than a pointer that points to the first element of the array. Therefore, if you dereference that pointer, you dereference the value stored at the first element of the array, which is 10. Dereferencing ara is exactly the same thing as referring to ara[0], because they both produce the same value.

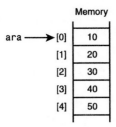

Figure 21.1: *Study how the array called* ara *appears in memory.*

You now see that you can reference an array with subscripts or with pointer dereferencing. Can you use pointer notation to print the third element of ara? Yes, and you already have the tools to do so. The following printf() prints ara[2] (the third element of ara) without using a subscript:

```
printf("%d",C1 *(ara+2) );        // Prints ara[2]
```

The expression *(ara+2) is not vague at all, if you remember that an array name is just a pointer that always points to the array's first element. *(ara+2) takes the address stored in ara, adds 2 to the address, and dereferences that location. The following holds true:

ara+0 points to ara[0]

ara+1 points to ara[1]

ara+2 points to ara[2]

ara+3 points to ara[3]

ara+4 points to ara[4]

Therefore, to print, store, or calculate with an array element, you can use either the subscript notation or the pointer notation. Because an array name contains the address of the array's first element, you must dereference the pointer to get the element's value.

INTERNAL LOCATIONS

C knows the internal data size requirements of characters, integers, floating-points, and the other data types on your computer. Therefore, because ara is an integer array, and because each element in an integer array consumes 2 to 4 bytes of storage, depending on the computer, C adds 2 or 4 bytes to the address if you reference arrays as just shown.

If you write *(ara+3) to refer to ara[3], C would add 6 or 12 bytes to the address of ara to get the third element. C does not add an actual 3. You do not have to worry about this, because C handles these internals. When you write *(ara+3), you are actually requesting that C add three integer addresses to the address of ara. If ara were a floating-point array, C would add three floating-point addresses to ara.

Pointer Advantages

Although arrays are really pointers in disguise, they are special types of pointers. An array name is a *pointer constant,* not a pointer variable. You cannot change the value of an array name, because you cannot change constants. This explains why you cannot assign an array new values during a program's execution. For instance, even if cname is a character array, the following is not valid in C:

```
cname = "Christine Chambers";   /* Invalid array assignment */
```

The array name, cname, cannot be changed because it is a constant. You would not attempt the statement

```
5 = 4 + 8 * 21;                     // Invalid assignment
```

because you cannot change the constant 5 to any other value. C knows that you cannot assign anything to 5, and C will print an error message if you attempt to change 5. C also knows that an array name is a constant and that you cannot change an array to another value. (You can assign values to an array only at declaration time, one element at a time during execution, or by using functions such as strcpy().)

This brings you to the most important reason to learn pointers: Pointers (except arrays referenced as pointers) are variables. You *can* change a pointer variable, and being able to do so makes processing virtually any data, including arrays, much more powerful and flexible.

EXAMPLE

1. By changing pointers, you make them point to different values in memory. The following program demonstrates how to change pointers. The program first defines two floating-point values. A floating-point pointer contains the address of the first variable, v1, and is used in the printf(). The pointer is then changed so that it points to the second floating-point variable, v2:

```
/* Filename: C21PTRCH.C
   Changes the value of a pointer variable */
#include <stdio.h>
main()
{
    float v1=676.54;                       // Defines two
    float v2=900.18;              // floating-point variables
    float * pV;            // Defines a floating-point pointer

    pV = &v1;                      // Makes pointer point to v1
    printf("The first value is %.2f \n", *pV);   // Prints
                                                 //   676.54

    pV = &v2;                  // Changes the pointer so that it
                               //   points to v2
    printf("The second value is %.2f \n", *pV);   // Prints
                                                  //   900.18

    return 0;
}
```

Because they can change pointers, most C programmers use pointers rather than arrays. Because arrays are easy to declare, C programmers sometimes declare arrays and then use pointers to reference those arrays. If the array data changes, the pointer helps to change it.

2. You can use pointer notation and reference pointers as arrays with array notation. The following program declares an integer array and an integer pointer that points to the start of the array. The array and pointer values are printed using subscript notation. Afterwards, the program uses array notation to print the array and pointer values.

Study this program carefully. You will see the inner workings of arrays and pointer notation:

```
/* Filename: C21ARPTR.C
   References arrays like pointers and
   pointers like arrays */
#include <stdio.h>
main()
{
```

```
int ctr;
int iara[5] = {10, 20, 30, 40, 50};
int *iptr;

iptr = iara;            // Make iptr point to array's first
                        // element. This would work also:
                        // iptr = &iara[0];

printf("Using array subscripts:\n");
printf("iara\tiptr\n");
for (ctr=0; ctr<5; ctr++)
    { printf("%d\t%d \n", iara[ctr], iptr[ctr]);   }

printf("\nUsing pointer notation:\n");
printf("iara\tiptr\n");
for (ctr=0; ctr<5; ctr++)
    { printf("%d\t%d \n", *(iara+ctr), *(iptr+ctr));   }

return 0;
}
```

OUTPUT

Here is the program's output:

```
Using array subscripts:
iara    iptr
10      10
20      20
30      30
40      40
50      50

Using pointer notation:
iara    iptr
10      10
20      20
30      30
40      40
50      50
```

Using Character Pointers

The ability to change pointers is best seen when working with character strings in memory. You can store strings in character arrays, or point to them with character pointers. Consider the following two string definitions:

```
char cara[] = "C is fun";    // An array holding a string
char *cptr = "C by Example";   // A pointer to the string
```

Figure 21.2 shows how C stores these two strings in memory. C stores both in basically the same way. You are familiar with the array definition. When assigning a string to a character pointer, C finds enough free memory to hold the string and assigns the address of the first character to the pointer. The previous two string definition statements do almost exactly the same thing; the only difference between them is the changeability of the two pointers (the array name and the character pointers).

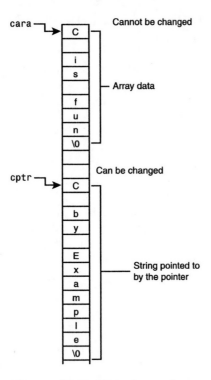

Figure 21.2: *This figure demonstrates the storage of two strings: one in an array and one pointed to.*

Because the %s control code prints strings, starting at the array or pointer name until the null zero is reached, you can print each of these strings with the following printf() statements:

```
printf("String 1: %s \n", cara);
printf("String 2: %s \n", cptr);
```

Notice that you print strings in arrays and strings pointed to in the same way. You might wonder what advantage one method of storing strings has over the other. The seemingly minor difference between these stored strings makes a big difference when you change them.

Suppose that you want to store the string Hello in the two strings. You cannot assign the string to the array like this:

```
cara = "Hello";                          // Invalid
```

Because you cannot change the array name, you cannot assign it a new value. The only way to change the contents of the array is by assigning the array characters from the string an element at a time, or by using a built-in function such as strcpy(). You can, however, make the character array point to the new string, like this:

```
cptr = "Hello";           // Change the pointer so that
                          // it points to the new string
```

TIP

If you want to store user input in a string pointed to by a pointer, first you must reserve enough storage for that input string. The easiest way to do this is to reserve a character array, and then assign a character pointer to the beginning element of that array, like this:

```
char input[81];           // Holds a string as long as
                          // 80 characters
char *iptr=input;         // Could also have done this:
                          // char *iptr=&input[0];
```

Now you can input a string by using the pointer:

```
gets(iptr);               // Make sure that iptr points to
                          //   the string typed by the user
```

You can use pointer manipulation, arithmetic, and modification on the input string.

EXAMPLE

1. Suppose that you want to store your sister's full name and print it. Instead of using arrays, you can use a character pointer. The following program does just that:

```
/* Filename: C21CP1.C
   Stores a name in a character pointer */
#include <stdio.h>
main()
{
    char *c="Bettye Lou Horn";

    printf("My sister's name is %s", c);
    return 0;
}
```

OUTPUT

This program prints the following:

```
My sister's name is Bettye Lou Horn
```

2. Suppose that you need to change a string pointed to by a character pointer. If your sister changed her last name to Henderson by marrying, your program could show both strings in the following manner:

```c
/* Filename: C21CP2.C
   Illustrates changing a character string */
#include <stdio.h>
main()
{
    char *c="Bettye Lou Horn";

    printf("My sister's maiden name was %s \n", c);

    c = "Bettye Lou Henderson";  // Assigns new string to c

    printf("My sister's married name is %s \n", c);
    return 0;
}
```

OUTPUT

The output is as follows:

```
My sister's maiden name was Bettye Lou Horn
My sister's married name is Bettye Lou Henderson
```

3. Do not use character pointers to change string constants. Doing so can confuse the compiler, and you probably will not get the results you expect. The following program is similar to those you just saw. Instead of making the character pointer point to a new string, this example attempts to change the contents of the original string:

```c
/* Filename: C21CP3.C
   Illustrates changing a character string improperly */
#include <stdio.h>
main()
{
    char *c="Bettye Lou Horn";

    printf("My sister's maiden name was %s \n", c);

    c += 11;             // Makes c point to the last name
                         // (the 12th character)
    c = "Henderson";     // Assigns a new string to c

    printf("My sister's married name is %s \n", c);
    return 0;
}
```

The program seems to change the last name from Horn to Henderson, but it does not. Here is the output of this program:

```
My sister's maiden name was Bettye Lou Horn
My sister's married name is Henderson
```

Why didn't the full string print? Because the address pointed to by c was incremented by 11, c still points to Henderson, so that was all that printed.

4. You might guess at a way to fix the last program. Instead of printing the string stored at c after assigning it to Henderson, you might want to decrement it by 11 so that it points to its original location, the start of the name. The code to do this follows, but it does not work as expected. Study the program before reading the explanation:

```c
/* Filename: C21CP4.C
   Illustrates changing a character string improperly */
#include <stdio.h>
main()
{
    char *c="Bettye Lou Horn";

    printf("My sister's maiden name was %s \n", c);

    c += 11;                     // Makes c point to the last
                                 // name (the 12th character)
    c = "Henderson";             // Assigns a new string to c
    c -= 11;                     // Makes c point to its
                                 //original location (???)

    printf("My sister's married name is %s \n", c);
    return 0;
}
```

This program produces garbage at the second printf(). There are actually two string constants in this program. When you first assign c to Bettye Lou Horn, C reserves space in memory for the constant string and puts the starting address of the string in c.

When the program then assigns c to Henderson, C finds room for another character constant, as shown in Figure 21.3. If you subtract 11 from the location of c, after it points to the new string Henderson, c points to an area of memory that your program is not using. There is no guarantee that printable data appears before the string constant Henderson. If you want to manipulate parts of the string, you must do so an element at a time, just as you must with arrays.

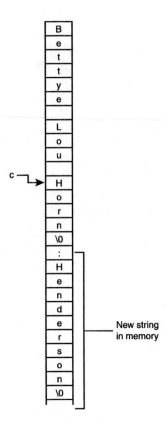

Figure 21.3: *Two string constants appear in memory because two string constants are used in the program.*

Pointer Arithmetic

You saw an example of pointer arithmetic when you accessed array elements with pointer notation. By now you should be comfortable with the fact that both of these array or pointer references are identical:

`ara[sub]` and `*(ara + sub)`

You can increment or decrement a pointer. If you increment a pointer, the address inside the pointer variable increments. The pointer does not always increment by 1, however.

Suppose that `fPtr` is a floating-point pointer that points to the first element of an array of floating-point numbers. You could initialize `fPtr` as follows:

```
float fara[] = {100.5, 201.45, 321.54, 389.76, 691.34};
fPtr = fara;
```

Figure 21.4 shows what these variables look like in memory. Each floating-point value in this example takes 4 bytes of memory.

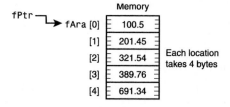

Figure 21.4: *A floating-point array appears to hold data; a pointer points to data.*

If you print the value of *fPtr, you see 100.5. Suppose that you increment fPtr by 1 with the following statement:

```
fPtr++;
```

C does not add 1 to the address in fPtr, even though it seems as though 1 should be added. In this case, because floating-point values take 4 bytes each on this machine, C adds 4 to fPtr. How does C know how many bytes to add to fPtr? C knows from the pointer's declaration how many bytes of memory pointers take. This is why the data type of pointers is so important.

After incrementing fPtr, if you were to print *fPtr, you would see 201.45, the second element in the array. If C added only 1 to the address in fPtr, fPtr would point only to the second byte of 100.5. This would output garbage to the screen.

NOTE
When you increment a pointer, C adds one data type size (in bytes) to the pointer, not 1. When you decrement a pointer, C subtracts one data type size (in bytes) from the pointer.

EXAMPLE

1. The following program defines an array with five values. An integer pointer is then initialized to point to the first element in the array. The rest of the program prints the dereferenced value of the pointer, and then increments the pointer so that it points to the next integer in the array.

   Just to show you what is going on, the size of integer values is printed at the bottom of the program. Because (in this case) integers take 2 bytes, C increments the pointer by 2 so that it points to the next integer. (The integers are 2 bytes apart from each other.)

   ```
   /* Filename: C21PTI.C
      Increments a pointer through an integer array */
   ```

```
#include <stdio.h>
main()
{
    int iara[] = {10,20,30,40,50};
    int *ip = iara;                     // The pointer points to
                                        // the start of the array

    printf("%d \n", *ip);
    ip++;                                   // 2 is actually added
    printf("%d \n", *ip);
    ip++;                               // 2 is actually added
    printf("%d \n", *ip);
    ip++;                               // 2 is actually added
    printf("%d \n", *ip);
    ip++;                               // 2 is actually added
    printf("%d \n\n", *ip);
    printf("The integer size is %d ",sizeof(int));
    printf("bytes on this machine");
    return 0;
}
```

OUTPUT

Here is the output from the program:

```
10
20
30
40
50
The integer size is 2 bytes on this machine
```

2. Here is the same program using a character array and a character pointer. Because a character takes only 1 byte of storage, incrementing a character pointer actually adds just 1 to the pointer; only 1 is needed because the characters are only 1 byte apart from each other:

```
/* Filename: C21PTC.C
   Increments a pointer through a character array */
#include <stdio.h>
main()
{
    char cara[] = {'a', 'b', 'c', 'd', 'e'};
    char *cp = cara;                    // The pointer points to
                                        // the start of the array
    printf("%c \n", *cp);
    cp++;                                   // 1 is actually added
    printf("%c \n", *cp);
```

```
    cp++;                           // 1 is actually added
    printf("%c \n", *cp);
    cp++;                           // 1 is actually added
    printf("%c \n", *cp);
    cp++;                           // 1 is actually added
    printf("%c \n\n", *cp);
    printf("The character size is %d ",sizeof(char));
    printf("bytes on this machine");
    return 0;
}
```

3. The next program shows the many ways you can add to, subtract from, and reference arrays and pointers. The program defines a floating-point array and a floating-point pointer. The body of the program prints the values from the array using array and pointer notation:

```
/* Filename: C21ARPT2.C
   Comprehensive reference of arrays and pointers */
#include <stdio.h>
main()
{
    float ara[] = {100.0, 200.0, 300.0, 400.0, 500.0};
    float *fptr;                        // Floating-point pointer

    /* Make pointer point to array's first value */
    fptr = &ara[0];                // Could also have been this:
                                   // fptr = ara;

    printf("%.1f \n", *fptr);                  // Prints 100.0
    fptr++;          // Points to next floating-point value
    printf("%.1f \n", *fptr);                  // Prints 200.0
    fptr++;          // Points to next floating-point value
    printf("%.1f \n", *fptr);                  // Prints 300.0
    fptr++;          // Points to next floating-point value
    printf("%.1f \n", *fptr);                  // Prints 400.0
    fptr++;          // Points to next floating-point value
    printf("%.1f \n", *fptr);                  // Prints 500.0

    fptr = ara;              // Points to first element again
    printf("%.1f \n", *(fptr+2) );   // Prints 300.00 but
                                     // does not change fptr

/* References both array and pointer using subscripts    */
    printf("%.1f   %.1f \n", (fptr+0)[0],
```

```
                         (ara+0)[0]);                        //  100.0   100.0
            printf("%.1f   %.1f \n", (fptr+1)[0],
                         (ara+1)[0]);                        //  200.0   200.0
            printf("%.1f   %.1f \n", (fptr+4)[0],
                         (ara+4)[0]);                        //  500.0   500.0

            /* References both array and pointer using subscripts.
               Notice that subscripts are based from addresses that
               begin before the data in the array and the pointer. */
            printf("%.1f   %.1f \n", (fptr-1)[2],
                         (ara-1)[2]);                        //  200.0   200.0
            printf("%.1f   %.1f \n", (fptr-20)[23],
                         (ara-20)[23]);                      //  400.0   400.0
            return 0;
        }
```

The following is the output from this program:

```
100.0
200.0
300.0
400.0
500.0
300.0
100.0    100.0
200.0    200.0
500.0    500.0
200.0    200.0
400.0    400.0
```

Arrays of Strings

You now are ready for one of the most useful applications of character pointers: storing arrays of strings. Actually, you cannot store an array of strings, but you can store an array of character pointers, and each character pointer can point to a string in memory.

By defining an array of character pointers, you define a *ragged-edge array*. Each row in the array contains a different number of characters.

The word *ragged-edge* derives from the use of word processors. A word processor typically can print text fully justified or with a ragged-right margin. The columns of this paragraph are fully justified, because both the left and the right columns align evenly. Letters you write by hand and type on typewriters (remember what a typewriter is?) generally have ragged-right margins. It is very difficult to type so that each line ends in exactly the same right column.

C supports two-dimensional tables which are fully justified. For example, if you declared a character table with five rows and 20 columns, each row would contain the same number of characters. You could define and initialize the table with the following statement:

```
char names[5][20]={ {"George"},
                    {"Michael"},
                    {"Joe"},
                    {"Marcus"},
                    {"Stephanie"} };
```

This table is shown in Figure 21.5. Notice that much of the table is wasted space. Each row takes 20 characters, even though the data in each row takes far fewer characters. The unfilled elements contain null zeros because C zeros out all elements you do not initialize in arrays. This type of table uses too much memory.

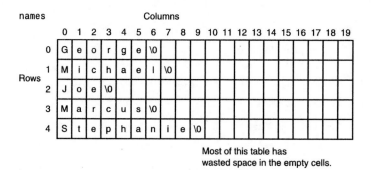

Figure 21.5: A fully justified table contains an equal number of cells in each row.

To fix the memory-wasting problem of fully justified tables, you should declare a single-dimensional array of character pointers. Each pointer points to a string in memory, and the strings do not have to be the same length.

Here is the definition for such an array:

```
char *names[5]={ {"George"},
                 {"Michael"},
```

```
        {"Joe"},
        {"Marcus"},
        {"Stephanie"} };
```

This array is single-dimensional. The definition should not confuse you, although it is something you have not seen. The asterisk before names makes this an array of pointers. The type of pointers is character. The strings are not being assigned to the array elements, but they are being pointed to by the array elements. Figure 21.6 shows this array of pointers. The strings are stored elsewhere in memory. Their actual locations are not critical because each pointer points to the starting character. The strings waste no data. Each string takes only as much memory as needed by the string and its terminating zero. This gives the data its ragged-right appearance.

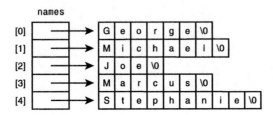

Figure 21.6: *The array that points to each of the five strings acts as if it held the string data.*

To print the first string, you would use this printf():

```
printf("%s", *names);              /* Prints George */
```

To print the second string, you would use this printf():

```
printf("%s", *(names+1));          /* Prints Michael */
```

Whenever you dereference any pointer element with the * dereferencing operator, you access one of the strings in the array. You can use a derefer-enced element any place you would use a string constant or character array (with strcpy(), strcmp(), and so on).

TIP

Working with pointers to strings is much more efficient than working with the strings. For instance, sorting a list of strings takes a lot of time if they are stored as a fully jus-tified table. Sorting strings pointed to by a pointer array is much faster. You swap only pointers during the sort, not entire strings.

---

1. Here is a full program that uses the pointer array with five names. The for loop controls the printf() function, printing each name in the string data. Now you can see why learning about pointer notation for arrays pays off:

```c
/* Filename: C21PTST1.C
   Prints strings pointed to by an array */
#include <stdio.h>
main()
{
    char *name[5]={ {"George"},      // Defines a ragged-edge
                    {"Michael"},  // array of pointers to
                    {"Joe"},         // strings
                    {"Marcus"},
                    {"Stephanie"} };
    int ctr;

    for (ctr=0; ctr<5; ctr++)
        { printf("String #%d is %s \n", (ctr+1), *(name+ctr)); }

    return 0;
}
```

The following is the output from this program:

```
String #1 is George
String #2 is Michael
String #3 is Joe
String #4 is Marcus
String #5 is Stephanie
```

2. The following program stores the days of the week in an array. When the user types a number from 1 to 7, the day of the week that matches that number (with Sunday being 1) displays by dereferencing the pointer that points to that string.

```c
/* Filename: C21PTST2.C
   Prints the day of the week based on an input value */
#include <stdio.h>
main()
{
    char *days[] = {"Sunday",    // The seven separate sets
                    "Monday",    // of braces are optional.
                    "Tuesday",
                    "Wednesday",
```

```
                         "Thursday",
                         "Friday",
                         "Saturday"};
        int dayNum;

        do
          { printf("What is a day number (from 1 to 7)? ");
            scanf(" %d", &dayNum);
          } while ((dayNum<1) || (dayNum>7));      // Ensures
                                                   // an accurate number


        dayNum--;                       // Adjusts for subscript
        printf("The day is %s\n", *(days+dayNum));
        return 0;
      }
```

What's Next

You deserve a break. You now understand the foundation of C's pointers
and array notation. As soon as you have mastered this section, you are on
your way to thinking in C as you design your programs. C programmers
know that C's arrays are pointers in disguise, and they program them
accordingly. As you progress into more advanced C concepts, you will appreciate the time you spent mastering pointer notation. The next chapter
introduces a new topic called *structures*. Structures enable you to store data
in a more unified manner than simple variables have allowed. Armed with
the pointer knowledge you now have, you will be able to write programs
that manipulate powerful data structures once you complete the next two
chapters.

Part VII

Advanced C

Introduction to Structures

Arrays of Structures

Simple C File Processing

Putting It All Together

22

Introduction to Structures

Using structures, you have the ability to group data and work with that data as a whole. Business data processing uses the concepts of structures in almost every program. Being able to manipulate several variables as a single group makes your programs easier to manage.

This chapter teaches you the following topics:

- Structure definitions
- Initializing structures
- The dot operator (.)
- Structure assignments
- Nested structures

Introducing Structures

A *structure* is a collection of one or more variable types. As you know, each element in an array must be the same data type, and you must refer to the entire array by its name. Each element (called a *member*) in a structure can be a different data type.

Suppose you wanted to keep track of your CD music collection. You might want to track the following pieces of information about each CD:

Title

Artist

Number of songs

Cost

Date bought

Five members would exist in this CD structure.

TIP

If you have programmed in other computer languages, or if you have ever used a database program, C structures are analogous to file records, and members are analogous to fields in those records.

After deciding on the members, you must decide what data type each member is. The title and artist would both be character arrays, the number of songs would be integer, the cost would be floating-point, and the date would be another character array. This information would be represented like this:

Member Name	Data Type
Title	Character array of 25 characters
Artist	Character array of 20 characters
Number of songs	Integer
Cost	Floating-point
Date bought	Character array of 8 characters

Each structure you define can have an associated structure name called a *structure tag*. Structure tags are not required in most cases, but it is generally best to define one for each structure in your program. The structure tag is not a variable name. Unlike array names that reference the array as variables, a structure tag is just a label for the structure's format.

You name structure tags yourself, using the same naming rules for variables. If you give the CD structure a structure tag named cdCollection, you are telling C that the tag called cdCollection looks like two character arrays, followed by an integer, a floating-point value, and a final character array.

A structure tag is actually a newly defined data type that you, the programmer, define. When you want to store an integer, you do not have to define to C what an integer is. C already knows what an integer is. When you want to store a CD collection's data, however, C does not know what format your CD collection will take. You have to tell C (using the example being described here) that you need a new data type. That data type will be your structure tag, called cdCollection in this example, and it will look like the structure previously described (two character arrays, integer, floating-point, and character array).

NOTE
No memory is reserved for structure tags. A structure tag is your own data type. C does not reserve memory for the integer data type until you declare an integer variable. C does not reserve memory for a structure until you declare a structure variable.

Figure 22.1 shows the CD structure, graphically representing the data types within the structure. Notice that there are five members and that each member is a different data type. The entire structure is called cdCollection because that is the structure tag.

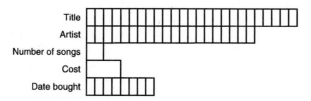

Figure 22.1: *This layout shows the* cdCollection *structure.*

NOTE
The mailing-list application in Chapter 25, "Putting It All Together," uses a structure to hold people's names, addresses, cities, states, and zip codes.

---

1. Suppose you were asked to write a program for a company's inventory system. The company had been using a card-file inventory system that tracked the following items:

   Item name

   Quantity in stock

   Quantity on order

   Retail price

   Wholesale price

This would be a perfect use for a structure containing five members. Before defining the structure, you would have to determine the data types of each member. After asking questions about the range of data (you must know the largest item name, and the most quantity that would ever be on order to ensure your data types will hold the data), you decide to use the following structure tag and data types:

Structure Tag: **Inventory Member**	**Data Type**
Item name	Character array of 20 characters
Quantity in stock	`long int`
Quantity on order	`long int`
Retail price	`double`
Wholesale price	`double`

2. Suppose the same company also wanted you to write a program that kept track of its monthly and annual salaries, printing a report at the end of the year that showed each month's individual salary and the total salary at the end of the year.

   What would the structure look like? Be careful. This type of data probably does not need a structure. Because all the monthly salaries will be the same data type, a floating-point or a double floating-point array will hold the monthly salaries nicely without the complexity of a structure.

   Structures are very useful for keeping track of data that must be grouped, such as inventory data, a customer's name and address data, or an employee data file.

Defining Structures

To define a structure, you must use the `struct` statement. The `struct` statement defines a new data type, with more than one member, for your program. The format of the `struct` statement is this:

```
struct [structure tag]
   {
      member definition;
      member definition;
         :
      member definition;
   } [one or more structure variables];
```

As mentioned earlier, the *structure tag* is optional (hence the brackets in the format). Each *member definition* is a normal variable definition, such as int i; or float sales[20]; or any other valid variable definition, including variable pointers if the structure requires a pointer as a member. At the end of the structure's definition, before the final semicolon, you can specify one or more structure variables.

If you specify a structure variable, you request C to reserve space for that variable. C knows that the variable is not integer, character, or any other internal data type; C knows the variable will be a type that looks like the structure. It might seem strange that the members themselves do not reserve storage, but they don't. The structure variables do. This is made very clear in the examples that follow.

Here is the way you would declare the CD structure:

```
struct cdCollection
    {
        char title[25];
        char artist[20];
        int numSongs;
        float price;
        char dateBought[9];
    } cd1, cd2, cd3;
```

Before going any further, you should be able to answer the following questions about this structure:

- What is the structure tag?
- How many members are there?
- What are the member data types?
- What are the member names?
- How many structure variables are there?
- What are their names?

The structure tag is called cdCollection. There are five members, two character arrays, an integer, a floating-point, and a character array. The member names are title, artist, numSongs, price, and dateBought. There are three structure variables—cd1, cd2, and cd3.

TIP

Many times, you can visualize structure variables as looking like a card-file inventory system. Figure 22.2 shows how you might keep your CD collection in a 3 by 5 card file. Each CD takes one card (representing each structure variable), and the information about each CD (the structure members) is on each card.

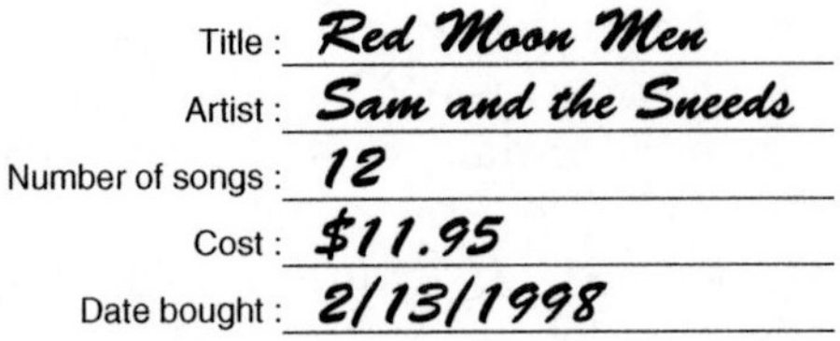

Title :	*Red Moon Men*
Artist :	*Sam and the Sneeds*
Number of songs :	*12*
Cost :	*$11.95*
Date bought :	*2/13/1998*

Figure 22.2: *Using structures is similar to using a card-based inventory filing system.*

If you had 1,000 CDs, you would have to declare 1,000 structure variables. Obviously, you would not want to list that many structure variables at the end of a structure definition. To help define structures for a large number of occurrences, you must define an *array of structures*—Chapter 23, "Arrays of Structures," shows you how to do that. For now, concentrate on familiarizing yourself with structure definitions.

EXAMPLE

1. Here is a structure definition of the inventory application described earlier in this chapter:

```
struct inventory
{
    char itemName[20];
    long int inStock;
    long int orderQty;
    float retail;
    float wholesale;
} item1, item2, item3, item4;
```

Four inventory structure variables are defined. Each structure variable—item1, item2, item3, and item4—looks like the structure.

2. Suppose a company wanted to track its customers and personnel. The following two structure definitions would create five structure variables for each structure. This example, having five employees and five customers, is very limited, but it serves to show how structures can be defined:

```
struct employees
{
    char empName[25];                  /* Employee's full name */
```

```
        char address[30];                    /* Employee's address */
        char city[10];
        char state[2];
        long int zip;
        double salary;                       /* Annual salary */
    } emp1, emp2, emp3, emp4, emp5;

    struct customers
    {
        char custName[25];                  /* Customer's full name */
        char address[30];                   /* Customer's address */
        char city[10];
        char state[2];
        long int zip;
        double balance;                     /* Balance owed to company */
    } cust1, cust2, cust3, cust4, cust5;
```

Each structure has very similar data. A little later in this chapter, you learn how to consolidate similar member definitions by creating nested structures.

TIP
Put comments to the right of members to document the purpose of the members.

Initializing Structure Data

There are two ways to initialize members of a structure. You can initialize members when you declare a structure, and you can initialize a structure within the body of the program. Most programs lend themselves to the latter method, because you do not always know structure data when you write your program.

Here is an example of a structure declared and initialized at the same time:

```
struct cdCollection
    {
    char title[25];
    char artist[20];
    int numSongs;
    float price;
    char dateBought[9];
    } cd1 = {"Red Moon Men", "Sam and the Sneeds",
            12, 11.95, "02/13/92"};
```

When first learning about structures, you might be tempted to initialize members individually inside the structure, such as

```
char artist[20]="Sam and the Sneeds";      // Invalid
```

You cannot initialize individual members because they are not variables. You can assign only values to variables. The only structure variable in this structure is cd1. The braces must enclose the data you initialize in the structure variables, just as they enclose data when you initialize arrays.

This method of initializing structure variables gets tedious when there are several structure variables (as there usually are). Putting the data into several variables, each set of data enclosed in braces, gets messy and takes too much space in your code.

More importantly, you usually will not even know the contents of the structure variables. Generally, the user enters data to be stored in structures, or you read them from a disk file.

A better approach to initializing structures is to use the *dot operator* (.). The dot operator is one way to initialize individual members of a structure variable within the body of your program. With the dot operator, you can treat each structure member almost as if it were a regular non-structure variable.

The format of the dot operator is

structureVariableName.memberName

A structure variable name must always precede the dot operator, and a member name must always appear after the dot operator. Using the dot operator is very easy, as the following examples show.

EXAMPLE

1. Here is a simple program that uses the CD collection structure and the dot operator to initialize the structure. Notice that the program treats members as if they were regular variables when combined with the dot operator:

```
/* Filename: C22ST1.C
   Structure initialization with the CD collection */
#include <stdio.h>
#include <string.h>
main()
{
    struct cdCollection
    {
        char title[25];
        char artist[20];
        int numSongs;
        float price;
```

```
        char dateBought[9];
    } cd1;

    /* Initialize members here */
    strcpy(cd1.title, "Red Moon Men");
    strcpy(cd1.artist, "Sam and the Sneeds");
    cd1.numSongs=12;
    cd1.price=11.95;
    strcpy(cd1.dateBought, "02/13/98");

    /* Print the data to the screen */
    printf("Here is the CD information:\n\n");
    printf("Title: %s \n", cd1.title);
    printf("Artist: %s \n", cd1.artist);
    printf("Songs: %d \n", cd1.numSongs);
    printf("Price: %.2f \n", cd1.price);
    printf("Date bought: %s \n", cd1.dateBought);

    return 0;
}
```

OUTPUT

Here is the output from this program:

```
Here is the CD information:
Title: Red Moon Men
Artist: Sam and the Sneeds
Songs: 12
Price: 11.95
Date bought: 02/13/98
```

2. By using the dot operator, you can get structure data from the keyboard with any of the data-input functions you know, such as scanf(), gets(), and getchar().

The following program asks the user for student information. To keep the example reasonably short, only two students are defined in the program:

```
/* Filename: C22ST2.C
    Structure input with student data */
#include <stdio.h>
#include <string.h>
main()
{
    struct students
    {
        char name[25];
```

```
        int age;
        float average;
    } student1, student2;

    /* Get data for two students */
    printf("What is first student's name? ");
    gets(student1.name);
    printf("What is the first student's age? ");
    scanf(" %d", &student1.age);
    printf("What is the first student's average? ");
    scanf(" %f", &student1.average);

    fflush(stdin);  /* Clear input buffer for next input */

    printf("\nWhat is second student's name? ");
    gets(student2.name);
    printf("What is the second student's age? ");
    scanf(" %d", &student2.age);
    printf("What is the second student's average? ");
    scanf(" %f", &student2.average);

    /* Print the data */
    printf("\n\nHere is the student information you
            entered:\n\n");
    printf("Student #1:\n");
    printf("Name:     %s\n", student1.name);
    printf("Age:      %d\n", student1.age);
    printf("Average: %.1f\n", student1.average);

    printf("\nStudent #2:\n");
    printf("Name:     %s\n", student2.name);
    printf("Age:      %d\n", student2.age);
    printf("Average: %.1f\n", student2.average);

    return 0;
}
```

OUTPUT

Here is the output from this program:

```
What is the first student's name? Joe Sanders
What is the first student's age? 13
What is the first student's average? 78.4

What is the second student's name? Mary Reynolds
What is the second student's age? 12
What is the second student's average? 95.3
```

```
Here is the student information you entered:

Student #1:
Name:      Joe Sanders
Age:       13
Average:   78.4

Student #2:
Name:      Mary Reynolds
Age:       12
Average:   95.3
```

3. Structure variables are passed by copy, not by address as with arrays. Therefore, if you fill a structure in a function, you must return it to the calling function in order for the calling function to recognize it, or use global structure variables, which is generally not recommended.

A good solution to the local/global structure problem is this: Define your structures globally without any structure variables. Define all your structure variables locally to the functions that need them. As long as your structure definition is global, you can declare local structure variables from that structure. All subsequent examples in this book use this method.

This is where structure tag plays an important role. Use the structure tag to define local structure variables. The following program is similar to the previous one. Notice that the student structure is defined globally with no structure variables. In each function, local structure variables are declared by referring to the structure tag. The structure tag keeps you from having to redefine the structure members every time you define a new structure variable:

```
/* Filename: C22ST3.C
   Structure input with student data passed to functions */
#include <stdio.h>
#include <string.h>
struct students fillStructs(struct students studentVar);
void prStudents(struct students studentVar);
void main(void);

struct students                         /* A global structure */
   {
      char name[25];
      int age;
      float average;
```

```
    };                              /* No memory reserved yet */

void main(void)
{
    struct students student1, student2;     /* Defines two
                                             local variables */

    /* Call function to fill structure variables */
    student1 = fillStructs(student1);          /* student1
                    is passed by copy, so it must be
                    returned for main() to recognize it */
    student2 = fillStructs(student2);

    /* Print the data */
    printf("\n\nHere is the student information you");
    printf(" entered:\n\n");
    prStudents(student1);  /* Print first student's data */
    prStudents(student2); /* Print second student's data */

    return 0;
}

struct students fillStructs(struct students studentVar)
{
    /* Get student's data */
    fflush(stdin);   /* Clear input buffer for next input */
    printf("What is student's name? ");
    gets(studentVar.name);
    printf("What is the student's age? ");
    scanf(" %d", &studentVar.age);
    printf("What is the student's average? ");
    scanf(" %f", &studentVar.average);

    return (studentVar);
}

void prStudents(struct students studentVar)
{
    printf("Name:    %s\n", studentVar.name);
    printf("Age:     %d\n", studentVar.age);
    printf("Average: %.1f\n", studentVar.average);
    return 0;
}
```

The prototype and definition of the fillStructs() function might seem complicated, but it follows the same pattern you have seen throughout this book. Before a function name, you must declare void or put the return data type if the function returns a value. fillStructs() does return a value, and the type of value it returns is struct students.

4. Because structure data is nothing more than regular variables grouped together, feel free to calculate using structure members. As long as you use the dot operator, you can treat structure members just as you would other variables.

The following example asks for a customer's balance and uses a discount rate, included in the customer's structure, to calculate a new balance. To keep the example short, the structure's data is initialized at variable declaration time.

This program does not actually require structures because only one customer is used. Individual variables could have been used, but they would not illustrate calculating with structures.

```
/* Filename: C22CUST.C
   Updates a customer balance in a structure */
#include <stdio.h>

struct customerRec
    {
        char custName[25];
        double balance;
        float disRate;
    } ;

main()
{
    struct customerRec customer = {"Steve Thompson",
                                   2431.23, .25};

    printf("Before the update, %s", customer.custName);
    printf(" has a balance of $%.2f\n", customer.balance);

    /* Update the balance */
    customer.balance *= (1.0[ms]customer.disRate);

    printf("After the update, %s", customer.custName);
    printf(" has a balance of $%.2f\n", customer.balance);
    return 0;
}
```

5. You can copy the members of one structure variable to the members of another as long as both structures have the same format. Some older versions of C require you to copy each member individually when you want to copy one structure variable to another, but ANSI C makes duplicating structure variables easy.

Being able to copy one structure variable to another will seem more meaningful when you read Chapter 23.

The following program declares three structure variables, but initializes only the first one with data. The other two are then initialized by assigning the first structure variable to them:

```c
/* Filename: C22STCPY.C
   Demonstrates assigning one structure to another */
#include <stdio.h>

struct student
{
   char stName[25];
   char grade;
   int age;
   float average;
};

main()
{
   struct student std1 = {"Joe Brown", 'A', 13, 91.4};
   struct student std2, std3;         /* Not initialized */

   std2 = std1;              /* Copies each member of std1 */
   std3 = std1;              /* to std2 and std3           */


   printf("The contents of std2:\n");
   printf("%s, %c, ", std2.stName, std2.grade);
   printf("%d, %.1f\n\n", std2.age, std2.average);

   printf("The contents of std3:\n");
   printf("%s, %c, ", std3.stName, std3.grade);
   printf("%d, %.1f\n", std3.age, std3.average);
   return 0;
}
```

Here is the output from the program:

```
The contents of std2
Joe Brown, A, 13, 91.4

The contents of std3
Joe Brown, A, 13, 91.4
```

Notice that each member of std1 was assigned to std2 and std3 with two single assignments.

Nested Structures

C gives you the ability to nest one structure definition within another. This saves time when you are writing programs that use similar structures. You have to define the common members only once in their own structure and then use that structure as a member in another structure.

The following two structure definitions illustrate this point:

```
struct employees
{
    char empName[25];            /* Employee's full name */
    char address[30];             /* Employee's address */
    char city[10];
    char state[2];
    long int zip;
    double salary;                        /* Annual salary */
};


struct customers
{
    char custName[25];           /* Customer's full name */
    char address[30];             /* Customer's address */
    char city[10];
    char state[2];
    long int zip;
    double balance;           /* Balance owed to company */
};
```

These structures hold different data. One structure is for employee data and the other holds customer data. Even though the data should be kept separate (you don't want to send a customer a paycheck!), the structure definitions have a lot of overlap and can be consolidated by creating a third structure.

Suppose you created the following structure:

```
struct addressInfo
{
    char address[30];          /* Common address information */
    char city[10];
    char state[2];
    long int zip;
};
```

This structure could then be used as a member in the other structures, like this:

```
struct employees
{
    char empName[25];              /* Employee's full name */
    struct addressInfo eAddress;   /* Employee's address */
    double salary;                     /* Annual salary */
};
```

```
struct customers
{
    char custName[25];             /* Customer's full name */
    struct addressInfo cAddress;   /* Customer's address */
    double balance;                /* Balance owed to company */
};
```

It is important to realize that there is a total of three structures, and that they have the tags addressInfo, employees, and customers. How many members does the employees structure have? If you answered three, you are correct. There are three members in both employees and customers. The employees structure has the structure of a character array, followed by the addressInfo structure, followed by the double floating-point member salary.

Figure 22.3 shows how these structures look.

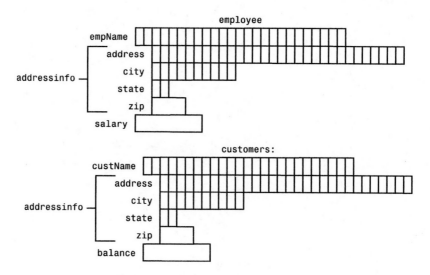

Figure 22.3: *You might nest structures inside other structures.*

As soon as you define a structure, that structure is then a new data type in the program and can be used anywhere a data type (such as int, float, and so on) can appear.

You can assign members' values using the dot operator. To assign the customer balance a number, you can type something like this:

```
customer.balance = 5643.24;
```

The nested structure might seem to pose a problem. How can you assign a value to one of the nested members? By using the dot operator, you must nest the dot operator just as you nest the structure definitions. You would assign a value to the customer's zip code like this:

```
customer.cAddress.zip = 34312;
```

To assign a value to the employee's zip code, you would do this:

```
employee.eAddress.zip = 59823;
```

What's Next

With structures you have the ability to group data in more flexible ways than arrays allow. Your structures can contain members of different data types. You can initialize the structures either at declaration time or during the program with the dot operator. Structures become even more powerful when you declare arrays of structure variables. The next chapter shows you how to declare several structure variables without giving them each a different name. By doing so, you can step through structures much quicker using C's loop constructs.

23

Arrays of Structures

This chapter shows you how to create different kinds of data structures. After creating an array of structures, you can store many occurrences of your data values. Arrays of structures are good for storing a complete employee file, inventory file, or any other set of data that fits within the structure format. Whereas arrays provide a handy way to store several values that are the same type, with arrays of structures you can store several values of different types together, grouped as structures. Dynamic memory allocation enables you to reserve memory when you need storage instead of having to define variables in advance.

This chapter teaches you the following topics:

- Creating arrays of structures
- Initializing arrays of structures
- Referencing elements from a structure array
- Dynamic memory allocation with `malloc()` and `free()`

Declaring Arrays of Structures

It is very easy to declare an array of structures. Specify the number of reserved structures, inside array brackets, when you declare the structure variable. Consider the following structure definition:

```
struct stores
     { int employees;
          int registers;
          double sales;
     } store1, store2, store3, store4, store5;
```

This structure should pose no problem for you to understand because no new commands exist in the structure declaration. This structure declaration creates five structure variables. Figure 23.1 shows how C stores these five structures in memory. Each of the structure variables has three members—two integers followed by a double floating-point value.

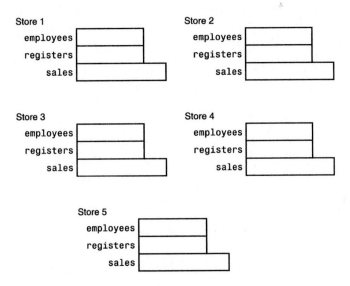

Figure 23.1: *The structure of* store1, store2, store3, store4, *and* store5 *structure variables are identical.*

If the fourth store increased its employee count by three, you could update the store's employee number with the following assignment statement:

```
store4.employees += 3;          /* Add 3 to this store's
                                   employee count */
```

Suppose that the fifth store just opened and you want to initialize its members with data. If the stores are a chain and the new store is similar to one of the others, you might begin initializing the store's data by assigning each of its members the same data as another store's, like this:

```
store5 = store2;              /* Define initial values
                                 for the store5 members */
```

Such structure declarations are fine for a small number of structures, but if the stores were a national chain, five structure variables would not be enough. Suppose there were 1,000 stores. You would not want to create 1,000 different store variables and work with each one individually. It would be much easier to create an array of store structures.

Consider the following structure declaration:

```
struct stores
     { int employees;
          int registers;
          double sales;
     } store[1000];
```

In one quick declaration, this code creates 1,000 store structures, each one containing three members. Figure 23.2 shows how the first four of these structure variables appear in memory. Notice the name of each individual structure variable: store[0], store[1], store[2], and so on. The name is the same and only the subscript distinguishes the variables.

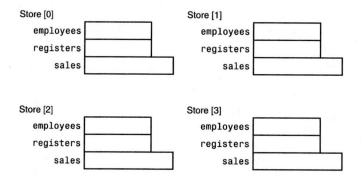

Figure 23.2: *An array of the* store *structures makes expansion simple.*

CAUTION

Be careful that your computer does not run out of memory when you create a large number of structures. Arrays of structures quickly consume valuable memory. You might have to create fewer structures, storing more data in disk files and less data in memory.

The element store[2] is an array element. This array element, unlike the others you have seen, is a structure variable. Therefore, it contains three members, each of which you can reference with the dot operator.

The dot operator works the same way for structure array elements as it does for regular structure variables. If the number of employees for the fifth store (store[4]) increased by three, you could update the structure variable like this:

```
store[4].employees += 3;      /* Add 3 to this store's
                                 employee count */
```

You can assign complete structures to one another using array notation also. To assign all the members of the 20th store to the 45th store, you would do this:

```
store[44] = store[19];     /* Copy all members from the
                              20th store to the 45th */
```

The rules of arrays are still in force here. Each element of the array called store is the very same data type. The data type of store is struct stores. As with any array, each element must be the same data type; you cannot mix data types within the same array. This array's data type happens to be a structure you created containing three members. The data type for store[316] is the same for store[981] and store[74].

The name of the array, store, is a pointer constant to the starting element of the array, store[0]. Therefore, you can use pointer notation to reference the stores. To assign store[60] the same value as store[23], you can reference the two elements like this:

```
*(store+60) = *(store+23);
```

You also can mix array and pointer notations, such as

```
store[60] = *(store+23);
```

and get the same results.

You can increase the sales of store[8] by 40% using pointer or subscript notation as well, as in

```
store[8].sales = (*(store+8)).sales * 1.40;
```

The extra pair of parentheses are required because the dot operator has precedence over the dereferencing symbol in C's hierarchy of operators (see Appendix B, "C's Precedence Table"). Of course, in this case, the code is not helped by the pointer notation. The following is a much clearer way to increase the sales by 40%:

```
store[8].sales *= 1.40;
```

KEEP YOUR ARRAY NOTATION STRAIGHT

You would never access the member sales like this:

```
store.sales[8] = 3234.54;          /* Invalid */
```

Array subscripts follow only array elements. sales is not an array; it was declared as being a double floating-point number. store can never be used without a subscript (unless you are using pointer notation).

Here is a corrected version of the previous assignment statement:

```
store[8].sales=3234.54;           /* Correctly assigns
                                       the value        */
```

The following examples build an inventory data-entry system for a mail-order firm using an array of structures. There is very little new you have to know when working with arrays of structures. Concentrate on the notation used when accessing arrays of structures and their members to get comfortable with the arrays of structures notation.

EXAMPLE

1. Suppose you work for a mail-order company that sells disk drives. You are given the task of writing a tracking program for the 125 different drives you sell. You must keep track of the following information:

   Storage capacity in megabytes

   Access time in milliseconds

   Vendor code (A, B, C, or D)

   Cost

   Price

   Because there are 125 different disk drives in the inventory, the data will fit nicely into an array of structures. Each array element is a structure containing the five members described in the list.

   The following structure definition defines the inventory:

   ```
   struct inventory
   {
        long int storage;
        int accessTime;
        char vendorCode;
        double code;
        double price;
   } drive[125];   /* Defines 125 occurrences of the structure */
   ```

2. When working with a large array of structures, your first concern should be how the data will be input into the array elements. The application determines the best method of data entry.

For instance, if you are converting from an older computerized inventory system, you will have to write a conversion program that reads the inventory file in its native format and saves it to a new file in the format needed by your C programs. This is no easy task. It requires that you have extensive knowledge of the system you are converting from.

If you are writing a computerized inventory system for the first time, your job is a little easier because you do not need to worry about converting the old files. You still must realize that someone has to type the data into the computer. You will have to write a data-entry program that receives each inventory item from the keyboard and saves it to a disk file. You should give the user a chance to edit inventory data to correct any data that he or she originally might have typed incorrectly.

One of the reasons this book waits until the last chapters to introduce disk files is that disk file formats and structures share a common bond. As soon as you store data in a structure, or more often, in an array of structures, you can very easily write that data to a disk file using straightforward disk I/O commands.

The following program takes the array of disk drive structures shown in the previous example and adds a data-entry function so that the user can enter data into the array of structures. The program is menu-driven. The user has a choice, when starting the program, to add data, print data to the screen, or exit the program. Because you have yet to see disk I/O commands, the data in the array of structures goes away when the program ends. As mentioned earlier, saving those structures to disk is an easy task after you learn C's disk I/O commands. For now, concentrate on the manipulation of the structures.

This program is longer than many you have seen in this book, but if you have followed the discussion of structures and the dot operator, you should have little trouble following the code:

```
/* Filename: C23DSINV.C
   Data-entry program for a disk drive company */
#include <stdio.h>
#include <stdlib.h>

struct inventory               // Global structure definition
{
    long int storage;
    int accessTime;
    char vendorCode;
    float cost;
    float price;
};               // No structure variables defined globally
```

```
void dispMenu(void);
struct inventory enterData();
void seeData(struct inventory disk[125], int numItems);
void main(void);

void main(void)
{
struct inventory disk[125];    // Local array of structures
    int ans;
    int numItems=0;                    // Number of total items
                                       // in the inventory

    do
      {
          do
            { dispMenu();    // Display menu of user choices
              scanf(" %d", &ans);      // Get user's request
            } while ((ans<1) || (ans>3));

            switch (ans)
        { case (1): { disk[numItems] = enterData(); // Enter
                                            // disk data
                    numItems++; // Increment number of items
                    break; }
          case (2): { seeData(disk, numItems);  // Display
                                            // disk data
                    break; }
          default : { break; }
        }
        } while (ans!=3);               // Quit program
                                        // when user is through
        return 0;
}

void dispMenu(void)
{

    printf("\n\n*** Disk Drive Inventory System ***\n\n");
    printf("Do you want to:\n\n");
    printf("\t1. Enter new item in inventory\n\n");
    printf("\t2. See inventory data\n\n");
    printf("\t3. Exit the program\n\n");
    printf("What is your choice? ");
    return 0;
}
```

```
struct inventory enterData()
{
    struct inventory diskItem;    // Local variable to fill
                                  //  with input

    printf("\n\nWhat is the next drive's storage in \
            mega bytes? ");
    scanf(" %ld", &diskItem.storage);
    printf("What is the drive's access time in ms? ");
    scanf(" %d", &diskItem.accessTime);
    printf("What is the drive's vendor code (A, B, C, \
            or D)? ");
    fflush(stdin);   /* Discard input buffer
                            before getting character */
    diskItem.vendorCode = getchar();
    getchar();   /* Discard carriage return */
    printf("What is the drive's cost? ");
    scanf(" %f", &diskItem.cost);
    printf("What is the drive's price? ");
    scanf(" %f", &diskItem.price);

    return (diskItem);
}

void seeData(struct inventory disk[125], int numItems)
{
    int ctr;
    printf("\n\nHere is the inventory listing:\n\n");
    for (ctr=0;ctr<numItems;ctr++)
        {
        printf("Megabyte storage: %ld\t", disk[ctr].storage);
        printf("Access time: %d\n", disk[ctr].accessTime);
        printf("Vendor code: %c\t", disk[ctr].vendorCode);
        printf("Cost: $%.2f\t", disk[ctr].cost);
        printf("Price: $%.2f\n", disk[ctr].price);
        }
    return 0;
}
```

The output from a sample run of this program appears next. An item is being entered into the inventory file:

OUTPUT

```
*** Disk Drive Inventory System ***

Do you want to:
```

```
1. Enter new item in inventory

2. See inventory data

3. Exit the program

What is your choice? 1

What is the next drive's storage in megabytes? 3500
What is the drive's access time in ms? 17
What is the drive's vendor code (A, B, C, or D)? A
What is the drive's cost? 121.56
What is the drive's price? 230.00
```

A few lines from the inventory listing produced from such data entry appears next. There are many features and error-checking functions you can add, but this program is the foundation of a more comprehensive inventory system. You can easily adapt it to a different type of inventory, a video tape collection, a coin collection, or any other tracking system just by changing the structure definition and the member names throughout the program.

```
Here is the inventory listing:

Megabyte Storage: 3500 Access time: 17
Vendor Code: A Cost: $121.56    Price: $230.00
```

Using Arrays as Members

Members of structures themselves can be arrays. Array members pose no new problems, but you have to be careful when you access individual array elements. Keeping track of arrays of structures that contain array members might seem like a great deal of work on your part, but there is really nothing to it.

Consider the following structure definition. This statement declares an array of 100 structures, each structure holding payroll information for a company. Two of the members, name and department, are arrays:

```
struct payroll
  { char name[25];              /* Employee name array */
    int dependents;
    char department[10];        /* Department name array */
    float salary;
  } employee[100];              /* An array of 100 employees */
```

Figure 23.3 shows what these structures look like. The first and third members are arrays. name is an array of 25 characters, and department is an array of 10 characters.

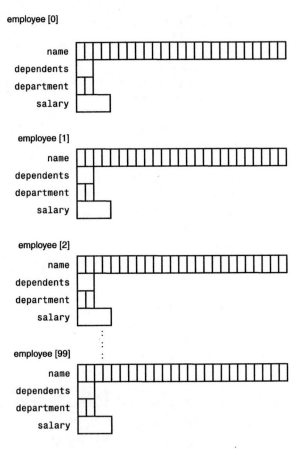

Figure 23.3: *Individual members can be arrays inside an array of structures.*

Suppose that you need to save the 25th employee's initial in a character variable. Assuming that initial is already defined as a character variable, the following statement assigns the employee's initial to initial:

```
initial = employee[24].name[0];
```

The double subscripts might look confusing, but the dot operator requires a structure variable on its left (employee[24]) and a member on its right (name's first array element). Being able to refer to member arrays makes the processing of character data in structures simple.

1. Suppose that an employee got married and wanted her name changed in the payroll file. (She happens to be the 45th employee in the array of structures.) Given the payroll structure described in the previous section, this would assign a new name to her structure:

```
strcpy(employee[44].name, "Mary Larson");   /* Assign
                                           a new name */
```

When you refer to a structure variable using the dot operator, you can use regular commands and functions to process the data in the structures.

2. Here is a very comprehensive example of the steps you might go through to write a C program. Assume that you have been hired by a local bookstore to write a magazine inventory system. You need to track the following:

> Magazine title (at most, 25 characters)
> Publisher (at most, 20 characters)
> Month (1, 2, 3,...12)
> Publication year
> Number of copies in stock
> Number of copies on order
> Price of magazine (dollars and cents)

Suppose that there is a projected maximum of 1,000 magazine titles that the store will ever carry. This means that you need 1,000 occurrences of the structure, not 1,000 magazines total. Here is a good structure definition for such an inventory:

```
struct magInfo
   { char title[25];
     char pub[25];
     int month;
     int year;
     int stockCopies;
     int orderCopies;
     float price;
   } mags[1000];               // Define 1000 occurrences
```

Because this program will consist of more than one function, it will be best to declare the structure globally, and the structure variables locally within the functions that need them.

This program needs three basic functions: a main() controlling function, a data-entry function, and a data printing function. You can add much more, but this is a good start for an inventory system. To keep the length of this example reasonable, assume that the user will want to enter several magazines, then print the magazine list. (To make the program more "usable," you would want to add a menu so that the user can control when he or she adds and prints the information, as well as add more error-checking and editing capabilities.)

Here is an example of the complete data-entry and printing program with prototypes. The arrays of structures are passed between the functions from main():

```c
/* Filename: C23MAG.C
   Magazine inventory program for adding and displaying
   a bookstore's magazines */
#include <stdio.h>
#include <ctype.h>

struct magInfo
    { char title[25];
      char pub[25];
      int month;
      int year;
      int stockCopies;
      int orderCopies;
      float price;
    };

struct magInfo fillMags(struct magInfo mag);
void printMags(struct magInfo mags[], int magCtr);
void main(void);

void main(void)
{
    struct magInfo mags[1000];
    int magCtr=0;               /* Number of magazine titles */
    char ans;

    do
    {                           /* Assumes that there will be
                                   at least one magazine filled */
        mags[magCtr] = fillMags(mags[magCtr]);
        printf("Do you want to enter another magazine? ");
        fflush(stdin);
        ans = getchar();
        fflush(stdin);          /* Discard carriage return */
        if (toupper(ans) == 'Y')
          { magCtr++; }
```

```
          } while (toupper(ans) == 'Y');
        printMags(mags, magCtr);
        return 0;               /* Return to operating system */
}


void printMags(struct magInfo mags[], int magCtr)
{
    int i;
    for (i=0; i<=magCtr; i++)
      { printf("\n\nMagazine %d:\n", i+1);    /* Adjust for
                                                  subscript */
        printf("\nTitle: %s \n", mags[i].title);
        printf("\tPublisher: %s \n", mags[i].pub);
        printf("\tPub. Month: %d \n", mags[i].month);
        printf("\tPub. Year: %d \n", mags[i].year);
        printf("\tIn-stock: %d \n", mags[i].stockCopies);
        printf("\tOn order: %d \n", mags[i].orderCopies);
        printf("\tPrice: %.2f \n", mags[i].price);
      }
    return 0;
}


struct magInfo fillMags(struct magInfo mag)
{
    puts("\n\nWhat is the title? ");
    gets(mag.title);
    puts("Who is the publisher? ");
    gets(mag.pub);
    puts("What is the month (1, 2, ..., 12)? ");
    scanf(" %d", &mag.month);
    puts("What is the year? ");
    scanf(" %d", &mag.year);
    puts("How many copies in stock? ");
    scanf(" %d", &mag.stockCopies);
    puts("How many copies on order? ");
    scanf(" %d", &mag.orderCopies);
    puts("How much is the magazine? ");
    scanf(" %f", &mag.price);
    return (mag);
}
```

Using `malloc()` and `free()` for Dynamic Memory Allocation

The difference between a beginning C programmer and an expert C programmer is the knowledge of *dynamic memory allocation*. Using dynamic memory allocation, you can request memory when you need it. Instead of giving the memory names as you do with variables, you create pointers that point to the newly allocated memory. Although you must define the pointers in advance, the memory that the pointers point to (such as an array of structures) doesn't consume memory until you need the memory.

The pool of memory your program draws from is called the *heap*. The heap is the unused memory not taken up by DOS, your programs, and your program variables.

NOTE

Local variables are reserved before your program ever begins, just as global variables are. Some people mistakenly believe that local variables are just as good as dynamically allocated data, but you must remember that local variables are not visible throughout an entire program. Local variables are reserved at the very beginning, when the program first begins running.

The size of the heap grows and shrinks as your program runs. Without using the heap and dynamic memory allocation, your program consumes the same amount of memory space for its entire run, Therefore, if a regular program uses a huge array of long character arrays in only a single function, that array consumes memory for the entire program. If you dynamically allocate the array space, however, the memory is only consumed for the lines that need the memory and the memory is released after the program is finished with it.

Dynamic memory allocation is especially important when you program in networked and windowed environments, as is more common every day. All the users and program tasks need to share the same computer's memory, so programs shouldn't reserve memory until they need it.

The `malloc()` function allocates memory from the heap and assigns it to your programs; `free()` releases your program memory back to the heap. The concept and use of `malloc()` is not difficult, but the syntax of `malloc()` looks intimidating to newcomers.

Looking at `malloc()` and `free()`

Here are the formats of `malloc()` and `free()`:

```
void * malloc(sizeToReserve)

free(pointerToHeap)
```

Of the two, `malloc()` takes a little more time to understand. Remember that both `malloc()` and `free()` are functions, not commands. `malloc()` returns a *void pointer*. A void pointer is a special kind of pointer that you *must* typecast. You've never typecast pointers before in this book, only regular data types such as `int`.

Here is an example of code that uses `malloc()`:

```
int * countPtr;    // Defines an integer pointer
countPtr = (int *)malloc(sizeof(int));
```

TIP

Read `malloc()` function calls from right to left.

Here is what the second statement does: `malloc()` needs to know exactly how much heap memory you want to grab. Because this code allocates a single integer from the heap, the `sizeof()` amount of an `int` is requested. (Integers take different amounts of memory on different computers, so you must use `sizeof` for any data allocated.)

After `malloc()` does its job grabbing enough heap memory to hold an integer, `malloc()` returns a void pointer that you must typecast to an integer pointer. The `(int *)` typecasts the pointer to an integer. (Without the `*`, the typecast can work only on nonpointer data.) Figure 23.4 shows what the `malloc()` function accomplished.

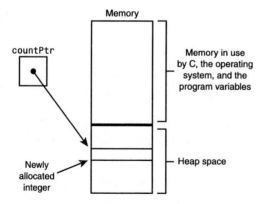

Figure 23.4: *The memory after you allocate a single integer.*

NOTE

If you reserve a `float` or a `double`, you must allocate the size of those data types instead of `int` as done here.

The integer pointer is your only access to the heap memory. `malloc()` does not assign a variable name to the allocated data, but returns only a pointer to the data. Therefore, if you want to store a value such as 17 in the heap's newly allocated value, you must do so through the pointer, like this:

```
*countPtr = 17;   // Store 17 on the heap
```

If you want to print the value on the heap, you can do so like this:

```
printf("The value is %d.\n", *countPtr);
```

After your program finishes with the heap value, it's much easier to give the memory back to the heap than it was to allocate it. Use `free()` like this:

```
free(countPtr);   // Gives the memory back to the heap
```

WHAT HAVE WE SAVED?

You might not think that much has happened, except that you've learned a difficult function. Although you've seen how to reserve an integer when you need it, the pointer to that integer (`countPtr`) had to be reserved for the entire program.

Remember that a pointer is no different from an array name. Therefore, with a single pointer, you can dynamically allocate an entire array when you need it!

Suppose that you needed an array of 100 floating-point values. Here is how to dynamically allocate the array (assuming that `fPtr` is already defined to be a `float` pointer):

```
fPtr = (float *)malloc(100 * sizeof(float));
```

Notice that `malloc()` is being instructed to reserve 100 floating-point values on the heap and to return, after the typecast, a floating-point pointer to the first of the 100 values. You now have an array. Here are a few things you can do:

```
for (i=6; i<100; i++)
   { fPtr[i] = 0.0; } // Zero the whole array on the heap
fPtr[20] = 23.54;     // store a value in the 21st element
*(fPtr+20) = 23.54;   // Store a value in the 21st element
```

The last two statements both do the same thing, except that one uses array subscript notation and the other uses pointer notation.

When you are through with the heap array, you can release the entire array back to the heap with this single `free()` function call:

```
free(fPtr);   // The free heap space will now grow
```

NOTE

C remembers how much memory you allocated with `malloc()` so that when you use `free()` with the same pointer, the entire memory space is freed.

You can even allocate structures and arrays of structures! Be sure to include the `sizeof()` information for whatever data element you want to reserve in the heap.

CAUTION
If you do not call `free()`, C frees the allocated memory back to the heap when your program ends. If, however, you are going to keep unused space allocated after you are done with it, making other tasks and users strain more for resources, you might as well not use dynamic memory allocation to begin with.

This section has only scratched the surface of dynamic memory allocation, but some examples that follow will help clear things up. The bottom line is this: Use dynamic allocation when you don't know in advance how many array elements you need, when you are getting user input into an array ragged-right edge array elements, or when you are working in a multitasking or multiuser environment. For example, you can declare an array of 100 structure pointers, but not waste the memory for each of the actual structures until the user is ready to enter data into the next structure.

TIP
Be sure to include `stdlib.h` in all programs that call `malloc()` and `free()`.

EXAMPLE

1. This example first defines three pointer variables and then stores data on the heap at the location of those pointers. If a pointer points to several heap values, you can treat the pointer as though it were a dynamically allocated array as done with this program's `myName` pointer:

```
/* Filename: C23DYN1.C */
/* Dynamically allocate simple
    variables on the heap then
    deallocate them */
#include <stdio.h>
#include <stdlib.h>
main()
{
    int *iPtr;
    float *fPtr;
    char *myName;
    iPtr = (int *)malloc(sizeof(int)),
    fPtr = (float *)malloc(sizeof(float));
    /* The name stored in myName can be as long
        as 20 characters */
    myName (char *)malloc(20 * sizeof(char));
    *iPtr = 25; /* Stores in the reserved heap */
    *fPtr = 3.14159;
    printf("What is your first name? ");
    /* Ordinarily, you couldn't gets() into a character
        pointer unless the pointer was originally
        defined as an array with ample space reserved */
    gets(myName);  /* User's name goes to the heap */
```

```
        printf("Here are the values:\n");
        printf("iPtr points to the heap at value %d.\n", *iPtr);
        printf("fPtr points to the heap at value %f.\n", *fPtr);

        /* No dereference on myName because it's printed with %s */
        printf("myName points to the heap at value %s.\n", myName);

        /* Always free everything back to the free heap space */
        free(iPtr);
        free(fPtr);
        free(myName);
        return 0;
    }
```

2. This example enables its user to accept 10 of the user's favorite songs
   into an array of character pointers (a ragged-edge array). If you did
   not understand dynamic memory allocation, you would have to first
   fill the array with enough blanks to hold each song.

   Now that you know about dynamic memory allocation, you only have to
   reserve the array of pointers and then allocate space for each song when
   the user enters that song. This program allocates the character pointer
   array and an extra character array that is 80 characters long. The extra
   array is used to grab a total of five song titles (up to 79 characters maximum with an 80th element for the null zero). The actual length of the
   song entered determines exactly how much heap space to allocate.

   The most important thing to remember about this code is that the
   space for each song is not reserved until the song is ready to be stored:

```
/* Filename: C23DYN2.C
/* Dynamically allocate favorite song titles */
#include <stdio.h>
#include <stdlib.h>
#include <string.h>
main()
{
    #define TOTALSONGS 5     // For more songs, change this
    char * songs[10]; // Ragged-edge array for the songs
    char newSong[80]; // Temporary holding place for song
    int i;

    for (i=0;i<TOTALSONGS;i++)
      { printf("What is your favorite song #%d? ",
                (i+1));
```

```
        gets(newSong);
        // sizeof tells the length of the song
        songs[i] = (char *)malloc((strlen(newSong)+1) *
                            sizeof(char));
        strcpy(songs[i], newSong);

    }
    printf("Here are the songs in reverse order:\n");
    for (i=(TOTALSONGS-1);i>=0;i--)
        { Printf("Song #%d: %s\n", (i+1), songs[i]);
            free(songs[i]); } // Dynamically deallocate when done
        return 0;

}
```

OUTPUT

Here is the program's output:

```
What is your favorite song #1? Cinque Terra, My Italian Riviera
What is your favorite song #2? My Bride's Gone
What is your favorite song #3? Red as a Rose
What is your favorite song #4? O' Say Can You C?
What is your favorite Song #5? Don't Mouse Around with my PC!
Here are the songs in reverse order:
Don't Mouse Around with My PC!
O' Say Can You C?
Red as a Rose
My Bride's Gone
Cinque Terra, My Italian Riviera
```

The songs take only as much memory (inside the heap) as the song titles consume, plus the character pointer in the songs array that points to each song. Also, even though as the program is close to ending, it does free each song.

There is a lot to dynamic memory allocation. Many beginning C books don't even cover the topic. However, mastering malloc() and free() is about all you have left to learn to master C.

What's Next

You have mastered structures and arrays of structures. Many useful inventory and tracking programs are ready to be written using structures. By being able to create arrays of structures, you can now create several occurrences of data. The next step in the process of learning C is to save those structures and other data to disk files. The next chapter explores the concepts of disk file processing in C.

24

Simple C File Processing

So far, every example in this book has processed data that resided inside the program listing or came from the keyboard. You assigned constants and variables to other variables and created new data values from expressions. The programs also received input with scanf(), gets(), and the character input functions. With the large volumes of data that most real-world applications need to process, however, you need a better way of storing that data. For all but the smallest computer programs, disk files offer the solution.

After storing data on the disk, the computer helps you enter, find, change, and delete the data. The computer and C are simply tools to help you manage and process data. This chapter focuses on disk and file processing concepts.

This chapter teaches you the following topics:

- An overview of disk files
- Types of files
- Sequential file access
- Random file access

Why Use a Disk?

If you've worked with computers very much, and if you've done some programming in other languages, you know the importance of file storage for data. The typical computer system has much less memory storage than hard disk storage. Your disk drive holds much more data than can fit in your computer's RAM. The disk memory, because it is *nonvolatile*, lasts longer because the disk retains its contents when you power-off your computer. Also, when your data changes, you (or more important, your users) do not have to edit the program and look for a set of assignment statements. Instead, the users run previously written programs that make changes to the disk data.

Types of Disk File Access

Your programs can access files two ways: through sequential access or random access. Your application determines the method you should choose. The access mode of a file determines how you read, write, change, and delete data from the file. Some of your files can be accessed in both ways, sequentially and randomly, as long as your programs are written properly and the data lends itself to both types of file access.

NOTE

Your C compiler might offer additional ways to access disk files with a library of specific I/O functions.

A sequential file must be accessed in the same order the file was written. This is analogous to cassette tapes: You play music in the same order it was recorded. (You can quickly fast-forward or rewind through songs that you do not want to listen to, but the order of the songs dictates what you do to play the song you want.) It is difficult, and sometimes impossible, to insert data in the middle of a sequential file. How easy is it to insert a new song in the middle of two other songs on a tape? The only way to truly add or delete records from the middle of a sequential file is to create a completely new file that combines both old and new songs.

It might seem that sequential files are limiting, but it turns out that many applications lend themselves to sequential file processing.

Unlike with sequential files, you can access random access files in any order you want. Think of data in a random access file as you would think of songs on a compact disc or a record; you can go directly to any song you want without having to play or fast-forward through the other songs. If you want to play the first song, the sixth song, and then the fourth song, you can do so. The order of play has nothing to do with the order in which the songs appear on the recording. Random file access sometimes takes more programming but rewards that effort with a more flexible file access method. You'll learn about both file storage methods in this chapter.

Learning Sequential File Concepts

There are three operations you can perform on sequential disk files. You can

- Create disk files
- Add to disk files
- Read from disk files

Your application determines what you need to do. If you are creating a disk file for the first time, you must create the file and write the initial data to it. Suppose that you wanted to create a customer data file. You would create a new file and write your current customers to that file. The customer data might originally be in arrays or arrays of structures, pointed to with pointers, or typed into regular variables by the user.

Over time, as your customer base grows, you can add new customers to the file. When you add to the end of a file, you *append* to that file. As your customers enter your store, you would read their information from the customer data file.

Customer disk processing brings up one disadvantage of sequential files, however. Suppose that a customer moves and wants you to change his or her address in your files. Sequential access files do not lend themselves well to changing data stored in them. It is also difficult to remove information from sequential files. Random files will provide a much easier approach to changing and removing data. The primary approach to changing or removing data from a sequential access file is to create a new one from the old one with the updated data.

NOTE
All file functions described in this chapter use the stdio.h header file.

Opening and Closing Sequential Files

Before you can create, write to, or read from a disk file, you must open the file. This is analogous to opening a file cabinet before working with a file stored in the cabinet. As soon as you are done with a cabinet's file, you close the file door. You must also close a disk file when you finish with it.

When you open a disk file, you must inform C only of the filename and what you want to do (write to, add to, or read from). C and your operating system work together to make sure that the disk is ready, and they create an entry in your file directory (if you are creating a file) for the filename.

When you close a file, C writes any remaining data to the file, releases the file from the program, and updates the file directory to reflect the file's new size.

To open a file, you must call the `fopen()` function (for "file open"). To close a file, call the `fclose()` function. Here is the format of these two function calls:

```
filePtr = fopen(fileName, access);
```

and

```
fclose(filePtr);
```

The `filePtr` is a special type of pointer that points only to files, not to data variables. You must define a file pointer with `FILE *`, a definition in the `stdio.h` header file. The examples that follow show you how to define a file pointer.

Your operating system handles the exact location of your data in the disk file. You do not want to worry about the exact track and sector number of your data on the disk. Therefore, you let the `filePtr` point to the data you are reading and writing. Your program only has to generically manage the `filePtr` while C and the operating system take care of locating the actual physical data.

The `fileName` is a string (or a character pointer that points to a string) containing a valid filename for your computer. If you are using a PC or a UNIX-based computer, the `fileName` can contain a complete disk and directory pathname. If you are using a mainframe, you must use the complete dataset name in the `fileName` string. Generally, you can specify the filename in uppercase or lowercase letters, as long as your operating system does not have a preference.

The value for `access` can be one of the mode values from Table 24.1. The updating `access` modes (those with a plus sign) are used in random file processing.

*Table 24.1: Possible **access** modes.*

Mode	Description
`"r"`	Opens a file for reading
`"w"`	Opens a file for writing (creates it)
`"a"`	Opens a file for appending (adding to it)
`"r+"`	Opens a file for update (reading and writing)
`"w+"`	Opens a file for update (creates it, then allows reading and writing)
`"a+"`	Opens a file for update (reads the entire file, or writes to the end of it)

Sometimes you see programs that contain a t or a b in the access mode, such as "rt" or "wb+". The *t* means *text file* and is the default mode; each of the access modes listed in Table 24.1 is equivalent to using *t* after the access mode letter ("rt" is identical to "r", and so on). A text file is an ASCII file, compatible with most other programming languages and applications. Text files do not always contain text, in the word processing sense of the word. Any data you need to store can go in a text file. Programs that read ASCII files can read data you create as C text files. The *b* in the access mode means *binary mode*.

BINARY MODES

If you specify *b* inside the access mode rather than *t*, C creates or reads the file in a binary format. Binary data files are "squeezed"—that is, they take less space than text files. The disadvantage of using binary files is that other programs cannot always read the data files. Only C programs written to access binary files (using the *b* access mode) can read and write to them. The advantage of binary files is that you save disk space because your data files are more compact. Other than the access mode in the fopen() function, you use no additional commands to access binary files with your C programs.

The binary format is a system-specific file format. In other words, not all computers can read a binary file created on another computer.

Here is a complete list of binary file access modes:

"rb" "wb" "ab" "ab+" "a+b" "wb+" "w+b" "ab+" "a+b"

If you open a file for writing (using access modes of "w", "wt", "wb", or "w+"), C creates the file. If a file by that name already exists, C overwrites the old file with no warning. When opening files, you must be careful that you do not overwrite existing data you want to save.

If an error occurs during the opening of a file, C does not return a valid file pointer. Instead, C returns a file pointer equal to the value NULL. NULL is defined in stdio.h. For example, if you open a file for output, but use a disk name that is invalid, C cannot open the file and will make the file pointer point to NULL. Always check the file pointer when writing disk file programs to ensure that the file opened properly.

TIP

Novice programmers seem to prefer to open all files at the beginning of their programs and close them at the end. This is not always best. Open files immediately before you access them and close them when you are done with them. This protects the files, keeping them open only as long as needed. A closed file is more likely to be protected in the unlikely (but possible) event of a power failure or a computer breakdown.

EXAMPLE

1. Suppose that you want to create a file for storing your house payment records for the last year. Here are the first few lines in the program that would create a file called house.dat on your disk:

```
#include <stdio.h>
```

```
main()
{
    FILE *filePtr;                 // Declares a file pointer
    filePtr = fopen("house.dat", "w"); // Creates the file
```

The rest of the program writes data to the file. The program never has to refer to the filename again. The program uses the `filePtr` variable to refer to the file. Examples in the next few sections illustrate how. There is nothing special about `filePtr`, other than its name (although the name is meaningful in this case). You can name file pointer variables XYZ or a908973 if you like, but these names are not meaningful.

You must include the `stdio.h` header file because it contains the definition for the FILE *declaration*. You do not have to worry about the physical FILE's specifics. The `filePtr` "points" to data in the file as you write it. Put the FILE *declaration*s in your programs where you declare other variables and arrays.

TIP
Because files are not part of your program, you might find it useful to declare file pointers globally. Unlike data in variables, there is rarely a reason to keep file pointers local.

Before finishing with the program, you should close the file. The following `fclose()` function closes the house file:

```
fclose(filePtr);           /* Closes the house payment file */
```

2. If you like, you can put the complete pathname in the filename. The following opens the household payment file in a subdirectory on the D disk drive:

```
filePtr = fopen("d:\mydata\house.dat", "w");  // Creates
                                              // the file
```

3. If you like, you can store a filename in a character array or point to it with a character pointer. Each of the following sections of code is equivalent:

```
char fn[] = "house.dat";    // Filename in character array
filePtr = fopen(fn, "w");               // Creates the file
char *myfile="house.dat";         // Filename pointed to
filePtr = fopen(myfile, "w");         // Creates the file
    /* Let the user enter the filename */
printf("What is the name of the household file? ");
gets(filename);                  // Filename must be an
                                 // array or character pointer
filePtr = fopen(filename, "w");       // Creates the file
```

This `fclose()` function closes the open file, no matter which method you used to open the file:

```
fclose(filePtr);          /* Closes the house payment file */
```

4. Check the return value from `fopen()` to ensure that the file opened properly. Here is code after `fopen()` that checks for an error:

```
#include <stdio.h>

main()
{
    FILE *filePtr;                    // Declares a file pointer
    filePtr = fopen("house.dat", "w"); // Creates the file
    if (filePtr == NULL)
        { printf("Error opening file.\n"); }
    else
        { /* Rest of output commands go here */ }
```

5. You can open and write to several files in the same program. Suppose that you wanted to read data from a payroll file and create a backup payroll data file. You would have to open the current payroll file using the `"r"` reading mode, and the backup file in the output `"w"` mode.

   For each open file in your program, you must declare a different file pointer. The file pointers that your input and output statements use determine which file they operate on. If you have to open many files, you can declare an array of file pointers.

   Here is a way you can open the two payroll files:

```
#include <stdio.h>
FILE *fileIn;                                    // Input file
FILE *fileOut;                                   // Output file

main()
{
    fileIn = fopen("payroll.dat", "r");  // Existing file
    fileOut = fopen("payroll.BAK", "w");        // New file
```

   When you finish with these files, be sure to close them with these two `fclose()` function calls:

```
fclose(fileIn);
fclose(fileOut);
```

Writing to a File

Any input or output function that requires a device performs input and output with files. You have seen most of these already. The most common file I/O functions are

getc() and putc()

fprintf()

fgets() and fputs()

There are a few more, but the most common I/O function left that you have not seen is the fscanf() function. fscanf() is to scanf() as fprintf() is to printf(). The only difference between fscanf() and scanf() is its first parameter. The first parameter to fscanf() must be a file pointer (or any C device, such as stdin and stdaux).

The following function reads three integers from a file pointed to by filePtr:

fscanf(filePtr, "%d %d %d", &num1, &num2, &num3);

As with scanf(), you do not have to specify the & before array variable names. The following fscanf() reads a string from the disk file:

fscanf(filePtr, "%s", name);

The fscanf() is not as potentially dangerous as the scanf() function. scanf() gets input from the user. The user does not always enter data in the format that scanf() expects. When you get data from a disk file, however, you can be more certain about the format because you probably wrote the program that created the file in the first place. Errors still can creep into a data file, and you might be wrong about the file's format when using fscanf(), but generally, fscanf() is more secure than scanf().

There is always more than one way to write data to a disk file. Most of the time, more than one function will work. For instance, if you write many names to a file, both fputs() and fprintf() will work. You also can write the names using putc(). You should use whichever function you are most comfortable with for the data being written. If you want a newline character (\n) at the end of each line in your file, the fprintf() and fputs() probably are easier than putc(), but all three will do the job.

NOTE

Each line in a file is called a *record*. By putting a newline character at the end of file records, you make the input of those records easier.

---

1. The following program creates a file called NAMES.DAT. The program writes five names to a disk file using fputs():

   /* Filename: C24WR1.C

```
    Writes five names to a disk file */
#include <stdio.h>

FILE *fp;

main()
{
    fp = fopen("NAMES.DAT", "w");   /* Creates a new file */

    fputs("Michael Langston\n", fp);
    fputs("Sally Redding\n", fp);
    fputs("Jane Kirk\n", fp);
    fputs("Stacy Grady\n", fp);
    fputs("Paula Hiquet\n", fp);

    fclose(fp);                      /* Release the file */
    return 0;
}
```

To keep this first example simple, no error checking was done on the
fopen(). The next few examples check for the error.

NAMES.TXT is a text data file. If you like, you can read this file into any
word processor such as the Windows WordPad (the file comes in as a
text-based ASCII file). If you were to view NAMES.TXT, you would see

```
Michael Langston
Sally Redding
Jane Kirk
Stacy Grady
Paula Hiquet
```

2. The following file writes the numbers from 1 to 100 to a file called
NUMS.1:

```
/* Filename: C24WR2.C
   Writes 1 to 100 to a disk file */
#include <stdio.h>

FILE *fp;

main()
{
    int ctr;
    fp = fopen("NUMS.1", "wt");   /* Creates a new file */
    if (fp == NULL)
        { printf("Error opening file.\n"); }
```

```
        else
          { for (ctr=1; ctr<101; ctr++)
            { fprintf(fp, "%d ", ctr); } /* Writes the data */
          }
        fclose(fp);
        return 0;
      }
```

The numbers are not written one per line, but with a space between each of them. The format of the fprintf() control string determines the format of the output data. When writing data to disk files, keep in mind that you will have to read the data later. You will have to use "mirror-image" input functions to read data you output to files.

Notice that this program opens the file using the "wt" access mode. This is equivalent to the "w" access mode because C opens all files as text files unless you specify a binary override access.

Writing to a Printer

The fopen() and other output functions were not designed to just write to files. They were designed to write to any device, including files, the screen, and the printer. If you need to write data to a printer, you can treat the printer as if it were a file. The following program opens a FILE pointer using the MS-DOS name for a printer located at LPT1 (the MS-DOS name for the first parallel printer port):

```
/* Filename: C24PRNT.C

   Prints to the printer device */
#include <stdio.h>
FILE *prnt;  /* Points to the printer */


main()
{
    prnt = fopen("LPT1", "w");
    fprintf(prnt, "Printer line 1\n");  // 1st line printed
    fprintf(prnt, "Printer line 2\n");  // 2nd line printed
    fprintf(prnt, "Printer line 3\n");  // 3rd line printed

    fclose(prnt);
    return 0;

}
```

Make sure that your printer is turned on and that it has paper before you run this program. When you run the program, you see this printed on the printer:

```
Printer line 1

Printer line 2

Printer line 3
```

Adding to a File

You can easily add data to an existing file or create new files by opening the file in append access mode. Data files on the disk rarely are static; they grow almost daily due to (with luck!) increased business. Being able to add to data already on the disk is very useful indeed.

Files you open for append access (using "a", "at", "ab", "a+b", and "ab+") do not have to exist. If the file exists, C appends data to the end of the file when you write the data. If the file does not exist, C creates the file (as is done when you open a file for write access).

EXAMPLE

The following program adds three more names to the NAMES.DAT file created in an earlier example:

```c
/* Filename: C24AP1.C
    Adds three names to a disk file */
#include <stdio.h>

FILE *fp;

main()
{
    fp = fopen("NAMES.DAT", "a");       // Adds to file

    fputs("Johnny Smith\n", fp);
    fputs("Laura Hull\n", fp);
    fputs("Mark Brown\n", fp);

    fclose(fp);                         // Release the file
    return 0;
}
```

If the file did not exist, C would create it and store the three names to the file. Here is what the file now looks like:

```
Michael Langston
Sally Redding
Jane Kirk
Stacy Grady
Paula Hiquet
Johnny Smith
Laura Hull
Mark Brown
```

Basically, you have to change only the `fopen()` function's access mode to turn a file creation program into a file appending program.

Reading from a File

As soon as the data is in a file, you must be able to read that data. You must open the file in a read access mode. There are several ways to read data. You can read character data a character at a time or a string at a time. The choice depends on the format of the data. If you stored numbers using `fprintf()`, you might want to use a mirror-image `fscanf()` to read the data.

Files you open for read access (using `"r"`, `"rt"`, and `"rb"`) must exist already, or C gives you an error. You cannot read a file that does not exist. `fopen()` returns NULL if the file does not exist when you open it for read access.

TIP
You can read a word at a time from a file using `fscanf()` with the `%s` control code.

Another event happens when reading files. Eventually, you read all the data. Subsequent reading produces errors because there is no more data to read. C provides a solution to the end-of-file occurrence. If you attempt to read from a file that you have completely read the data from, C returns the value EOF, defined in `stdio.h`. To find the end-of-file condition, be sure to check for EOF when performing input from files.

1. This program asks the user for a filename and prints the contents of the file to the screen. If the file does not exist, the program displays an error message:

```
/* Filename: C24RE1.C
   Reads and displays a file */
#include <stdio.h>
```

```
FILE *fp;

main()
{
    char filename[12];               // Holds user's filename
    int inChar;                        // Input character

    printf("What is the name of the file you want to see? ");
    gets(filename);

    if ((fp=fopen(filename, "r"))==NULL)
      { printf("\n\n*** That file does not exist ***\n");
        exit();                        // Exits program
      }

    inChar = getc(fp);          // Reads first character
    while (inChar != EOF)
      { putchar(inChar);
        inChar = getc(fp);
      }
    fclose(fp);
    return 0;
}
```

Notice that the program reads the input character in two places. It is possible, although rare, that a file with no data could exist. In such a file, the first character read would result in the end-of-file condition. Therefore, this program reads the first character and prints it as long as it is not EOF.

Although the program is written to help illustrate file input, most C programmers combine the file input with the test for EOF. This might seem like too much to do at once, but it is so common in C programs that you should become familiar with the algorithm. Here is a rewritten version of the previous program's I/O routine that is more common:

```
while ((inChar = getc(fp)) != EOF)        /* Reads first */
  { putchar(inChar); }                    /* character   */
```

OUTPUT

Here is the NAMES.DAT file. Newline characters are in the file at the end of each name so the names appear one per line in the file.

```
What is the name of the file you want to see? names.dat
Michael Langston
Sally Redding
Jane Kirk
```

```
Stacy Grady
Paula Hiquet
Johnny Smith
Laura Hull
Mark Brown
```

If you were to attempt to read a file that does not exist, the program displays the following message:

```
*** That file does not exist ***
```

2. The following program reads one file and copies it to another. You might want to use such a program to back up important data in case the original file gets damaged.

The program must open two files—the first for reading and the second for writing. The file pointer determines which of the two files is being accessed:

```c
/* Filename: C24RE2.C
   Makes a copy of a file */
#include <stdio.h>

FILE *inFp;
FILE *outFp;

main()
{
    char inFilename[12];        /* Holds original filename */
    char outFilename[12];        /* Holds backup filename */

    int inChar;                            /* Input character */

    printf("What is the name of the file you want
            to back up? ");
    gets(inFilename);

    printf("What is the name of the file ");
    printf("you want to copy %s to? ", inFilename);
    gets(outFilename);

    if ((inFp=fopen(inFilename, "r"))==NULL)
      { printf("\n\n*** %s does not exist ***\n",
               inFilename);
        exit();                              /* Exits program */
      }
    if ((outFp=fopen(outFilename, "w"))==NULL)
```

```
    { printf("\n\n*** Error opening %s ***\n",
            outFilename);
      exit();                               /* Exits program */
    }

  printf("\nCopying...\n");          /* Waiting message */
  while ((inChar = getc(inFp)) != EOF)    /* Gets input
                                              character */
    { putc(inChar, outFp); }    /* Writes the character
                                    to the backup file */

  printf("\nThe files are copied.\n");

  fclose(inFp);
  fclose(outFp);
  return 0;
}
```

Random File Records

Random files exemplify the power of data processing with C. Sequential file processing is slow unless you read the entire file into arrays and process them in memory. Random files provide you a way to read individual pieces of data from a file in any order needed and process them one at a time.

Generally, you read and write file *records*. A record to a file is analogous to a C structure. A record is a collection of one or more data values (called *fields*) that you read and write to disk. Generally, you store data in structures and write the structures to disk, where they are called records. When you read a record from disk, you generally read that record into a structure variable and process it with your program.

Unlike some other programming languages, not all C-read disk data has to be stored in record format. Typically, you write a stream of characters to a disk file and access that data either sequentially or randomly by reading it into variables and structures.

The process of randomly accessing data in a file is simple. Consider the data files of a large credit card organization. When you make a purchase, the store calls the credit card company to get an authorization. Millions of names are in the credit card company's files. There is no quick way the credit card company could read every record sequentially from the disk that comes before yours. Sequential files do not lend themselves to quick access. In many situations, looking up individual records in a data file with sequential access is not feasible.

The credit card companies must use a random file access so that their computers can go directly to your record, just as you go directly to a song on a compact disc or a record album. The functions you use are different from the sequential functions, but the power that results from learning the added functions is worth the effort.

Reading and writing files randomly is similar to thinking of the file as a big array. With arrays, you know that you can add, print, or remove values in any order. You do not have to start the first array element, sequentially looking at the next one, until you get the element you need. You can view your random access file in the same way, accessing the data in any order.

Most random file records are fixed-length records. That is, each record (usually a row in the file) takes the same amount of disk space. Most sequential files you read and wrote in the previous chapter were variable-length records. When you are reading or writing sequentially, there is no need for fixed-length records because you input each value one character, word, string, or number at a time, looking for the data you want. With fixed-length records, your computer can better calculate exactly where the search record is located on the disk.

Although you waste some disk space with fixed-length records (because of the spaces that pad some of the fields), the advantages of random file access compensate for the "wasted" disk space.

TIP
With random access files, you can read or write records in any order. Therefore, even if you want to perform sequential reading or writing of the file, you can use random-access processing and "randomly" read or write the file in sequential record number order.

Opening Random Access Files

Just as with sequential files, you must open random access files before reading or writing to them. You can use any of the read access modes mentioned in the last chapter (such as "r", "rt", and "rb") if you are going to only read a file randomly. To modify data in a file, however, you must open the file in one of the update modes, which Table 24.2 reviews.

Table 24.2: Random access update modes.

Mode	Description
"r+"	Opens a file for update (reading and writing)
"w+"	Opens a file for update (creates it, and then allows reading and writing)
"a+"	Opens a file for update (reads the entire file, or writes to the end of it)
"r+t"	Opens a text file for update (reading and writing; same as "r+")
"w+t"	Opens a text file for update (creates it, and then allows reading and writing; same as "w+")
"a+t"	Opens a text file for update (reads the entire file, or writes to the end of it; same as "a+")
"r+b"	Opens a binary file for update (reading and writing)
"w+b"	Opens a binary file for update (creates it, and then allows reading and writing)
"a+b"	Opens a binary file for update (reads the entire file, or writes to the end of it)

You can randomly read a file, even if the file was opened without an update +. Therefore, there is really no physical difference between sequential files and random files in C. However, the methods you use to access and update them differ.

EXAMPLE

1. Suppose that you want to write a program to create a file of friends' names. The following fopen() function call will suffice, assuming that fp is declared as a file pointer:

```
if ((fp = fopen("NAMES.DAT", "w"))==NULL)
    { printf("\n*** Cannot open file ***\n"); }
```

No update fopen() access mode is needed if you are only creating the file. However, what if you wanted to create the file, write names to it, and give the user a chance to change any of the names before closing the file? You would have to open the file like this:

```
if ((fp = fopen("NAMES.DAT", "w+"))==NULL)
    { printf("\n*** Cannot open file ***\n"); }
```

This enables you to create the file, and then change data that you wrote to the file.

2. As with sequential files, the only difference between using a binary fopen() access mode and a text fopen() access mode is that the file you create with the binary fopen() will be more compact and will save disk space. You could not, however, read that file from other programs as an ASCII text file. The previous fopen() function can be rewritten

to create and allow updating of a binary file. All other file-related commands and functions work for binary files just as they do for text files.

```
if ((fp = fopen("NAMES.DAT", "w+b"))==NULL)
    { printf("\n*** Cannot open file ***\n"); }
```

3. Suppose that you want to read a binary inventory file, and want to change some of the data to reflect new pricing. The following `fopen()` function call suffices for such a file that you want to read and update:

```
if ((fp = fopen("INVENT.JUN", "r+b"))==NULL)
    { printf("\n*** Cannot open file ***\n"); }
```

The `fseek()` Function

C provides a function that enables you to read to a specific point in a random access data file. This is the `fseek()` function. The format of `fseek()` is

```
fseek(filePtr, longNum, origin);
```

The `filePtr` is the pointer to the file that you want to access, initialized with an `fopen()` statement. The `longNum` is the number of bytes in the file you want to skip. C does not read this many bytes, but literally skips the data by the number of bytes specified in `longNum`. Skipping the bytes on the disk is much faster than reading them. If `longNum` is negative, C skips backward in the file (this allows for rereading of data several times). Because data files can be large, you must declare `longNum` as a long integer to hold a large number of bytes.

The `origin` is a value that tells C where to begin the skipping of bytes specified by `longNum`. The `origin` can be any of the three values shown in Table 24.3.

Table 24.3: Possible **origin** *values.*

Description	Named Origin	Constant
Beginning of file	SEEK_SET	0
Current file position	SEEKCUR	1
End of file	SEEK_END	2

The words SEEK_SET, SEEKCUR, and SEEK_END are defined in `stdio.h` as the constants 0, 1, and 2, respectively. That is why it does not matter which (the defined constants or the numeric constants) you use as the `origin`.

NOTE

Actually, the file pointer plays a much more important role than just "pointing to the file" on the disk. The file pointer continually points to the exact location of the next byte to read or write. In other words, as you read data, from either a sequential or a random access file, the file pointer increments with each byte read. By using `fseek()`, you can move the file pointer forward or backward in the file.

EXAMPLE

1. No matter how far into a file you have read, the following `fseek()` function positions the file pointer back at the beginning of a file:

```
fseek(fp, 0L, SEEK_SET); // Positions the file pointer
                         // at the beginning
```

The constant `0L` passes a long integer `0` to the `fseek()` function. Without the `L`, C would pass a regular integer that would not match the `fseek()` prototype, which is located in `stdio.h`. Chapter 3, "Variables and Constants," explains the use of data type suffixes on numeric constants, but the suffixes have not been used since then until now.

This `fseek()` function literally reads "move the file pointer 0 bytes from the beginning of the file."

2. The following example reads a file named MYFILE.TXT twice, once to send the file to the screen and once to send the file to the printer. Three file pointers are used, one for each device (the file, the screen, and the printer). The device names for the screen and the printer are MS-DOS compatible. If you run this program on a minicomputer or a mainframe, substitute your operating system's code for your local screen and printer in the `fopen()` function calls for these devices:

```
/* Filename: C24TWIC.C
   Writes a file to the screen, rereads it,
   and sends it to the printer */
#include <stdio.h>
FILE *inFile;                    /* Input file pointer */
FILE *scrn;                      /* Screen pointer */
FILE *prnt;                      /* Printer pointer */

main()
{
    int inChar;
    if ((inFile = fopen("MYFILE.TXT", "r"))==NULL)
      { printf("\n*** Error opening MYFILE.TXT ***\n");
        exit();  }

    scrn = fopen("CON", "w");       /* Open screen device */
```

```
        while ((inChar=getc(inFile))!=EOF)
            { putc(inChar,scrn); }          /* Output characters
                                                to the screen */


        fclose(scrn);                        /* Close screen because
                                           it is no longer needed */


        fseek(inFile, 0L, SEEK_SET);              /* Reposition
                                                 file pointer */
        prnt = fopen("LPT1", "w");    /* Open printer device */
        while ((inChar=getc(inFile))!=EOF)
            { putc(inChar,prnt); }          /* Output characters
                                               to the printer */


        fclose(prnt);         /* Always close all open files */
        fclose(inFile);


        return 0;
    }
```

You also can close then reopen a file to position the file pointer back at the beginning, but using `fseek()` is a more efficient method.

Of course, you could have used regular I/O functions such as `printf()` to write to the screen, instead of having to open the screen as a separate device.

3. The following `fseek()` function positions the file pointer at the 30th byte in the file. (The next byte read is the 31st byte.)

```
fseek(filePtr, 30L, SEEK_SET); // Positions file pointer
                               // at the 30th byte
```

This `fseek()` function literally reads "move the file pointer 30 bytes from the beginning of the file."

If you write structures to a file, you can quickly seek any structure in the file by using the `sizeof()` function. Suppose that you want the 123rd occurrence of the structure tagged with `inventory`. You would search using the following `fseek()` function:

```
fseek(filePtr, (123L * sizeof(struct inventory)), SEEK_SET);
```

4. The following program writes the letters of the alphabet to a file called ALPH.TXT. The `fseek()` function is then used to read and display the ninth and 17th letters (I and Q).

```
/* Filename: C24ALPH.C
   Stores the alphabet in a file,
```

```
                  then reads two letters from it */
#include <stdio.h>
FILE *fp;
main()
{
    int ch;                             // Holds A through Z

    /* Opens in update mode so that you can read
       the file after writing to it */
    if ((fp=fopen("alph.txt", "w+"))==NULL)    // Creates
                                               // alphabet file
      { printf("\n*** Error opening file ***\n");
        exit(); }

    for (ch=65; ch<=90; ch++)
       { putc(ch, fp); }                // Writes letters

    fseek(fp, 8L, SEEK_SET);            // Skips 8 letters,
                                        // points to I
    ch=getc(fp);
    printf("The first character is %c\n",ch);
    fseek(fp, 16L, SEEK_SET);          // Skips 16 letters,
                                       // points to Q
    ch=getc(fp);
    printf("The second character is %c\n",ch );

    fclose(fp);
    return 0;
}
```

5. To point to the end of a data file, you can use the `fseek()` function to position the file pointer at the last byte. Subsequent `fseek()`s should then use a negative `longNum` value to skip backward in the file. The following `fseek()` function makes the file pointer point to the end of the file:

```
fseek(filePtr, 0L, SEEK_END);  // Positions file pointer
                               // at the end
```

This `fseek()` function literally reads "move the file pointer 0 bytes from the end of the file." The file pointer now points to the end-of-file marker, but you can then `fseek()` backward to get to other data in the file.

6. The following program reads the `ALPH.TXT` file (created in Example 4) backward, printing each character as it skips back in the file:

```
/* Filename: C24BACK.C
   Reads and prints a file backward */
#include <stdio.h>
FILE *fp;
main()
{
    int ctr;    // Steps through the 26 letters in the file
    int inChar;

    if ((fp = fopen("ALPH.TXT", "r"))==NULL)
      { printf("\n*** Error opening file ***\n");
        exit(); }

    fseek(fp, 1L, SEEK_END);    // Points to the last byte
                                // in the file
    for (ctr=0;ctr<26;ctr++)
      {
      inChar = getc(fp);
      fseek(fp, -2L, SEEKCUR);
      putchar(inChar); }

    fclose(fp);
    return 0;
}
```

This program also uses the SEEKCUR origin value. The last fseek() in the program seeks 2 bytes backward from the current position, not from the beginning or the end as the previous examples do. The for loop toward the end of the program performs a "skip 2 bytes back, read 1 byte forward" method to skip through the file backward.

7. The following program performs the same actions as Example 4 (C24ALPH.C), with one addition. When the letters I and Q are found, an fputc() writes the letter x over the I and Q. The fseek() must be used to back up 1 byte in the file to overwrite the letter just read.

```
/* Filename: C24CHANG.C
   Stores the alphabet in a file, reads two letters from
   it, and changes those letters to x's */
#include <stdio.h>
FILE *fp;
main()
{
    int ch;                             /* Holds A through Z */

    /* Opens in update mode so that you can read
```

```
          the file after writing to it */
  if ((fp=fopen("alph.txt", "w+"))==NULL)        /* Creates
                                                    alphabet file */
    { printf("\n*** Error opening file ***\n");
      exit(); }

  for (ch=65; ch<=90; ch++)
    { putc(ch, fp); }                  /* Writes letters */

  fseek(fp, 8L, SEEK_SET);                /* Skips 8 letters,
                                             points to I */
  ch=getc(fp);

  /* Changes the I to an x */
  fseek(fp, -1L, SEEKCUR);
  fputc('x', fp);

  printf("The first character is %c\n",ch);
  fseek(fp, 16L, SEEK_SET);               /* Skips 16 letters,
                                             points to Q */
  ch=getc(fp);
  printf("The second character is %c\n",ch );

  /* Changes the Q to an x */
  fseek(fp, -1L, SEEKCUR);
  fputc('x', fp);

  fclose(fp);
  return 0;
}
```

OUTPUT

The file named ALPH.TXT now contains this:

ABCDEFGHxJKLMNOPxRSTUVWXYZ

This program forms the basis of a more complete data file management program. After you master the `fseek()` functions and become more familiar with disk data files, you will begin to write programs that store more advanced data structures and access them.

The mailing list application in Chapter 25, "Putting It All Together," is a good example of what you can do with random file access. The user is given a chance to change names and addresses that are already in the file. You can use the program to change selected data without having to rewrite the entire disk file. Simply use random access to seek data and write to it.

Other Helpful I/O Functions

Several more disk I/O functions are available that you might find useful. They are mentioned here for completeness. As you write more powerful programs in C, you will find a use for many of these functions when performing disk I/O. Each of these functions is prototyped in the stdio.h header file:

- feof(*fp*) can be used to test for an end-of-file condition when reading binary files. Unlike text files, C might mistake the binary data for the end-of-file marker. The feof() function ensures that the end-of-file condition is properly tested.

- fread(*array, size, count, fp*) reads the amount of data specified by the integer *count*, each data size being *size* in bytes (use the sizeof() function), into the array or pointer specified by *array*. fread() is called a *buffered I/O* function. fread() enables you to read much data with a single function call.

- fwrite(*array, size, count, fp*) writes *count array* elements, each being size *size*, to the file specified by *fp*. fwrite() uses a buffered I/O function. fwrite() enables you to write much data in a single function call.

- remove(*fp*) erases the file pointed to by *fp*. remove() returns 0 if the file was erased successfully and –1 if an error occurred.

- rewind(*fp*) positions the file pointer at the beginning of the file.

Many of these (and other built-in I/O functions that you will learn in your C programming career) are helpful functions that you can duplicate using what you already know. For instance, the rewind() function simply positions the file pointer at the beginning of a file. rewind() is the third method you have seen that does this. These three methods all position the file pointer at the beginning of the file:

```
fclose(fp);
fopen(fp, "r");            // Reopening a file always
                           // reinitializes the pointer
```

and

```
fseek(fp, 0L, SEEK_SET);
```

and

```
rewind(fp);
```

The buffered I/O file functions enable you to read and write entire arrays (including arrays of structures) to the disk in a single function call.

EXAMPLE

1. The following program requests a filename from the user and uses the remove() function to erase the file from the disk:

```
/* Filename: C24ERAS.C
    Erases the file specified by the user */
#include <stdio.h>
FILE *fp;
main()
{
    char filename[12];

    puts("What is the filename you want me to erase? ");
    gets(filename);

    if (remove(filename) == -1)
        { printf("\n*** I could not remove the file ***\n"); }
    else
        { printf("\nThe file %s is now removed\n", filename); }
    return 0;
}
```

2. The following program reads a binary file, a character at a time, until feof() returns a true condition. (The regular end-of-file defined constant works only for text files.)

```
/* Filename: C24READ.C
    Reads and displays a binary file */
#include <stdio.h>

FILE *fp;

main()
{
    char filename[12];          /* Holds user's filename */
    int inChar;                 /* Input character */

    printf("What is the name of the file you want to see? ");
    gets(filename);

    if ((fp=fopen(filename, "rb"))==NULL)
      { printf("\n\n*** That file does not exist ***\n");
        exit();                              /* Exits program */
      }
```

```
            while (!feof(fp))
               { inChar = getc(fp);
                 putchar(inChar); }

            fclose(fp);
            return 0;
         }
```

3. The following function would be part of a larger program that gets inventory data, in an array of structures, from the user. This function is passed the array name and the number of elements (structure variables) in the array. The fwrite() function then writes the complete array of structures to the disk file pointed to by fp:

```
void writeStr(struct inventory items[], int invCnt)
{
    fwrite(items, sizeof(struct inventory), invCnt, fp);
    return 0;
}
```

If the inventory array had 1,000 elements, this one-line function would still write the entire array to the disk file. You could use the fread() function to read the entire array of structures from the disk in a single function call.

What's Next

You can now perform one of the most important requirements of data processing: writing and reading to and from disk files. Before this chapter, you could only store data in variables. The short life of variables (they last only as long as your program is running) makes long-term storage of data impossible. You can now save large amounts of data in disk files to process them later. The mailing-list application that appears next offers a complete example of random access file manipulation along with most of the other concepts you learned in this book. The program enables the user to enter names and addresses, store them to disk, edit them, change them, and print them from the disk file. The mailing-list program is your final monster example that "puts it all together."

25

Putting It All Together

This chapter differs from all the other chapters in the book. Instead of describing topics, one at a time, and showing small examples, this entire chapter is one large example. Although no attempt is made to re-teach you the concepts presented in the example, you'll find that the chapter includes a well-documented program, set up in modular form, that contains ample comments that explain what is occurring in the code. Much of the program is *self-documenting*, meaning the code is formatted and variable names are such that you will be able to read the code in a straightforward manner and easily determine what much of the program does at each step.

This chapter teaches you the following topics:

- The organization of a large C program

- How data, control statements, and data structures work together to form an application

- Review and feedback of the knowledge you've gained from the earlier chapters

Program Overview

This chapter's complete C program is one that includes most of the commands and functions you learned throughout the book. This program manages a mailing list for your personal or business needs. In today's world of windowed environments, the program's text-based nature might seem hampering, but the only difference between this program and one that you'll eventually write using compiler-specific windowing commands is the method of screen I/O. In addition, the text-based I/O functions you've learned will be fundamentally important as you tackle the windowed environments of the C-based C++ and Java languages.

The Program's Features

When you run the program, you are presented with a menu of choices that guide you through the program's operation. Comments throughout the program offer improvements you might want to make. As your knowledge and practice of C improves, you might want to expand this mailing list application into an entire contact database.

The program currently features

- A menu-based user-selection process
- The ability to enter, edit, and maintain a C-based mailing list
- A more elegant screen or window clearing method using a function that your compiler should support
- Data-entry error-checking
- Printing of the mailing list

Future Enhancements

If you want to continue honing your C skills, try your hand at the following enhancements you can make with the skills you already possess:

- Add an entry for the code member to track different types of names and addresses (that is, business codes, personal codes, and so on)
- Search for a partial name (that is, type **Sm** to locate all names beginning with Sm, such as *Smith*, *Smitty*, and *Smythe*).
- When searching for name matches, ignore case (that is, type **smith** instead of **Smith** to find *Smith*).
- Allow for the sorting of the listing of names and address by zip code for bulk mailing.

The Program

Next is the listing of the mailing list program. Between each function is a set of comments that divide the functions visually, with a row of asterisk-based comments, so you can distinguish the separate functions. The asterisk-based comments are used extensively in the code due to their more visible nature when you read through the program as opposed to the double-slash comments which are easier to type.

```c
/* Filename: MAILING.C
   * Mailing List Application *
   -------------------------


   This program enables the user to enter, edit, maintain,
   and print a mailing list of names and addresses.


   All commands and concepts included in this program are
   explained throughout the text of C By Example.        */


/* Header files used by the program */
/* These header files contain function prototypes
   needed by the called functions. */
#include <stdio.h>
#include <ctype.h>


/* Global structure of a name and address */
struct mail_struct
   { char name[25];               /* Name stored here should
                                      be last, first order */
     char address[25];
     char city[12];
     char state[3];               /* Save room for null zero */
     char zipcode[6];
     char code[7];    /* For additional expansion. You
                         might want to use this member for
                         customer codes, vendor codes, or
                         holiday card codes */
   };
/* Global file pointer */
FILE *fp;
```

```
/* Defined constants */
/* MAX is the total number of names allowed
    in memory for reading mailing list */
#define MAX 250
#define BELL '\x07'
#define FILENAME "ADDRESS.DAT"

/* Prototype all of this program's functions */
void main(void);
void disp_menu(void);
void clear_sc(void);
void enter_na(void);
void change_na(void);
void print_na(void);
void err_msg(char err_msg[]);
void add_to_file(struct mail_struct item);
void pause_sc(void);
void pr_data(struct mail_struct item);
void get_new_item(struct mail_struct *item);
void getzip(char zipcode[]);

/**********************************************************/
void main(void)
{
    struct mail_struct list[MAX];
    char ans;
    do
      { disp_menu();        /* Display menu for the user */
        scanf(" %d", &ans);
        switch (ans)
        {   case (1) : { enter_na();
                    break; }
            case (2) : { change_na();
                    break; }
            case (3) : { print_na();
                    break; }
            case (4) : { break; }
            default  : { err_msg("*** You need to enter");
```

```
                            printf(" 1 through 4 ***");
                    break; }
        }
    } while (ans!=4);
    return 0;
}


/**********************************************************/
void disp_menu()  /* Display main menu of the program */
{
    clear_sc();                  /* Clear either the screen
                                    or the output text window */
    printf("\t\t*** Mailing List Manager ***\n");
    printf("\t\t   --------------------\n\n\n");
    printf("Do you want to:\n\n\n");
    printf("\t1. Add names and addresses to the list\n\n\n");
    printf("\t2. Change names and addresses in the list\n\
            \n\n");
    printf("\t3. Print names and addresses in the list\n\
            \n\n");
    printf("\t4. Exit this program\n\n\n");
    printf("What is your choice? ");
    return 0;
}


/**********************************************************/
void clear_sc()              /* Clear the screen by sending
                                25 blank lines to it */
    /** Your compiler probably has a compiler-specific
        function that clears the screen in a more elegant
        style. This program is generic for all types of
        computers (PCs or mainframes), so the screen is
        cleared here by printing several newlines **/
{
    int ctr;              /* Counter for the 25 blank lines */
    for(ctr=0;ctr<25;ctr++)
        { printf("\n"); }
    return 0;
}
```

```
/***********************************************************/
void enter_na(void)
{
    struct mail_struct item;
    char ans;
    do
    { fflush(stdin);                    /* Clear input buffer
                                           before getting strings */
      printf("\n\n\n\n\nWhat is the name? ");
      gets(item.name);
      printf("What is the address? ");
      gets(item.address);
      printf("What is the city? ");
      gets(item.city);
      printf("What is the state? (2-letter abbreviation \
              only) ");
      gets(item.state);

      getzip(item.zipcode);        /* Ensure that zip code
                                           is all digits */

      strcpy(item.code, " ");  /* Null out code member */
      add_to_file(item);           /* Write new information
                                              to disk file */
      printf("\n\nDo you want to enter another name");
      printf(" and address? (Y/N) ");
      ans=getchar();
      getchar();                   /* Discard carriage return */
    } while (toupper(ans)=='Y');

    return 0;
}


/***********************************************************/
void change_na(void)
{
    /* This search function can be improved by using the  */
    /* code member to assign a unique code to each person */
```

```
/* in the list. Names are difficult to search for    */
/* because there are so many variations (such as      */
/* Mc and Mac, and St. and Saint).                          */

struct mail_struct item;
int ans, s;                    /* Holds size of structure */
int change_yes = 0;              /* Will be True if user
                                    finds a name to change */
char test_name[25];

printf("\nWhat is the name of the person you want");
printf(" to change? ");
fflush(stdin);   /* Clear out all in input buffer */
gets(test_name);
fflush(stdin);

s = sizeof(struct mail_struct);    /* To ensure that
                                  fread() reads properly */
if((fp=fopen(FILENAME, "r+"))==NULL)
   { err_msg("*** Read error--ensure file
              exists ***");
   return 0; }
do
  { if(fread(&item, sizeof(struct mail_struct), 1,
             fp)!=s)
   { if(feof(fp))               /* If EOF, quit reading */
       { break; }
   }
   if (strcmp(item.name, test_name)==0)
    { pr_data(item);     /* Print name and address */
       printf("\nIs this the name and address to");
       printf(" change? (Y/N) ");
       ans=getchar();
       getchar();        /* Discard carriage return */
       if (toupper(ans)=='N')
          { continue; }          /* Get another name */
       get_new_item(&item);     /* Let user type new
                                      information */
```

```
                fseek(fp, (long)-s, SEEK_CUR);    /* Back up
                                                     one structure */
                fwrite(&item, s, 1, fp);          /* Rewrite
                                                       information */
                change_yes = 1;                   /* Changed flag */
                break;                            /* Finished */
            }
        } while (!feof(fp));
    fclose(fp);
    if (!change_yes)
        { err_msg("*** End of file--couldn't find\
                    name ***"); }
    return 0;
}


/**********************************************************/
void print_na(void)
{
    struct mail_struct item;
    int s, linectr=0;

    s = sizeof(struct mail_struct);    /* To ensure that
                                          fread() reads properly */
    if((fp=fopen(FILENAME, "r"))==NULL)
        { err_msg("*** Read error--ensure \
                    file exists ***");
      return 0; }
    do
        { if(fread(&item, sizeof(struct mail_struct), 1,
                    fp)!=s)
          { if(feof(fp))             /* If EOF, quit reading */
              { break; }
          }
          if (linectr>20)                  /* Screen is full */
          { pause_sc();
            linectr=0; }
          pr_data(item);      /* Print name and address */
          linectr+=4;
```

```c
        } while (!feof(fp));
    fclose(fp);
    printf("\n- End of list -");
    pause_sc();                 /* Give user a chance to see
                                   names remaining onscreen */
    return 0;
}


/***********************************************************/
void err_msg(char err_msg[])
{
    printf("\n\n%s\n", err_msg);
    printf("%c", BELL);
    return 0;
}


/***********************************************************/
void add_to_file(struct mail_struct item)
{
    if((fp = fopen(FILENAME, "a"))==NULL)  /* Open file in
                                              append mode */
        { err_msg("*** Disk error--please check \
                   disk drive ***");
      return 0; }
    fwrite(&item, sizeof(item), 1, fp);    /* Add structure
                                              to the file */
    fclose(fp);
    return 0;
}


/***********************************************************/
void pause_sc()
{
    char ans;
    fflush(stdin);              /* Remove any extra characters
                                   from the input buffer */
    printf("\nPress the Enter key to continue...");
    ans=getchar();
```

```
        fflush(stdin);              /* Remove any extra characters
                                        from the input buffer */

    return 0;
}


/**********************************************************/
void pr_data(struct mail_struct item)
{
    /* Prints the name and address sent to it */
    printf("\nName    : %-25s\n", item.name);
    printf("Address: %-25s\n", item.address);
    printf("City    : %-12s\tState: %-2s  zipcode: %-5s\n",
            item.city, item.state, item.zipcode);
    return 0;
}


/**********************************************************/
void get_new_item(struct mail_struct *item)
{
    struct mail_struct temp_item;     /* Holds temporary
                                          and changed input */
    printf("\nEnter new name and address information");
    printf(" below\n(Press the ");
    printf("Enter key without typing data to retain old");
    printf(" information)\n\n");
    printf("What is the new name? ");
    if (strlen(gets(temp_item.name))>0)    /* Save new data
                                               only if user */
      { strcpy((*item).name, temp_item.name); } /* presses
                                               Enter key */
    printf("What is the address? ");
    if (strlen(gets(temp_item.address))>0)
      { strcpy((*item).address, temp_item.address); }
    printf("What is the city? ");
    if (strlen(gets(temp_item.city))>0)
      { strcpy((*item).city, temp_item.city); }
    printf("What is the state? (2-letter abbreviation \
            only) ");
    if (strlen(gets(temp_item.state))>0)
      { strcpy((*item).state, temp_item.state); }
    printf("What is the zip code? ");
```

```
    if (strlen(gets(temp_item.zipcode))>0)
      { strcpy((*item).zipcode, temp_item.zipcode); }
    (*item).code[0] = 0;    /* Null out code member
                                (unused here) */

    return 0;  /* Return structure with changed member(s) */
}


void getzip(char zipcode[])         /* Ensure that zip code
                                        is all digits */
{
    int ctr, bad_zip;

    do
      { bad_zip = 0;
        printf("What is the zip code? ");
        gets(zipcode);
        for(ctr=0;ctr<5;ctr++)
      { if (isdigit(zipcode[ctr]))
          { continue; }
        else
          { err_msg("*** The zip code must be digits \
                    only ***");
          bad_zip = 1;
          break; }
      }
      } while (bad_zip);
    return 0;
}
```

What's Next

Next, you should begin making money at your career of C programming. Seriously, you now know as much as most C programmers know about the C programming language. You now need to study your C compiler's specific (and non-standard) functions so you can begin to build more powerful programs from the tools your compiler supplies. In addition, you should begin looking in the C++ or Java languages if you want to springboard your C knowledge into other languages.

Part VIII

Appendixes

Memory Addressing, Binary, and Hexadecimal

C's Precedence Table

ASCII Table

Glossary

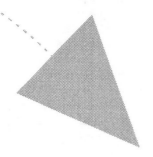

Appendix A

Memory Addressing, Binary, and Hexadecimal

You do not have to understand the concepts in this appendix to become well-versed in C. You can master C, however, only if you spend some time learning about the "behind-the-scenes" roles played by binary numbers. The material presented here is not difficult, but many programmers do not take the time to study it; hence, there are a handful of C masters who learn this material and understand how C works "under the hood," and there are those who will never be as expert in the language as they could be.

You should take the time to learn about addressing, binary numbers, and hexadecimal numbers. These fundamental principles are presented here for you to learn, and although a working knowledge of C is possible without knowing them, they will greatly enhance your C skills (and your skills in every other programming language).

After reading this appendix, you will better understand why different C data types hold different ranges of numbers. You also will see the importance of being able to represent hexadecimal numbers in C, and you will better understand C array and pointer addressing.

Computer Memory

Each memory location inside your computer holds a single character called a *byte*. A byte is any character, whether it is a letter of the alphabet, a numeric digit, or a special character such as a period, question mark, or even a space (a blank character). If your computer contains 32 *megabytes* of memory, it can hold a total of approximately 32 million bytes of memory. This means that as soon as you fill your computer's memory with 32 million bytes, there is no room for an additional character unless you overwrite something else.

Before describing the physical layout of your computer's memory, it might be best to take a detour and explain exactly what 32 megabytes, or 32 *meg*, really means.

Memory and Disk Measurements

A few years ago, when memory space began increasing, computer manufacturers would append *K* (from the metric word *kilo*) to memory measurements so they would not have to attach as many zeros to the end of numbers for disk and memory storage that measured in thousands. The K stands for approximately 1000 bytes. As you will see, almost everything inside your computer is based on a power of 2. Therefore, the K of computer memory measurements actually equals the power of 2 closest to 1000, which is 2 to the 10th power, or 1,024. Because 1024 is very close to 1000, computer people often think of K as meaning 1000, even though they know it only approximately equals 1000.

NOTE

A computer standards committee called the *IEEE Standards Board* has plans to adopt new abbreviation standards for memory measurements. *Mega* would mean exactly 1 million, and shorter abbreviations such as *Ki* and *Gi* would become standard for measurements such as kilobyte and gigabyte. In short, more confusion may result during the adoption but the standards board hopes that consistent measurements in computer specifications and advertising will eventually become the result.

Think for a moment about what 640K, an older standard for PC memory, exactly equals. Practically speaking, 640K is about 640,000 bytes. To be exact, however, 640K equals 640 times 1024, or 655,360. A few years ago, if you ran the PC DOS command CHKDSK, the result would be 655,360 as your total memory (assuming that you have 640K of RAM) rather than 640,000.

Because today's memory and disk drives can hold such a large amount of data, typically several million characters, there is an additional memory measurement shortcut often written as *M,* which stands for meg, or megabytes. A megabyte is approximately 1 million bytes, just as a kilobyte is approximately 1000 bytes. Therefore, 64M is approximately 64,000,000 characters, or bytes, of storage. As with K, the M literally stands for 1,048,576 because that is the closest power of 2 (2 to the 20th power) to 1 million.

How many bytes of storage is 64 megabytes? It is approximately 64 million characters, or 67,112,960 characters to be exact.

A *gigabyte*, or *gig*, or *G* as it's often written, steps up the memory ante once more to represent 1 billion characters of data. Therefore, an 8-gigabyte hard disk holds approximately 8 billion characters of data and exactly holds the closest power of 2 to 8 billion.

Memory Addresses

Each memory location in your computer, just as with each house in your town, has a unique *address*. A memory address is simply a sequential number, starting at 0, which labels each memory location. Figure A.1 shows how your computer memory addresses are numbered if you have 32M of RAM.

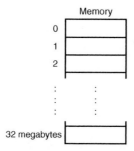

Figure A.1: *Here are some memory addresses for a 32M-based computer.*

By using unique addresses, your computer can keep track of memory. When the computer stores a result of a calculation in memory, it finds an empty address, or one matching the data area where the result is to go, and stores the result at that address.

Your C programs and data share computer memory with the operating system, such as Windows. Windows must always reside in memory while you operate your computer. Otherwise, your programs would have no way to access disks, printers, the screen, or the keyboard. In addition, your C compiler and your C program (in source code format) might be in memory also. Once you compile and run your C program, your program and the operating system will reside in memory together.

Bits and Bytes

You already know that a single address of memory might contain any character, called a byte. You know that your computer holds many bytes of information, but it does not store those characters in the same way that humans think of characters. For example, if you type a letter **W** on your keyboard while working in your C editor, you see the W on the screen, and you also know that the W is stored in a memory location at some unique address. Actually, your computer does not store the letter W; it stores electrical impulses that stand for the letter W.

Electricity, which is what runs through the components of your computer, making it understand and execute your programs, can exist in only two states—on or off. As with a lightbulb, electricity is either flowing (it is on) or it is not flowing (it is off). Even though you can dim some lights, the electricity is still either on or off.

Today's modern digital computers employ this on-or-off concept. Your computer is nothing more than millions of on and off switches. You might have heard about integrated circuits, transistors, and even vacuum tubes that computers have contained over the years. These electrical components are nothing more than switches that rapidly turn electrical impulses on and off.

This two-state on-and-off mode of electricity is called a *binary state of electricity*. Computer people use a 1 to represent an on state (a switch in the computer that is on) and a 0 to represent an off state (a switch that is off). These numbers, 1 and 0, are called *binary digits*. The term binary digits is usually shortened to *bits*. A bit is either a 1 or a 0 representing an on or an off state of electricity. Different combinations of bits represent different characters.

Several years ago, someone listed every single character that might be represented on a computer, including all uppercase letters, all lowercase letters, the digits 0 through 9, the many other characters (such as %, *, {, and +), and some special control characters. When you add the total number of characters that a PC can represent, you get 256 of them. The first 127 of these characters are listed in Appendix C's ASCII (pronounced *ask-ee*) table.

The order of the ASCII table's 256 characters is basically arbitrary, just as the telegraph's Morse code table is arbitrary. With Morse code, a different set of long and short beeps represent different letters of the alphabet. In the ASCII table, a different combination of bits (1s and 0s strung together) represent each of the 256 ASCII characters. The ASCII table is a standard table used by almost every PC in the world. ASCII stands for American Standard Code for Information Interchange. (Some minicomputers and mainframes use a similar table called the EBCDIC table.)

It turns out that if you take every different combination of eight 0s strung together, to eight 1s strung together (that is, from 00000000, 00000001, 00000010, and so on until you get to 11111110, and finally, 11111111), you will have a total of 256 of them. (256 is 2 to the 8th power.) Each memory location in your computer holds 8 bits each. These bits can be any combination of eight 1s and 0s. This brings us to the following fundamental rule of computers.

NOTE

Because it takes a combination of eight 1s and 0s to represent a character, and because each byte of computer memory can hold exactly one character, 8 bits equals 1 byte.

To bring this into better perspective, consider that the bit pattern needed for the uppercase letter A is 01000001. No other character in the ASCII table "looks" like this to the computer because each of the 256 characters is assigned a unique bit pattern.

Suppose that you press the **A** key on your keyboard. Your keyboard does not send a letter A to the computer; rather, it looks in its ASCII table for the on and off states of electricity that represent the letter A. When you press the A key, the keyboard actually sends 01000001 (as on and off impulses) to the computer. Your computer simply stores this bit pattern for A in a memory location. Even though you can think of the memory location as holding an A, it really holds the byte 01000001.

If you were to print that A, your computer would not send an A to the printer; it would send the 01000001 bit pattern for an A to the printer. The printer receives that bit pattern, looks up the correct letter in the ASCII table, and prints an A.

From the time you press the A until the time you see it on the printer, it is not a letter A. It is the ASCII pattern of bits that the computer uses to represent an A. Because a computer is electrical, and because electricity is easily turned on and off, this is a nice way for the computer to manipulate and move characters, and it can do so very quickly. Actually, if it were up to the computer, you would enter everything by its bit pattern, and look at all results in their bit patterns. This would not be good, so devices such as the keyboard, screen, and printer know that they have to work part of the time with letters as we know them. That is why the ASCII table is such an integral part of a computer.

There are times when your computer treats 2 bytes as a single value. Even though memory locations are typically 8 bits wide, many CPUs access memory 2 bytes at a time. If this is the case, the 2 bytes are called a *word* of memory. On other computers (commonly mainframes), the word size might be 4 bytes (32 bits) or even 8 bytes (64 bits).

SUMMARIZING BITS AND BYTES

A bit is a 1 or a 0 representing an on or an off state of electricity.

Eight bits represents a byte.

A byte, or 8 bits, represents one character.

Each memory location of your computer is 8 bits (a single byte) wide. Therefore, each memory location can hold one character of data. Appendix C is an ASCII table listing all possible characters.

If the CPU accesses memory 2 bytes at a time, those 2 bytes are called a word of memory.

The Order of Bits

To further understand memory, you should understand how programmers refer to individual bits. Figure A.2 shows a byte and a 2-byte word. Notice that the bit on the far right is called bit 0. From bit 0, keep counting by ones as you move left. For a byte, the bits are numbered 0 to 7, from right to left. For a double-byte (a 16-bit word), the bits are numbered from 0 to 15, from right to left.

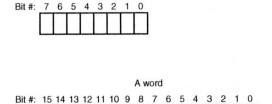

Figure A.2: This illustrates the order of bits in a byte and a 2-byte word.

Bit 0 is called the *least-significant bit,* or sometimes the *low-order bit.* Bit 7 (or bit 15 for a 2-byte word) is called the *most-significant bit,* or sometimes the *high-order bit.*

Binary Numbers

Because a computer works best with 1s and 0s, its internal numbering method is limited to a *base-2* (binary) numbering system. People work in a *base-10* numbering system in the real world. The base-10 numbering system is sometimes called the decimal numbering system. There are always as many different digits as the base in a numbering system. For example, in the base-10 system, there are 10 digits, 0 through 9. As soon as you count to 9 and run out of digits, you have to combine some that you already used. The number 10 is a representation of 10 values, but it combines the digits 1 and 0.

The same is true of base 2. There are only two digits, 0 and 1. As soon as you run out of digits, after the second one, you have to reuse digits. The first seven binary numbers are 0, 1, 10, 11, 100, 101, and 110.

It is okay if you do not understand how these numbers were derived; you will see how in a moment. For the time being, you should realize that no more than two digits, 0 and 1, can be used to represent any base-2 number, just as no more than 10 digits, 0 through 9, can be used to represent any base-10 number in the regular "real-world" numbering system.

You should know that a base-10 number, such as 2981, does not really mean anything by itself. You must assume what base it is. You get very used to working with base-10 numbers because that is what the world uses. However, the number 2981 actually represents a quantity based on powers of 10. For example, Figure A.3 shows what the number 2981 actually represents. Notice that each digit in the number represents a certain number of a power of 10.

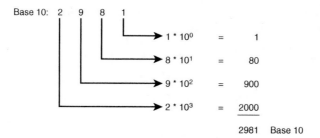

Figure A.3: *The base-10 breakdown of the number 2,981.*

This same concept applies when you work in a base-2 numbering system. Your computer does this, because the power of 2 is just as common to your computer as the power of 10 is to you. The only difference is that the digits in a base-2 number represent powers of 2 and not powers of 10. Figure A.4 shows you what the binary numbers 10101 and 10011110 are in base-10. This is how you convert any binary number to its base-10 equivalent.

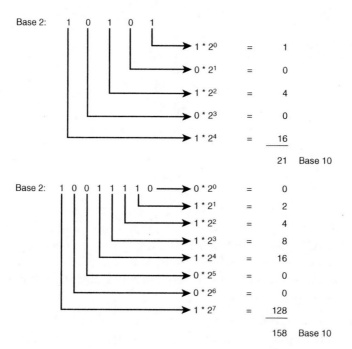

Figure A.4: *The base-2 breakdown of the numbers 10101 and 10011110.*

A base-2 number contains only 1s and 0s. To convert any base-2 number to base-10, add each power of 2 everywhere a 1 appears in the number. The base-2 number 101 represents the base-10 number 5. (There are two 1s in the number, one in the 2 to the 0 power, which equals 1, and one in the 2 to the second power, which equals 4.) Table A.1 shows the first 18 base-10 numbers and their matching base-2 numbers.

Table A.1: The first 17 base-10 and base-2 (binary) numbers.

Base-10	Base-2
0	0
1	1
2	10
3	11
4	100
5	101
6	110
7	111
8	1000
9	1001
10	1010
11	1011
12	1100
13	1101
14	1110
15	1111
16	10000
17	10001

You do not have to memorize this table; you should be able to figure the base-10 numbers from their matching binary numbers by adding the powers of two for each 1 (on) bit. Many programmers do memorize the first several binary numbers, however, because it comes in handy in advanced programming techniques.

What is the largest binary number a byte can hold? The answer is all 1s, or 11111111. If you add the first eight powers of 2, you get 255.

A byte holds either a number or an ASCII character, depending on how it is accessed. For example, if you were to convert the base-2 number 01000001 to a base-10 number, you would get 65. However, this also happens to be the ASCII bit pattern for the uppercase letter *A*. If you check the ASCII table, you will see that the *A* is ASCII code 65. Because the ASCII table is so closely linked with the bit patterns, the computer knows whether to work with a number 65 or a letter *A*—by the context of how the patterns are used.

A binary number is not limited to a byte, as an ASCII character is. Sixteen or 32 bits at a time can represent a binary number (and usually do). There are more powers of 2 to add when converting that number to a base-10 number, but the process is the same. By now you should be able to figure out that 1010101010101010 is 43,690 in base-10 decimal numbering system (although it might take a little time to calculate).

To convert from decimal to binary takes a little more effort. Luckily, you rarely need to convert in that direction. Converting from base-10 to base-2 is not covered in this appendix.

Binary Arithmetic

At their lowest level, computers can only add and convert binary numbers to their negative equivalents. Computers cannot truly subtract, multiply, or divide, although they simulate these operations through judicious use of the addition and negative-conversion techniques.

If a computer were to add the numbers 7 and 6, it could do so (at the binary level). The result is 13. If, however, the computer were instructed to subtract 7 from 13, it could not do so. It can, however, take the negative value of 7 and add that to 13. Because –7 plus 13 equals 6, the result is a simulated subtraction.

To multiply, computers perform repeated addition. To multiply 6 by 7, the computer adds seven 6s together and gets 42 as the answer. To divide 42 by 7, a computer keeps subtracting 7 from 42 repeatedly, using the addition of a negative 7 method, until it gets to a 0 answer (or less than 0 if there is a remainder), and then counts the number of times it took to reach 0.

Because all math is done at the binary level, the following additions are possible in binary arithmetic:

```
0 + 0 = 0
0 + 1 = 1
1 + 0 = 1
1 + 1 = 10
```

Because these are binary numbers, the last result is not the number 10, but the binary number 2. (Just as the binary 10 means "no ones, and carry an additional power of 2," the decimal number 10 means "no ones, and carry a power of 10.") No binary digit represents a 2, so you have to combine the 1 and the 0 to form the new number.

Because binary addition is the foundation of all other math, you should learn how to add binary numbers. You will then understand how computers do the rest of their arithmetic.

Using the binary addition rules shown previously, look at the following binary calculations:

```
01000001 (65 decimal)
+00101100 (44 decimal)
------------
01101101 (109 decimal)
```

The first number, 01000001, is 65 decimal. This also happens to be the bit pattern for the ASCII A, but if you add with it, the computer knows to interpret it as the number 65 rather than the character A.

The following binary addition requires a carry into bit 4 and bit 6:

```
00101011 (43 decimal)
+00100111 (39 decimal)
------------
01010010 (82 decimal)
```

Typically, you have to ignore bits that carry past bit 7, or bit 15 for double-byte arithmetic. For example, both of the following binary additions produce incorrect positive results:

```
10000000 (128 decimal)          1000000000000000 (65536 decimal)
+10000000 (128 decimal)        +1000000000000000 (65536 decimal)
------------                   --------------------
00000000 (0 decimal)            0000000000000000 (0 decimal!)
```

There is no 9th or 17th bit for the carry, so both of these seem to produce incorrect results. Because the byte and 16-bit word cannot hold the answers, the magnitude of both these additions is not possible. The computer must be programmed, at the bit level, to perform *multiword arithmetic,* which is beyond the scope of this book.

Binary Negative Numbers

Because subtracting requires understanding binary negative numbers, you need to learn how computers represent them. The computer uses *2's complement* to represent negative numbers in binary form. To convert a binary number to its 2's complement (to its negative) you must

1. Reverse the bits (the 1s to 0s and the 0s to 1s).

2. Add 1.

This might seem a little strange at first, but it works very well for binary numbers. To represent a binary –65, you need to take the binary 65 and convert it to its 2's complement, such as

```
01000001 (65 decimal)
10111110 (Reverse the bits)
    +1 (Add 1)
```
```
10111111 (-65 binary)
```

By converting the 65 to its 2's complement, you produce –65 in binary. Though it doesn't seem like 10111111 would be –65, the 2's complement definition it what actually makes it so.

If you were told that 10111111 is a negative number, how would you know which binary number it is? You perform the 2's complement on it. Whatever number you produce is the positive of that negative number. For example:

```
10111111 (-65 decimal)
01000000 (Reverse the bits)
    +1 (Add 1)
```
```
01000001 (65 decimal)
```

Something might seem wrong at this point. You just saw that 10111111 is the binary –65, but isn't 10111111 also 191 decimal (adding the powers of 2 marked by the 1s in the number, as explained earlier)? It depends whether the number is a *signed* or an *unsigned* number. If a number is signed, the computer looks at the most significant bit (the bit on the far left), called the *sign bit*. If the most significant bit is a 1, the number is negative. If it is 0, the number is positive.

Most numbers are 16 bits long. That is, 2-byte words are used to store most integers. This is not always the case for all computers, but it is true for most PCs.

In the C programming language, you can designate numbers as either signed integers or unsigned integers (they are signed by default if you do not specify otherwise). If you designate a variable as a signed integer, the computer interprets the high-order bit as a sign bit. If the high-order bit is on (1), the number is negative. If the high-order bit is off (0), the number is positive. If, however, you designate a variable as an unsigned integer, the computer uses the high-order bit as just another power of 2. That is why the range of unsigned integer variables goes higher (generally from 0 to 65535, but it depends on the computer) than for signed integer variables (generally from –32768 to +32767).

After so much description, a little review is in order. Assume that the following 16-bit binary numbers are unsigned:

```
0011010110100101
1001100110101010
1000000000000000
```

These numbers are unsigned, so the bit 15 is not the sign bit, but just another power of 2. You should practice converting these large 16-bit numbers to decimal. The decimal equivalents are

13733

39338

32768

If, on the other hand, these numbers are signed numbers, the high-order bit (bit 15) indicates the sign. If the sign bit is 0, the numbers are positive and you convert them to decimal in the usual manner. If the sign bit is 1, you must convert the numbers to their 2's complement to find what they equal. Their decimal equivalents are

+13733

-26198

-32768

To compute the last two binary numbers to their decimal equivalents, take their 2's complement and convert it to decimal. Put a minus sign in front of the result and you find what the original number represents.

TIP

To make sure that you convert a number to its 2's complement correctly, you can add the 2's complement to its original positive value. If the answer is 0 (ignoring the extra carry to the left), you know that the 2's complement number is correct. This is like saying that decimal opposites, such as −72 + 72, add up to zero.

Hexadecimal Numbers

All those 1s and 0s get confusing. If it were up to your computer, however, you would enter everything as 1s and 0s. This is unacceptable to people because we do not like to keep track of all those 1s and 0s. Therefore, a *hexadecimal* numbering system (sometimes called *hex*) was devised. The hexadecimal numbering system is based on base-16 numbers. As with other bases, there are 16 unique digits in the base-16 numbering system. Here are the first 19 hexadecimal numbers:

```
0  1  2  3  4  5  6  7  8  9  A  B  C  D  E  F  10  11  12
```

Because there are only 10 unique digits (0 through 9), the letters A through F represent the remaining six digits. (Anything could have been used, but the designers of the hexadecimal numbering system decided to use the first six letters of the alphabet.)

To understand base-16 numbers, you should know how to convert them to base-10 so that they represent numbers people are familiar with. Perform the conversion to base-10 from base-16 the same way you did with base-2, but instead of using powers of 2, represent each hexadecimal digit with powers of 16. Figure A.5 shows how to convert the number 3C5 to decimal.

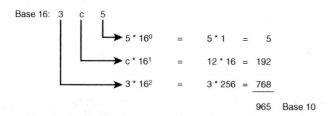

Figure A.5: *Converting hexadecimal 3C5 to its decimal equivalent.*

TIP

Calculators exist that convert numbers between base-16, base-10, and base-2, and also perform 2's complement arithmetic.

You should be able to convert 2B to its decimal 43 equivalent, and E1 to decimal 225 in the same manner. Table A.2 shows the first 20 decimal, binary, and hexadecimal numbers.

Table A.2: The first 20 base-10, base-2 (binary), and base-16 (hexadecimal) numbers.

Base-10	Base-2	Base-16
1	1	1
2	10	2
3	11	3
4	100	4
5	101	5
6	110	6
7	111	7
8	1000	8
9	1001	9
10	1010	A
11	1011	B
12	1100	C
13	1101	D
14	1110	E

continues

Table A.2: continued

Base-10	Base-2	Base-16
15	1111	F
16	10000	10
17	10001	11
18	10010	12
19	10011	13
20	10100	14

Why Learn Hexadecimal?

Because of its close association to the binary numbers your computer uses, hexadecimal notation is extremely efficient for describing memory locations and values. It is much easier for you (and more importantly at this level, for your computer) to convert from base-16 to base-2 than from base-10 to base-2. Therefore, you sometimes want to represent data at the bit level, but using hexadecimal notation is easier (and requires less typing) than using binary numbers.

To convert from hexadecimal to binary, convert each hex digit to its 4-bit binary number. You can use Table A.2 as a guide for this. For example, the following hexadecimal number

5B75

can be converted to binary by taking each digit and converting it to four binary numbers. If you need leading zeros to "pad" the four digits, use them. The number becomes

0101 1011 0111 0101

It turns out that the binary number 0101101101110101 is exactly equal to the hexadecimal number 5B75. This is much easier than converting them both to decimal first.

To convert from binary to hexadecimal, reverse this process. If you were given the binary number

1101000011110111111010

you could convert it to hexadecimal by grouping the bits into groups of four, starting with the bit on the far right. Because there is not an even number of groups of four, pad the one on the far left with zeros. You then have the following:

0011 0100 0011 1101 1111 1010

Now you only have to convert each group of four binary digits into their hexadecimal number equivalent. You can use Table A.2 to help. You then get the following base-16 number:

```
343DFA
```

The C programming language also supports the base-8 *octal* representation of numbers. Because octal numbers are rarely used with today's computers, they are not covered in this appendix.

How Binary and Addressing Relates to C

The material presented here may seem foreign to many programmers. The binary and 2's complement arithmetic reside deep in your computer, shielded from most programmers (except assembly language programmers). Understanding this level of your computer, however, explains everything else you learn.

Many C programmers learn C before delving into binary and hexadecimal representation. For them, much about the C language seems strange, but it could be explained very easily if they understood the basic concepts.

For example, a signed integer holds a different range of numbers than an unsigned integer. You now know that this is due to the sign bit's being used in two different ways, depending on whether the number is designated as signed or unsigned.

The ASCII table also should make more sense to you after this discussion. The ASCII table is an integral part of your computer. Characters are not actually stored in memory and variables; rather, their ASCII bit patterns are. That is why C can move easily between characters and integers. The following two C statements are allowed, whereas they probably would not be in another programming language:

```
char c = 65;    // Puts the ASCII letter A in c
int ci = 'A';   // Puts the number 65 in ci
```

The hexadecimal notation taught to many C programmers also makes much more sense if they truly understand base-16 numbers. For example, if you see in a C program the line

```
char a = '\x041';
```

you could convert the hex 41 to decimal (65 decimal) if you want to know what is being assigned. Also, C systems programmers find that they can better interface with assembly language programs when they understand the concepts presented in this appendix.

If you gain only a cursory knowledge of this material at this point, you will be very much ahead of the game when you program in C and the languages developed from C.

Appendix B

C's Precedence Table

NOTE

This table contains every C operator. Some, most notably the bitwise operators, are not extensively covered in this book due to their esoteric nature. Nevertheless, no language's operator precedence table would be complete without a full listing of operators.

Precedence

Level	Symbol	Description	Associativity
1	++	Prefix increment	Left to right
	--	Prefix decrement	
	( )	Function call and subexpression	
	[ ]	Array subscript	
	->	Structure pointer	
	.	Structure member	
2	!	Logical negation	Right to left
	~	1's complement	
	-	Unary negation	
	+	Unary plus	
	(type)	Type cast	
	*	Pointer dereference	
	&	Address of	
	sizeof	Size of	
3	*	Multiplication	Left to right
	/	Division	
	%	Modulus (integer remainder)	

continues

continued

Level	Symbol	Description	Associativity
4	+	Addition	Left to right
	–	Subtraction	
5	<<	Bitwise left shift	Left to right
	>>	Bitwise right shift	
6	<	Less than	Left to right
	<=	Less than or equal to	
	>	Greater than	
	>=	Greater than or equal to	
7	==	Equal test	Left to right
	!=	Not equal test	
8	&	Bitwise AND	Left to right
9	^	Bitwise exclusive OR	Left to right
10	¦	Bitwise inclusive OR	Left to right
11	&&	Logical AND	Left to right
12	¦¦	Logical inclusive OR	Left to right
13	?:	Conditional test	Right to left
14	=	Assignment	Right to left
	+=	Compound add	
	–=	Compound subtract	
	*=	Compound multiply	
	/=	Compound divide	
	%=	Compound modulus	
	<<=	Compound bitwise left shift	
	>>=	Compound bitwise right shift	
	&=	Compound bitwise AND	
	^=	Compound bitwise exclusive OR	
	¦=	Compound bitwise inclusive OR	
15	,	Sequence point	Left to right
	++	Postfix increment	
	––	Postfix decrement	

Appendix C

ASCII Table

Dec X_{10}	Hex X_{16}	Binary X_2	ASCII Character
000	00	0000 0000	null
001	01	0000 0001	☺
002	02	0000 0010	☻
003	03	0000 0011	♥
004	04	0000 0100	♦
005	05	0000 0101	♣
006	06	0000 0110	♠
007	07	0000 0111	•
008	08	0000 1000	◘
009	09	0000 1001	○
010	0A	0000 1010	◙
011	0B	0000 1011	♂
012	0C	0000 1100	♀
013	0D	0000 1101	♪
014	0E	0000 1110	♫
015	0F	0000 1111	☼
016	10	0001 0000	►
017	11	0001 0001	◄
018	12	0001 0010	↕
019	13	0001 0011	‼
020	14	0001 0100	¶
021	15	0001 0101	§
022	16	0001 0110	▬
023	17	0001 0111	↨
024	18	0001 1000	↑

continues

continued

Dec X_{10}	Hex X_{16}	Binary X_2	ASCII Character
025	19	0001 1001	↓
026	1A	0001 1010	→
027	1B	0001 1011	←
028	1C	0001 1100	∟
029	1D	0001 1101	↔
030	1E	0001 1110	▲
031	1F	0001 1111	▼
032	20	0010 0000	space
033	21	0010 0001	!
034	22	0010 0010	"
035	23	0010 0011	#
036	24	0010 0100	$
037	25	0010 0101	%
038	26	0010 0110	&
039	27	0010 0111	'
040	28	0010 1000	(
041	29	0010 1001	)
042	2A	0010 1010	*
043	2B	0010 1011	+
044	2C	0010 1100	´
045	2D	0010 1101	-
046	2E	0010 1110	.
047	2F	0010 1111	/
048	30	0011 0000	0
049	31	0011 0001	1
050	32	0011 0010	2
051	33	0011 0011	3
052	34	0011 0100	4
053	35	0011 0101	5
054	36	0011 0110	6
055	37	0011 0111	7
056	38	0011 1000	8
057	39	0011 1001	9

Dec X_{10}	Hex X_{16}	Binary X_2	ASCII Character
058	3A	0011 1010	:
059	3B	0011 1011	;
060	3C	0011 1100	<
061	3D	0011 1101	=
062	3E	0011 1110	>
063	3F	0011 1111	?
064	40	0100 0000	@
065	41	0100 0001	A
066	42	0100 0010	B
067	43	0100 0011	C
068	44	0100 0100	D
069	45	0100 0101	E
070	46	0100 0110	F
071	47	0100 0111	G
072	48	0100 1000	H
073	49	0100 1001	I
074	4A	0100 1010	J
075	4B	0100 1011	K
076	4C	0100 1100	L
077	4D	0100 1101	M
078	4E	0100 1110	N
079	4F	0100 1111	O
080	50	0101 0000	P
081	51	0101 0001	Q
082	52	0101 0010	R
083	53	0101 0011	S
084	54	0101 0100	T
085	55	0101 0101	U
086	56	0101 0110	V
087	57	0101 0111	W
088	58	0101 1000	X
089	59	0101 1001	Y
090	5A	0101 1010	Z
091	5B	0101 1011	[

continues

continued

Dec X_{10}	Hex X_{16}	Binary X_2	ASCII Character
092	5C	0101 1100	\
093	5D	0101 1101	]
094	5E	0101 1110	^
095	5F	0101 1111	_
096	60	0110 0000	`
097	61	0110 0001	a
098	62	0110 0010	b
099	63	0110 0011	c
100	64	0110 0100	d
101	65	0110 0101	e
102	66	0110 0110	f
103	67	0110 0111	g
104	68	0110 1000	h
105	69	0110 1001	i
106	6A	0110 1010	j
107	6B	0110 1011	k
108	6C	0110 1100	l
109	6D	0110 1101	m
110	6E	0110 1110	n
111	6F	0110 1111	o
112	70	0111 0000	p
113	71	0111 0001	q
114	72	0111 0010	r
115	73	0111 0011	s
116	74	0111 0100	t
117	75	0111 0101	u
118	76	0111 0110	v
119	77	0111 0111	w
120	78	0111 1000	x
121	79	0111 1001	y
122	7A	0111 1010	z
123	7B	0111 1011	{
124	7C	0111 1100	¦

Dec X_{10}	Hex X_{16}	Binary X_2	ASCII Character
125	7D	0111 1101	}
126	7E	0111 1110	~
127	7F	0111 1111	Δ
128	80	1000 0000	Ç
129	81	1000 0001	ü
130	82	1000 0010	é
131	83	1000 0011	â
132	84	1000 0100	ä
133	85	1000 0101	à
134	86	1000 0110	å
135	87	1000 0111	ç
136	88	1000 1000	ê
137	89	1000 1001	ë
138	8A	1000 1010	è
139	8B	1000 1011	ï
140	8C	1000 1100	î
141	8D	1000 1101	ì
142	8E	1000 1110	Ä
143	8F	1000 1111	Å
144	90	1001 0000	É
145	91	1001 0001	æ
146	92	1001 0010	Æ
147	93	1001 0011	ô
148	94	1001 0100	ö
149	95	1001 0101	ò
150	96	1001 0110	û
151	97	1001 0111	ù
152	98	1001 1000	ÿ
153	99	1001 1001	Ö
154	9A	1001 1010	Ü
155	9B	1001 1011	¢
156	9C	1001 1100	£
157	9D	1001 1101	¥
158	9E	1001 1110	₧

continues

continued

Dec X_{10}	Hex X_{16}	Binary X_2	ASCII Character
159	9F	1001 1111	ƒ
160	A0	1010 0000	á
161	A1	1010 0001	í
162	A2	1010 0010	ó
163	A3	1010 0011	ú
164	A4	1010 0100	ñ
165	A5	1010 0101	Ñ
166	A6	1010 0110	ª
167	A7	1010 0111	º
168	A8	1010 1000	º
169	A9	1010 1001	¿
170	AA	1010 1010	⌐
171	AB	1010 1011	¬
172	AC	1010 1100	½
173	AD	1010 1101	¼
174	AE	1010 1110	¡
175	AF	1010 1111	«
176	B0	1011 0000	»
177	B1	1011 0001	▒
178	B2	1011 0010	▓
179	B3	1011 0011	■
180	B4	1011 0100	│
181	B5	1011 0101	┤
182	B6	1011 0110	╡
183	B7	1011 0111	╢
184	B8	1011 1000	╖
185	B9	1011 1001	╕
186	BA	1011 1010	╣
187	BB	1011 1011	║
188	BC	1011 1100	╗
189	BD	1011 1101	╝
190	BE	1011 1110	╜
191	BF	1011 1111	╛

Dec X_{10}	Hex X_{16}	Binary X_2	ASCII Character
192	C0	1100 0000	⌐
193	C1	1100 0001	└
194	C2	1100 0010	⊥
195	C3	1100 0011	⊤
196	C4	1100 0100	├
197	C5	1100 0101	─
198	C6	1100 0110	+
199	C7	1100 0111	╞
200	C8	1100 1000	╟
201	C9	1100 1001	╚
202	CA	1100 1010	╔
203	CB	1100 1011	╩
204	CC	1100 1100	╦
205	CD	1100 1101	╠
206	CE	1100 1110	=
207	CF	1100 1111	╬
208	D0	1101 0000	⊥
209	D1	1101 0001	╨
210	D2	1101 0010	╥
211	D3	1101 0011	╙
212	D4	1101 0100	╘
213	D5	1101 0101	╒
214	D6	1101 0110	╓
215	D7	1101 0111	╫
216	D8	1101 1000	╪
217	D9	1101 1001	┘
218	DA	1101 1010	┘
219	DB	1101 1011	┌
220	DC	1101 1100	■
221	DD	1101 1101	▪
222	DE	1101 1110	▮
223	DF	1101 1111	▌
224	E0	1110 0000	▪
225	E1	1110 0001	α

continues

continued

Dec X_{10}	Hex X_{16}	Binary X_2	ASCII Character
226	E2	1110 0010	β
227	E3	1110 0011	Γ
228	E4	1110 0100	π
229	E5	1110 0101	Σ
230	E6	1110 0110	σ
231	E7	1110 0111	μ
232	E8	1110 1000	γ
233	E9	1110 1001	Φ
234	EA	1110 1010	θ
235	EB	1110 1011	Ω
236	EC	1110 1100	δ
237	ED	1110 1101	∞
238	EE	1110 1110	ø
239	EF	1110 1111	∈
240	F0	1110 0000	∩
241	F1	1111 0001	≡
242	F2	1111 0010	±
243	F3	1111 0011	≥
244	F4	1111 0100	≤
245	F5	1111 0101	⌠
246	F6	1111 0110	⌡
247	F7	1111 0111	÷
248	F8	1111 1000	≈
249	F9	1111 1001	°
250	FA	1111 1010	•
251	FB	1111 1011	·
252	FC	1111 1100	√
253	FD	1111 1101	ⁿ
254	FE	1111 1110	²
255	FF	1111 1111	■

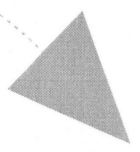

Glossary

address—A sequential number, beginning with zero, of each memory location.

ANSI C—A term used to represent the standard C programming language as accepted by the ANSI (*American National Standards Institute*) committee.

argument—The value sent to a function or procedure. This can be a constant or a variable. C's arguments are always enclosed in parentheses.

array—A list of variables, sometimes called a *table*.

ASCII—Abbreviation for *American Standard Code for Information Interchange*. This defines a unique number for each character the computer can produce.

ASCII file—A file containing characters that programs can access. Also called a *text file*.

backup file—A copy of a file that preserves your work in case the original file is damaged. Often, backup files reside on tape, CD-ROM, or other large-capacity storage devices.

binary—A numbering system based on two digits: 0 and 1. See also *bit*.

binary zero—Another name for *null zero*.

bit—Abbreviation for *binary digit*, the smallest unit of storage on a computer. Each bit has a value of 0 or 1, indicating the absence or presence of an electrical signal. See also *binary*.

bitwise operators—C operators that manipulate the internal binary representation of data.

block—One or more statements treated as if they are a single statement. C blocks are always enclosed within braces.

bubble sort—An easy-to-code sorting routine that sorts arrays of values.

bug—An error in a program that prevents the program from running correctly. This term originated when a moth short-circuited a printer's connection, preventing the computer from printing.

byte—A basic unit of data storage and manipulation. A byte is equivalent to eight bits and can contain a value ranging from 0 through 255.

C++—A programming language, strongly based on C, which includes support for object-oriented programming (OOP).

code—A set of instructions written in a programming language. See also *source code*.

comments—Programmer-supplied remarks that help explain and clarify parts of a program.

compile—To translate a program written in a programming language, such as C or Java, into machine language that your computer understands.

compiler—The utility that converts source code into a machine language.

concatenation—The process of attaching one string to the end of another or combining two or more strings into a longer string.

conditional loop—A series of C instructions that occurs a fixed number of times.

constant—Data that remains the same during a program run, sometimes called a *literal*.

debug—The process of locating an error (bug) in a program and removing it.

debugger—A program that helps the programmer locate errors in code.

default—A predefined action or command that a computer or programming language chooses unless you specify otherwise.

dereference—The process of finding a value pointed to be a pointer variable.

editor—The tool used by programmers to write and correct source code.

element—An individual item in an array.

execute—To run a program.

file—A collection of data stored as a single unit on a disk or other storage device. Files always have a filename that identifies them.

fixed-length records—A record in which each field takes the same amount of space, even if that field's data value does not fill the field.

floating-point numbers—See *real numbers*.

format string—A string that describes the look of a program's output.

free-form language—A programming language, such as C, that enables the programmer to put code in whatever starting position desired and with as much white space as will make the program more readable.

function—A self-contained program segment designed to do a specific task. All C programs must have at least one function called `main()`. Some functions are built-in routines, inside a programming language, that manipulate data.

function call—The execution of one function from another part of a program.

gigabyte (GB or gig)—Approximately one billion bytes.

global variable—A variable that can be seen from (and used by) every statement in a program.

hard copy—The printout of a program (or its output).

hardware independent—The ability of a program to run on different kinds of computers.

hexadecimal—A numbering system based on 16 elements. Digits are numbered 0 through F as follows: 0, 1, 2, 3, 4, 5, 6, 7, 8, 9, A, B, C, D, E, F.

hierarchy of operators—See *order of operators.*

high-level language—A programming language, such as C, that enables the programmer to write programs using familiar commands and operators.

infinite loop—The never-ending repetition of a block of statements.

integer—A whole number without a decimal point, such as 77, 0, and –15.

integer variables—Variables that can hold integers.

I/O—Abbreviation for *Input/Output.*

Java—A C-like programming language used to activate Web pages.

JCL—Abbreviation for *job control language* used by mainframe programmers. JCL was the source for the `//` coding convention used by C programmers to begin comments.

kilobyte (KB)—A unit of measurement that is equal to 1,024 bytes.

least significant bit—The rightmost bit of a byte. For example, a binary 00000001 would have a 1 as its least significant bit.

linking—Also called *link-editing.* Refers to the part of the compiler that initially converts the programmer's source code to a temporary and pre-object machine code stage called object code.

literal—See *constant.*

local variable—A variable that can be seen from (and used by) only the block in which it is defined.

loop—The repeated circular execution of one or more statements.

low-level language—A programming language, such as machine language, that requires the programmer to write programs in cryptic instructions that the computer can execute.

machine language—The series of binary digits that a computer executes to perform individual tasks. People seldom, if ever, program in machine language today due to the complexity and tedium that accompanies programming in such a low-level language.

main module—The first function of a modular program, called `main()` in C, that controls the execution of the other functions.

maintainability—The ability to change and update programs that were written in a simple and clear style.

math operator—A symbol used for addition, subtraction, multiplication, division, and other calculations.

megabyte (MB or meg)—Approximately one million bytes.

member—A piece of a structure variable that holds a specific type of data.

memory—The storage area inside a computer which is used to store data temporarily.

menu—A list of commands or instructions displayed on the screen to organize commands and make programs easier to use.

modular programming—The process of writing your programs in several modules rather than as one long program. By breaking a program into several smaller routines, you can isolate problems better, write correct programs faster, and produce programs that are much easier to maintain.

modulus—The integer remainder of division.

multidimensional arrays—Arrays with more than one dimension. As two-dimensional arrays, they are sometimes called *tables* or *matrices*, which have rows and columns.

nested loop—A loop that appears within another loop.

null zero—The string-terminating character. All C string constants and string variables end in null zero. The ASCII value for null zero is 0.

null string—An empty string, the first character of which is the null zero and the length of which is zero.

numeric function—A built-in function that manipulates numbers.

object code—A halfway step between source code and executable machine language. Object code consists mostly of machine language; however, it is not directly executable by the computer. Object code must first be linked in order to resolve external references and set up proper addresses.

object-oriented programming—Also called *OOP*. A method of utilizing a specially designed programming language to create objects that contain both data and procedures. These objects eliminate much of the tedium from coding that non-OOP languages sometimes require.

OOP—See *object-oriented programming*.

operator—An operator manipulates data and might perform mathematical calculations or change the data to other data types.

order of operators—Sometimes called the *hierarchy of operators* or the *precedence of operators*, the order of operators determines exactly how C computes formulas.

parallel arrays—Two or more arrays, working side-by-side. Each element in each array corresponds to one in the other array at the same location.

parameter—A list of variables enclosed in parentheses that follow the name of a function. Parameters indicate the number and data type of arguments that will be sent to the function.

passing by address—When an argument (a local variable) is passed by address, the variable's memory address is sent to, and is assigned to, the receiving function's parameter list. A change made to the parameter within the function will also change the value of the argument variable.

passing by value—By default, all C variable arguments are passed by value. When the value contained in a variable is passed to the parameter list of a receiving function, changes made to the parameter within the routine will not change the value of the argument variable.

pointer—A variable that holds the address of another variable.

precedence of operators—See *order of operators*.

preprocessor—The part of the compiler that interprets preprocessor directives and makes changes to the source code before compilation.

preprocessor directive—A command, preceded by a #, that you place in your source code that directs the compiler to modify the source code in some fashion.

program—A group of instructions that tell the computer what to do.

program listing—A printed program.

program template—An existing program that a programmer changes to create a new program.

programmer—A person who writes computer programs.

programming language—A set of rules and grammar for writing computer instructions.

random access file—Records in a file that can be accessed in any order.

real numbers—Numbers that have a decimal point and a fractional part to the right of the decimal.

record—An individual row in a file.

relational operators—Operators that compare data; they tell how two variables or constants relate to each other.

scientific notation—A shortcut method of representing numbers of extreme magnitudes.

sequential-file access—A file that has to be accessed one record at a time beginning with the first record.

single-dimensional arrays—Arrays that have only one subscript and represent a list of values.

sorting—A method of putting data in a specific order (such as alphabetical or numerical order), even if that order is not the same order in which the elements were entered.

source code—A programming language's instruction, such as C's, written and understood by programmers that the compiler translates into object and ultimately into machine language code.

spaghetti code—A term used when too many occurrences of goto appear in a program. If a program branches all over the place, it is difficult to follow the program's logic. The logic's travel resembles a bowl of spaghetti.

stream—A sequence of characters, one following another, flowing between devices in your computer.

string constant—One or more groups of characters that end in a null zero.

string literal—Another name for *string constant*.

structure—A unit of related information containing one or more numbers, such as an employee number, employee name, employee address, and so on.

subscript—A number inside brackets that differentiates one element of an array from another.

syntax error—A misspelling or bad programming language grammar usage. Syntax errors are the most common errors a programmer makes.

text file—See *ASCII file*.

truncation—The process of removing the fractional part of a number (the part to the right of the decimal point) and leaving only the part to the left of the decimal point.

two's complement—A method your computer uses to take the negative of a number.

unary operator—The addition or subtraction operator used before a single variable or constant.

UNIX—A multiuser operating system.

variable—A named storage location for data whose value can change as the program progresses.

variable scope—Sometimes called the *visibility of variables*, variable scope describes how variables are seen by your program. A variable's scope defines whether the variable is a local variable or a global variable.

variable-length record—A record that consumes no wasted disk or memory space. As soon as a field's data value is saved to the files, the next field's data value is stored immediately after it. There is usually a special separating character between the fields so that your programs know where a field begins and ends.

weakly typed language—A programming language that does not police data type usage.

white space—The empty parts of a program, such as blank lines and extra spacing, that programmers include to make a program more readable and maintainable.

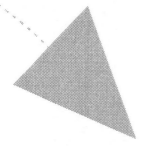

Index